Live & Work
in Brussels

D1572300

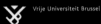

Live & Work in Brussels

Derek Blyth

crimson

**BRUSSELS
RELOCATION**
the key to your life in Belgium

TEL +32 2 353 21 01
FAX +32 2 353 06 42
e-mail brussels.relocation@skynet.be
www.brussels-relocation.com

LIVE & WORK IN BRUSSELS
by Derek Blyth

First edition 2008

Copyright © Crimson Publishing, a division of Crimson Business Ltd 2008

ISBN 978-1-85458-383-3

Typeset by Nicki Averill Design & Illustration
Photographs © iStock, Shutter Stock and Derek Blythe
Printed and bound in Turkey by Mega Printing

Contents

TIME OFF

ABOUT BELGIUM

APPENDICES

Introduction

Let's not be coy. Brussels isn't the world's sexiest destination. Many people see it as a dull place where petty Eurocrats draft regulations that will drive traditional Stilton cheese makers out of business and force Third World farmers to grow straight bananas. Add to that bad driving, rain, surly officials, high taxes and an absurd little statue of a peeing boy that has somehow been adopted as the city's image and you might wonder if there is anything good to say about Brussels.

But wait a minute. Brussels is the capital of Europe, the centre of power of a 27-nation federation that some call the United States of Europe. The city must have something in its favour to make it appeal to international leaders, politicians, diplomats and the world's press. Some people think that Brussels is the EU capital for no better reason than compromise. Its only merit, they argue, is that it is not Paris or Berlin. Yet others believe that there are deeper reasons that justify Brussels' international role.

The city has a geographical advantage, lying at the crossroads of ancient land routes dating back to Roman times. It has always been a meeting place, where merchants have exchanged goods, philosophers have talked ideas and diplomats have tried to stop wars. Karl Marx wrote most of the Communist Manifesto while living in a Brussels suburb and the ground rules of the European Economic Community were debated in an isolated castle on the forest's edge.

Now it is one of the world's political centres, where politicians and civil servants work away on regulations that will affect a region that stretches from the Atlantic Ocean to the borders of Russia, and from the twilight north of Finland to the hot shores of the Mediterranean. Europe has been united many times before, but this is the first time it has been done without force, without one life being lost. And Brussels has been at the centre of this unique experiement almost from the beginning.

Some people may find Brussels boring or bureaucratic, but many more are energised by the working atmosphere, the diversity of languages, the cultural vitality and the constant flow of people. There are few cities in the world where you can hear a dozen different languages on your way to work, sit in a café next to a delegation of Chinese business leaders or join a gym where 30 different nationalities work out.

But Brussels is more than just a political centre. It's an old European city soaked in history and culture where you can spend endless weekends exploring the old quarters, wandering around the superb art galleries or taking a look around the distinctly odd Atomium. If you ever get tired of the city, there are high speed trains to Paris or Amsterdam, cheap flights to almost every capital in Europe and splendid Flemish cities like Antwerp and Ghent just half an hour away.

Admittedly, it takes time to discover all the good things about Brussels. You have to wander through the back streets of the Marolles, visit artists' studios in Saint-Gilles during the annual open days, sneak into normally-closed churches during Mass, take long tram rides out to the woods, track down contemporary dance venues in Molenbeek, stand on a chilly winter afternoon eating frites on Place St Josse, join the queue waiting to get inside the royal greenhouses and try a dozen different restaurants before you find the perfect *croquettes aux crevettes*. It's a slow process, but some people end up liking Brussels so much that they never leave.

Derek Blyth, Brussels, November 2007

Acknowledgements

The author owes thanks to countless people in Brussels who, over many years, have helped, advised and directed him to hidden parts of the city. Most notably, Brigid Grauman and Cleveland Moffett of The Bulletin, Ans Persoons of the Brussels-Europe Liaison Office, Ana Baptista of the Brussels Enterprise Agency, An Van Hamme of the Brussels Public Transport Authority and Guy Bellefroid of the Fondation des Arts. Many others have provided useful information on specialised areas, including Marie Dumont, Clare Thomson and André De Vries. I am grateful, too, to everyone who took time to answer questions connected with the book, including Carolina Di Girolamo of the British School of Brussels, Leen Daems of Bozar and Line Couvreur of Toque Toc. I would also like to thank my editor, David Woodworth, who suggested many improvements to the text and worked through a Bank Holiday weekend to get the final text ready on time. And special thanks to Katharine Mill, Julie Anne Verbeelen, Nicola Lennon and Richard Tuffs for agreeing to participate in the case studies. Finally, I would like to thank my wife, Mary, for putting up patiently with endless trips to odd locations, my daughter Anna for invaluable insights into nightlife, Rose for introducing me to some unexpected shops, and the twins, Thomas and Daniel, for never once complaining as we went in search of yet another fragment of lost city wall.

A Word on Street Names

Brussels is a bilingual city. Every street name has a French and Dutch version. The two names are sometimes run together, where this can be done, to create a single name, like Rue Washingtonstraat. In this guide, simply for the sake of clarity, the French name has been used throughout, even though the author personally considers Beenhouwersstraat a far richer and more potent name than plain old Rue des Bouchers.

Why Live & Work in Brussels

- Brussels is the hub of the world's largest political zone, and contains more diplomats than any other city in the world.
- Behind the first impression of plain office blocks and grey houses lies an older Brussels of quirky charm.
- The city has outstanding architecture, some of the finest of which dates back to the fifteenth century.
- Over one third of the residents of Brussels are not Belgian, and even the Belgians are divided into French and Flemish communities.
- The city's diversity makes Brussels a comfortable city to live and work in, with neighbourhoods to suit any lifestyle.
- Brussels is divided into nineteen municipal councils, each with its own mayor, town hall and municipal services.
- The city survived two world wars comparatively unscathed, but since then construction projects have destroyed large parts of the city's fabric.
- Much of modern Brussels is the result of leaving architecture and planning to property speculators.
- The tide has now turned, and in recent years some existing skyscrapers have actually been reduced in height.

About Brussels

Cosmopolitan Capital

Brussels is a sophisticated city, boasting smart hotels, inspiring shops and spectacular restaurants. Much of the energy that flows through the city streets now comes from its role as the official capital of Europe, although an older and slower city survives in many parts.

It commands international attention, if not always respect, because of its role as the political hub of the world's largest economic zone. The leading politicians of 27 European countries gather four times a year in the blushing pink Justus Lipsius building to make decisions affecting the future of 500 million EU citizens (and, occasionally, the entire planet). After the summits, news broadcasters invariably announce that 'Brussels has decided to...' It isn't strictly true. The decisions are made by the national governments. Brussels is just the place where they meet. But the city has become linked in people's minds with impersonal bureaucracy and unpopular rules.

Brussels has been looking for an international role since the 1950s and has worked hard to attract the European institutions, Nato, European regional offices and NGOs. As a result, it has changed from a rather provincial national capital into a vibrant international city, whose distinguishing features are traffic jams, helicopters and the sound of wheeled suitcases on cobblestones.

More than 170,000 non-Belgian EU citizens now work in Brussels out of a total population of one million. The European Commission employs about 22,000 people while other EU organisations account for a further 4,200 jobs. The city has more diplomats than anywhere else in the world (2,200) and more foreign journalists than even media-soaked Washington (1,200 and rising). It also hosts 2,000 international companies, 1,700 charities and pressure groups, and some 200 expatriate groups.

Take the metro any morning and you will hear a good dozen languages being spoken. Sit in a café and you will be surrounded by foreign voices from all over the globe. Some expatriates only stay for a few years, but others meet partners, have children and settle in Brussels for the rest of their lives.

The sheer scale of the international community now threatens to transform Brussels. Locals can't afford the rents any more, the traffic gets increasingly chaotic, and Belgians feel chased out of their own haunts. It doesn't help that expatriates often live in their own enclaves, indifferent to the city where they live. As a result, many Belgians are still not convinced that they want their capital turned into a hub of international power, although it isn't certain that they have a say in the matter any more.

Ten Reasons to Live in Brussels

Easy housing It's easy to find a house in Brussels. The problem is choosing where to live. You can settle for an urban loft, a Parisian-style apartment, a suburban villa on the forest's edge, or a turreted castle set in a vast estate. Rented housing is cheaper than it was five years ago, and there are countless places to be found at half the price of London or Paris.

Good food Brussels is a city where people believe in eating well. It has elegant restaurants for special occasions, but also modest neighbourhood places where you can eat a good lunch for less than €10. Some are typically Belgian, others offer Japanese, Thai or Greek cooking. But wherever you eat in Brussels, the cooking is invariably excellent.

Cosmopolitan buzz Brussels is one of the greatest multicultural cities in the world. You can experience its unique cosmopolitan atmosphere in the cafés on Place du Luxembourg, the trams that run down Avenue Louise, the Moroccan shops on the Rue de Brabant and the restaurants in the Marolles. Few cities in Europe are home to so many different nationalities and languages. Yet it is only in the past 50 years that Brussels has evolved into an international hive and many areas of the city remain stubbornly Belgian.

Classy culture Brussels has all the culture you need in a relatively compact area. You can listen to the world's best musicians, wander around galleries filled with Flemish art, find a film in an almost extinct language and listen to the freshest new bands from London. Ticket prices are cheap, queues are manageable and distances not too great, making Brussels one of the most relaxed cultural cities in Europe.

Cool lifestyle Brussels is hard working from Monday to Friday, but it has a cool nightlife and a relaxed weekend mood. It's a good city for sleepy bars, friendly food markets and unexpected festivals.

Childcare Brussels is one of the best cities in Europe for bringing up children. It has subsidised crèches in every neighbourhood, big parks within walking distance, and a huge choice of summer activities. Belgians are fairly strict parents, yet a Belgian childhood has its own special charm, involving summers at the Flemish coast, steaming waffles on winter afternoons, and long family lunches in Ardennes restaurants.

Healthcare Belgium has one of the world's best healthcare systems. It is expensive to maintain, but ensures that everyone has access to doctors, dentists and hospitals without having to queue.

Quality education Belgium takes education very seriously. It has one of the world's best state school systems, producing high results in areas like maths and languages. Anyone who settles in Brussels has access to excellent universities, business colleges and language schools, making it the ideal city to add a new language or skill to your CV.

Inspiring travel Brussels is close to some inspiring places that can be easily reached by train or car. You can spend a romantic weekend in Bruges, tramp through the Ardennes in autumn, or set off on a bike ride across the Flemish polders. It's also easy to get over the border to France, Germany or the Netherlands for a complete change of lifestyle.

Quirky charm Brussels may be a serious political centre, but that doesn't stop people having fun. Look out for the cartoon murals, the odd statues (including one of a dog peeing in the street) and the eccentric posters advertising Kaaitheater productions. Brussels has always been an unconventional city, making it the perfect home for artists, anarchists, students and the occasional oddball.

A City with an Identity Problem

Despite its international role, Brussels is seen by most people as boring. The city rarely makes the news except as the source of dull EU regulations. Its buildings seem grey to someone who steps off the Eurostar from London; the people seem sullen to anyone who breezes in from Dublin and the streets look decidedly shabby to a Finn who caught a flight that morning in Helsinki.

To add to its low esteem, the city has rarely been praised by writers or poets. Charlotte Brontë was miserable for two years in Brussels. The French poet Charles Baudelaire complained endlessly about everything: the smell of soap in the streets, the fat women, the insipid beer. The American travel writer Bill Bryson added to the general consensus by grumbling about the litter, the freeways and the absence of a river.

Brussels is really not an easy city to love. Most people are disappointed that it is not as beautiful as Paris or as harmonious as Bruges. The people of Brussels are partly to blame for the way the city looks. They perversely seem to like the city to be unloved and slightly dingy. Some decide not to paint the front of their house in case it attracts the attention of burglars.

People often change their mind about Brussels when they stop being a tourist and start living as a resident. Victor Hugo was extremely contented in Brussels, but then he kept a mistress in the Galerie des Princes and enjoyed the plentiful supply of prostitutes near his home, noting in his diary that *'at 2 Rue du Rempart du Nord, behind the Place des Barricades, you can get a cigar, a glass of gin, a cup of coffee, and a woman, all for 25 centimes'.*

As a resident, you discover that an older Brussels survives beyond the glass office blocks and grey houses. It is still a city with a certain quirky charm. Go beyond the well-worn routes and you become aware of the odd details, like the modern art in the metro stations, the bizarre shops, the old women walking strangely diminutive dogs.

You might even come to like the chaos of Brussels: the street names in two languages (or even three in the Marolles), the streets dug up for years on end, the fact

Grand Place lamp-post

Eglise Notre-Dame des Riches Claires

that no one is in charge, no one knows what is going on, and no one knows what language to talk. It is often baffling, occasionally maddening, but never predictable.

Two Cultures It is hardly surprising that Brussels has no clear identity. The possibility of a homogeneous city is virtually ruled out by the fact that the population is divided into French and Dutch communities. They have separate schools, theatres, bookshops, libraries, cafés and neighbourhoods. In addition, Brussels is split into 19 municipal councils, each with its own town hall, mayor, police force and social services.

The fact that one third or more of Brussels' residents are not Belgian means that diversity is inevitable. The migrants have come at different times, for different reasons – Italians and Moroccans came north after the Second World War; Hungarian dissidents fled to Brussels following the failed 1956 uprising; Congolese students started arriving in the 1960s; American executives came in the boom years of the 1960s and 1970s; Spanish and Portuguese migrants arrived in the late 1960s; British and Irish civil servants put down roots in the 1970s; Scandinavians began to arrive in the 1990s; and East Europeans came here in the early 21st century. Scattered through the city are any number of Irish pubs, Spanish tapas bars, British bookshops, Moroccan butchers, Congolese bars, Japanese restaurants and Scandinavian design boutiques. Each community has brought its own culture to Brussels, adding another layer of complexity, another way of doing business, and helping to create one of the most culturally diverse cities in the world.

This diversity helps to make Brussels a comfortable city for living and working. It has neighbourhoods to suit almost any lifestyle. You can rent a Parisian-style apartment off the Grand'Place and shop in small Flemish corner stores or live in an American-style home in the suburbs and drive to the hypermarket every Saturday. You can paint your face green on St Patrick's Day or sign up as a pantomime dame with a local British dramatic society. There is no pressure to become Belgian; in fact, no one really knows what it means to be Belgian, least of all Belgians, who are either Flemish, or Walloon, or Brussels Flemish, or European, or citizens of the world.

While the foreign population is tolerated, it is not particularly loved. The vague hostility towards outsiders has its roots in history. For centuries, Brussels was a city under foreign occupation. The Burgundians in the 15th century were succeeded by the Spanish in the 16th century. Then came the Austrians, followed by the French, followed by the Dutch, followed by independence, followed by two periods of German occupation.

The Impact of Europe Many locals see the European Union as the latest in a line of foreign occupations. They resent the well-paid civil servants from other countries, blaming them for everything from rising house prices to traffic congestion. Yet the Brussels economy profits immensely from its European role. The EU is one of the biggest employers in Brussels, providing jobs for thousands of local people. Its presence has helped to turn an old industrial city into the second most prosperous region of Europe.

The international community has changed the basic character of Brussels. Some expatriate communities have been particularly active, like the Galicians who have restored the abandoned La Tentation department store, and the Asturians who rescued from ruin the Presse Socialiste building. Others are less visible, like the British, who often prefer to live in the countryside, or the French, who simply blend in with the Belgians.

The city is still changing, sometimes in unexpected directions. A Brussels mayor recently decided that the skyscrapers put up in the 1960s and 1970s were a bad idea. He introduced new height restrictions that have resulted in a city of vanishing towers. The city has also started to remove petrol stations from residential neighbourhoods, plant more trees, reduce traffic speeds and introduce cycle lanes.

It still has some way to go, yet Brussels is a much more attractive city than many people imagine. Anyone who takes time to explore the city will find lost medieval chapels, cobbled country lanes and secluded parks where the citizens of Brussels walk their dogs. There are also buildings, old Flemish inns and corners of the city that look almost like Bruges (like the Rue du Bois Sauvage behind the Cathedral).

Individualism It possibly won't ever make sense to you as a city. There are too many individuals in Brussels, each with their own ideas about the city. One person wants Brussels to be more like Paris. Another wants it to be more like Antwerp. Someone wants to put giant cartoon murals on the walls. Someone else believes that the city needs glass skyscrapers. Everyone has a say in the city.

Sometimes they get it badly wrong. Most people now agree that the road tunnels built in the 1950s were a bad idea. And the parking garages in the city centre hardly add to the city's beauty. Some things in the city are truly shocking. The lovely cobbled Rue de Rollebeek leads to one of the worst – a bowling alley built above a petrol station next to a fragment of the old city wall. 'How could they do this?' newcomers inevitably ask.

One possible explanation is that Brussels is a city that tries to accommodate. It tries to be a city that has bowling alleys, petrol stations *and* ancient walls. Other cities would have made a choice. An American city might have gone for the bowling alley. A French city would have sacrificed everything to protect its ancient wall. Brussels tries as far as it can to please everyone. That, perhaps, is why the capital of Europe is here and nowhere else.

The City Wall

Brussels had two city walls. The second wall has vanished, torn down in the 19th century to build the boulevards, leaving just the isolated Porte de Hal. The first wall is shorter – just 4km long – and crops up in the most unlikely places. There's a tower next to the Novotel on Place Sainte Catherine, a stretch of wall next to a bowling alley on Boulevard de l'Empereur, another stretch of wall looking down on a school playground in the Rue des Alexiens, the remains of a turret inside a shop on Rue des Chartreux; and, strangest of all, a long stretch that cuts through the lobby of the SAS Hotel and its underground car park.

One City, 19 Mayors

Tourists are hardly aware that Brussels is a city with 19 mayors, each with authority over their local commune. Yet foreign residents soon learn the power of the commune in Belgian life. The mayor is in charge of the police, local schools, social welfare, some traffic regulations and certain town planning rules. The local town hall is where you go to get an identity card, register as a voter, request planning permission or publish your marriage banns.

The system has certain advantages. It creates a sense of local democracy, say its supporters. You may find that your local

Street Names

Brussels has some evocative street names from the Middle Ages, like the Quai au Bois à Brûler (Firewood Quay), and the Rue des Six Jeunes Hommes (Six Young Men Street). But some of the most exotic street names are simple mistakes. When the French took over Brussels in 1795, they translated all the street names from Dutch to French, but they didn't always get it right. So Wilde Woudestraat, named after a man called Wilde Woude, became the Rue du Bois Sauvage (since *woud* is Dutch for wood). Likewise, the Wolvengracht, originally named after a man called De Wolf, became the Rue du Fossé aux Loups, or Wolves Ditch Street.

policeman comes to your door to welcome you to the municipality, or that your town hall organises a reception for newly-arrived foreigners. Or you may not. It depends where you live. The smaller or richer municipalities tend to be the most welcoming. The poorer communes have more pressing problems.

The communes give Brussels much of its urban variety, as each of the 19 municipalities has its own urban style. The local authorities can decide to adopt a different style of street lighting, or parking meter or tree variety. As a result, you can almost always tell when you cross the boundary from one commune to another, if only because the metal street name sign is in a different style.

The system ensures that the Hôtel de Ville plays an important part in everyday life. Most town halls in Brussels are grand 19th-century buildings designed to convey a sense of civic pride. The poorest districts of Brussels, oddly enough, often have the grandest town halls. The residents of Saint-Gilles commune deal with their local administration in a spectacular building modelled on a Loire château. Those who live in central Brussels, including the poorest parts of the Marolles, have the right to marry in the ancient Gothic town hall on Grand'Place.

Yet many people in Brussels would like the communes to be abolished. They argue that the system is inefficient and incoherent. They point to the case of the European Quarter, where planning decisions often require the consent of three local mayors, each one with a different political agenda.

For a foreigner, it is certainly confusing. You may well find it absurd that Avenue Louise forms part of Brussels 1000 commune, or that parking regulations change midway along a street because of a commune boundary. But the communes possibly have a role in a city of one million people. They create a sense of being part of a small town, with manageable problems.

Architecture

Brussels is a city of one million stubborn individualists. Everyone has their own ideas here, which is why no two buildings are the same, no two doors are alike, no two letterboxes identical.

The city has some outstanding architecture, like the baroque guild houses on Grand'Place and the Art Nouveau townhouses in the residential streets of Saint-Gilles and Ixelles. At its best, Brussels can produce astonishing structures, like the Horta House in Rue Américaine and the Atomium at Heysel. Its architects are often skilled in several styles. They have to be, because Belgium is a country of individuals. Some clients want modern architecture, while others want tradition.

Many of the best buildings in Brussels date from the 15th century. They were designed in the elaborate style known as Brabant Gothic. There are scattered relics of the period dotted around the old city, like the town hall on Grand'Place, the lovely Eglise Notre Dame du Sablon built by the guild of archers, and the Eglise Notre Dame de la Chapelle where Pieter Bruegel the Elder is buried. But the city has swept away most of its Medieval past, leaving just a few stone relics in the city museum on Grand'Place.

The city went through a building boom in the 19th century, fuelled by the industrial revolution and the wealth of the Congo. The architects were bold, imaginative and eclectic, drawing on international architectural styles and using new materials like iron and glass.

The suburbs grew under the doctrine of liberalism. Nothing much was planned (unlike the socialist Netherlands where nothing was left to chance). Everything in Brussels was left to the enlightened citizen. The city streets became lined with a bewildering variety of architectural styles. There were turreted Medieval fantasies next to sober neo-classical houses, Art Nouveau convolutions alongside mock Greek temples. The Brussels streets, as a result, look messy compared to the boulevards of Paris, but they are at least interesting, odd, alive.

This period of architectural activity ended in the spectacular Art Nouveau style which exploded in Brussels seven years before the end of the 19th century and fizzled out just before the First World War.

After the war, everything was muted, including architecture. Houses were more plain, less fanciful, simply because of a lack of skilled craftsmen. Oweners became unhappily obsessed with brown tiled façades, clean lines, sober looks. Belgians wanted modern houses with wide windows and garages. But they wanted them in the city, on a narrow plot of land. The result was a hideous confusion of styles, with tall apartment blocks rising above discreet family houses, petrol stations next to churches, parking garages destroying the visual harmony of a 500-year-old Gothic church.

Town Hall

In the past 50 years, architects in Brussels have barely risen above the mediocre. But they are now becoming more imaginative, less timid, finally aware that they are designing for a world capital. There is talk of exciting skyscrapers, new waterfront developments, a Library of Europe. Architecture in Brussels is once again moving in interesting directions.

Palais de Justice

The Destruction of Brussels

Brussels has been lucky in war. The city survived two world wars virtually undamaged. Yet it has been less fortunate in peace. Over the past 150 years, at least five huge construction projects have caused enormous damage to the city fabric: the Palais de Justice destroyed large areas of the Marolles; a rail tunnel left a path of destruction through the centre; the Mont des Arts, just before the First World War, obliterated an entire quarter dating back to the middle ages; the road tunnels in the 1950s and 1960s destroyed most of the city's tree-lined boulevards; and the European Quarter obliterated a beautiful 19th-century residential quarter.

The destruction of Brussels began under Leopold II, when large areas of the old town were torn down to build prestigious projects like the Mont des Arts, the Palais de Justice and the north-south rail tunnel. The locals were not enthusiastic and Leopold often had to use bribes to force people out of their homes. One of his favourite ploys was to pay an agent to buy up properties that stood in the way of his project, and then leave them to rot until they were beyond saving. More than a century later, property speculators in the European Quarter were still using Leopold's trick, although the authorities have recently brought in new measures to end the worst abuses.

The city is now more aware of the need to protect its architectural heritage, but the turnaround came too late to save Victor Horta's Maison du Peuple. Built during 1895-99 as a socialist meeting hall and restaurant, this was considered a masterpiece of Art Nouveau architecture. Yet it was torn down in 1966, despite a petition signed by some of the world's leading architects. Many other Horta houses suffered the same fate in the 1960s and 1970s, providing sites for anonymous office buildings.

Architects invented the term 'Bruxellisation' to describe this process in which the city leaves architecture and planning to the property speculators. There's nothing that can be done now, as much of the urban fabric has been destroyed forever, with six-lane roads cutting through old residential quarters and concrete offices looming over quiet city parks.

The city finally began to take note of its critics in the late 1980s. The new Brussels Region, fired with enthusiasm, began to draw up a list of protected monuments. Yet the property developers then came up with a new ruse, almost as bad as Bruxellisation. They would save the façade of a protected building, but gut the interior, then construct a modern office building (with underground parking) behind the façade. The critics called this façadism. The Place des Martyrs is pure façadism, with modern interiors concealed behind a neo-classical skin. The result is a strange city of buildings that are not what they seem.

Bringing Down the Skyscrapers

The skyline of Brussels changed dramatically in the 1960s and 1970s when skyscrapers began to appear along the main avenues. But the view changed again in the early 21st century when the skyscrapers began to disappear. The Brussels mayor François Xavier de Donnea was unhappy with the view from the balcony of the town hall. He liked to take his foreign visitors there to show them the beautiful Grand'Place, but they inevitably commented on the ugly skyscrapers looming above the baroque gables. De Donnea finally cracked. He had a Prince Charles moment, and decided to deal with the 'horrible towers which disfigure the city'. The result was a new rule on building height which newspapers called the 'balcony syndrome'. The skyscrapers had to be reduced in size so that they were invisible from the balcony of the town hall. The Madou Plaza was one of the first to be cropped. Others are now being brought down to size.

The Best Views

Brussels is not a city of sublime views that take the breath away. The beauty of the city lies in unexpected details and secret interiors. The more of the city you see, the less harmonious it becomes. Yet there are some places where you can get an impression of the city's diverse architecture and tormented history.

Grand'Place
The Grand'Place is beautiful at any time, but especially in the early morning, before it gets too crowded, and late at night, when the architectural details are illuminated. For the best view, enter the square by the Rue Chair et Pain, admire the spire at the end of the street, and settle in one of the cafés that look out on the square. The Aroma Coffee Lounge at No. 37 has four little tables on the first floor that look out on the square. Failing that, the Roi d'Espagne at No. 1 has a row of tables next to the small barred windows on the mezzanine.

Mont des Arts
For the best view of the old town, position yourself in front of Alexander Calder's *Whirling Ear* sculpture on the Rue Montagne de la Cour. The view includes the spire of the town hall on Grand'Place and the gardens of the Mont des Arts.

Place Poelaert
Stand on the balustrade in front of the Palais de Justice for a sweeping view of the city. Down below are the red tiled roofs of the Marolles where Pieter Bruegel the Elder once painted. Turn to the right and you see the towers of the Minimes church and Notre-Dame de la Chapelle. On the far horizon, the nine spheres of the Atomium might just be visible.

Marolles square

Cinquantenaire Arch
Visit the army museum in the Cinquantenaire Park and look for signs pointing to the Arcades. Take the lift to the rooftop terrace for an unexpected view of the steel and glass buildings of the European Quarter and the Avenue de Tervuren heading off towards the woods.

Museum of Musical Instruments Roof Terrace
Take the lift to the top floor of the Museum of Musical Instruments for an inspiring view of Place Royale, the royal palace and the park.

Place du Petit Sablon
Stand at the top end of the Petit Sablon, behind the statues of Egmont and Hoorn, for a view of the little romantic park and its statues of illustrious Belgians.

What Happened to the River?

The mayor's office in Brussels town hall is decorated with romantic paintings of Brussels that make the city look as wistful as Bruges or Venice. You see a river meandering past crumbling brick houses, old stone bridges and overgrown quaysides. So what happened to the river?'

King Leopold II is to blame. He wanted to make the Belgian capital more beautiful. That meant more like Paris and less like Bruges. Hundreds of old brick houses were torn down and long straight boulevards were created in the Napoleon III Style.

The River Senne was a narrow and stinking river that bred cholera. In 1871 Burgomaster Anspach had the meandering river vaulted over. It vanished below the elegant boulevard named after Anspach, soon fading from the public memory. But not everyone approved. Charles Baudelaire complained: 'What good is a city without a river in which one can drown oneself?'

The Senne can still occasionally be seen. It meanders through the fields outside the city (where it is called the Zenne), passes under the motorway to Paris and disappears into a tunnel in industrial Anderlecht. It emerges again north of Evere and follows the Avenue de Vilvoorde until it returns again to the Flemish countryside. The river also appears unexpectedly in the city centre in a courtyard off the Place St Géry (go through the gate at No 23). But this is a fake river. Look at the water long enough and you can see that it isn't flowing anywhere.

A group of eccentric locals now wants the Brussels river to be restored. They call themselves the *Zennezotten* in Dutch and *Les Fous de la Senne* in French. They are, as the name implies, totally mad. The river is now part of the city sewer system. It could never be restored. Yet the Zennezotten keep up the pressure, hoping that the city will at least listen to some of their ideas. *'A murmuring river running between the houses would make Brussels a completely different city,'* said one Senne lunatic.

The Zennezotten (who are mainly Flemish Brusselers) have already scored some modest victories. You will see a thin trickle of water running across the pavement outside Notre-Dame du Bon Secours, as a reminder of the river that once flowed past the church walls. In the summer of 2006, the Zennezotten called for a stretch of water in the Parc Maximilien, not far from the canal. The city authorities were unexpectedly enthusiastic about the idea. Maybe Brussels will soon have a river where miserable French poets can drown themselves.

Notable Buildings

Town Hall

The town hall on Grand'Place, while not exactly symmetrical, is an impressive Brabant Gothic building. The 300 statues were carved by 19th-century Belgian sculptors, but so convincingly that almost everyone thinks they are 15th century originals. The spire, which rises to 96.6m, was praised by Victor Hugo, who lived in a hotel opposite, as *'the equal of Chartres'*.

Cathedral

The Cathedral stands, somewhat awkwardly, on sloping ground above the old town, next to a modern office building with a strange Gothic-inspired façade. The interior was recently restored, perhaps a little too enthusiastically, creating a gleaming white space that looks more like a Dutch Reformed church. But there are mysterious underground spaces where archaeologists have uncovered the remains of a much older church.

Galeries Saint Hubert

The beautiful Galeries St Hubert was built by Jean-Pierre Cluysenaar in 1847. It was the first covered shopping gallery in Europe, and remains one of the most impressive. Its fake marble columns and marble statues were recently restored.

Palais de Justice

Most tourists don't dare step inside the Palais de Justice. The building is simply too terrifying to approach. It was designed by Leopold II to strike fear into the unruly Marolles workers. Built on the old gallows hill, looming over the working class district, it serves as a permanent reminder of the rule of law. The architect Joseph Poelaert created this monstrous edifice of stone and glass. It has endless corridors, numberless windows and dark corners where the dust has gathered for more than a century. You can wander around freely, following signs to mysterious parts of the building, discovering vistas that resemble Piranesi's architectural fantasies. There are huge empty staircases that descend to the lower levels, signs pointing to obscure courtrooms, black-gowned lawyers whispering to their clients, desperate young mothers waiting for a verdict. It's easy to imagine getting lost in this building, wandering hopelessly in search of the Tribune of the First Instance, room 0.4. It's easy to imagine all sorts of things, none of them very pleasant. Place Poelaert, *open Monday to Friday during office hours*.

Musée Horta

Victor Horta built some of the most sublime houses in Europe in the 1890s. Some of them are still standing, barely noticed in the quiet streets of Ixelles and Saint-Gilles. The Musée Horta at Rue Américaine 25 is now a museum. Stand in the street to admire the curling railings, then push open the front door. Everything in the house was designed by Horta, down to the door handles and radiator pipes. The basement is a cold room lined with enamelled brickwork, but the mood becomes warmer and more sensual as one climbs the staircase, culminating in a gorgeous space at the top of the house bathed in a mysterious golden light. The adjoining house, originally

Maison St Cyr – Art Nouveau detail

Horta's studio, now contains a small collection of drawings, models and architectural fragments, some rescued from buildings that were torn down in the 1970s. *Rue Américaine 25, Saint-Gilles; ☎ 02.543.04.90; www.hortamuseum.be*

Atomium

Possibly the world's strangest building, the Atomium was built for the 1958 Brussels World Fair and represents an atom of iron magnified 165 billion times. The structure consists of nine steel spheres linked by tubes that are big enough to walk through. It looks best at night when the nine spheres are lit by thousands of tiny lights. Be careful if you take a photograph. The building is protected by strict copyright laws and anyone who posts their photographs on the internet risks a massive bill. *Heysel; ☎ 02.475.47.77; www.atomium.be*

The Spirit of '58

1958 was the year of the space race, the launch of Barbie dolls and the first Ikea store in Sweden. It was also the year when 50 million people visited the World Fair in Brussels. Expo 58 was the first world fair since the 1930s. The organisers wanted something bold and inspiring, something to symbolise progress and peace after the war. They commissioned a young Belgian engineer, André Waterkeyn, to design an upside down Eiffel Tower. It was a ridiculous idea, he told them, but perhaps they would like to consider a large steel structure based on the nine atoms of an iron crystal. Waterkeyn produced a tiny prototype using knitting needles and chewing gum. He gave it a Latin-sounding name – Atomium – so that American visitors could pronounce it. The committee was impressed. It was modern. It was shiny. It had balls (quipped the journalists).

Expo 58 showed the shape of the future. There was a Sputnik bleeping away in the Soviet hall, clam chowder in the American pavilion, cable cars floating above the crowds, an abundance of new sensations. The fair attracted artists, film stars and dictators. Among the visitors were General de Gaulle, Alain Delon, Romy Schneider and Snow White and the Seven Dwarfs. The fair even produced a new style – the 'Atomic Style'. Everything was bright, modern, light and new. Even the materials were fresh – everything traditional was considered old fashioned, replaced by aluminium, leatherette, plastic, polyester.

A mere two years later, it all started to fall apart. The Congo was lost. Then the language war erupted. The Belgian dream was over almost as soon as it began. There are relics of this brief moment of optimism scattered around Belgium, some lovingly preserved, others rusting away. Not far from the Atomium, a strange restaurant called Salon 58 occupies a round building with a domed roof built for Expo 58 by the Belgian roofing industry. A mobile designed for the

American pavilion by Alexander Calder now sits in the centre of a pool on the Mont des Arts, near the Museum of Fine Arts.

Many of the city's road tunnels were built for Expo 58, including the long Leopold III Tunnel that leads to the Ostend motorway. Expo 58 also marked the beginning of a car park building boom in the city centre. The most obvious relic is Parking 58 near Place Sainte Catherine, a striking concrete building with a strange bar squeezed under a sloping ramp.

Some Expo buildings have ended up in the strangest places. The Uccle gym La Pavillon is located in a structure rescued from the World Fair, while a Chinese restaurant on the N1 near Wijrijk occupies a cavernous building that was originally a Bavarian beer hall. The English Catholic Church of St Anthony's in Kraainem was a chapel for Expo visitors, although the original iron altar has been demoted to a table that stands in the entrance hall. The little blue cable cars that were one of the main attractions of Expo 58 ended up in Namur carrying tourists up to the Citadel. They now lie abandoned following a fire.

How they got on: personal stories

Katharine Mill

Katharine Mill, 37, moved to Brussels in summer 1998 to work as a sub-editor for *The Bulletin*. She went on to work as a media officer for the Greenpeace European Unit and now works as a freelance journalist and consultant. She lives in Saint-Gilles near the Gare du Midi.

Why did you decide to relocate to Brussels?
For quality of life and an interesting job opportunity. I came to Brussels because I wanted to be back in a French-speaking environment. I had been in Bordeaux five years previously for two years. After four years back in London, where I am from, I wanted to combine the francophone environment with doing what I enjoyed working in the media.

What about red tape – any problems?
No.

What were your first impressions of Brussels?
Very good. It was World Cup 98 and on my first night my new colleagues took me to the Bank pub on Rue du Bailli, to watch that night's England game. I walked home afterwards up Rue Washington looking at all the lighted windows and thought, 'hmm, I could live here'. The next night I went downtown, ate near the Grand'Place and then went to a café in the Quartier Saint-Jacques, where I got talking to two friendly Belgians at the neighbouring table who enhanced the warm feeling I was developing about the place. It certainly helped that it was a very balmy mid June.

Where in Brussels do you live and why?
I live in lower Saint-Gilles near the Gare du Midi. I bought a house here four years ago: I like Saint-Gilles for it's boho atmosphere, lack of pretension and great public transport connections.

Was it hard to find accommodation? What is accommodation like in Brussels?
When I first arrived I rented a flat in Brussels 1000 near Porte de Namur for four years, living behind the Brussels equivalent of Bond Street: Boulevard de Waterloo. It was a modest flat so the rent was affordable, but the location was amazing. I was delighted to be able to rent my own place after flat sharing in London for years.

How did you go about finding work?
I found work before I came. That was the reason I moved here. I hadn't been planning to move to Belgium: it happened quite by chance.

How do you find working there compared with home?
I found the basic working hours rather long – 9am–6pm compared to 9am–5pm. Even though you're supposed to leave early on Fridays, it doesn't happen that way.

Did it take long to acclimatise?
No.

How does the quality of life compare to other countries you have lived in? Do you find it expensive to live here?
Very good quality of life – the city is compact and accessible; the quality of entertainment (culture, dining out) is very high, it is extremely well connected and easy to leave to walk in nearby countryside. Unlike in many capital cities, the time spent commuting to work need not be long, and the city centre is affordable and pleasant to live in.

Regarding costs, accommodation is cheaper, but food can be more expensive, although eating out is not overpriced, and the service is included. The public transport – train, metro, tram, bus - is excellent value.

What is the social life like – is it easy to make friends?
It very much depends on you and your situation. I was lucky to be working with other British people who knew what it was like to move here alone and helped me settle in. I made friends with other foreigners who arrived at around the same time as I did. I met friends while taking Dutch classes – also foreigners who had recently arrived, like me, and were keen to invest some time in getting to know Belgium, so we had that in common. Eight years later, we're still good friends. We didn't keep up with the Dutch classes though.

Do you find locals welcoming to foreigners?
I would say they are accepting without being particularly welcoming. I have heard of hostility expressed by Belgians to expats buying property – 'pushing up the prices', 'changing the "character" of the neighbourhood', but in my neighbourhood we're mostly foreigners of one description or another, so I've never had a problem. After over eight years here, most of my good friends are non-Belgian – French, Austrian, British, Irish. But I do have one good Belgian friend.

What do you like best about Brussels?
I like the fact that it's the meeting place of northern European and Latin cultures: with the Flemish and French-speaking cultures vying for cultural space, I think it has the best of both worlds for an outsider. It has everything a city needs – bar, perhaps, a river.

What do you like least about Brussels?
1. There is a general shortage of civic attitude, particularly on the part of motorists, but also from many local residents, young or old. They are neither generous nor

gracious towards those outside their close circle. This translates onto the street as a lack of smiling good-natured humanity and not much sense of humour. However, they are quite good at respecting the 10 o'clock no-noise rule.
2. Men urinating in the street.

What is your favourite place in Brussels?
The Kaaitheater. It features some of the most amazing performing arts around. In fact, any of the major cultural venues and festivals.

What is you least favourite place in Brussels?
Soi-disant chic boutiques staffed by unpleasant and frosty ladies, mainly francophone it has to be said.

What aspects of your new environment/lifestyle have caused you most problems?
Not having family nearby means that familiar support networks are not present. It is easy to feel lonely.

Do you think you will stay in Brussels/Belgium?
Probably not, but I will not leave without regrets. I would particularly miss the health service, the public transport, progressively 'greener' local government policies, and the accessible and affordable cultural activities.

Do you have any regrets about leaving your home country?
Not many. There are pluses and minuses all the way; nowhere is perfect.

What advice would you give someone thinking of coming to live and work in Brussels?
Find out what is going on, make sure to learn a local language, and explore and enjoy the good things that the city has to offer. There are plenty of them.

Nicola Lennon

Nicola Lennon was born in Ireland and moved to Belgium with her family in 1974 when she was nine years old. She went to the European School in Brussels and then returned to Ireland for four years to study at university. She returned to Brussels in 1986 and now runs a small bookshop near Avenue Louise selling English-language books from around the world.

Why did you decide to relocate to Brussels?
I returned to Brussels to look for a job, since it was very difficult to find work in Ireland in the 1980s. Finding work in Brussels was very easy at that time. For 17 years I worked in various small-sized companies in administrative and then management positions. In the early 2000s, I decided to start my own business. This was much less complicated than I thought it would be. There are a certain number of administrative procedures to follow and tasks to complete, but the state has simplified things considerably in recent years. What still remains to be done is to offer more financial incentives to small businesses to help them through the first three to five years. Belgium is still a country that favours large companies and the employee status over the entrepreneur and freelance status; the result of this is that a very large number of small companies go bankrupt within the first five years of business.

What about red tape – any problems?
Having found a job very quickly, it was very easy for me to apply for an identity card. I received an ID for a three-month period twice before the commune issued me with the five-year card, which I have renewed every five years since or every time I change domicile! I have been pretty lucky with minimum red tape problems – it was just getting used to dealing with the people working in the administrations that took a while. I must admit that there has been a great improvement over the years, which is probably a result of the fact that there are more and more Belgians of foreign origin occupying these positions, and not exclusively native Belgians.

What were your first impressions of Brussels?
When I was 9, I hated it! Coming from Dublin where we lived on a housing estate and we played outside all the time, to being limited to our home and garden with no friends in the neigbourhood, was awful! When I came back after university, what I found the most difficult to get used to was the unfriendliness and, to a certain extent, the rudeness of the Belgians. In Dublin, it was common to speak to people you didn't know, on the bus, at the shop, even in the streets. Back in Brussels, I remember one incident where I was at a tram stop I would go to every day at around the same time and where I would see the same people. On this particular day, I spontaneously greeted someone I had seen the day before. The person just looked through me as if I wasn't there. Then it really hit me that I was in Belgium and not in Ireland! I have hundreds of anecdotes about this aspect of the Belgians, things that have happened to me or friends. I could fill a book with them!

Where in Brussels do you live and why?
I live in Ixelles now, but I have previously lived in a variety of communes since 1986. I chose Ixelles specifically, because it has the most diverse population. I try my best to keep away from communes which are nearly exclusively inhabited only by Belgians as I find those neighbourhoods too depressing.

Was it hard to find accommodation? What is accommodation like in Brussels?
It has become more difficult over the years to find nice and reasonably priced accommodation in Brussels. I visited some dumps before finding a beautiful apartment near the Place Flagey. I had been a house owner before, so I was surprised by the considerable increase in rents within a 10-year period. I had paid 20,000 BEF (€500) for the two-bedroom apartment I rented in the mid 1990s compared to the €750 I pay today. The increase is considerable even taking into account inflation. In general though, I think Brussels is just catching up with its neighbouring European cities, and there are some beautiful apartments and houses here which one doesn't find in other cities.

How did you go about finding work?
When I first started working in Brussels I would apply to ads in the local newspapers. As I said, it was very easy to find employment in the 1980s and every time I got bored with my job, I would resign and find a new job really quickly. In the 1990s, things started to change and finding interesting work became a bit more difficult (so I stopped my spontaneous resignations and became a more mature job seeker – find the new job first, then resign!). However, I had noticed a pattern: I always ended up getting frustrated with the directors or the owners of the companies that I worked for, thinking that I could do the job better than they could! That's when the seed of self employment was planted. It took me until the early 21st century to become clear as to what I would like to run as a business, and the rest is history!

How do you find working here compared with home?
I have only ever worked in Brussels, never in Ireland.

Did it take long to acclimatise?
I don't think I will every really acclimatise myself to Belgium. I also don't think I could settle back in Ireland now. I feel like an 'apatride' who has no home, though I do still feel very much Irish. I guess the world's my oyster and I'll settle where my heart takes me one day!

How does the quality of life compare to other countries you have lived in? Do you find it expensive to live here?
When I hear friends who live in Dublin, London or Paris talk about cost of living, I think most expats are very lucky here in Brussels. We have a comfortable lifestyle, with relatively reasonable rents and many quality services which you don't find in other European cities (namely health services and schools).

What is the social life like – is it easy to make friends?

When mixing with fellow expats, making friends is relatively easy. Trying to get to know your neighbours (especially if they're Belgian, but not only) is much more difficult. I have made some 'Belgian' friends over the years, but they are all either half some other nationality, or of foreign origin!

Do you find locals welcoming to foreigners?

In general, not really, but I have met some locals who are friendly enough. There are always exceptions to the rule!

What do you like best about Brussels?

I like the fact that there are a lot of foreigners who live in Brussels, and I like its size, not too big, not too small. I like some of its architecture and beautiful buildings. I also like its green spaces, the various *bois* and the Forêt de Soignes. I like the cinemas which show films in the original language (unlike Paris or Rome, for example, where films are dubbed). I like the great choice of restaurants.

What do you like least about Brussels?

There are too many dogs and unconscious dog owners who allow them to shit on the footpaths, so that I have to walk looking down in order to avoid walking in dog shit! There are now too many cars in Brussels, which results in the city feeling very polluted (noise and air) especially during the summer. There are too many rude and aggressive drivers, which makes driving in Brussels very stressful. Road and building works are a major disaster in Brussels. Authorities seem to love to start *chantiers* at the worst times, some seem never ending (Place Flagey is a wonderful example!) and the coordination of them is a catastrophe (adding to the mayhem of driving in Brussels!). Finally, I dislike intensely the locals complaining about everything. Complaining is definitely a national pastime!

What is your favourite place in Brussels?

Les Etangs d'Ixelles. On a sunny day, walking around the lakes is very pleasant and there are some beautiful buildings to admire.

What is you least favourite place in Brussels?

Rond Point Schuman, Rue de la Loi, Rue Belliard – the concrete jungle!

What aspects of your new environment/lifestyle have caused you most problems?

Having to do anything which requires some administrative procedure is generally a problem in Belgium. This is mainly because people are so unhelpful and bureaucratic. Either they do not know, or else it is not their responsibility. This attitude is found not just in the public administration offices, but also in service companies, like telephone, TV, post office, utility companies, etc.

Having to send registered letters to confirm all official actions is difficult to get used to. And having to go to the commune to get various forms for various reasons (*bonne vie et mœurs, composition de ménage*, etc.) is all part of the bureaucratic procedures that Belgium seems to excel in!

Phoning a public administration office is always daunting. The phone often rings for ages before someone picks up. If you are lucky enough and someone does pick up, you can be relatively sure not to reach the right place first time. Obtaining the correct information you are looking for is also not guaranteed. Even after having been here so long and being relatively well oiled to the various procedures, I'm still amazed at the general feeling of confusion and apathy I find at the different administrations. As a result, I have adopted the attitude of the less often I have to deal with them, the better!

The weather, of course, can be very depressing at times, with the low lying grey clouds and the infamous drizzle (*drache nationale*) that can go on for days without a glimpse of a blue sky or the sun. Perhaps this explains the side of the Belgian's personality that is unfriendly and complaining!

Do you think you will stay in Brussels/Belgium?
Good question! When I came back in the 1980s I hadn't planned to stay long! But I'm still here and I have a 12-year-old son who was born here and whose life is really here. Now I have my bookshop, so I'll stay here for some time longer. But I do not see myself retiring here.

Do you have any regrets about leaving your home country?
I had many, but that was a long time ago, and I don't believe in holding on to regrets. My motto is: If you don't like something, change it. If you can't change it, accept it or change the way you think about it. But whatever you do, don't complain!

What advice would you give someone thinking of coming to live and work in Brussels?
They need to arm themselves with a lot of patience and a good sense of humour. And then keep an open mind and be prepared to be surprised. You never know when you will meet a helpful and welcoming local!

Julie Anne Verbeelen

Julie Anne Verbeelen is from an Iowa farm in the United States. After studying Graphic Design in Springfield, Missouri, she moved to Finland in 1998 to study art and design. She met a Belgian, Pieter Verbeelen, an interior architect, in Helsinki and moved to Brussels in 2000. After two children and a major house/studio renovation, Julie followed her dream and set up a children's design studio called 'The turtle dreams of wind and wings'.

Why did you decide to relocate to Brussels?
Pieter was born in Brussels, so we moved back with his parents and stayed in their attic while we applied for jobs and decided where to live. We were not thinking to stay in Belgium, but when I became pregnant the idea of living close to family was very important, so we decided to stay.

What about red tape – any problems?
Well, not after we got married, but the paperwork to get married was a nightmare. In Belgium you have to present all kinds of papers that we do not have in the States. Like proof that you are not married.

What were your first impressions of Brussels (compared with Helsinki)?
This is a difficult question as I fell immediately in love with Helsinki. It was exciting as I was a student and fell in love there, so part of my heart will always remain in Helsinki. But I have fallen in love with Brussels as well, although the weather doesn't allow you to become too passionate about it. What I noticed right off I guess would be the languages. In Helsinki they also have two cultures and two languages (Finnish and Swedish), but they have managed to narrow the divide between these cultures. Schools are together and everyone needs to learn both languages from the very beginning. I found (and still find) the divide between French and Flemish very difficult.

Where in Brussels do you live and why?
We actually live very close by where we started, which was in Pieter's parent's attic in Ixelles. After having our first son and the first grandson, we started a project to renovate the old horse stable behind Pieter's parents' house. This process took over two years, but we have lived and worked in our house/studio now for almost three years and I am very happy with the location. There are many international families in Ixelles and we're close to Pieter's family. It is wonderful for our boys to see their grandparents daily and also my relationship with my mother-in-law is more of a friendship than anything else.

Was it hard to find accommodation? What is accommodation like in Brussels?
For us it was unique. We just squatted in Pieter's parent's attic. I don't know about other places.

How did you go about setting up your design studio?

It started during my master's thesis work on designing children's learning environments in Helsinki. After graduating and moving to Brussels I searched and searched for my dream job of designing for children. But I never found it so I would just sit with my sketchbook at a cafe down the street from my house thinking, observing and dreaming. The cafe was called *La Vache Qui Regarde Passer Les Trains* (The Cow that Watches the Trains Pass By). I called it the cow-cafe. I loved this idea of a nonsense sentence as a company name, so I came up with the name 'The turtle dreams of wind and wings'. That was in 2001. I continued sketching and working on occasional projects. Pieter was working at the time as a freelance interior architect and we sat for many hours dreaming and sketching, but never really doing. It was in January 2006 that we got a big push from a project to design an exhibition for the International School of Brussels. After this project everything seemed possible, especially for me because of being able to do the project in English. We then pushed ourselves to make all our dreams and sketches real and created a company.

Was it easy to set up a company in Belgium?

This is much more of a risk and an investment than in the States and it is quite scary in the beginning. Additionally, taxes and Belgium bureaucracy are amazingly complicated. They definitely do not favour the small business owners. But this was our dream and we knew it wouldn't exist unless we made it happen. Our studio is in our home, which we had in mind when we renovated it so it works really well. I am very happy to have found my dream job and the best thing is I am the boss – well, I guess I am half the boss and Pieter is the other half.

How do you find working here compared with home?

Frustrating! This has a lot to do with language, but also because of the lack of customer service in Brussels. It still shocks me from time to time! But, seriously I wouldn't have my company anywhere else. I love the diversity here.

Did it take long to acclimatise?

It did take me a long time, but I am quite introverted and I didn't really make an effort to find friends until my first son was seven months old. I then joined an organisation for English-speaking mothers (BCT) and after that it seemed very easy to settle down and find my place here.

How does the quality of life compare to other countries you have lived in? Do you find it expensive to live here?

Helsinki was expensive. Brussels is relatively cheap compared to other central European countries and that is one reason why we chose to stay here. I also really love the quality of life that most Europeans enjoy. I like the consciousness of most people I meet here towards politics, environmental issues, family, etc. I feel the large international population in Brussels makes it possible to realise our company's dreams and ideas.

What is the social life like – is it easy to make friends?

Again, because of the large international community here, it seems that you can make friends effortlessly once you get into the right circles. It is also nice to be in a large city with so many cultural opportunities and events that allow you to network and meet new people – both international and Belgian.

Do you find locals welcoming to foreigners?
It depends on the context, but attempting to learn French and Flemish and respecting their cultural diversity is a start to feeling welcome. It is important, even though Brussels is very international, to realise you are in Belgium and it is up to you to try and fit in with their way of doing things even if you don't really agree.

What do you like best about Brussels?
Brussels has changed a lot in the six and a half years that I have lived here and I like it more and more each day. I like most that it is finally acting like the capital that it is and representing more culturally diverse events and initiatives. I like most the diverse and international population here.

What do you like least about Brussels?
Rain, poop on the sidewalks, right of way from the right, inconsiderate people and the divide between French and Flemish speaking people.

What is your favourite place in Brussels?
We are quite local and we like to walk to the places we go, so we stay mostly in our own neighbourhood, which is in the Châtelain and Flagey areas.

What is you least favourite place in Brussels?
Right now it is the trams, because I am very irritated they raised their prices when they should be almost free in order to persuade people to leave their cars behind.

What aspects of your new environment/lifestyle have caused you most problems?
Climate! I can't and will never get use to the fact that when it finally warms up in May it doesn't continue to warm up throughout the summer until you are wishing for cool weather. Here, June could be as cold as February and then July might be even colder. I think the thing I miss most from Iowa is the predictable hot sunny summer days!

Do you think you will stay in Brussels/Belgium?
Yes, until I find a way to relocate to the south of France!

Do you have any regrets about leaving your home country?
None. I sometimes have to pinch myself to make sure I am really living this life and it is not just a dream.

What advice would you give someone thinking of coming to live and work in Brussels?
Connect with the international community, but don't miss out on getting to know both the French and Flemish culture as well.

Richard Tuffs

Richard Tuffs was born in Ipswich 1952 and grew up in a rural environment. Following a first degree from the University of Sussex, he worked as a town planner and then did a Masters course in planning at Birmingham Polytechnic. Following a disappointing two years in Ipswich working as a town planner at Suffolk County Council, he moved to Paris with his French girlfriend, intending to improve his French and experience French culture. He found a job in a language school and stayed for five years, then returned to Birmingham to do a Masters course in Applied Linguistics. He moved to Brussels in 1987 as an assistant at the ULB, teaching English at the Solvay Ecole de Commerce. He later moved to the Open University in Brussels and now works as European Policy Manager for West Midlands in Europe.

Why did you decide to relocate to Brussels?
I wanted to return to Paris, but my French girlfriend did not! One of my lecturers invited me to apply for a post in Brussels. We saw it as a compromise – French language, good food, near the UK and France.

What about red tape – any problems?
Amazing – this was 1987. Queuing for a *Carte de Sejour*, getting electricity and gas, waiting six months for a phone, etc…My first year in Brussels was just red tape! However I had experienced this in France so was able to speed things along better than many of my Anglo-Saxon colleagues!

What were your first impressions of Brussels?
Very bad indeed. Getting off the train at the Gare du Midi, there were no directions and the *pre-metro* was dark and dirty. Quite negative and this put us off selling our house in Birmingham just in case we wanted to leave.

Where in Brussels do you live and why?
Boitsfort. We found a small house near the forest. It has good connections to the E411 – my wife works in Louvain-la-Neuve – and I could take the 94 tram to the ULB.

Was it hard to find accommodation? What is accommodation like in Brussels?
When I first came to Brussels on a limited budget I found it hard to find a flat to rent in Ixelles with a courtyard for the cat! Our first flat was a typical Brussels experience – corrupt landlord and poor accommodation. Then by chance we met a Belgian friend and she opened us up to a network of contacts. We eventually found a better flat and my girlfriend found a job. Crisis over…

How did you go about finding work?
I had a job before I came at the ULB.

How do you find working there compared with home?
This was my first full-time university post. I found it hierarchic and a little old-fashioned, which I believe is still the case with the ULB.

Did it take long to acclimatise?
Yes longer than I expected – I would say about two years.

How does the quality of life compare to other countries you have lived in? Do you find it expensive to live here?
I think the quality of life compares well, especially for public transport and health care. Accommodation is cheaper than the UK but some areas are more expensive. In general I don't think Brussels is unduly expensive except for car insurance and local taxes.

What is the social life like – is it easy to make friends?
I have a good expat network but I have found it hard to make a lot of Belgian friends – those Belgian friends that I have, have often lived abroad themselves and so are more open to international contacts. My lack of Dutch means that I have a limited number of friends from Flanders, but I do have quite a few Dutch-speaking friends with whom I communicate in English.

Do you find locals welcoming to foreigners?
Tolerant but not welcoming.

What do you like best about Brussels?
Food, beers, diversity, surrealism, and the lack of health and safety worries, which makes life more spontaneous than the UK. Belgians are generally cheerful and well educated and open. I like the internationalism of the population, if not the politicians, and the multiculturalism which enriches my life. I find the UK arrogant and don't like the way that it insists that it is better than most nations. This manifests itself in a constant flow of anti-Belgian jokes, which I find insulting. I also prefer Belgium's approach to Europe, rather than the rampant anti-Europe stance in the UK.

What do you like least about Brussels?
As a town planner, I am depressed at the way Brussels has destroyed itself by poor governance and just does not seem to care about its appearance. 'Bruxellisation' is sadly all too evident, although things have improved in the past few years. Linked to this is a complete lack of pride regarding the city and no appreciation of the fact that outsiders visit the city and need direction signs. I am also ashamed at the poor image that Brussels projects to outsiders – slightly dull and bourgeois.

What is your favourite place in Brussels?
Lots of places. Boitsfort market on a sunny day, the Grand'Place in all weathers, Place Ste-Catherine and Quai aux Briques for the fish restaurants, the cafés Greenwich and Archiduc and Mort Subite, Place Flagey and the lakes. I also like the Forêt de Soignes, strolling along Rue Blaes to the Jeu de Balle.

What is your least favourite place in Brussels?
The Maison Communal in Ixelles. I still shudder over the wasted hours and aggressive service when I first arrived. Any supermarket – they are all poorly designed, with bad service and difficult parking. The Rue des Bouchers is just a tourist trap. I also dislike Rue Neuve, Gare du Nord and the northern part of Brussels, along with the appalling office suburbs around Zaventem, built without any planning whatsoever.

Do you think you will stay in Brussels/Belgium?
Yes.

Do you have any regrets about leaving your home country?
No – after the first two years of admin difficulties, I have found Brussels welcoming, providing me with excellent health care, and a full social and cultural life.

What advice would you give someone thinking of coming to live and work in Brussels?
Come. Brussels is a great place to live with a good quality of life but you need to be flexible, adaptable, and relaxed. Rules are made to be broken! I appreciate the laid back attitude of Belgians, which means that anything might be possible.

The Grand'Place

Flemish Renaissance building in the Rue du Bois Sauvage

Moving to Brussels: Before you Go

Belgium is no longer a bureaucratic nightmare for foreigners, but there remain some preparations to be made before you arrive especially for non-EU nationals. Some municipalities in Belgium insist on a certificate of good conduct (certificat de bon moeurs/bewijs van goed gedrag) before they will issue a residence permit. You should go to the local town hall to register as a resident within eight days of arriving in Belgium. Children may find it hard to adapt to life at a Belgian state school because of the two national languages.

Dealing with the paperwork

Brussels has stylish shops, sophisticated apartments and outstanding restaurants. But before you can enjoy any of that, you have to find a job, rent an apartment and spend several hours dealing with the bureaucracy. Here is how to do it.

A Guide to Red Tape

Belgium is no longer a bureaucratic nightmare for foreigners. The administration has been streamlined and many procedures can be done online. But it's important that you follow the steps in the right order, or you could be caught in a Kafkaesque nightmare.

Before you Leave Home

Moving to a new country is never easy. Belgium is no exception, but you can deal with many of the basic problems before you arrive.

Three Months Before you Leave

Language Lessons Start learning the language. You will probably find French useful if you are living and working in Brussels, but Dutch might be a better option if you are moving to Flanders.

Talk to Children Your children need to be told about the reasons for moving to Brussels. Young ones might feel more positive about the move if you tell them that Tintin comes from Brussels and house walls in the city are painted with giant cartoon murals. Teenage children might appreciate the fact that Belgium has some of Europe's best summer rock festivals and Antwerp is famous for its cool style. Suggest they look at the website www.noctis.com to get an idea of the parties, raves and bars that make Belgium one of Europe's clubbing hotspots. Promise to buy everyone a Belgian waffle as soon as you arrive in Brussels.

Formalities Contact the Belgian Embassy or Consulate in your home country and ask for the latest information on the formalities applicable for living, studying or working in Belgium. The website of the Belgian Embassy in Washington DC (www.diplobel. us) covers many of the familiar problems for non-EU citizens such as obtaining a visa and a work permit.

Police Certificate Some municipalities in Belgium insist on a certificate of good conduct (*certificat de bon moeurs/bewijs van goed gedrag*) before they will issue a residence permit. The aim is simply to establish that you don't have a serious criminal record. But it can be difficult to get hold of the correct document. Try asking the Belgian embassy in your home country what exactly is needed. You might be able to get a

Hergé mural in Marolles

certificate from a police station in your home country. American citizens need an FBI criminal history. They get this from the Federal Bureau of Investigation. The procedure has to be done by post, and takes eight to ten weeks; contact FBI CJIS Division (Record Request), 1000 Custer Hollow Road, Clarksburg, WV 26306.

Two Months Before you Leave

Passport You need to have a valid passport to enter Belgium, although citizens of EU countries can travel with just a valid ID card.

Visa Nationals from European Economic Area (EEA) countries (15 EU countries plus Iceland, Norway and Liechtenstein) are allowed to stay in Belgium for three months without any formalities. Citizens from the US and many other countries can also stay for three months, provided that they have a passport or identity papers accepted by the Belgian authorities, a return air ticket and proof of adequate means of support. Newcomers planning to stay for more than three months need to get their papers in order - ideally before leaving home. Nationals from the EEA do not require a visa, but nationals from a non-EEA country have to apply to a Belgian embassy or consulate in their home country for a Schengen visa. This document allows them to enter all 15 countries of the Schengen area.

The Schengen Visa

The Schengen agreement (www.eurovisa.info) abolished border controls between most EU countries. Travellers now pass between these countries without any passport checks or baggage examination. Anyone from outside Europe who applies for a visa for one of these countries is automatically issued with a Schengen Visa, which allows them to travel freely between all the Schengen countries without any further formalities, although everyone is required to carry an ID card or passport.

The Schengen agreement applies to air travel, with the result that flights between member countries are treated as if they are domestic flights. Most European airports have been modified to create separate zones for Schengen travellers (who are normally not checked) and others (who have to show passports).

The treaty is named after a small town on the Luxembourg border where the agreement was signed in 1985. The Schengen zone currently contains 15 countries including Belgium, France, Germany, Italy and the Netherlands. But Britain and Ireland are not members and so all travellers have to produce a passport when travelling to these countries. Those with a Schengen visa will need to apply for a second visa from the British or Irish authorities.

The application form can be downloaded from the Schengen website (www.eurovisa.info), but you will have to go in person to an embassy or consulate to collect the visa. You need to produce a passport valid for at least 15 months, a certificate of good conduct, a medical certificate issued by an approved doctor, and a work permit. You are also expected to provide proof that you have sufficient funds for the period of stay, evidence of somewhere to stay and a return ticket. Married applicants also have to provide a marriage certificate, while parents must produce legalised birth certificates for all their children. The visa application normally takes at least three weeks to process. The procedure costs $49 in the US and a similar amount in other countries. A single fee covers spouses and all children.

Work Permit No work permit is needed if you come from one of the countries belonging to the European Economic Area (EEA). You can settle in Belgium along with your spouse and children without any formalities. The EEA currently covers 18 countries - Austria, Belgium, Denmark, Finland, France, Germany, Greece, Iceland, Ireland, Italy, Lichtenstein, Luxembourg, Netherlands, Norway, Portugal, Spain, Sweden and the United Kingdom.

All citizens from non-EEA countries must have a work permit before they move to Belgium to take up a job. This includes citizens from 10 of the 12 countries that joined the EU in 2004 and 2007. The Belgian government only allows citizens of Malta and Cyprus to work in Belgium without a work permit. This regulation is unlikely to be relaxed until April 2009 at the earliest. Check the European job mobility portal for up to date information on Belgian regulations as they apply to each of the new EU countries (www.europa.eu.int/eures).

The work permit has to be obtained by the employer, who applies to the Belgian authorities. A permit is normally only granted if there are no Belgian or EU nationals available to fill the post. You should allow at least four weeks for the application to be processed.

Obtain Legalised Documents Foreigners often run into problems with the Belgian authorities when they are asked to produce a birth certificate or marriage certificate. The Belgian authorities (like most other administrations) only accept foreign documents that have been legalised. This involves a rather obscure certificate known as the *apostille* which is attached to an official copy of the original document by the issuing authority. You can request this once you are in Belgium, but it is much simpler to do so before you leave. You will need a legalised marriage certificate, for example, if one partner has been granted a work permit in Belgium but the other has no job. The certificate has to be translated into one of the official languages of Belgium by a certified translator (unless it is already in French, Dutch or German).

Documents originating in the UK are dealt with centrally by the Legalisation Office (www.fco.gov.uk, look under 'legalisation'). Citizens of the US and Australia must have documents legalised by the issuing state, rather than a national authority. Several companies in the US can, in return for a fee, get you the required certificates and legalised translations for Belgium.

Obtain Legalised Translations Non-EU citizens should obtain legalised translations of important official documents such as a marriage certificate or academic degree before moving to Belgium.

One Month Before you Leave

Accommodation Find a temporary place to stay in Brussels. Most large Brussels estate agents have websites with photographs of properties to rent. You may simply want to book a hotel room or an apartment hotel for a few days. You need to book well ahead if you arriving at a busy period of the year (September to December or March to June).

Certificates Collect all your educational and professional certificates and qualifications. You should also take copies of birth certificates, marriage documents, divorce papers and any legal papers regarding custody of children. This saves the trouble of applying for them when you are living in Belgium.

Tax and Banking Records It might be useful to create a file of recent tax records and bank statements to show the Belgian authorities, especially if you plan to be self employed or set up a company.

Medical Records Collect medical and dental records. Non-EU citizens should take out temporary medical insurance to cover the interim period before they sign up with a Belgian insurance company. Citizens of EU countries are covered by their existing national health insurance for the first six months.

Open a Bank Account Contact a Belgian bank to open an expat account before you move. This can often be done online, though you will not be able to get a full range of services until you are legally resident in Belgium.

Find a Removal Company You will probably need to find a company to ship your furniture to Belgium. Make sure you are fully insured.

Final Week Before you Leave

Pet Passport You need to get a pet passport if you are bringing an animal into Belgium. Contact your vet to get a certificate of good health, which has to be issued no more than eight days before moving to Belgium. You will also need a recent rabies certificate, dated not less than one month before travelling.

Becoming Belgian

Citizenship Rules Simplified

The government has simplified the formalities for becoming a Belgian citizen and obtaining a Belgian passport. Anyone who has lived in the country for at least seven years and has been granted official residency can apply for citizenship. The procedure is now fairly rapid compared to many other countries. Candidates simply have to make a declaration of citizenship in French or Dutch before an official in their local town hall. That is all. The Belgian government doesn't insist on its new nationals knowing the name of the prime minister or the words of the national anthem.

Children of a marriage with one Belgian parent are granted automatic Belgian citizenship, as are third-generation immigrants. Children born in Belgium with two foreign parents are eligible for Belgian nationality from birth if their parents have lived legally in Belgium for at least 10 years. The application can be made up to the child's 12th birthday. Other children born in Belgium can also obtain Belgian citizenship between the ages of 18 and 30 simply by signing a declaration at their local town hall, as long as they have lived in Belgium since birth.

People who become naturalised Belgian citizens can keep their original nationality if this is allowed by the other country. The British and US governments let you keep both nationalities.

Learning the Languages

It is difficult to integrate in Brussels if you don't speak at least some French and perhaps even a few sentences of Dutch. You can, of course, get along perfectly well just speaking English, but you will miss out on social contacts and the cultural vitality of a bilingual city.

So you probably need to think about signing up for a language course. Brussels offers an enormous choice of courses and activities, from serious lessons that aim to give you a firm grounding in the subjunctive tense to relaxed sessions that allow you to chat in the new language.

The cheapest courses are offered by the local commune (or *gemeente*). They are often heavily subsidised, but can be dull and traditional in their methods. The private schools, though expensive, often use more exciting teaching methods.

Most private language schools are located in business districts such as Avenue Louise and the European Quarter, whereas municipal schools are often in residential districts. For total immersion, you can sign up for a week course in a residential school in the Ardennes.

Living in a polyglot city like Brussels, you can pick up the basics of many languages without setting foot in a classroom. You can listen to Spanish on the tram, tune in to FM Brussel radio for Dutch or turn on the television to watch a Portuguese TV soap.

Learning French

Alliance Française de Bruxelles-Europe Set up in Brussels in 1945, the Alliance Française belongs to a worldwide network of French language institutes. The Brussels branch teaches about 5,000 students every year, many of them EU staff and diplomats. Highly recommended for those who want a no-nonsense course. Rue de la Loi 26; ☎ 02.732.15.92; email: info@alliancefr.be; www.alliancefr.be

Amira A friendly school that teaches French communication skills in small groups. Avenue Louise 283; ☎ 02.640.68.50; email info@amira.be; www.amira.be

Call International Relaxed lessons in comfortable surroundings using a method known as accelerated learning. Branches in Brussels, Waterloo, Tournai and Lille. Rue des Drapiers 25; ☎ 02.644.95.95; www.callinter.com

Ceran Intensive French residential courses in a manor house deep in the Ardennes. Aimed at professionals, Ceran courses get fast results, but they aren't cheap. Avenue des Petits Sapins 27, Spa; ☎ 087.79.11.22; www.ceran.com

Chambre de Commerce The Brussels Chamber of Commerce has been organising language courses at the VUB university campus in Etterbeek since 1970. Courses focus on grammar and communication skills. Students are also offered e-learning. Building D, VUB, Pleinlaan 2; ☎ 02.629.39.08; www.vub.ac.be

CPAB Language school based in Ixelles with a range of classes in French, including individual lessons. One of the least expensive schools in Brussels, but classes are big. Galeries de la Toison d'Or 29-31 (off the Chaussée d'Ixelles); ☎ 02.511.01.09 ; www.cpab.net

Fondation 9 Language school set up in 1989 by Brussels University ULB and the Chamber of Commerce to teach European languages. At the time there were just nine official languages, but the EU now struggles with more than 20. This school concentrates on the main languages (French, Dutch, German and English), with classes in the morning and after work. Avenue Louise 485; ☎ 02.627.52.52; email fondation9@ulb.ac.be; www.ulb.ac.be/assoc/fondation9

Thema Small and friendly language school in Ixelles with classes in French, Dutch, Italian and English. Offers courses in business language taught by specialists. Rue Tenbosch 63; ☎ 02.640.59.82; email: info@themalingua.be; www.themalingua.be

Learning Dutch

Huis van het Nederlands The Huis van het Nederlands (Dutch House) provides information on all Dutch language courses in Brussels. Located in the centre of Brussels, this is a good place to begin searching for a course. Rue Philippe de Champagne 23; ☎ 02.501.66.60; www.huisnederlandsbrussel.be

De Rand Organises Dutch language courses in several community centres in the Flemish belt. The emphasis is on teaching everyday Dutch and introducing newcomers to Flemish culture. Kaasmarkt 17, Wemmel; ☎ 02.456.97.80; email info@derand.be; www.derand.be

Oefen hier je Nedelands An inspired attempt in the Flemish belt to encourage people to speak more Dutch. Flemish shopkeepers put up signs in their window inviting customers to: 'Oefen hier je Nederlands' (Try out your Dutch here). Shops participating in the scheme are listed on the website www.oefenhierjeNederlands.be

Babbelut Relaxed language cafés where you can talk Dutch with other foreigners. Organised by Bru-taal at the Elzenhof Flemish Centre in Ixelles and five other cultural centres in Brussels. No need to book, just turn up on the night. ☎ 02.501.66.90; email info@bru-taal.be; www.bru-taal.be

Learning other Languages

Det Danske Kultur Institut The Danish Cultural Institute organises Danish language courses in its cultural centre in the European Quarter. Rue du Cornet 22; ☎ 02.230.73.26; www.dkibenelux.org

Goethe Institut The German government provides serious German language courses in a townhouse in the heart of the European Quarter. Courses are expensive but thorough. Rue Belliard 58; ☎ 02.230.39.70; www.goethe.de/bruessel

Instituto Cervantes Run by the Spanish government, the Instituto Cervantes offers a range of Spanish courses in a townhouse close to the European institutions. Avenue de Tervuren 64; ☎ 02.737.01.90; www.bruselas.cervantes.es

Instituto Italiano di Cultura The Italian Cultural Institute offers serious Italian language courses in an 1880s townhouse near Avenue Louise. The centre has a library, newspaper reading room and cinema. Rue de Livourne 38; ☎ 02.533.27.20; www.iicbruxelles.be.

The Scandinavian Language School Offers language courses at the Danish Cultural Institute in Danish, Finnish, Swedish, Norwegian and Islandic. Rue du Cornet 22; ☎ 02.230.73.26; www.dkibenelux.org

Children's Language Courses

Children tend to pick up languages much faster than adults. Several organisations in Brussels help them master the new language while having fun at the same time.

Kiddy and Junior Classes Language classes for children of all ages, combined with fun activities. Rue du Taciturne 50; ☎ 02.218.39.20; email: info@kiddyclasses.net; www.kiddyclasses.net

Kid's Computer Club Inspiring language lessons for children aged four to 18 years. Lessons in several languages combined with computer courses and sports. Avenue René Gobert 31; ☎ 02.374.27.08; email: secretariat@kidscomputer.be; www.kidscomputer.be

Banking

Belgium's banks are quietly efficient organisations that often lead the world in technological innovation. Belgians have been able to use cash machines since the 1970s and advanced forms of electronic payment are now widely available. Most banks welcome expatriate customers and some offer a specialised expat service. The largest banks produce brochures, forms and web pages in English. The main Belgian banks are listed on the website of the Belgian Bankers' and Stockbrokers' Association (www.abb-bvb.be). Local branches are listed in the Brussels Yellow Pages (*Gouden Gids/Pages d'Or*) under the heading *Banken/Banques*. The information can also be found online in English at www.goldenpages.be.

Belgian Banks

Dexia: ☎ 02.222.12.01; www.dexia.be

Fortis: (expat desk) ☎ 02.413.56.49; www.fortisbank.be/expats

ING: ☎ 02.464.66.64; www.ing.be/expats

KBC: (expat desk) ☎ 02.429.18.57; www.kbc.be/expats

Banque de Post/Postbank: Post office bank. www.bpo.be

Foreign Banks in Belgium

Banca Monte Paschi Belgio: ☎ 02.220.72.11; www.montepaschi.be

Citibank: ☎ 02.626.53.96; email expatriatebanking.belgium@citigroup.com; www.citibank.be

Triodos: Dutch ethical bank. ☎ 02.548.28.28; www.triodos.com

Opening an Account

Most Belgian banks are smart and efficient, but they offer different types of services. It is worth doing some preliminary research before you open an account, since it's very difficult to change your bank once you have complex arrangements in place. You should find out how much the bank charges in annual fees, as these can vary considerably. Some smaller banks offer better rates, but provide a less extensive network of branches. The best branches for expatriates are located in the main business districts such as Schuman and Avenue Louise. Banks in the suburbs sometimes have less experience in dealing with expatriate clients, though they may offer a more friendly service than big city branches. Banks' hours are normally open Monday to Saturday 9.30am to 4pm.

Opening a current account (*zichtrekening/compte à vue*) is normally straightforward. You simply go along to a branch taking proof of identity. Most banks will accept a passport, but some ask for a Belgian ID card. You can even open an online account without setting foot in a bank. Some of the large banks offer an expat service that

The Euro

Belgium was one of 12 European countries that abolished their national currency in favour of the euro (€) on 1 January 2002. The original Eurozone members were Austria, Belgium, France, Germany, Greece, Ireland, Italy, Luxembourg, Spain, Portugal and The Netherlands. The currency is issued in coins of one cent, two cents, five cents, 10 cents, 20 cents, 50 cents, €1 and €2, and notes of €5, €10, €20, €50, €100, €200 and €500. The notes are uniform across the Eurozone, illustrated with rather dull generic images symbolising lofty European values. The coins are potentially more interesting, as each country is allowed to puts its own design on one side of the coin. Austria has put an edelweiss on its two-cent coin, Italy has Dante on the €2 coin and Finland has two swans flying over a lake on its €1 coins. Belgium unfortunately confirms its dull national image abroad by putting King Albert, rather than Magritte or Rubens, on all eight denominations.

The euro has turned out to be one of the EU's biggest success stories. The currency was adopted by Slovenia in 2007 and most of the other new member states plan to convert to the euro as soon they have met the entry conditions. The small countries are almost ready to convert, but Poland and Hungary are still a long way off. Despite the success of the common currency, Britain, Sweden and Denmark refuse to give up their national currency.

The main problems with the introduction of the euro have been relatively minor – the Finns have stopped using the fiddly one cent coins, and many shops refuse to accept €200 and €500 notes because of forgeries. The euro is also blamed for rising prices and many people still make calculations in the old currencies. In a recent survey, more than half of French people said they wanted the French Franc to be restored. Yet the euro has become a powerful world currency that could one day overtake the dollar.

allows you to open the account online before you move to Belgium, but you will eventually have to go along the bank in person (once you have a residence permit).

Most banks will include an overdraft facility on your current account (*aller en negative/onder nul gaan*). But they will need proof of your income, such as a contract of employment or three successive salary slips. Some banks limit the overdraft to €250, while others will allow customers a negative balance of over €1,200.

Once your account is opened, the bank will send you a Bancontact/Mister Cash debit card. You will then receive a second letter with your secret PIN code (a four digit number).

You can also open a savings account (*compte d'épargne/spaarrekening*). Banks offer different rates of interest on savings accounts, ranging from 1.5% to 3%, though some offer higher rates to attract new customers. Money can be transferred to savings accounts using self banking machines. Interest on savings accounts is non-taxable below €1,600.

Expat Services

Some of the larger Belgian banks such as ING and Fortis have compiled useful information packages for expats in Belgium. They sometimes offer an optional comprehensive service to expats (which involves an annual charge). This includes a current account, debit card, credit card and transfer forms, but also advantageous financial and insurance packages geared towards foreign residents.

Cash

It's almost possible to live in Belgium without ever using cash. Most shops have Bancontact machines which can be used for electronic payments, and many allow you to make small payments using Proton.

If you do need cash, you can usually find a cash dispenser (ATM) outside a bank. These are equipped to take Bancontact/Mister Cash cards issued by local banks, as well as credit cards and foreign cards with a Maestro chip.

Customers of Belgian banks can use any Bancontact machine without charge. They can also use self bank machines located inside banks, even if they belong to a rival bank. The self bank centres are open longer hours than banks, normally 5am to 11.30pm. Access is provided by swiping your card.

People without Belgian bank accounts often complain about the scarcity of cash machines on the street. This leads to long queues, especially in central Brussels on Saturday afternoons. The machines carry a limited amount of cash, and are frequently empty by Saturday evening, so that it is sometimes impossible to get hold of cash on Sundays.

The large Belgian supermarkets have come up with a solution. When paying with Bancontact, you can ask the cashier for cash from the till. The sum is then deducted from your card. You can do this on Sundays at Delhaize City shops.

Paying Bills

Most bills are sent in the form of an orange bank transfer form (*overschrijving/virement*) with the name of the payee, account number and amount already printed. You simply have to put in your bank account number, sign the form and give it to your bank. You can post the form, hand it to the cashier or drop it in the special deposit box inside the bank marked *virement/overschrijving*.

You can also pay bills by electronic transfer using your Bancontact card in a self bank machine belonging to your bank. This method is faster and more reliable. Most banks also offer home banking, which allows customers to manage their banking on a home computer.

Payment by cheques has virtually disappeared in Belgium. It can still be done, but is generally expensive.

Standing Orders You can set up a standing order (*ordre permanent/doorlopende opdracht*) authorising your bank to pay fixed monthly sums such as rent. The standing order can be created electronically using self bank, and cancelled at any time.

Authorised Payments Many bills are not for fixed amounts, such as electricity, gas and phone bills. You can pay these automatically by setting up an authorised payment (*domicilisation/domiciliëring*). This system allows the authorised organisation to deduct the money automatically from your account. You have to give your consent in writing to the payee, who then sends the bills directly to the bank. The bank then removes the amount from your account. The payee sends you notification of the bill on a standard transfer form, but you do not need to do anything.

Debit Cards You can pay for most items in Belgium using a debit card issued by your bank (Bancontact/Mister Cash). You need to type in a four-digit code when you use the card. The money is deducted almost immediately from your account. You can also ask your bank to add the Maestro function to your Bancontact card, which allows you to withdraw money or make electronic payments at foreign cash machines displaying the Maestro logo.

Proton Some Belgians pay a small additional charge to have their Bancontact card equipped with Proton. This allows them to load the card electronically with a small amount of credit (€5-€125), which can be used to make small payments, like buying a newspaper or a baguette. The money is deducted without the need for a pin code, which means that you lose all the money if your card is lost. Proton can also be used in phone boxes and parking meters.

Credit Cards Most credit cards are accepted in Belgium, though not always in restaurants and small shops. You may have to show your identity card when paying by credit card. The most popular cards in Belgium are Visa and MasterCard, which are used like debit cards. The full balance is automatically deducted from your current account every month. Some banks also offer conventional credit cards such as American Express and Diners, but these are not widely accepted in Belgium. Most Belgian credit cards can only be used with a four-digit PIN code, but some retailers require nothing more than a signature.

Internet Banking Most banking transactions can be done by internet once you have set up a home banking scheme. You can also arrange to do your banking by telephone, which allows you to carry out transactions using a touch-tone phone anywhere in the world.

International Transfers Transferring money from abroad can be expensive and slow, but you can speed up the process by asking for a Swift transfer and quoting the Swift number of your Belgian bank (BIC). Transferring money from one European country to another in euro should cost the same as a domestic transaction. The process is speeded up if you quote the international code of your Belgian bank (IBAN) and its Swift code. Some banks charge extra fees if the information is not scrupulously correct.

Lost Card If your bank card is lost or stolen, you should have it stopped immediately by calling 070.344.344. You should also contact your branch as soon as possible.

Bank Charges Belgian banks charge an annual fee for services such as Proton, Bancontact and Maestro. The average Belgian family pays about €65 a year in charges, which is the second lowest rate in Europe. The Dutch pay less, but Italians pay three times as much.

Savings Accounts Most Belgian banks offer low rates of interest on savings accounts (*compte d'épargne/spaarboekje*). Some Dutch banks have begun to poach Belgian customers by offering much better rates for online savings accounts if you keep the money in the account for a certain period. The main Dutch banks looking for Belgian customers are Rabobank (www.rabobank.be) and ABN-AMRO (www.abnamro.be).

Getting to Brussels

Brussels is one of Europe's most accessible cities. It sits at the centre of a network of railway lines, motorways and airline routes. You can take a high-speed train from Paris in 75 minutes, or drive from London via the Channel Tunnel in under five hours. The existing infrastructure is impressive, and new projects are now in the pipeline to improve international rail links and upgrade Brussels Airport.

Travel by Air

Brussels Airport

The main Belgian airport is at Zaventem, 14km north east of the city centre. The airport authority has made major improvements in recent years, with the result that Brussels is ranked as one of the best airports in Europe. But it is not perfect. Parking is often difficult, and you may spend 30 minutes searching for a space. The airport is also much bigger, so it takes longer to reach check-in, especially if you are flying from the new Terminal A. Most European flights leave from this terminal, but flights to the United States and Britain are from the older Terminal B.

The airport has flights to most major European cities, along with an extensive network of long-haul destinations. It was, until recently, difficult to find low-cost flights

from Brussels, but cheap flights are now offered by Brussels Airlines and EasyJet. The duty-free area has a good range of shops, including several selling Belgian chocolates. But prices are high, even without VAT, except for alcohol and cigarettes.

Transport from Brussels Airport

The easiest way to get to the airport from central Brussels is by train. The Airport City Express runs every 20 minutes to Gare du Midi, with stops at Gare Centrale and Gare du Nord. The service is not as fast as the name suggests, taking 20 minutes to reach the city centre. The trains are also shabby, but prices are cheap, with a single ticket costing just €2.60. The first train to the airport leaves Bruxelles Midi station at 4.50am and the last train leaves from the airport at 11.21pm.

The rail authority is now working on a new link that will connect the European Quarter with Brussels Airport in just 12 minutes. Until the new line opens (probably in 2012), the simplest way to travel between the European institutions and the airport is to use the bus service operated by the Brussels transport authority. The service begins at Place du Luxembourg, near the European Parliament, and stops at Rond Point Schuman, close to the Berlaymont building, before continuing through Schaerbeek and Evere. A single ticket bought from the driver costs €3, but frequent travellers can buy a cheaper 10-ride ticket for €21.

The airport bus is, in principle, a useful connection, linking the European Quarter with the airport in about 30 minutes. But it can get stuck in traffic during rush hours. It also, mysteriously, changes number on certain days. It is number 12 from Monday to Friday, but number 11 on Saturday, Sunday and weekends, when it follows a slightly modified route.

A taxi ride from the airport to the centre costs about €30 and takes about 20 minutes when the traffic is flowing. But during rush hours (7am-9am and 5pm-7pm) the journey can take twice as long and cost a lot more. There is often a long queue at the official taxi rank in front of the main arrivals hall.

Brussels Airlines

Belgium suffered a national trauma when the national airline, Sabena, went bankrupt in November 2002. The response was to create a much smaller business airline, SN Brussels Airlines, serving major European cities, along with destinations in Africa and North America. Five years later, the airline merged with Virgin Express to create Brussels Airlines. The new company aims to attract both business and budget travellers by a two-tier fare structure. The executives will be offered b.flex tickets, while low-cost travellers can buy b.light tickets for as little as €49 one-way. With guaranteed cheap fares to almost 50 European airports, Brussels Airlines could turn into a serious rival to Ryanair.

Cheap Flights

Once seen as an expensive business–class destination, Brussels Airport is rapidly repositioning itself as a low-cost hub. The East European airline Sky Europe offers cheap flights from Brussels to Prague, Vienna, Budapest and Krakow, while easyJet began flights from Brussels to Geneva in the summer of 2007. The low-budget Spanish airline Vueling operates to Valencia and Barcelona, and the Finnish airline Blue1 flies to Helsinki.

Charleroi Airport

Charleroi Airport has become a major hub for low-cost flights across Europe. The main operator is Ryanair, which currently offers cheap flights to 19 destinations (Dublin, Shannon, Glasgow, Stockholm, Venice, Rome, Pisa, Milan, Carcassonne, Girona, Valladolid, Salzburg, Malaga, Faro, Nîmes and Valencia). The fares are often unbelievably low, but the Irish airline is frequently criticised for poor customer service. If your flight is cancelled, you may have to wait a whole day for a replacement plane to turn up.

Passengers also have to bear in mind that many Ryanair airports are a long way from the nearest city. Charleroi Airport (which Ryanair has successfully renamed Brussels South Charleroi) is 46km south of Brussels. There is a shuttle bus service from Bruxelles Midi Station which takes about one hour, but you need to catch it at least three hours before the departure time to be sure of catching your flight. Tickets cost €10.50 and are sold by the driver. The Ryanair bus leaves from the Rue de France, at the back of the station, near the Eurostar terminal. Watch out for a scam in which taxi drivers tell Ryanair passengers that the bus has broken down, and offer to take them to the airport for a ludicrous fare.

There is an alternative. You can take a direct train from Bruxelles Midi Station to Charleroi, then catch TEC bus 68 to the airport. The train takes 45 minutes and the bus takes a further 10 minutes, so this looks like a promising option. But the buses only run every hour at weekends, so the Ryanair coach might realistically be the most efficient option.

The Walloon authorities are currently investing heavily in Charleroi Airport and plan to open a new terminal building in 2007. A second low-cost airline, Wizz Air (www.wizzair.be) now offers flights from Charleroi to Budapest, Warsaw and Ljubljana.

Other International Airports

The high-speed train network makes it possible to catch a flight from an international airport in a neighbouring country. Thalys trains run from Brussels to Paris Charles de Gaulle airport in one hour and 15 minutes. There are also regular train services to Amsterdam Schiphol airport taking one hour and 40 minutes, and ICE trains to Frankfurt airport taking about three hours and 25 minutes.

Amsterdam Schiphol is a major hub for low-cost flights to European destinations. Flights are operated by easyJet, which generally offers a more customer-friendly service than Ryanair.

How to get the Cheapest Fares

Low-cost carriers don't always offer the cheapest fares. You normally get the best deals on Ryanair and other budget operators if you book several weeks ahead. It also helps if you can avoid popular times such as departing from Belgium on a Friday evening or arriving back on a Sunday evening. Fares also rise steeply as the departure date approaches and it can be cheaper to travel at short notice with a regular airline such as Brussels Airlines or Aer Lingus.

Flight Contacts

Brussels Airport: ☎ 02.753.4200; www.brusselsairport.be
Charleroi Airport: ☎ 071.251.211; www.charleroi-airport.com
Brussels Airlines: ☎ 070.35.11.11; www.brusselsairlines.be
Ryanair: www.ryanair.com
Aer Lingus: www.aerlingus.com
Sky Europe: www.skyeurope.com
easyJet: www.easyjet.com
Vueling: www.vueling.com
Blue1: www.blue1.com

Travel by Rail

Belgian Railways

Belgium opened the first railway line on Continental Europe in 1835, just four years after the world's first trains ran in Britain. The country went on to build the world's densest railway network, with lines running across the flat Flemish polders to the coast and penetrating deep into the Ardennes. The 19th-century Belgian network has survived almost intact, providing a cheap and efficient travel option for those without cars. Some of the local routes involve old rattling carriages, but trains operating on mainline routes are among the most modern in Europe.

High Speed

Belgium has invested heavily over the past decade in constructing new tracks for high-speed trains. The work is at an end, and Brussels now lies at the hub of a network of fast trains that run to the heart of some of the main cities of Europe.

Eurostar Grey and yellow Eurostar trains link Brussels with London in just 1hr 50mins. You have to check in 30 minutes before the train leaves and go through passport and security checks. Eurostar trains travel at 300 km/hour, taking 20 minutes to pass through the Channel Tunnel. Some trains stop at Lille in northern France and at Ebbsfleet off the M25. There are nine trains a day on weekdays, and seven at weekends.

Eurostar tickets are not particularly cheap, but there are occasionally special deals. Return fares start at roughly €30 for a single, if you book ahead and travel at a non-peak period, but the price rises steeply if you want to travel on a weekday at short notice. Tickets are valid for travel to any

Belgian city, so you can take a Belgian train as far as Arlon in the south or Ypres in the west.

Business travellers are wooed with various incentives, such as a Corporate Programme and a Eurostar Frequent Traveller programme. Those travelling first class can wait in a lounge designed by Philippe Starck. The waiting areas for second-class passengers at Brussels are fairly basic.

The Ashford Revolt

A major change happened on 14 November 2007 when Eurostar moved its London terminal from Waterloo to St Pancras International in northern London. The striking new terminal provides easy connections for train services to northern Britain, including York, Hull, Glasgow and Edinburgh. The shortest journey time between Brussels and London is now under two hours. Not everyone is pleased with the new timetable. Trains will stop at a new Stratford International station, close to the Canary Wharf office district and the 2012 Olympics site. Some services will also stop at Ebbsfleet International station, which will mainly serve people arriving by car. But trains from Brussels will no longer stop at Ashford International. The decision to cut Ashford has sparked off a protest campaign. Various petitions have been circulated, gathering thousands of signatures. At the time of writing Eurostar remained committed to its plan to axe all Brussels to Ashford services (so passengers will have to change at Lille).

Thalys Maroon-liveried Thalys trains take just one hour and 22 minutes from Brussels to Paris. This service is immensely popular, with up to 25 trains a day connecting the capitals. Tickets for the Paris metro are sold on the train.

Thalys trains also run from Brussels to Amsterdam, and from Brussels to Cologne, though the high-speed lines on these routes are still not completed. The current journey time to Amsterdam by Thalys is two hours and 40 minutes, hardly any faster than conventional services. The journey time to Cologne is two hours and 20 minutes.

TGV High-speed French TGV trains run from Brussels to more than 30 destinations in France, including Disneyland Paris, Charles-de-Gaulle airport, Provence and the French Riviera. You can leave Brussels at 7.04am and be in Bordeaux by 1pm, just in time for lunch. Or you can take a train from Brussels at 8.32am that gets you to Avignon by 12.30pm.

There are also frequent TGV and Eurostar services to Lille in northern France. The train takes just 38 minutes and drops you in the heart of a modern business district designed by the Dutch architect Rem Koolhaas. But if gleaming modernity isn't your thing, you can walk for 10 minutes to reach the beautifully restored Vieux Lille quarter.

ICE German Inter City Express (ICE) trains operate a high-speed service between Brussels and Frankfurt, taking three hours and 45 minutes, with stops at Liège, Aachen, Cologne and Frankfurt airport. Trains run three times a day. Once in

Frankfurt, you can connect with a high-speed train to Berlin taking about four hours and 10 minutes.

EC Brussels is a hub for EuroCity (EC) international trains. Slower than TGVs, these trains run to cities such as Milan and Warsaw.

IC and IR A large number of InterCity (IC) trains connect Brussels with the main cities in Belgium, while slower and older IR trains serve small stations.

Night Trains

Many night train services have been abolished, but you can still board a train in Brussels in the early evening and wake up the next morning in the heart of Berlin. You can even travel further east on the Jan Kiepura, which leaves Brussels every evening bound for Warsaw and Moscow.

Luxurious Spanish Elipsos trains leave from the Gare du Lyon in Paris every night bound for Barcelona. The Italian Artesia trains offer a similar level of comfort, with services from Paris to Milan, Venice and Rome.

Gare du Midi

The Gare du Midi (Zuidstation in Dutch) is the main Brussels station for high-speed trains. The Eurostar terminal is here, and all Thalys trains stop at Midi (but not at Centrale or Nord stations). The station building, which dates from the 1930s, was recently modernised, and now contains an attractive shopping arcade. But the station lies in a neglected quarter of Brussels, a long and not particularly attractive walk from the city centre.

Midi does have very good public transport connections and can be reached by metro, tram or bus. The fastest route to the centre is by underground tram (known in Brussels as the pre-metro). Trams 52, 56 and 81 run from the station to the city centre. Be careful that the tram is going in the right direction. A taxi to the centre costs about €15.

Other Brussels Stations

The three main station in Brussels are Gare du Midi, Gare Centrale and Gare du Nord (also known by the Dutch names *Zuidstation, Centraal Station and Nordstation*). The stations are linked by a tunnel known as the North-South Junction that runs below broad boulevards. The Gare Centrale is the most central station, just five minutes walk from Grand'Place. It is also close to the Parc de Bruxelles, which can be reached through the Galerie Ravenstein shopping arcade and two sets of steps.

Gare Centrale Brussels Central Station was designed by the architect Victor Horta, though he did not live to see it completed. The Art Deco building was finally opened in 1952, marking the end of the North-South Junction project. It is linked to the metro system and various bus routes.

Gare du Nord The North Station is close to the Quartier Nord office district. It does not have a metro station, but can be reached by underground trams 52, 55, 56, 81 and 90.

Gare du Luxembourg The old Luxembourg Station has closed down, but a new underground rail station has been built nearby, reached from the open square in front of the European Parliament. The station lies on the line to Namur and Luxembourg.

Gare Schuman Schuman Station is currently a small commuter station with direct trains to the suburbs and some southern Belgian cities. The station is to be upgraded into a major transport interchange in 2012.

Tickets and Timetables

Belgium's national railway network (SNCB/NMBS) is heavily subsidised by the government and train tickets are not particularly expensive. Many people pay nothing at all, as all government employees are given a free season ticket. Even if you have to pay, you can often find a special bargain fare. All weekend return tickets are half price if you leave after 7pm on a Friday and return by Sunday night.

Tickets for high-speed trains can be bought at most Belgian stations, some travel agents or at the SNCF rail booking shop in Galerie Louise. You can also order international train tickets online (www.b-rail.be), and then collect them at the Railtour desk at Gare du Midi. Remember to take along the credit card used to make the online booking, as you will have to show this when you collect the ticket.

Tickets for travel in Belgium are sold at stations, but can also be bought online at the Belgian rail site (www.b-rail.be). Once you have made the booking, you simply print out the email confirmation, which is used instead of a ticket.

Commuters can buy various types of season ticket, including a school student rail card (*Carte Train Scolaire*), a daily commuter ticket on a particular route (*Carte Train Trajet*), a daily commuter ticket on a particular network (*Carte Train Reseau*) and a card aimed at part-time workers (*Railflex*). The different options are explained in English on the Belgian railways website under the heading *Railcards*.

People over 65 are particularly fortunate in Belgium. For just €4, they can buy a ticket that allows them to travel between any two Belgian stations on the same day, as long as they begin the journey after 9am.

The rail operator also offers a broad range of special deals for day trips or weekends away. Many of these are package deals, including rail fare and entrance ticket to a museum or exhibition. The deals are listed in the brochure B-Excursions.

Taking a bicycle on a train is not particularly encouraged, but you can instead rent bikes cheaply at many stations. You can buy a special ticket (*Trein+Vélo/Train+Fiets*) which covers a return ticket and bike rental for a day. The bike is booked at the same time as you buy the ticket, and so is waiting for you when you arrive. The scheme is limited to stations in tourist areas such as the coast, the Ardennes and the Westhoek.

The main rail services, including the Airport City Express, are listed in the booklet *IC-IR de poche/IC-IR Treinwijs*. This can be picked up free at any railway station. Times of particular trains can be found online at www.b-rail.be.

Channel Tunnel

Eurotunnel carries cars on a train shuttle through the Channel Tunnel. The connection takes just 35 minutes, with departures every 30 minutes during the day. The price of a crossing depends on the time of day. The most popular slots can cost up to €279 for a single ticket, whereas a crossing at 2am on a Tuesday can be as little as €49. Prices are lower if you book in advance. There are also cheap deals for short trips of five days or less. The ticket covers a car plus up to nine passengers. Driving time from the Channel Tunnel to Brussels is about two hours.

Rail Contacts

Belgian Railways: ☎ 02.528.28.28; www.b-rail.be
Eurostar: ☎ 01233 617 575 (UK); www.eurostar.com
Thalys: ☎ 02.528.28.28; www.thalys.com
Eurotunnel: ☎ 08705 35 35 35 (UK); ☎ 070.22.32.10 (Belgium); www.eurotunnel.com

Travel by Sea

Ferries

Many people expected that the Channel Tunnel would replace ferry services between Britain and France, but the ferry companies responded creatively to the challenge by introducing glamorous modern ferries with beautiful lounges and restaurants. The investment paid off, and cross-Channel ferries still carry millions of people from Dover to Calais. The main operators are P&O and Sealink. Both companies offer low fares and special deals, so it pays to check their websites before making a booking. Crossings take one hour and 30 minutes.

The port of Ostend is only one hour from Brussels, but it now has limited services to Britain. Transeuropa Ferries runs 3-4 sailings a day from Ramsgate to Ostend taking four hours. Norfolkline runs a service between Dover and Dunkirk in northern France taking one hour and 45 minutes.

P&O Ferries operates nightly crossings between Hull and Zeebrugge, near Bruges. The crossing takes about 12 hours. The ships are modern, with attractive restaurants, bars and discos. Most people book a cabin for the night, though the budget option is to book a reclining seat.

The Greek company Superfast Ferries operates a night crossing between Zeebrugge and Rosyth, near Edinburgh, every second day. The crossing takes about 17 hours. The ships are modern, with restaurants and bars, but the entertainment is minimal compared to P&O. Driving time from Brussels to Zeebrugge is about one hour and 30 minutes.

Ferry Contacts

Seafrance: ☎ 0870 443 1653 (UK); www.seafrance.com
P&O Ferries: ☎ 070.70.77.71 (Belgium); email customer.services@poferries.com;
www.poferries.com
Transeuropa Ferries: ☎ 01843 595522 (UK); 059.34.02.60 (Belgium);
www.transeuropaferries.com.
Norfolkline: ☎ 0870 870 10 20 (UK); ☎ 02.719.90.92 (Belgium);
email doverpax@norfolkline.com; www.norfolkline.com
Superfast Ferries: ☎ 0870 234 22 22 (UK); ☎ 050.252.252 (Zeebrugge, Belgium);
www.superfast.com

Travel by Road

Motorways

Brussels lies at the heart of Belgium's dense motorway network. Motorways are well maintained, lit at night and generally safer than other roads in Belgium. Some stretches of motorway are regularly blocked at rush hours, including main routes into Brussels and the ring roads around Brussels and Antwerp, while traffic on the E40 motorway to the coast is often reduced to a crawl at weekends in the summer.

Coaches

Eurolines express coaches (www.eurolines.com) offer a cheap way to travel between Brussels and other European cities. The coach from London to Brussels takes six to nine hours and costs €49. The coach station in Brussels is close to the Gare du Nord.

Buses

Travelling on local buses in Belgium can be frustrating and complicated. The main services are provided by TEC in Wallonia (www.infotec.be) and De Lijn in Flanders (www.delijn.be). Both companies have websites with timetable information and route planners, but these can be difficult to use. Some services are infrequent, and many do not run on Sundays. But there are some useful bus routes.

Those who live in the Flemish suburbs around Brussels can use De Lijn buses to commute into Brussels. Services used to be sporadic, but they have now been improved. A new bus lane on the E411 motorway has sped up bus services from Overijse to Delta metro station.

The historic city of Bruges has an excellent bus network which uses small buses to serve the old town and suburbs. Buses leave from outside the railway station.

Brussels facts

Size
Brussels measures 161 sq km.

Population
The city has a population of just over one million inhabitants, or 9.6% of the Belgian population, including 263,000 foreigners. Of those, 154,000 are European, 45,000 come from North Africa and 12,000 are from Turkey.

Density
The population density is 6,237 people per sq km.

Wealth
Brussels is the third richest region in Europe with a gross domestic product of €53.381 per head. Only the City of London and Luxembourg score higher.

Highest Point
The highest point is Altitude Cent in Forest, 100m above sea level.

Urban Details
Brussels has 1,900km of roads, 31 tunnels, 77 bridges, 17 viaducts, 487 sets of traffic lights, 7,000 pedestrian crossings, 18,500 traffic signs and 26,000 lamp posts.

Most Expensive Restaurant Dish
Filet de bar de ligne 'dos bleu' (tartiné au caviar d'Iran Osciètre); filet of sea bass 'blue back' (covered with Iranian Oscietra caviar). Restaurant Bruneau, Ganshoren, €195.

The Bottom Line

What Does it Cost to Live in Brussels?

Monthly rent of a one-bedroom apartment in a good area	€600
Dinner for two in a fashionable restaurant	€100
Lunch for two	€20
Cinema ticket	€7
Single journey on the metro	€1.50
Visit to the doctor	€20
Espresso	€2

Planning an international move

Removal Companies

Allied Arthur Pierre: Global movers. ☎ 0800.23.311 (freephone); email info@alliedap.be; www.allied.com

Capital Worldwide: Small British company specialising in moves between the UK and Belgium. ☎ 01622 766380 (UK), 02.535.74.30 (Belgium); email moving@capital-worldwide.com; www.capital-worldwide.com

Gosselin: Belgian company. ☎ 02.772.34.87; email comm.@gosselin.be; www.gosselin.be

Silogics: Small company based in Brussels. ☎ 02.735.91.14; email sales@silogics.com; www.silogics.com

Relocation Agencies

AM & PM Relocation: Specialists offering help with registration, schooling and integration. ☎ 016.58.07.90; email info@am-pm.be; www.am-pm.be

Art of Living: Offers a range of relocation packages aimed at company executives moving to Belgium. ☎ 02.653.00.37; email artofliving@artofliving.be; www.artofliving.be

Brussels Relocation: Small agency that helps families find a home and integrate in the community. ☎ 02.353.21.01; email brussels.relocation@skynet.be; www.brussels-relocation.com

Map Relocations: Friendly agency that offers advice on immigration, schools and settling down in Belgium. ☎ 02.658.80.80; email info@map-relocations.com; www.map-relocations.com

When you Arrive

Moving to Belgium used to be a bureaucratic nightmare. It is less so now, but you should still be prepared for problems and delays. Every country has its rules. Belgium is not the worst country in the world for red tape. Take along a book to read while you wait in line.

First Week in Belgium

Accommodation Meet your landlord if you are renting a place and sign a lease. Ask if you can take over the utility bills from the previous tenant. Write down the meter readings. Write your name on a label and stick it next to the outside doorbell.

Kafka

A city of bureaucrats can sometimes seem a forbidding place. But the Belgian government is now struggling to curb the power of its bureaucracy by drastically reducing the number of regulations, forms and petty rules. The project is named Kafka in honour of the Czech novelist who showed the pitiless cruelty of the Hapsburg bureaucracy. Headed by a bureaucrat called Vincent Van Quickenborne, the Kafka project is gradually replacing tedious bureaucratic processes with online procedures. This has cut the time needed to set up a Belgian company to just three days. Belgians can now do much of their administration online, but foreigners without an electronic ID card have to do things the old way.

Get a Job Contract Ask your employer for an employment contract.

Passport Photos Go to a photo booth in a metro station and get at least six passport photographs for every member of your family.

Contact Your Town Hall Phone your local town hall to find out the documents required for registering as a resident.

Apply for Residence Permit Go to the local town hall to register as a resident within eight days of arriving in Belgium. You will need to take along a valid passport or national ID card, three passport photographs for each family member, and a job contract or proof of sufficient means of support (some recent bank statements should be enough). Some municipalities also require a birth certificate, a certificate of good conduct, a copy of your rental agreement and proof of civil status. A few administrations even take fingerprints. You will be charged a small fee, probably about €5–€20. Once you have registered, a local police officer will go to your house within a few days to check that your name is next to the doorbell.

EU staff can, if they prefer, apply for a special European Commission identity card. They can pick this up at the Commission office, and so avoid any contact with the local town hall. But this special ID is only valid within Belgium; a passport is still required for trips abroad.

Book a Parking Space You may have to book a parking space for a removal van in front of your house or apartment. Apply to the police in your local municipality several days before the space is needed. You will be charged a fee. Ask the police for a contact number in case the space is occupied on the day you have booked it. Check that the no parking signs are put in place on the preceding day.

Get Connected Contact electricity, gas and water suppliers to arrange appointments for connections to be made. You will need to provide some form of identification such as a residence permit or passport. Check this when you book an appointment.

Collect Residence Permit You will receive a letter calling you to the town hall to pick up your residence permit (*carte de séjour*). This is normally valid for five months.

Five Months after Arriving

Renew Residence Permit Go to the town hall to renew your residence permit. After five months, EU nationals should be eligible for a Belgian ID card as long as they have proof of employment or self-employment and membership of a social security fund. The ID card is initially valid for one year, after which you are issued with a five-year card. Once you have an ID card, your name is entered on the population register. You have to carry the ID card (or a passport) at all times. Children under 12 do not get issued with an ID, but they receive a small card with their name on it. They should wear this around their neck when they are not with their parents.

Brussels Help Desk

No one enjoys the business of moving to a new country. There are phone calls to make, forms to complete, dozens of little details to sort out in an unfamiliar country. Some employers will help you out. Or you can turn to colleagues who know how things work. There are also expatriate organisations that can help to make the transition as smooth as possible, such as the American Women's Club and the British & Commonwealth Women's Club. But if all else fails EU citizens can get in touch with the Brussels-Europe Liaison Office, set up by Brussels Region in 1991 to provide advice to Europeans settling in Brussels. It employs specialists who can advise on registration formalities, legal issues and childcare facilities. They also send out a monthly email newsletter with local news and details of cultural highlights (www. blbe.be/news). The office is located at Avenue d'Auderghem 63, close to Schuman metro station. The website (www.blbe.be) has a great deal of useful information in English.

Electronic ID

The Belgian government is gradually replacing the old system of paper ID cards with new electronic cards (e-ID). Most Belgian nationals have already been issued with the electronic ID cards, which are modelled on bank cards and incorporate a chip containing some personal details such as date of birth and address. The holder can use the card (which has a pin code) to carry out many administrative formalities online, including filing tax returns, paying parking fines, ordering a car number plate and voting. The government now plans to issue electronic ID cards to the one million foreign nationals living in Belgium.

EU nationals will get an ID card identical to Belgians, while non-EU citizens will get a slightly different type. Foreigners living in the Uccle commune were the first to be issued with the cards in early 2007.

EU Help Desks

Solvit EU citizens can now ask for help if they find themselves caught in a bureaucratic nightmare. The Solvit network is a free EU online service that helps citizens who experience problems in moving between EU countries or setting up a business in another country. They claim to be able to find a solution within 10 days. www.ec.europa.eu/solvit

Europe Direct The EU's free phoneline can advise EU citizens on problems such as residence permits or getting professional qualifications recognised. ☎ 00800.6789.1011 (free from any EU country). www.europa.eu/europedirect

Consumer Protection

Belgian shops have a reputation for poor customer service, but consumers are at least protected by EU consumer legislation. This provides a minimum guarantee of two years on all goods. The Belgian consumer watchdog Test-Achats (Test Aankoop in Flanders) regularly surveys products on sale in Belgium and offers legal advice to its members. ☎ 02.542.33.00; www.test-achats.be

The European Consumer Centre in Brussels can help consumers with problems connected to cross-border transactions in Europe. The staff can, for example, provide free legal advice to airline passengers involved in disputes with low-cost airlines like Ryanair. ☎ 02.542.33.46; email info@eccbelgium.be; www.eccbelgium.be

Q&A

Desperately seeking information? You can often find the answer on the Q&A forum on www.xpats.com. People post several dozen questions every day, though most of the activity happens Monday to Friday. You get the best results by posting a question early on Monday morning. Some replies are more useful than others, but several regulars are clued up on a wide variety of topics. By Friday afternoon, the forum is winding down, and little activity happens over the weekend.

Setting Up Home

- Rental prices in Brussels are lower than in most other European capitals, especially London.
- There is currently a glut of apartments in Brussels and rents have fallen by 10% in recent years, while house prices have doubled.
- Prices start at around €300 a month for a one room apartment in a student area, or €1,200 for a three bedroom apartment.
- There is a wide range of accommodation to be found, from loft apartments in converted factories to large villas in the Flemish countryside.
- Rental prices are highest in the leafy districts of southern Brussels where diplomats and professionals live.
- You should look into public transport connections when searching for a home as the metro does not cover all parts of the city.
- Many choose to rent cheaply in the countryside around Brussels where prices are low, but half a million people commute into Brussels daily and journey times are slow.
- Anyone wanting to speak French on a daily basis should look in the French-speaking communes of Walloon Brabant.
- Those planning to settle in the Flemish region should be prepared to learn Dutch.

A guide to the housing market

Urban Buzz or Suburban Calm?

Brussels offers something for just about everyone, at a price well below most European capitals. You can live in a loft apartment in a converted factory, or retreat to a large villa in the Flemish countryside. The city has appealing neighbourhoods where you find specialised food shops, street markets and cobbled squares. But some people prefer to live out in the Brabant countryside with a field of cows as their closest neighbour. Brussels is one of the few world capitals that allows you to live in any way you want.

Some Brussels neighbourhoods have a busy urban mood, while others are quiet districts with anonymous apartment buildings where you can live for years without meeting your neighbour. Single people who like going out should take a look at apartments in the Dansaert, Stépanie, Châtelain or the Porte de Namur quarters. Young professionals with a decent income should think about hunting for a stylish apartment in the Sablon or Etangs d'Ixelles areas.

Familes have different needs. They often want a big apartment in a quieter neighbourhood, or a house with a garden in the suburbs. It's relatively easy to find an attractive suburban house that costs no more than a two-room apartment in the city, but more difficult to find somewhere out of town that is well served by public transport.

The commuter belt extends for about 50 miles around Brussels, although most expatriates live within 10-20km of the city. The distances are relatively short, but commuting can often take one to two hours because of dense traffic. Expatriates can sometimes feel isolated in the suburbs if they do not

House near Parc Egmont

speak the language or have family links in the area. Public transport is often poor, and parents may have to spend a lot of time driving their children around.

It is worth asking around for advice, trying out public transport, and checking the area at night, before you agree to sign a long lease.

Costs

While Londoners and New Yorkers pay a huge part of their income on rent, Brussels residents can fairly easily find an affordable apartment that leaves most of their monthly salary intact. A young professional who takes home €3,000 a month in Brussels will be able to find a very attractive apartment for €1,000 a month. Someone on €1,500 a month should have no trouble finding a one-bedroom apartment for €500-€600.

While prices have crept up in recent years, they are still far below the monthly sums required to secure a similar place in Paris or London. The highest prices occur in the leafy districts of southern Brussels where European bureaucrats and international professionals like to live. Other areas of the city, like peaceful Jette, or slightly scruffy Schaerbeek, have ample apartments and houses to let at a fraction of London or Paris prices.

The reason is simple. There is currently a glut of apartments in Brussels, and more are being built all the time. As a result, rents in Brussels have fallen by 10% over the past five years, even though house prices have more than doubled.

Red House on the Rue du Midi

House-hunting

Brussels is one of the world's easiest cities for house-hunting. You just have to stroll around your favourite neighbourhoods looking for the bright orange A *Louer/Te Huur* signs. Or you can check the apartments and houses to let in local estate agent windows. Several big agencies are based on Avenue Louise. Some agencies are very efficient, while others provide an uninspired service.

The city has two free weekly newspapers that list property for rent - the French-language *Vlan*, which is distributed on Thursday, and the Dutch-language *Brussel deze Week*, which can be picked up in the Flemish library, Flemish cultural centres and tourist offices. An extended edition of Vlan with a separate property magazine is sold in newsagents on Saturdays.

The *Bulletin*, an English language magazine published every Thursday, carries an extensive listing of properties for rent, but these are mainly at the upper end of the market (and sometimes overpriced for the expatriate market).

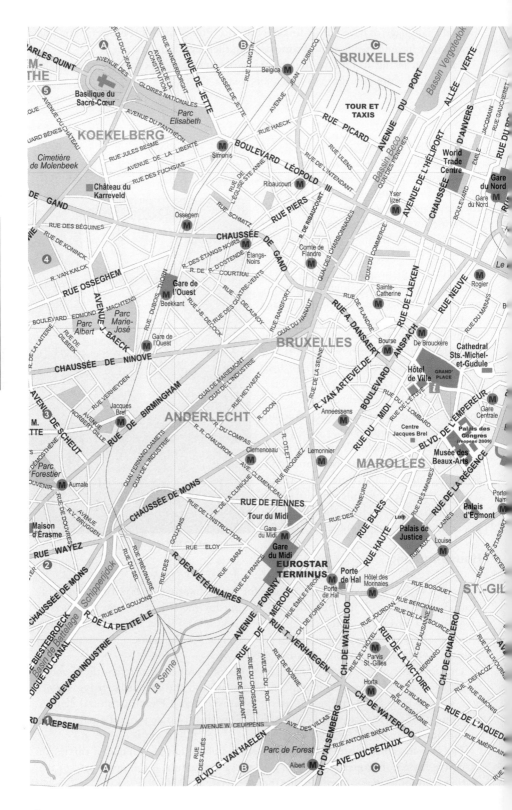

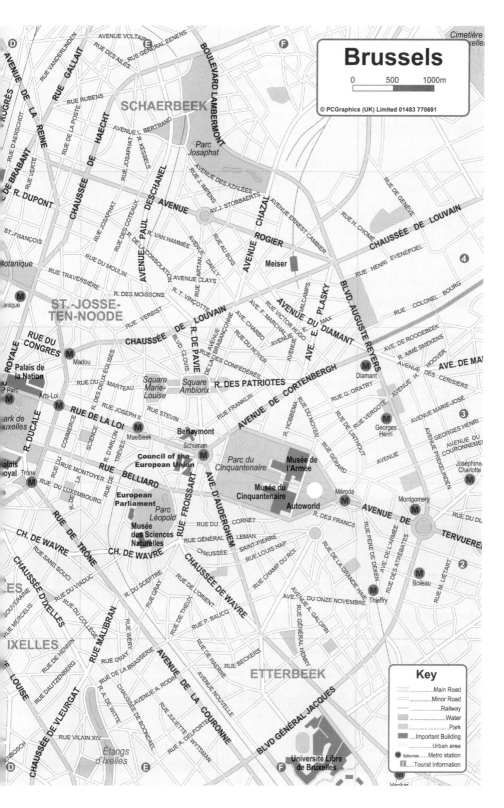

Brussels

0   500   1000m

© PCGraphics (UK) Limited 01483 770691

Cimetière
xelles

SCHAERBEEK

Parc
Josaphat

AVENUE VOLTAIRE
RUE DES AILES
RUE GÉNÉRAL EENENS

BOULEVARD LAMBERMONT

AVENUE DE LA REINE
RUE VANDERLINDEN
RUE GALLAIT
RUE RUBENS
RUE DE LA POSTE
RUE VERTE
RUE D'AERSCHOT
DE BRABANT
R. DUPONT
ST.-FRANÇOIS
otanique

CHAUSSÉE DE HAECHT
AVENUE L. BERTRAND
AVENUE PAUL DESCHANEL
RUE JOSAPHAT
R. KESSELS
RUE DES COTEAUX
R. DE CONSOLATION
RUE DU MOULIN
RUE TRAVERSIÈRE

AVENUE DES AZALÉES
AV. J. IMPENS
AV.-J. STOBBAERTS
AVENUE ERNEST CAMBIER

AVENUE CHAZAL
AVENUE ROGIER

Meiser

CHAUSSÉE DE LOUVAIN
RUE DE GENÈVE
RUE H. CHOMÉ
RUE HENRI EVENEPOEL

④

anique

ST.-JOSSE-
TEN-NOODE

RUE DU CONGRES
ROYALE
Palais de
la Nation
Parc
Arts-Loi
alais
oyal
ark de
uxelles
R. DUCALE
RUE DE LA LOI
RUE MONTOYER
RUE DE LUXEMBOURG

RUE JOSAPHAT
R. DES COTEAUX
R. VAN HAMMÉE
AVENUE DAILLY
AVENUE CLAYS
R.T. VINÇOTTE
R. DES MOISSONS
RUE VERBIST
CHAUSSÉE DE LOUVAIN
R. DE PAVIE
BLVD. CLOVIS
RUE DES DEUX ÉGLISES
RUE DU MARTEAU
RUE JOSEPH II
RUE STEVIN
RUE DE LA SCIENCE
R. DARLON
R. DE TRÈVES

Madou
Botanique
Square
Marie-
Louise
Square
Ambiorix
R. DES PATRIOTES
RUE FRANKLIN
AVENUE DE CORTENBERGH

AVENUE DE LACKEN
AVENUE DES CELTES
RUE AU BOIS
AVENUE TARTAN
RUE DE LA BRABANÇONNE
RUE CHARBO
RUE DU NOYER
RUE DES CONFÉDÉRÉS

AVENUE DE TERVUEREN

AVENUE DU DIAMANT
AV. F. MARCHAL
RUE VICTOR HUGO
AV. E. PLASKY
RUE ELLIPS
BLVD. AUGUSTE REYERS
RUE HENRI
Diamant
RUE G. GRATRY
Georges
Henri
③

AVE. DE ROODEBEEK
AVENUE HOOVER
AVE. DE MAI
R. AIMÉ SMEKENS
AVENUE H. DES CERISIERS
AVENUE MARIE-JOSÉ
AVENUE GEORGES HENRI
AVENUE DE COURONNEMEN
Joséphine-
Charlotte

Berlaymont
Maelbeek
Schuman
Council of the
European Union

European
Parliament
Parc
Léopold
Musée
des Sciences
Naturelles

RUE DE LA LOI
RUE COMMERCE
RUE BELLIARD
AVE. FROISSART
AVE. D'AUDERGHEM
RUE DU CORNET
RUE GÉNÉRAL LEMAN
CHAUSSÉE
SAINT-PIERRE
RUE LOUIS HAP

Parc du
Cinquantenaire

Musée de
l'Armée
Musée du
Cinquantenaire
Autoworld
R. DES FRANCS

Mérode
Montgomery
AVENUE DE
RUE DU DU
TERVUERE
②
Boileau
RUE M. LIETART

CH. DE WAVRE
CHAUSSÉE D'IXELLES
RUE DE TRÔNE
RUE SANS SOUCI
CH. DE WAVRE
RUE DU VIADUC

CHAUSSÉE DE WAVRE
RUE DU SCEPTRE
RUE GRAY
RUE DE L'ORIENT
RUE DE THÉLY
RUE P. BALICQ

AVENUE DE L'ARMÉE
RUE PÈRE DE DEKEN
RUE DE LA GRANDE HAIE
RUE CHAMP DU ROI
AVENUE DU ONZE NOVEMBRE
RUE A. GALOPIN
Thieffry

RUE DES ATRÉBATES

IXELLES
LOUISE
SOUVERAINE
RUE MERCELIS
RUE DE HENNIN
RUE DAUTZENBERG
RUE MALIBRAN
RUE GRAY
RUE WERY
RUE DE LA BRASSERIE
AVENUE A. RODIN
CHAUSSÉE DE BOONDAEL
R.-A. DE WITTE
RUE JULIETTE DELPORTE
RUE A. DE WYTSMAN

AVENUE DE LA COURONNE
RUE DE HAERNE
RUE BECKERS
AVENUE NOUVELLE
RUE GÉNÉRAL HENRY

ETTERBEEK

CHAUSSÉE DE VLEURGAT
NBOSCH
RUE VILAIN XIV

Étangs
d'Ixelles

BLVD GÉNÉRAL JACQUES

Université Libre
de Bruxelles

Hénkei

Key

........Main Road	
........Minor Road	
........Railway	
........Water	
........Park	
........Important Building	
........Urban area	
Ⓜ Schuman ......Metro station	
🅸 ....Tourist Information	

You can also use a relocation company to find a suitable property for rent, while people working for the European institutions can check for properties on the intranet.

But the most popular way to search is on the internet. There are several Belgian sites with good search engines and useful photos. You will still have to visit places, but you can at least eliminate unsuitable properties.

Which Language?

Living in the countryside outside Brussels can seem idyllic. But you have to communicate with the locals. Most of the suburban belt is Dutch-speaking, apart from Waterloo and a few other towns to the south, which are French-speaking. You find the same style of houses and the same rents on both sides of the language divide, yet the two regions have different languages and cultures. Anyone who seriously wants to use French as their everyday language should look for a house in the French-speaking communes of Walloon Brabant. Someone who decides to settle in the Flemish Region should make an effort to learn Dutch.

Getting to Work

Brussels is a difficult city to get around during the rush hour. The main roads into the city are normally jammed from about 7am-10am. The metro is the most reliable option for getting to work, but it is overcrowded and doesn't serve all areas of the city. You can check the best public transport route from home to work using the route planner at www.stib.be.

Some small towns outside Brussels have train stations. Use the route planner at www.planitram.be to find out the journey time to work. You should also try the journey out once before you sign the lease to see how long it takes. Make sure you travel on a weekday morning at 8am to find out whether the journey is tolerable. Note that many suburban train services are reduced or even cut altogether at weekends.

Houses on mural on the Rue du Trône

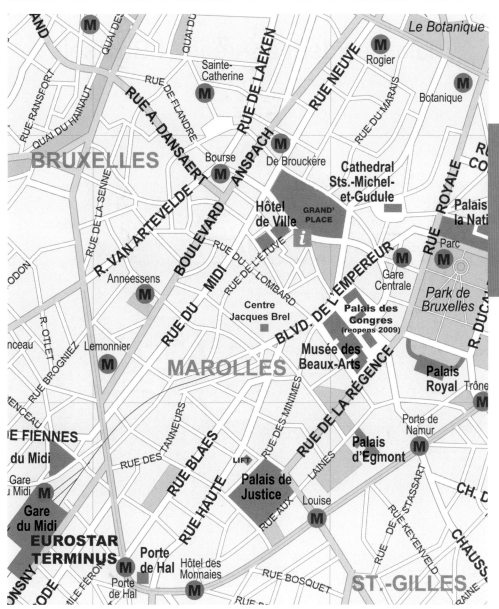

Neighbourhoods

Main Residential Areas of Brussels

Downtown

Dansaert

This is the fashionable quarter for anyone who wants to live in the heart of Brussels. Grand old apartments with beautiful period details can be found, along with some recently converted industrial spaces. You can find an impressive apartment in a 19th-century building for €600, but a loft space is likely to cost at least €1,000. People who live in this neighbourhood can drink coffee on the shady Place du Vieux Marché-aux-Grains, wander around the seriously fashionable shops on Rue Dansaert, and perhaps watch a Japanese cult movie on the rooftop of the Beursschouwburg in the summer. This area is immensely popular with single expatriates on short-term contracts because of the buzzing nightlife,

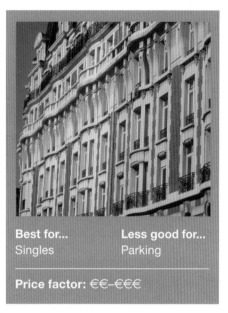

Best for... Singles

Less good for... Parking

Price factor: €€–€€€

but families could find living here a bit stressful. The quarter is not without a few drawbacks, such as late-night noise, impossible parking and tourists hogging the café tables. But it's possibly worth the struggle to be able to say that you live in the same neighbourhood as some of Belgium's coolest film-makers and rock musicians.

Vlaams Schouwburg

Best for... Culture

Less good for... Familes

Price factor: €–€€

This is a downtown area popular with young Flemish residents and immigrant families. The housing stock ranges from smart new apartments with high-security entrances on the Rue de Laeken to large 19th-century buildings that have not been improved in the past twenty years. Metro stations are nearby, but parking is difficult. The area around the Vlaams Schouwburg has long suffered from street prostitution. The city recently imposed high taxes on short-stay hotels used for casual sex, but the problem persists. Prices in this neighbourhood are generally lower than the Dansaert area.

Marolles

This is an old Brussels neighbourhood that goes back to the city's earliest days. Pieter Bruegel worked in this quarter in a brick house with a crow-stepped gable that is still standing (but doesn't admit visitors). Some patchy gentrification has happened in recent years, but it's still a solid working class district of old cafés with neon signs and narrow cobbled streets where rubbish gathers. This is where you come to find craftsmen who can repair a damaged violin or supply a single stair banister. Young artists settle here because of the low rents, alongside Moroccan families and the occasional adventurous loft dweller. The prices vary enormously, from €400 for a studio apartment to at least €1,000 for a new loft space. The Porte de Hal metro station is nearby and Grand'Place is just five minutes away on foot, but finding a parking space can be a challenge.

Best for...   **Less good for...**
Eating out   Families

Price factor: €€–€€€

Best for...   **Less good for...**
Eating out   Culture

Price factor: €

Saint-Catherine

This is an attractive downtown Brussels neighbourhood located around the old fish market, with good restaurants and local shops. The area is quieter than Dansaert and parking is easier, but this can be a difficult area to raise children as there are no parks or squares in the neighbourhood. Prices are cheaper than the Dansert neighbourhood, although they have risen in recent years.

Tour et Taxis

This old canalside zone is being redeveloped as a new urban district with apartments, museums and restaurants. The Tour et Taxis complex is the setting for concerts and events, but not much else goes on in the neighbourhood and at nights the streets

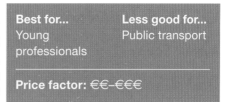

have a raw industrial edge. But that could soon change. The Brussels Region recently announced an ambitious plan to create a new waterfront leisure zone, with an open-air swimming pool due to open in 2010. Most of the investment at the moment involves converting old industrial buildings into stylish (and expensive) lofts. Parking is not too difficult, but public transport is limited. Expect to pay at least €1,000 for a loft in this area.

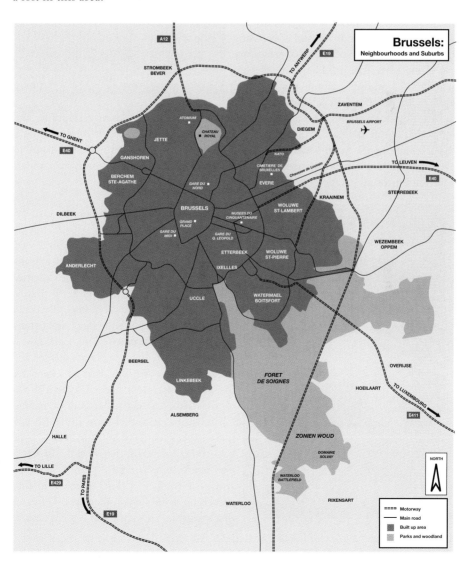

Upper Town

Avenue Louise

The long avenue that runs from Place Louise to the Bois de la Cambre has always been the smartest address in Brussels, but irreparable damage was done in the 1950s and 1960s when the avenue was turned into a six-lane highway and tall office blocks were built at major intersections. The elegant avenue of 19th-century townhouses may be a thing of the past, but Louise is still one of the most vibrant areas of town. This is a neighbourhood where American law firms and advertising agencies have their offices, so prices are not going to be cheap. There are elegant apartment buildings along the avenue, some with penthouses that look out over

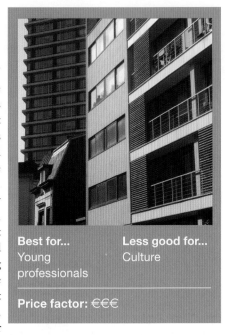

Best for... Young professionals

Less good for... Culture

Price factor: €€€

the rooftops of Ixelles. Those who live here have access to smart restaurants and shops that count Belgian royalty among their customers. As a result Avenue Louise has become popular with wealthy diplomats and French tax exiles, who are happy to pay €800 for a one-room apartment. Parking is a problem, though many apartments have underground garages.

Best for... Eating out

Less good for... Students

Price factor: €€–€€€

Châtelain

This is a desirable Ixelles neighbourhood close to Avenue Louise with handsome 19th-century townhouses. The quarter has good shops on the Rue du Bailly, a picturesque market on the Place du Châtelain every Wednesday and some fashionable restaurants, but parking is difficult and the quarter is not well located for EU offices. So why is it so expensive to rent an apartment here? It comes down to that elusive Belgian notion of *charme*. Châtelain has it. Other areas don't. So you must expect to pay €800 for even a basic two-room apartment that would cost €600 two blocks away, or €1,200 for a cramped attic that is labelled 'loft'. Don't leap into a decision without considering other areas that are just as appealing but less expensive.

Alice Jolly, British novelist writing in *The Bulletin* – *Châtelain is a whole world: you can live here for weeks and not go anywhere else, because it has everything you need.*

Stéphanie

A stylish quarter at the city end of Avenue Louise with big townhouses and some of the city's smartest hotels. The back streets can be tatty, and street prostitution is sometimes a problem at weekends, but this remains a safe neighbourhood with a good range of affordable restaurants, several city supermarkets and three cinema complexes. The nearest metro is at Louise, while trams rumble down the main arteries. But parking is inevitably difficult, unless you can find a garage or qualify for a *Bruxelles-Ville* parking permit. This is a good area for young single people hunting for an interesting one-room apartment. You might not want to stay in the neighbourhood for ever, but it's the perfect location for someone new to the city. It doesn't take much hunting to find a

Best for...
Singles

Less good for...
Parking

Price factor: €€–€€€

bright apartment in a converted 19th-century house for as little as €500. You can also find some surprising properties in this neighbourhood, including secret houses hidden behind grander buildings, sometimes costing as little as €800 a month. But prices rise sharply for apartments in the Louise Village development, off Avenue Louise, where you will pay €1,300 for a two-room apartment because it is *de standing*.

Best for...
Eating out

Less good for...
Students

Price factor: €€–€€€

Sablon

Probably the most civilised quarter in Brussels, the Sablon is a neighbourhood of lovingly restored townhouses, cobbled streets, antique shops and romantic restaurants. The neighbourhood is perfect for culture, with the fine art museum and the music conservatory on your doorstep, along with an elegant little park and some of the city's best restaurants. You might have thought that this would be a super-rich enclave, but rents are surprisingly affordable, especially in the streets heading towards the Marolles. You can rent a freshly painted one-room apartment with a view of the Gothic church for €750, or a snug apartment in a converted 17th-century attic for €600. Most apartments are fairly small, but perfect for young people who like to go out. Parking is inevitably a headache, but the Sablon is well-served by buses and trams, so a car is really not necessary. The quarter looks its best at the weekend, when antique dealers organise a market on the Square, and during the Nocturnes du Sablon in December, when concerts are held in some of the quarter's sublime interiors.

Flagey

Best for...	Less good for...
Eating out	Public transport

Price factor: €€

Living in the Flagey area means finding a flat in an Art Deco apartment block or renting a house close to the Ixelles ponds. This neighbourhood has long been a hive of Portuguese immigrants, Moroccan shopkeepers and Belgian artists, but the area received an image boost in 2002 with the opening of the Flagey cultural centre in the old Belgian radio building. Despite the almost inevitable funding crisis, Flagey has developed into a buzzing arts centre offering an inspiring monthly programme of films, concerts and literary readings. Mainly because of the new centre, rents are gradually rising, slowly nudging out the artists, actors and craftsmen who give the area much of its charm. Public transport is less than perfect, with the crowded bus 71 providing the fastest link to the centre. Yet there are many factors that make this neighbourhood feel like home, like drinking coffee in Café Belga, eating dinner in the friendly Le Grain de Sel, hearing Fado music drift out of a Portuguese café and shopping for rare French cheeses at the Sunday market.

Best for...	Less good for...
Families	Students

Price factor: €€€–€€€

Ixelles Ponds

Two ponds are all that remain of a river that once meandered past Ixelles village. The slopes above the Etangs d'Ixelles (Ixelles Ponds) became a desirable quarter at the end of the 19th century, when progressive lawyers and entrepreneurs commissioned daring Art Nouveau houses, while more conventional Belgians put up classical townhouses. You can still, if you are utterly determined, find an Art Nouveau house signed by Ernest Blérot or a beautifully proportioned family home with a period interior. You can also find luxurious spaces in 1930s Art Deco apartment buildings overlooking the ponds. But this is an increasingly desirable neighbourhood, its appeal boosted by the opening of Flagey arts centre. A growing cohort of French tax exiles is adding to the pressure. The cheapest rents are on the east side of the ponds, heading towards Ixelles hospital, but a small apartment with a view of the ponds could easily cost €800.

Abbaye de la Cambre

This is a sophisticated urban quarter of Ixelles with handsome apartment buildings from the 1930s overlooking a beautiful Cistercian abbey. The quarter has pleasant streets and good restaurants, and lies within walking distance of the Bois de la Cambre. Apartments here are expensive, but they generally offer attractive features such as marble fireplaces and high ceilings. The neighbourhood is increasingly popular with French tax exiles, which pushes prices up even higher. It's consequently hard to find an apartment for under €1,000 a month.

Best for...
Young professionals

Less good for...
Culture

Price factor: €€–€€€

Place St Boniface

Best for...
Young professionals

Less good for...
Quiet

Price factor: €€–€€€

St Boniface used to be a forgotten square with not much more than a mussels restaurant, an old camera shop and a dilapidated church. But then people started to notice the Art Nouveau façades and the convenient location on the edge of the European Quarter. As a result, St Boniface is now one of the city's most attractive corners, with a neighbourhood charm all of its own. Those who live here can sit on the terrace of the Ultime Atome, watch the sun glint on the gold fleck of a faded fresco, listen to the neighbourhood chatter, watch a delivery van unloading tea for Comptoir Florian, and try once again to catch the eye of the beautiful but frighteningly cool waitresses. The Boniface neighbourhood has some wonderful restaurants, along with useful shops selling flowers and pastries, but prices continue to rise, making it hard for Belgians to live here. Parking is difficult around the square, but bus 71 provides a fast connection into the centre.

Ma Campagne

Not a lot of campagne left in this 19th-century corner of Saint-Gilles, but the old name has survived. It's very much *upper* Saint-Gilles, with generously portioned houses, tree-lined streets and discreet Belgian restaurants. The English Gothic turrets of Saint-Gilles prison loom above the rooftops, but this is nevertheless a safe neighbourhood. Trams 91 and 92 provide a useful link to the centre, but it is a longish haul to the European Quarter. Prices are still modest here, with a decent two-room apartment costing about €600.

Saint-Gilles

Saint-Gilles has the most spectacular town hall in Brussels. It's an enormous red brick Flemish Renaissance building from 1904 with sweeping staircases, magnificent hallways and a distinguished collection of 19th-century Belgian paintings. You may wonder whether this small Brussels municipality really needs such a palace. Yet there was once money in Saint-Gilles, and you can still spend a pleasant day wandering the

Best for...	Less good for...
Singles	Public transport

Price factor: €€

streets in search of neglected Art Nouveau architecture. It is now a bit shabby, but slowly regenerating itself. The Socialist mayor, Charles Picqué, has done much to make Saint-Gilles more attractive. Those who live here speak fondly of the local football team, the Saturday market on Parvis de Saint-Gilles and the quiet hazy light that fills the Café Verscheuren. This is an area that appeals to artists and students because of the affordable apartments. A studio flat in a converted house can be found for as little as €400.

Katharine Mill comments
I live in lower Saint-Gilles near the Gare du Midi. I bought a house here four years ago: I like Saint-Gilles for it's boho atmosphere, lack of pretension and great public transport connections.

Best for...	Less good for...
Students	Culture

Price factor: €€

Forest

The commune of Forest rises up the slopes from the Gare du Midi, gradually becoming more desirable as it gains height. The upper area around Parc Duden is one of the most attractive residential neighbourhoods in the city, yet prices are lower than in neighbouring Uccle. Down towards the station, the streets are more shabby and prices consequently lower. Your Belgian colleagues may tell you that Forest is dangerous, but they are probably remembering isolated riots from many years ago. This is now a relaxed multicultural area that could become as fashionable as Flagey once the new Wiels arts centre is fully operational. Prices vary enormously: a sunny apartment with two bedrooms can be found for €550, but an attractive family house with three bedrooms and a view of Parc Duden could cost as much as €1,400.

Best for...
Singles

Less good for...
Public transport

Price factor: €€–€€€

Matonge

Best for...
Nightlife

Less good for...
Parking

Price factor: €€

This is a lively African Quarter close to the Porte de Namur where you can find a decent apartment for €450. The mood is relaxed and friendly, with unusual African vegetables on sale in the local shops and people out on the streets until late at night. But it can get noisy and occasionally unpleasant, especially in areas where soft drugs are regularly traded. Parking is virtually impossible, but the metro is nearby and the EU institutions just ten minutes on foot, so doing without a car would hardly hurt at all.

SETTING UP HOME

ULB

The 19th-century streets around the university campus in Ixelles are popular with expatriates looking for a lively quarter with restaurants and cafés. There are some attractive houses for rent, although much of the accommodation is aimed at Belgian students looking for a small single room. Noise can be a problem and parking is difficult, but there are good transport links by tram and bus. A studio apartment can be found for less than €400, while a two-roomed apartment might cost no more than €600.

Best for... Students
Less good for... Parking

Price factor: €€–€€€

Roosevelt/Bois

The area on the east side of the Bois de la Cambre is popular with diplomats and international executives. Most people live in apartment buildings in quiet neighbourhoods close to the woods. Parking is normally not a problem, but public transport is limited.

Best for... Quiet
Less good for... Singles

Price factor: €€€

Trams 93 and 94 will get you into town, but they are often slowed down by traffic. Prices here are not too extravagant and you can find an attractive apartment with two bedrooms and a terrace looking out on the woods for €700.

European Quarter

Cinquantenaire

The 19th-century streets around the Berlaymont have recently become a property hotspot. While many families still prefer to hunt out a villa in the leafy suburbs, younger people are now snapping up apartments and houses that are within walking distance of the European institutions. The skyline is consequently thick with cranes as new apartments with deep underground garages go up on every available building site. This neighbourhood is well placed for getting to the airport and is served by the metro and two railway stations. The spacious Cinquantenaire Park, currently undergoing a major renovation, provides green space and a small playground perfect for small children. For evening action, the neighbourhood is thick with international restaurants and Irish pubs, but cinemas and theatres are a 10-minute metro ride away. Apartments in this area are generally priced for expatriates on high salaries. As commuting problems get steadily worse, these locations are likely to become even more desirable, so prices could soon reach London levels. Already, rents are well above the average Belgian budget – the term *proximité CEE* (near the EU) allows owners to charge outrageous prices for apartments that have little or no character. An apartment with two bedrooms, a garden and a garage can easily cost €1,500 a month. Other areas such as Louise and the Sablon often offer much better deals while still being close to the EU institutions.

Best for...
Families

Less good for...
Students

Price factor: €€€

Best for...
Young
professionals

Less good for...
Students

Price factor: €€€€–€€€€€€

Montgomery

The streets around the Montgomery roundabout have some of the most expensive apartments in Brussels. They were mostly built in the 1930s in a grand classical style and many of the buildings have basement garages. But the main appeal of the neighbourhood is that it is within walking distance of the European institutions. The apartments are often unusually large for Brussels, making it possible to live here with a family. But it won't be a cheap option. Expect to pay €1,100-€1,500 for a three-bedroom apartment in a 1930s building.

Place Jourdan

A friendly Brussels neighbourhood within walking distance of the European institutions. This is mainly an area of apartments, but the occasional townhouse can sometimes be found. It's a good

Best for...
Young
professionals

Less good for...
Families

Price factor: €€

neighbourhood for specialised shops and local cafés, but it can be quiet at weekends. A standard two-room apartment might cost no more than €600.

Best for...
Families

Less good for...
Students

Price factor: €€€

La Chasse

A solid neighbourhood of 19th-century townhouses, friendly local restaurants and the occasional antique warehouse. Not a particularly fashionable quarter, but houses are expensive because of the location, just a 10-minute walk from the European institutions. This is a respectable Belgian quarter, with good local shops but little nightlife. Young single people might prefer the buzz of other neighbourhoods.

Schaerbeek

Schaerbeek was one of the grand 19th-century quarters of Brussels, spreading itself across a landscape of gentle hills and cherry orchards. The town hall is a spectacular Renaissance-style building with an interesting collection of Belgian art and a signed photograph of Dwight D. Eisenhower thanking the locals for making him an honourary citizen in September 1945. Yet the grandeur has not convinced Belgians to stay around. They have largely abandoned Schaerbeek for the greener suburbs, and the area now has a large Turkish and Moroccan population. Some streets look neglected, but the quarter around Parc Josaphat has grand houses overlooking a romantic landscaped park, while the quarter around Place De Jamblinne de Meux attracts expatriates because of its closeness to the EU institutions. Your neighbours could be a friendly Moroccan family or EU civil servants attracted by the cosmopolitan atmosphere. The public transport network is not exceptional, but tram 23 rumbles reliably along the outer boulevards. Parking is less of a problem than other communes.

Best for...
Young professionals

Less good for...
Public transport

Price factor: €€

Dailly

An upcoming neighbourhood with large 19th century townhouses on the edge of Schaerbeek. This is a mixed district, where EU officials live happily next door to ethnic shops. The EU institutions are within walking distance, but there is not much green space available. Parking is difficult and the metro is a bit of a hike away. Yet this is an area to consider, as property prices are considerably lower here because of the Schaerbeek postcode. You should be able to find a small studio for €400 or a two-roomed apartment for €500. But rents are rising, and the area is likely to become more desirable when the old army barracks on Place Dailly are converted into luxury apartments.

Best for...
Families

Less good for...
Singles

Price factor: €€

Chant d'Oiseau

This is a quarter popular with EU staff, though you might wonder why. It seems at first fairly anonymous and dull, but there is a strong sense of community, and you soon get to know your neighbours. The area is supremely quiet and has good local shops on the Chaussée de Wavre. You can rent a sunny two-room apartment for about €800, or a modern terraced house for €1,200. Parking is relatively easy, as most houses and apartments have their own garages, and the metro is not far off.

Best for...	Less good for...
Families	Culture

Price factor: €€€–€€€€€

St Josse

St Josse always comes bottom in the annual survey of Belgium's wealthiest and poorest municipalities. This is a tightly-packed immigrant district, with plenty of Turkish restaurants and Moroccan shops. Most Belgians wouldn't dream of settling here, but housing is cheap and the location is not at all bad, just ten minutes on foot from the EU institutions. There are some exceptional houses waiting to be restored, like the 1883 townhouse that Karin Dhadamus turned into a sublime B&B (see the picture gallery at www.phileasfogg.be).

Best for...	Less good for...
Singles	Quiet

Price factor: €–€€

The Forest's Edge

Auderghem

Auderghem is an appealing residential district with quiet neighbourhoods and grand townhouses. Popular with international executives and EU officials, this is inevitably an expensive quarter. Residents enjoy the leafy streets, rambling parks and the big shopping centre. Parking is usually easy, and the metro runs straight to Schuman from Herrmann Debroux station.

Best for...	Less good for...
Families	Students

Price factor: €€€–€€€€

Boitsfort

This is a compact commune on the forest's edge with a slight bohemian atmosphere. The centre of the commune feels like a village, with narrow cobbled lanes, a pond and some country-style restaurants. But the calm is brutally disturbed by a busy avenue that cuts across the commune. Houses here can be very small, and prices are very high. Yet Boitsfort is much in demand and properties change hands within hours of going on the market, so you really have to be alert to find a house to let. Those who manage to settle here praise the friendly atmosphere, local shops and almost rural atmosphere. The main disadvantage is that it takes time to get into the town centre, though tram 94 now connects Boitsfort with the metro terminus at Herrmann Debroux, providing a fast link to Schuman. Count on paying €1,200 for an apartment with two bedrooms and at least €1,500 for a modest house.

Best for... Families

Less good for... Singles

Price factor: €€€€–€€€€€€

Best for... Families

Less good for... Public transport

Price factor: €€€–€€€€

Coin du Balai

A cluster of family houses on the forest's edge that feel a bit cut off from the rest of Brussels. It has something of the mood of an Ardennes village, with cats prowling the lanes, back gardens filled with fruit trees, and the smell of woodsmoke in the air. The artist Rik Wouters lived in this quarter in the early 20th century. It is still idyllic, attracting bohemians, ecologists and teachers. The only drawbacks are that housing is hard to find and public transport is limited to bus 95. You can find a villa in this quarter with lots of charming features for €1,300 a month, but you would have to snap it up on the spot.

Dani Klein, Belgian singer with Vaya Con Dios
I love Boitsfort because it is friendly and green and yet no more than ten minutes from the centre of town by car.

Best for...	Less good for...
Public transport	Singles

Price factor: €€–€€€€€€€€€€

Stockel

This is an immensely popular area with large modern villas and attractive shops around Place Dumont. The quarter even has its own local cinema offering a mixture of French and US movies. There are excellent public transport links by metro, tram and bus, and yet Stockel is conveniently close to the forest for Sunday rambles and cycle rides. This is an expensive area of Brussels, where the cheapest one-bedroom apartment costs at least €500 and a small two-bedroom house will be at least €1,200. It's also an area where prices can easily rise to €5,000 for a large house in a secluded location.

Uccle

Uccle is a large commune with a wide variety of housing types, from beautiful villas with wisteria climbing the walls to plain modern apartments with gloomy rooms. This is one of the most desirable areas of Brussels, at least among Belgians. They like Uccle for its parks, its tree-lined avenues and the general atmosphere of good breeding. But it can be snobbish. Public transport is limited, although there is a good tram link into town along Avenue Albert. Almost everything in Uccle is overpriced. A small one-room apartment close to the town hall can easily cost €500, while a basic two-room apartment close to the European School could rise to €1,000. Don't sign a lease without checking other areas of town. You perhaps have to be Belgian to see the point of paying so much.

Best for...	Less good for...
Families	Public transport

Price factor: €€–€€€€€

Place Brugmann

A sophisticated corner of Ixelles with some grand townhouses located around a pleasant Brussels square with a bookshop, bakery and florist. Parking is not impossible and frequent trams run down Avenue Brugmann towards Avenue Louise. Rents are generally high, with a two-room apartment likely to cost €800 a month and anything possessing the smallest hint of *charme* likely to be over €1,000.

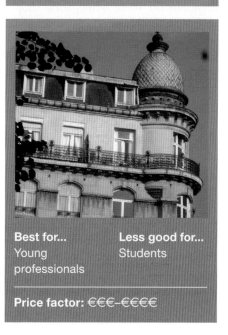

Best for...	Less good for...
Young professionals	Students

Price factor: €€€–€€€€

Woluwe St-Pierre

A cosmopolitan district popular with diplomats and senior EU bureaucrats. The local commune provides a wide range of amenities, including one of the city's best sports centres. Public transport connections are good to Schuman and the centre, and parking is rarely a problem. But the commune is fairly dull. Single people who enjoy going out at night should look to the Sablon or Louise rather than Woluwe. A plain modern two-bedroom apartment will cost €750 while a two-room apartment with a view of the Parc de Woluwe and a garage could easily be €1,200. A family home will cost much more, from €1,400 for a plain villa to €5,000 for a large mansion.

Best for... Families

Less good for... Students

Price factor:
€€€€€€€€-€€€€€€€€€€

Woluwe St Lambert

Best for... Public transport

Less good for... Students

Price factor: €€€€

A residential area popular with foreigners, mainly offering modern houses and apartments, though some older houses can be found, especially in the picturesque quarter around the Place St Lambert, which still has something of the mood of a Brabant village. The American-style Woluwe shopping centre opened in Woluwe St Lambert in the 1960s, but failed to drive out the more quirky local shops. The commune had little culture until the new Wolubilis cultural centre opened in 2006, but residents can now see exciting international theatre and drama without leaving the neighbourhood. There are good public transport links to the centre, and parking is rarely difficult. You can find a stylish duplex in a converted townhouse for €750, but family houses are much more expensive.

Northern and Western Suburbs

Anderlecht

Best for... Public transport

Less good for... Singles

Price factor: €

A mixed industrial and residential quarter that has never appealed to the expatriate community. The problem is that it lies on the wrong side of town, too far from the international hub for most people. Yet it has some elegant villas and good metro connections.

Molenbeek

Far from fashionable, Molenbeek is where immigrants find cheap housing. Some industrial buildings close to the canal have recently been converted into expensive lofts, but this is not the safest quarter of the city.

Best for...	Less good for...
Adventurous singles	Families

Price factor: €–€€

Jette

This is a quiet area of northern Brussels with attractive townhouses on well-kept streets. It lacks the excitement of Ixelles, but many Belgians love its melancholy dullness. It is not really an expat area at present, but the demographics could soon change, following the recent decision by the Belgian government to construct a fourth European School in Laeken on the site of a former military barracks. Smart young property developers are now converting old buildings into luxury apartments and lofts, hoping for a sudden surge in interest. Some quarters of Jette are served by metro, but most people prefer to use their car and parking is easy.

Best for...	Less good for...
Families	Culture

Price factor: €€–€€€

Susan Carroll, Irish journalist
quoted in *The Bulletin*
Jette is only 15 minutes from the city centre, but it sometimes feels like a country village.

Out of Town – Flanders

Tervuren

The small Flemish town of Tervuren woos foreigners with its location in the heart of the forest. It has been a favourite country retreat since the 18th century, and has a fine heritage of castles, lakes and parkland. Some townhouses lie in the centre, but most people live in large modern villas on leafy suburban streets. The presence of the British School makes this a favourite with English-speaking families. The attractions are many, including vast areas of wild forest, quiet streets and an attractive town square. Residents can take tram 44 to Montgomery metro station, but most people who live here use their cars for every journey.

Overijse

Overijse began as a Flemish village on the edge of the Forêt de Soignes. A statue in the main square commemorates the philosopher Justus Lipsius, who was born here in 1547. The old village is now surrounded by sprawling suburbs closely modelled on the American pattern. Houses here are popular with foreign families looking for a modern villa on a quiet street. There are regular De Lijn buses into Brussels, but no

Best for...	Less good for...
Families	Young singles

Price factor: €€€€–€€€€€€€€

train station nearby. A few people commute by bicycle through the forest, but most use their cars, even though this inevitably involves sitting in a traffic jam. A large modern house with four bedrooms and a garden costs about the same price as a two-bedroom apartment in Woluwe. You can pay as little as €1,100 a month for a modern family home with three bedrooms, while a monthly rent of €1,500 will get you an attractive new villa with four bedrooms. But teenagers might find it boring living out here and many parents eventually tire of having to drive everywhere.

Kraainem

Kraainem is a pleasant Flemish suburb on the eastern edge of the city, with a large stock of modern houses. It lies within the ring road and somehow feels closer to Brussels than other Flemish *gemeenten*.

Best for...	Less good for...
Public transport	Students
Price factor: €€–€€€€€€€	

Kraainem is increasingly in demand with expatriates because it is one of the few suburbs with good transport connections to Brussels (by tram and metro). Houses in Kraainem tend to be plain modern buildings, but prices are high. You might be able to find an acceptable two-bedroom apartment for under €600, but a four-bedroom house is likely to cost at least €2,000. Watch out for any house that costs less than expected. The reason may be that it lies under a flight path. Only a small area is affected by aircraft noise, but it can be intolerable for the unlucky few.

Hoeilaart

The small Flemish town of Hoeilaart has a rambling rural charm, yet it lies close to the city, just beyond the Brussels Ring. You can find lovely old Belgian villas with period charm for €1,100 a month, and even

Best for...	Less good for...
Families	Public transport
Price factor: €€€€–€€€€€€€	

the occasional mansion with a swimming pool and tennis court for under €2,500. Trains run to Brussels from Hoeilaart station, but most people prefer to drive into the city through the beech forest every day.

Linkebeek

A compact Flemish community on the southern edge of Brussels with some charming old houses surrounded by rambling gardens. The commute into town is slow and train services from

Best for...	Less good for...
Families	Singles
Price factor: €€€€€	

Linkebeek station are infrequent. Yet many people are prepared to make the sacrifice for Linkebeek's genuine rural atmosphere and attractive local restaurants.

Sterrebeek

A peaceful Flemish town a few kilometers beyond Tervuren. It attracts expatriate families looking for large villas on quiet streets. The modern villas in Sterrebeek are sometimes more imaginative than those in Overijse or Kraainem. You might find a romantic Arts and Crafts house with five bedrooms and an enormous garden for €1,800 a month. The town has an authentic Flemish atmosphere, including several good bakeries. Commuting into Brussels is slow by car but reasonably painless by train.

Best for...	Less good for...
Families	Public transport
Price factor: €€€€€€€€€	

Wezembeek-Oppem

Best for...	Less good for...
Families	Students
Price factor: €€€€€€€	

An appealing Flemish village east of Kraainem with attractive modern villas and the occasional old Brabant farmhouse for rent. Many Germans settle here to be close to the Deutsche Schule. It's also popular with British expatriates because of its rural charm. Some houses are conveniently close to the route of tram 39, which provides a reliable but slow link to Montgomery metro station. A modern house with three bedrooms costs at least €1,500 a month, but places are hard to find. Watch out for houses affected by aircraft noise.

Out of Town – Wallonia

Waterloo

Best for...	Less good for...
Families	Public transport
Price factor: €€€€€€–€€€€€€€€	

Waterloo is famous for its battlefield, but that's not the reason why foreigners settle in this area. They are more interested in the big modern villas, quiet suburban streets and enormous supermarkets. The town appeals particularly to Americans because of the presence of St John's International School and the relatively easy driving conditions. Many Nordic families are drawn to Waterloo because of the Scandinavian school on the outskirts. The beautiful Walloon Brabant countryside is another factor that tempts people here. Waterloo estate agents always have a large number of modern villas on their books, ranging in price from €1,200 a month for a basic three-bedroom house to €2,400 for a luxury villa with character. Yet people who live in Waterloo face some serious transport problems. The main public transport into Brussels is by bus W, although there are some trains from Waterloo station. Most people choose to use their car, which leads to dense traffic in Waterloo centre and increasingly long journey times into Brussels on the clogged Chaussée de Waterloo.

Rixensart

Best for...	Less good for...
Families	Students
Price factor: €€€€€–€€€€€€€	

An old village with a castle located in the Walloon Brabant countryside. Most expatriates live in large modern villas on quiet roads. The commute into Brussels can be slow on the E411 motorway, but trains run from Rixensart station. The prices here are lower than Waterloo. Expect to pay €1,300 for an attractive villa with five bedrooms and a big garden, or €1,800 for an English-style house with five bedrooms.

Genval

Best for...	Less good for...
Quiet	Culture

Price factor: €€€€

Genval was founded in the rolling Walloon Brabant landscape in the early 20th century as a spa town. The old quarter around the lake has lovely rambling villas on winding lanes, but most of the houses date from the 1960s and 1970s. Houses out here are hard to find, but you might be able to rent a secluded villa with two bedrooms for as little as €900 a month. A modern two-bedroom apartment costs about the same price. There are direct trains every 30 minutes to Schuman station, with the journey taking about 25 minutes, but the service drops to one train an hour at weekends.

Lasne

Best for...	Less good for...
Countryside	Public transport

Price factor:
€€€€€€€–€€€€€€€€

Located 24km south of Brussels, Lasne regularly comes top in surveys as the wealthiest commune in Belgium. It's not difficult to see why. This neat Walloon Brabant village has an old church and narrow cobbled lanes leading to whitewashed farmhouses. But Lasne is only for the seriously rich. A two-bedroom house costs at least €1,600 a month, a stylish modern villa well over €2,000. You also need to be prepared to commute daily into Brussels by car, as public transport is not an option.

Braine l'Alleud

Best for...	Less good for...
Families	Students

Price factor: €€€€€

Braine l'Alleud is a pleasant town spread out over the rolling fields and woods of Walloon Brabant. The commune includes a large part of the Waterloo battlefield and many street names have historical echoes, such as the Avenue Wellington and the Avenue de la Garde Impériale. Most houses are large and modern, with big gardens and sometimes a swimming pool. The only drawbacks are scarce public transport and a long commute into Brussels. Expect to pay at least €1,400 for a modern villa with four bedrooms and a basketball hoop attached to the garage.

Out of Town – Bilingual

Rhode-St-Genèse

Best for...	Less good for...
Families	Students

Price factor: €€€€

This is a bilingual municipality just beyond the southern limits of Brussels. It appeals to families looking for large houses on quiet streets, but public transport barely exists. Prices are generally high, though you can still track down a three-bedroom house for €900 with a bit of looking.

Mind your language

Anyone settling in the small towns outside Brussels should take into account the language tensions in the Flemish belt around Brussels. The city is encircled by Flemish territory where the official language is Dutch. Some expatriates live here happily without speaking a word of Dutch, but others face serious practical problems when they have to deal with the public administration. Bear in mind that all bills and official letters will be in Dutch. You may also have to deal with Dutch-speaking officials in the local town hall, although the staff in your local bank will almost certainly speak excellent English. If you send your children to a local school, they will have to learn to speak perfect Dutch (and in some schools they will not be allowed to speak any other language in the playground). At the very least, your life will be much easier if you learn at least some basic Dutch.

Village in the Ardennes

Commuting into Brussels

Many people choose to live in the countryside around Brussels, where large villas can be found for relatively cheap rents. But there can be problems. Half a million people travel into Brussels every day. Two thirds commute for work, while the rest are tourists or students. Some travel into the city by train, but most arrive by car, clogging the motorways and main roads into the city and reducing the average car speed in Brussels during rush hours to 11 km/hour, barely faster than a bicycle.

Brussels is a French–speaking city, yet 70% of its 360,000 commuters come from Flanders. The reason is simple. Most jobs in Brussels are in the public sector. Almost all require a fluency in Dutch and French. The Flemish are prepared to learn French to get a good job, but the same determination to learn Dutch doesn't exist in Wallonia.

The character of Brussels changes during office hours. You hear Dutch widely spoken in the streets and restaurants up until 6pm, but less so in the evening. Most Flemish workers leave the city as soon as the working day ends and Flemish theatres and cultural institutions struggle to fill seats in the evening. Some put on lunchtime events for commuters, such as *Boterhamen in het Park*, which offers summer concerts and poetry readings for the civil servants who work around the park.

The Flemish government is now making an effort to persuade more Dutch speakers to settle in Brussels, but the results so far have been disappointing. Most people still prefer to live in their linguistic territory, rather than be treated as outsiders in their own capital, as often happens with Dutch-speakers.

But the commuters aren't just Belgians. Many of the cars stuck in traffic at 8.55am on a Monday morning belong to European civil servants and international executives who have chosen to live in a spacious villa outside Brussels. They are prepared to crawl into Brussels every day for the sake of a house with a garden. The government, at least at present, has no plans to discourage this habit.

Aircraft Noise

The Flemish suburbs east of Brussels seem like the perfect location for families. They offer large villas and spacious gardens within easy reach of the European Quarter. Yet some districts suffer from intolerable aircraft noise at certain times of the day. The problem originally affected Flemish suburbs to the north of Brussels such as Vilvoorde, Meise and Grimbergen, but in 2002 the government changed flight routes so that more aircraft now take off above the communes of Kraainem, Sterrebeek and Wezembeek-Oppem. Many believe the move was political, as the northern communes have a strongly Flemish population while eastern communes are favoured by French-speakers and expatriates. Yet the basic problem is that Brussels Airport is located in a densely-populated area. Several attempts have been made to disperse flight paths over a wider area, rather than concentrate them over a single route. Yet a final agreement has proved elusive because the problem involves two separate regions, Brussels and Flanders, which have separate aviation policies. Anyone looking for a house on the east side of Brussels should therefore do some preliminary research on aircraft noise levels before agreeing to let or buy a house.

Short-term stays

Apartment Hotels

Brussels has a large floating population of politicians, lobbyists, consultants and interns. They sometimes stay for a week or a few months, and don't want to go to the trouble of looking for an apartment or signing a three-year lease. The solution for many is to stay in a furnished room in an apartment hotel (or flathotel). These are designed for expatriates looking for short-term accommodation and offer the comfort of a private apartment along with the 24-hour services of a hotel. The apartments can be rented for variable periods, ranging from a few days to a month or more. They are more expensive than a normal apartment but cheaper than a hotel room. Most include service and a desk receptionist to deal with practical problems.

The cheapest one-bedroom studio flat in the European Quarter can cost as little as €700 a month, but average prices are about €1,500-€2,000 for one bedroom, €2,000-€3,000 for two bedrooms, and €2,000-€3,000 for three.

Some apartment hotels are fairly basic, but others are furnished luxuriously and include the use of a fitness room, sauna and business centre. You might even be offered help with practicalities such as registering with the authorities.

Several international hotel chains offer furnished apartments, including Marriott. Most apartment hotels are located in the business districts such as Avenue Louise and the European Quarter, though a few lie in the quieter suburbs. They generally occupy modern apartment buildings, but the 105 furnished apartments in Rue du Souveraine are located in 20 brightly painted townhouses in the heart of Ixelles.

Check with the agency how much they charge for damage, as the bill for a single broken vase can sometimes come as a shock.

Bed and Breakfast

You can discover some of Brussels most interesting living spaces by staying in bed and breakfast accommodation. These often offer attractive rooms in lively quarters for about half the price of a hotel room. Some places offer luxurious rooms aimed at professionals, while others provide cheaper options for interns. Rates drop significantly for longer stays.
www.bnb-brussels.be

Houses in the European Quarter

Long-term renting

Renting

SETTING UP HOME

The Brussels property market offers a wide variety of rented accommodation. A studio flat is normally small and modern, while an apartment can be anything from a neat Art Deco interior to a series of grand rooms carved out of an old townhouse. The term 'villa' normally means a detached house with a garden, while loft apartments are normally one-room spaces created in old industrial buildings.

Staff employed by the European institutions can often find a house within walking distance of their office, though many prefer to live outside the city in peaceful residential districts of Tervuren, Overijse and Waterloo.

People with children often choose a house with a garden close to an international school, whereas single people are often drawn by the urban excitement of Ixelles or downtown Brussels. Anyone who feels the need for green space should bear in mind that residents of central Brussels have just one square metre of greenery per head, whereas those in the suburbs have 20 sq m each.

Prices have gone up in recent years, but you can still find a decent one-room apartment in the student quarter near the ULB university campus for as little as €300 a month, though anything with character is likely to cost at least €600 a month. The cheapest two-bedroom apartments cost around €700, while three-bedroom apartments begin at about €1,200.

Charges

Always ask about charges before you sign a lease. Most listings give the price without charges, but you may have to pay a monthly supplement to cover common facilities such as staircase lighting and cleaning. Some monthly charges are negligible, but you may have to pay €100 or more a month in a luxury apartment building. The charges are usually revised by the landlord at the end of each year. You might suddenly find yourself paying a lot more, though the landlord will have to provide bills to justify the increase.

Taxes

Tenants and home owners have to pay a regional tax every year to Brussels Capital Region. The bill is sent to the 'head of household' registered as living in the apartment or house on 1 January of that year. The tax was reduced from €179 to €89 in 2007 after Brussels Region introduced various cost-cutting measures. The tax covers services such as rubbish collection and street lighting. It also includes the TV and radio licence, though you still have to pay an annual subscription to a cable company.

Lofts

Young professionals in good jobs are sometimes attracted by the idea of living in a loft. Loft living is a relatively new concept in Brussels, but it is now a booming sector. Most loft spaces are located in old industrial spaces in central Brussels, but you can also find lofts in suburbs such as Ixelles, Uccle and Jette. Not all are in industrial buildings; some are simply apartments that have been renovated to look more like a loft. Some of the most authentic lofts are in the Tour et Taxis neighbourhood. But loft living is not for everyone. While they offer unusual living spaces, the lofts are often in run-down post-industrial areas. It is important to walk around the streets after dark to get an impression of the neighbourhood. If you don't feel safe, don't sign the lease. Lofts are also relatively expensive places to live and it is hard to find anything in this category for under €1,000 a month.

Studios

Single people on modest salaries can often find a studio apartment in an attractive location. Studios are smaller than apartments, with a single living area and a bedroom, so guests may have to sleep on the sofa. They are sometimes located in attics of converted houses with interesting views across the rooftops, but some can be oppressively small. Expect to pay about €350-€400 a month.

House Sharing

Belgians like to rent their own unfurnished apartment, but that usually means signing a lease for three years. For expatriates on short-term contracts, it's often easier to find someone with a room in a townhouse or apartment going spare. Most places are already furnished, and house-sharers normally accept short-term lets. Since the lease has already been negotiated, you don't have to worry about dealing with a landlord. Most flat shares are in Ixelles or Saint-Gilles. Many are organised by students at Brussels University.

A room in a house in the European Quarter is likely to cost €400-€450 a month, but you might find something for as little as €250 a month in less fashionable Saint-Gilles. Look in the classified ads section of www.xpats.com under 'homeshares', or try putting up a notice in your office.

Renting a Garage

Many areas of Brussels have many more cars than parking spaces, particularly in central Brussels, Ixelles and Etterbeek. You can save yourself a lot of trouble by renting a garage in the neighbourhood. The price you pay depends on the neighbourhood, but the normal rate is about €100-€120. Make sure if you drive a large car that it fits into the garage, as some parking spaces are a tight squeeze. Contact your insurance company if you rent a garage, as most companies offer a substantial reduction if the car is parked there overnight.

What Determines the Price

Certain features can push up the price of a house or apartment in Brussels. They include parquet floors, closeness to a European School, an American kitchen, an Uccle postcode, a location close to the European institutions (*proximité CEE*), a loft interior or a garage. An apartment *de standing* will inevitably be a lot more expensive than a normal apartment.

Making the move

Signing the Lease

Once you have found a place to rent, you will have to sign a lease. Here you have a choice. You can opt for a three-year lease or a nine-year contract. Many foreigners feel more comfortable with a three-year lease, especially if they are in Belgium for a limited period. This type of lease fixes the rent for three years, but the tenant has to pay for the entire period. If you leave before the end of the contract, you have to find someone else to take over the lease or pay a penalty.

A nine-year lease is more advantageous, because it can be broken at any time. You simply have to give three months' notice, although there is a penalty to pay if you leave within three years (three month's rent if you leave in the first year, two months' rent in the second year and one month's rent in the third year).

The rent in both cases is fixed for the period of the contract, but it increases every year by a small amount determined by the official Belgian cost of living index. The tenant has security of tenure, unless the landlord or a family member wants to occupy the property, or extensive repairs are required. The landlord in this case has to give the tenant six months' notice by registered letter.

You can download a standard rental agreement at the estate agent websites www.immoweb.be or www.pim.be. You can also buy standard lease contracts in some Brussels bookshops.

Many apartments include a service charge (*provision pour charges/vooruitbetaling*) to cover shared costs, such as cleaning common stairs, lifts, lighting in hallways and maintaining a common garden. This is normally calculated every year and divided among the tenants.

The landlord has to register the lease within two months of the contract being signed. If he fails to do so, the tenant can leave at any time without giving notice.

Brussels has a plentiful supply of rented property, so you don't need to take the first apartment you see. Insist on the landlord carrying out major repairs before you sign anything. You might also be able to negotiate a lower rent or ask for a shorter contract if the landlord is desperate to rent the property.

The tenant is liable for insuring the building and contents against fire. You are also obliged to have chimneys swept and gas boilers cleaned every year. This is necessary for insurance, but it is also vital for your own safety, as faulty gas appliances claim several lives every year in Belgium. You should ask the landlord for the name of an official engineer qualified to service your appliances.

Etat des Lieux

A high number of tenants in Brussels get a nasty shock at the end of the lease when they are presented with a massive bill for damages. The best way to protect yourself is to arrange for an official inventory (*état des lieux/plaatsbeschrijving*) before you sign the lease. This provides a detailed description of the state of the property, sometimes with photographs attached, which is signed by the landlord and tenant.

SETTING UP HOME

Don't be coy about doing this. Even the most courteous Belgian landlord can turn nasty at the end of a lease and claim unreasonable amounts for the slightest blemish. Take no chances and insist that the survey is carried out by an independent expert (*expert immobilier/vastgoedexpert*). You will have to pay the bill for both entry and exit surveys, but a good expert knows what to check in making the survey. Normal wear and tear is acceptable at the end of the lease, but the degree of acceptable damage is often a matter of dispute. The expert knows the law, and can ensure that you are not charged unfairly. The fee charged for a single survey depends on the size of the property. A one-room studio apartment might cost about €85, whereas a large villa could cost over €200. You can find a list of property surveyors on the website www. pap.be, under *'Addresses Utiles'*.

Security Deposit

Your landlord will normally ask for a deposit equal to three months rent to cover damage to the property, or breach of contract (such as early termination of the lease). You should ask your bank to put the deposit in a 'blocked account', which needs the signatures of both landlord and tenant before any money can be withdrawn. The deposit is your money, and earns you interest when the lease ends.

Furnishing an Apartment

Most people rent unfurnished apartments. So where do you buy cheap furniture? The answer for most people is Ikea. Brussels has a large floating population of students and business executives who need to furnish a place for a few years. Ikea provides an easy place to buy cupboards, beds and plates. The company has three superstores in the Brussels area, including a new branch in the Brussels suburb of Anderlecht.

There are other options for those who want to be different. You can find furniture shops in the Marolles that sell tables, chairs and beds. They can be pricey, but most will deliver to your place.

You can also pick up used furniture at garage sales. These are listed in the classified ads section of www.expat.com. Most of the sellers live in the suburbs, so a car is necessary.

Or you can do things on the cheap. The Petits Riens charity shop on Rue Américaine has rooms filled with discarded furniture. Some of it is beyond repair, but you might spot an old item that fits your interior (www.petitsriens.be).

Some people are in Brussels for such a short period that they simply rent furniture rather than shipping their own from home or buying new items. Several agencies in Brussels specialise in renting furniture to expatriates. You simply look through a catalogue, pick what you like and wait for delivery.

Housing Problems

The Brussels-Europe Liaison Office employs housing specialists who provide free advice to expatriate tenants in Brussels. You can avoid many common problems by talking to one of their specialists before signing the lease. They will also advise you on the procedure to follow if your landlord behaves unreasonably. (Avenue d'Auderghem 63; ☎ 02.280.00.80; email blbe@blbe.irisnet.be; www.blbe.be)

Brussels property listings

Newspapers and Magazines

The Bulletin: English language magazine almost exclusively devoted to expensive properties to rent or buy. www.thebulletin.be

Vlan: Free city newspaper with extensive property listings and useful property website (in English). www.vlanimmo.be

Estate Agents

Clairière: Agency based at Avenue Louise 195, with extensive list of apartments in Ixelles and the European Quarter. ☎ 02.640.40.60; email immoclairiere.be; www.immoclairiere.be

Crescendimmo: Belgian agency with apartments and houses in Brussels and surrounding districts. ☎ 02.660.50.50; email info@crebrussels.be; www.cre.be

Find a Home: Agency based in Overijse with houses and apartments to rent in popular expatriate areas of Flemish Brabant. ☎ 02.657.11.99; email info@findahome. be; www.findahome.be

Globali: Brussels agency specialising in luxury lofts and suburban villas on the east side of town, with many expatriate clients on its books. ☎ 02.775.08.50; email info@globali.be; www.globali.be

Immo Regard: Specialises in upmarket villas outside Brussels. ☎ 02.653.09.40; email contact@immoregard.be; www.immoregard.be

Louise Properties: Upmarket agency on Avenue Louise with apartments and villas in Brussels and surrounding countryside. ☎ 02.644.05.05; email info@louiseproperties. be; www.louiseproperties.be;

MacNash: Large estate agent active in the expatriate market. ☎ 02.347.11.47; email info@macnash.com; www.macnash.com;

Multimmo: Estate agents covering the leafy suburbs south of the city, including Linkebeek and Sint-Genesius Rode. ☎ 02.378.40.40; email info@multimmo.be; www.multimmo.be

Office des Propriétaires: The oldest estate agents in Brussels, dating back to the late 19th century and mainly interested in upmarket properties. Sells a standard lease agreement used by many landlords. ☎ 02.626.08.26; www.op.be; email info@op.be.

Omnium: International group with modern two and three bedroom apartments to rent in Brussels. ☎ 02.743.24.24; email location@omnium.be; www.omnium.be

Otimmo: Agency based at Avenue Louise 223 with extensive list of properties in Ixelles and other desirable areas. ☎ 02.646.59.59; email otimmo@otimmo.com; www.otimmo.com

Victoire: Upmarket apartments and houses mainly in Woluwe, Uccle and Auderghem. ☎ 02.771.12.40; email rent@victoire.be; www.victoire.be

Websites

Immoweb: Extensive Belgian property website popular with house hunters. www.immoweb.be

Ximmo: New Belgian site for property listings. www.ximmo.be

PAP: Property owners' website. www.pap.be

Expats.com: The Bulletin's expat website, with a list of property ads from the current issue of The Bulletin. www.xpats.com

Easy Expat: Expatriate website with a limited number of apartments to rent. www.easyexpat.com

Craigslist: Online listings with housing section. brussels.www.craigslist.org

Crescendimmo: Belgian agency with apartments and houses in Brussels and surrounding districts. ☎ 02.660.50.50; email info@crebrussels.be; www.cre.be

Furnished Flats

Brussels Business Flats: Stylish furnished flats in excellent locations, such as the European Quarter, Avenue Louise and the Sablon. Prices start at about €800 a month for a studio flat. ☎ 02.733.49.45; email info@bbf.be; www.bbf.be

Home in Brussels: Manages some 500 different apartments in Brussels, ranging from simple studios to luxurious penthouses. ☎ 02.732.00.00; email info@homeinbrussels.be; www.homeinbrussels.be

Marriott: The hotel chain has 50 luxury apartments in the European Quarter. ☎ 02.505.29.29; email Brussels@execapartments.com; www.execapartments.com

Phileas Flathotel: Karin Dhadamus, who runs the Phileas Fogg guesthouse, has four furnished apartments in a Brussels townhouse. They are stylish little places with odd details, located within walking distance of the EU institutions. Monthly rents from €600 to €800. ☎ 02.217.83.38; email phileas.fogg@belgacom.net; www.phileasfogg.be

Rue Souveraine: Luxury apartments in a street of renovated townhouses in Ixelles. Residents have access to a health club and communal gardens. There is even a Rue Souveraine blog, helping to create a village atmosphere among residents. But prices are high, with the cheapest one-room apartment costing just over €1,500 a month. ☎ 02.626.07.76; www.ruesouveraine.com

Renting Furniture

Furniture Rental: Wide choice of furniture for rent including low-cost options. ☎ 02.216.48.79; email furnitrent@skypro.be; www.furniture-rental.be

Interior Rent: From single items to harmonised interiors. ☎ 03.860.77.00; www.interiorrent.com

Buying Furniture

Ikea: Swedish furniture superstore with three outlets in the Brussels area. www.ikea.be

Petits Riens: Huge warehouse space filled with old furniture, some of it beyond repair. Profits go to charity. ☎ 02.537.30.26; email info@petitsriens.be; www.petitsriens.be

Understanding The Property Ads

A vendre/Te koop: for sale

A louer/Te huur: for rent

Appartement: a flat with a separate living room, kitchen and at least one bedroom

Flat/Studio: a single room used as a living room and bedroom, with a separate small kitchen and bathroom

Loft: an open living space with a separate bathroom, not always a genuine loft, and often overpriced for the neighbourhood

Maison/Huis: a traditional Belgian house

Maison de maître: an elegant 19th-century townhouse

Maison bourgeoise: a townhouse

Villa: a detached or semi-detached modern suburban house with garden

Living: living room

Chambre/Kamer: bedroom

Cuisine/Keuken: kitchen

Cuisine Américaine: a modern open kitchen, often separated from the living room by an eating bar

Cour: courtyard

Box: a small garage

Utilities, telephones, television and internet

Most utility companies require a Belgian ID card before they will make a connection, though some will accept a passport if your have just arrived in the country. If you are renting, you can often arrange informally to take over the utilities contracts from the previous tenant without the inconvenience of the supply being disconnected and then reconnected.

Utility bills are normally sent out monthly. The meter is read once a year, and the monthly charge is calculated on the basis of the previous year's consumption. If you take over a rented property, your initial bills will be based on the previous tenant's consumption.

You have three weeks to pay before being disconnected, but it is easy to run over the time limit if you are away on holiday. The safest method of payment is to arrange with your bank to pay by automatic direct debit. You can do this electronically using a self-bank machine.

Energy

The Brussels energy market was liberalised at the beginning of 2007, which means that consumers can now choose their supplier. At least they could if there was another serious supplier available. The main supplier is Electrabel Customer Solutions (www.electrabel.be), a former state monopoly now owned by the Suez group. The only competing operator in Brussels Region is the small Belgian company Lampiris (www.lampiris.be), though new companies are expected to enter the market eventually.

The energy market in Flanders was liberalised in 2003, but prices continued to rise, pushed upwards by the global energy crisis. The energy market in Wallonia was liberated at the same time as Brussels, bringing several new companies into the market.

Even if prices don't go down in Brussels, consumers should eventually be able to choose a green supplier who generates energy by wind turbines or solar power. The website www.brugel.be was set up by Brussels Region to provide consumers with information on the different suppliers in Brussels Region and has an online calculator to compare prices, though this seems a relatively pointless exercise given the lack of serious competition.

Plugs

The electricity supply in Belgium is 220 volts. Most plugs have two round pins plus a hole for a third socket pin, though smaller appliances have just two round pins. You can plug in electrical equipment from most other EU countries without any problem, though people from Britain and Ireland need an adaptor plug to use with three-pin plugs. Anyone bringing equipment from the United States will need to buy a transformer to convert a 110 volt supply to 220 volts. Check with a local electrician before you do anything.

Adaptors are sold in branches of Brico and at shops selling travel accessories. But you should eventually take off the old plugs and rewire using Belgian plugs, as some insurance companies may not accept a claim if damage was caused by an appliance connected using an adaptor.

The Invisible Killer

Every winter several people die in Brussels because of carbon monoxide poisoning. This is usually the result of a faulty gas water heater or gas central heating system. If a chimney is blocked, or the flame fails to burn properly, the carbon monoxide will remain in the room undetected. The initial effects are fatigue and headaches, followed by unconsciousness. It is therefore vital to have all gas appliances checked every year by a certified engineer. This is the tenant's responsibility in rented accommodation.

Water

The water supply in Brussels is provided by a single company that recently changed its name to Vivaqua (www.vivaqua.be). The company supplies water to two million consumers in Brussels and the surrounding towns and villages. Water is paid for annually depending on the amount used.

Is Brussels Water Safe To Drink?

Belgium has a bad environmental reputation. In a 2003 United Nations report, Belgian water quality was ranked as the worst in the world in a survey of 122 countries, below even the poorest African countries. The Belgian water authorities argued that the report was flawed, but most Belgians don't take any chances. They regularly carry home bottled water brought by truck from the Ardennes or the mountains of France. But is this necessary?

The Brussels water authority Vivaqua insists that it is not. Most of the city's tap water is piped from the Ardennes. The main catchment area lies in the grounds of Modave Castle, far from any polluting industry. It originates in rain that falls on the Hautes Fagnes moors and is collected in deep caves before being brought to Brussels in a network of underground pipes.

Most of the city's water in fact comes from the same source as Spa bottled water. But the bottled version is 100 times more expensive and causes far greater environmental damage, Vivaqua argues. Admittedly, some of the city's tap water is recycled. It is treated with chlorine, which gives the water a slightly unpleasant taste. But this can be removed by using a water filter. Bottled water is really not necessary.

Telephones

Getting a phone installed in Belgium used to take months, but you can now get connected in five working days. This is what happens when a creaky state monopoly is challenged by the free market. The main operator is Belgacom (www.belgacom.be), a sleek modern company that replaced the old state operator. Its main competitors are the Swedish-owned Tele2 (www.tele2.be) and Telenet (www.telenet.be). The rival companies claim to offer the same services as Belgacom at lower rates. In addition, three operators (BT, Colt and MCI) offer phone services aimed at Belgian business users, but many Belgians are unwilling to change, and remain loyal to Belgacom.

One advantage is that you find Belgacom shops in most main shopping streets. You can pick up phones, faxes and modems in these outlets, as well as arranging for a phone or broadband connection. The shops are listed at the Belgacom website (www.belgacom.be) and in phone directories. Belgacom also provides a helpful English-speaking service on the freephone line 0800.55.800.

With the introduction of competition, Belgacom has been forced to entice customers with special offers. The latest deal is the Happy Time International tariff, which offers cheap calls to a single country. The list of options includes the UK and USA. You have to make your calls from 5pm-8am on weekdays or any time during the weekend. If you can organise your life around these hours, you pay just €1 per call no matter how long you talk.

The Belgacom/Proximus company X-Bo (www.x-bo.be) offers expatriates a one-stop telecom service, which bundles together almost all communication needs, including a fixed phone line, mobile phone, internet, digital TV and home alarm systems. The staff explain everything in fluent English.

Mobile Phones

It takes no time at all to get set up with a Belgian mobile phone (known in Belgium as a GSM). Most European mobile phones will work in Brussels, but you pay heavy charges for calls in Belgium with a foreign phone. The European Commission has tried to cut these charges within Europe, but with limited success. It's generally worth buying a new mobile when you move to Belgium, rather than make roaming calls on your old mobile. A new phone can cost as little as €49.

The next decision is whether to sign a contract with a Belgian operator and pay a monthly bill or simply recharge your phone when the credit runs low. Frequent users are likely to find that a contract works out cheaper and easier, but occasional users are probably better off with a pre-paid credit card. Phones can easily be recharged using cards sold at phone shops, newsagents and supermarkets. You can also top up your credit from your bank account using your own mobile phone.

There are three operators in Belgium - Proximus (owned by Belgacom), Mobistar and Base. Each company has an extensive network of phone shops in main streets. While call charges are roughly the same, each operator tries to attract customers with different special offers. It is worth doing some research in advance to find out the service that best suits your needs. You can begin by looking at the three websites, which all have information in English (www.proximus.be, www.mobistar.be, www.base.be).

Television

Belgium has one of the best television services in the world. A basic cable subscription costs about €130 a year and provides access to at least 24 TV channels. About 97% of houses in Belgium are covered by cable TV. You activate the service when you move into your house by contacting the local supplier. The basic package in Brussels includes BBC 1 and BBC 2, three Belgian French channels, five Belgian Dutch channels, five French channels, three German channels, three Dutch channels, and Italian, Portuguese, Spanish, Turkish and Moroccan channels.

Viewers looking for English programmes have a huge choice. They have the two BBC channels (seen in Belgium one hour later due to the time difference), along with CNN, CNBC and BBC World. But they can also turn to the Flemish and Dutch channels, which often screen British and American films and series in the original language with subtitles.

The Flemish channels buy up some of the best British programmes, so you can often catch an ITV or Channel 4 series in Belgium just a few months after it has been broadcast in Britain. The Flemish channel Canvas buys some of the best UK and US productions, like *The Sopranos*, *Desperate Housewives* and *The Office*. It also regularly screens quality British and American movies, along with rather elderly episodes of *Inspector Morse*. The commercial channel TV4 is a good bet for US police dramas, reality shows and Hollywood movies.

The Flemish and Dutch have an insatiable appetite for British TV detective series like *Inspector Morse* and *Spooks*. But they also have a weakness for absurd British comedy like *Fawlty Towers* and *Little Britain*.

The French channels are probably less interesting to English speakers, as they dub all foreign programmes and films into French. Your children might get a kick out of watching *The Simpsons* in French (where the accents closely follow the originals), but only the saddest of the sad would watch an old John Wayne movie with a monotonous French voice over.

There are two local channels serving Brussels – Tele Bruxelles in French and TV Brussel in Dutch. TV Brussel tries to attract an international audience by subtitling its evening programmes in English and broadcasting an English programme on Sunday evenings. The international Euronews gets around the language problem by broadcasting news pictures without any commentary at all.

Those living outside Brussels have a different choice of programmes, depending on the cable provider. Viewers in Flanders are served by Telenet (www.telenet.be), which excludes some of the smaller French channels, while viewers in Wallonia have to live without the Flemish channels VTM, KanaalTwee and VT4. You might not mind, but children living in Waterloo can be intensely jealous of friends in Brussels who can watch *The Simpsons* in English on VT4.

Most foreigners ignore programmes in Dutch, yet Flemish channels produce some excellent documentaries and TV series. It's worth signing up for a Dutch language course so that you can follow *Flikken* (a police series set in Ghent), *Windkracht 10* (helicopter rescue series set in Koksijde) and *Matroeskas* (a raw look at Russian prostitutes in Antwerp).

Cable Companies

Four cable companies operate in Brussels, but there is no choice of supplier, as each company holds a monopoly in certain communes.

Brutéle: Serves Auderghem, Evere, Ixelles, Uccle, Saint-Gilles and Woluwe-St-Pierre. Offers digital TV and internet services. ☎ 02.500.99.11; www.brutele.be

UPC: Etterbeek, Schaerbeek, Jette, Forest, Berchem St-Agathe, Koekelberg and Ganshoren. The package includes the Flemish channel Vijf TV, which is not available in other areas of Brussels. Offers an internet service called Chello. ☎ 02.240.08.00; email info@upcbelgium.be; www.upcbelgium.be

Coditel: Serves Anderlecht, Brussels (including the Louise and Loi districts), Laeken, St Josse and Watermael-Boitsfort. ☎ 02.226.52.00; www.coditel.be

Wolu-TV: Serves Woluwe-St-Lambert. ☎ 02.736.77.89; email wolutv@chello.be; www.wolutv.be

Radio 4

The BBC mandarins caused an almighty row in Belgium a few years ago when they decided to move Radio 4 from long wave to FM. This meant that listeners in Brussels could no longer catch favourite programmes like the *Archers* or *Women's Hour*. The decision led to angry letters and a petition to the BBC. The BBC replied that listeners in Brussels did not pay a license fee and so had no right to complain. Yet the director-general eventually caved in to pressure and the BBC now broadcasts Radio 4 on both FM and long wave 198. Problem solved? Not quite. The BBC sometimes uses its long wave frequency to broadcast cricket matches that can go on for several days. The result: more angry letters to the BBC. But there is now a solution. You can listen to crystal clear FM broadcasts on your computer using a broadband internet connection (www.bbc.co.uk/radio4).

Digital TV

Belgians are now beginning to switch to digital TV. More than 100,000 subscribers have already signed up for Belgacom's interactive internet service Belgacom TV. This system works with most modern TVs, but you need a broadband connection, a decoder and a remote control for each TV set. The cheapest package costs just under €10 per month, but prices go up for packages that include sport and movies. The basic package on offer at the time of writing isn't too impressive for expatriates. You don't get BBC 1 or BBC 2, just BBC World. Belgacom is still trying to negotiate broadcasting rights, so it's best to wait until they have signed some more deals.

Satellite TV

Satellite TV is popular with Turkish and Moroccan communities, along with Americans who want to follow baseball games. But Belgians rarely feel the need to install a dish on their house.

The Sky digibox offers access to over 100 different channels, mainly British and American, but an additional subscription is required to watch US sports programmes.

You will probably need planning permission from the local town hall to put up a large satellite dish on your house. Several companies in Brussels will come to your house and install a dish correctly.

Internet

After a slow start, Belgium is now one of the world's leading countries for internet access. The market is dominated by high-speed internet connections, which represent 73% of residential use and 90% of business use.

Several cable TV companies offer an internet service using the existing TV connection. The cable companies Brutélé, Telenet (in Flanders) and Chello (www. chello.be) have interesting internet offers. Subscribers pay a flat rate which allows them to stay online all day, without having to use the telephone line. The other option is to sign up for a high-speed connection through Belgacom. Its Turbo Line service offers speeds of up to 4 megabites per second, allowing you to download huge files of images and music. You will need to buy a Belgacom modem, but your telephone line remains free.

Internet Hotspots

Brussels has about 180 internet hotspots, mainly located in hotels and cafés. Most require some form of payment, but some are free. Brussels currently lags behind cities like Amsterdam and London in wifi hotspots, but Brussels Region has an ambitious plan to provide free wifi access across the entire city. As a modest start, it has installed 22 internet posts on busy squares like Place Stéphanie and Place Flagey. The posts have touch screens and can be used to send emails, consult public transport timetables and read Le Soir. They also serve as wifi hotspots providing free internet access for anyone with a laptop within a radius of about 500m. Free wifi is also available in the Marché St Géry and at Recyclart's café.

Anyone with a Belgacom broadband subscription (such as Belgacom ADSL or Skynet Go) can surf for free in a Belgacom hotspot for a limited period (3-5 hours a month). You simply log on using your login name and password. Otherwise you can buy a 60-minute wireless surf card for €7,50.

Internet Café

Dotspot A funky digital centre that offers internet, laser printing, scanning, computer classes and coffee. Rue du Lombard 83, central Brussels; ☎ 02.513.61.03; www.dotspot.be. Open Monday to Saturday 11am-9pm, Sunday 2pm-6pm.

Help in the home

Cleaners

The Belgian government recently introduced a new system for paying for home helps which eliminates the black market and ensures that cleaners get a decent legal wage and social benefits. Under the system, the cleaner is paid with 'service vouchers' (*titres-services/dienstcheques*) rather than cash in hand. They then get paid every week for their hours by an official employment agency.

The system involves a minimum of red tape. The householder employing a cleaner simply has to register with the temp agency Accor Services. This can be done online at www.dienstencheques.be. The cleaner has to be registered with an officially approved organisation (usually a temp agency).

You then order a batch of cheques to pay your cleaner. The cheques can be used for certain specified tasks, such as cleaning or ironing but not babysitting. Each cheque costs €6,70 and equals one hour of work.

The employer normally pays the cleaner with cheques at the end of each week. But it's also possible to make the weekly payment online or by calling a freephone number. The details are set out on the website.

Accor receives €21 from the government per cheque. This money goes towards paying the cleaner a monthly salary, along with health insurance and pension contributions. The system has been a huge success in Belgium, but it is heavily subsidized by the government and the price of cheques may soon have to rise.

House Sitters

Taxistop offers an online service that matches house sitters with people going on holiday. You pay an annual subscription of €60 to cover administration costs and €12.50 to join Taxistop, but no other payment is involved. Most house sitters will happily look after your pets and cut the lawn. Your house is fully insured for damage. www.taxistop.be; email oppas@taxistop.be.

Moving on

New Address in Belgium

Moving house is as traumatic in Belgium as anywhere else. Yet there are a few simple rules that can help to make the move go more smoothly. The first step is to contact your landlord three months before you plan to leave by registered letter. Some landlords can get difficult at this stage and insist that you give a full three months notice. That means a letter has to arrive before the first day of a month for that month to count. Once the landlord has received notice, he can start showing new tenants around the house, so you may want to tell him what times are convenient.

You should then cancel cable and broadband subscriptions (best done by registered letter) and book appointments with the electricity, gas and water companies so that they can read the meters on the day you leave.

It can be stressful, but there is a way to avoid much of the hassle. A service provided by the Belgian post office called DoMyMove will take care of much of the administration. You simply fill in a form available at all post offices or download it from the website www.post.be. Information is given in the English section 'manage your mail' under 'receiving services'. The post office will redirect mail to your new address, cancel electricity, gas and cable contracts, arrange for utilities to be turned on at your new address, and notify your phone company, internet provider, bank, insurance company and dozens of other companies about your change of address. The service costs €20 for four months.

The post office doesn't do everything. You will still have to notify the local town hall that you are leaving and possibly go to the local traffic police to reserve a parking space for a removal truck to stop in front of your house.

Leaving Belgium

Moving out of Belgium is slightly more complicated, as you have to notify the tax authorities and make sure that you are removed from the population register. Otherwise, you may find yourself involved in a prolonged dispute with the tax authorities, who will assume that you are still a resident in Belgium.

The post office will take care of much of the basic administration if you sign up for its DoMyMove service. The service costs €70 for four months for a move out of Belgium.

It's relatively easy to sell unwanted furniture by placing a classified ad on the website www.xpats.com. You can also phone your local commune to collect unwanted furniture, or donate usable stuff to Les Petits Riens.

Your last contact with Belgian bureaucracy will probably be a trip to the town hall to have your name removed from the population register. You may then be asked to return your ID card and those of other family members.

Daily Life

- Many parents on short-term contracts prefer to send their children to international schools where they can learn in their own language.
- Belgium has one of the best systems of childcare in Europe, providing a range of facilities mainly aimed at working parents.
- Belgium has one of the best health services in the world, but you have to pay about 13% of your income into a compulsory healthcare fund and then still have to pay a certain amount for every visit to a doctor, dentist or hospital.
- You cannot build up a long-term debt on a Belgian credit card: the full outstanding balance is deducted every month.
- Brussels is generally a safe place to live, but as elsewhere there are some areas best avoided.
- You can get along perfectly well in Brussels just speaking English, but you will miss out on social contacts and the cultural vitality of a bilingual city.
- Restaurant prices include a service charge so you don't have to leave a gratuity, but you should tip the usherette in a cinema.

Culture shock

It takes time to adapt to a new country, especially if language is a problem. Yet Brussels is a relatively manageable capital city where telephones work, trains run on time and rubbish is collected twice a week. Anyone who longs for home can easily find the comfort of friends in one of the 200 expatriate groups. They include a Belgian branch of the National Trust, a Brussels Brontë Society, a Brussels Cricket Club, an Icelandic Club and an Irish Hurling Club.

For the British, food is the one thing they miss most intensely. The BBC correspondent Mark Mardell longed for fresh lemon grass and a properly pulled pint. Others miss Marmite, Shredded Wheat and possibly (though they should be ashamed of this in Belgium) Cadbury's Dairy Milk chocolate. Most of these items can be found in Brussels supermarkets such as Delhaize and Carrefour, or at the Stonemanor shop in Everberg.

Americans also miss certain types of food, such as peanut butter and proper blinis. They possibly also miss the open spaces of America, the safe driving and the friendly rituals of neighbourhood life. Many are struck by the apparent lack of courtesy in everyday transactions.

American parents are sometimes shocked when they take their kids to see a children's film in Belgium, since cinemas have a fairly undiscriminating approach to screening trailers. The result is that small children can be exposed to some fairly explicit sex and violence while waiting for the latest Disney film. Yet this is not seen as a problem by Belgian parents.

People from other English-speaking countries also grumble about customer service in Brussels. It's true that sales assistants often seem to spend a lot of time talking to their colleagues, rather than serving customers with Anglo-American promptness, but this is not the same as rudeness. It is part of the Belgian way of life, where work is not taken too seriously. Small shops such as bakeries and greengrocers are often more friendly than supermarkets. Shopkeepers greet customers with a cheery 'Bonjour' when they come into the shop. As they leave, the greeting can vary from 'Au revoir' to 'Bon soirée' to 'Bon weekend'.

Belgian driving habits are likely to annoy people from Scandinavia, Britain and America. But people from South America or Greece have no particular complaints about the driving habits. They are much more likely to grumble about the damp Belgian weather.

Many people from Britain and America are irritated by Belgian bureaucracy, but the system has its advantages. Once you have a Belgian ID, you have the same rights as everyone else. All the benefits of the Belgian system are open to you, including state crèches, public schools and free public transport for children.

Madame Pipi

Most public toilets in Belgium are supervised by a woman known fondly as Madame Pipi. She will often be found sitting at a table by the entrance reading a copy of *Libelle* magazine, with a saucer containing a few small coins. The women often rely entirely on tips for their income and occasionally have to pay for cleaning materials out of their own pocket. It is only fair in the circumstances to pay the modest amount requested, usually 30-50 cents.

How to Meet Locals

Almost every expatriate finds it difficult to meet Belgians in Brussels. Belgians generally like to spend evenings with their families, while weekends are taken up with visits to older relatives in the Ardennes or rural Flanders. Nor do Belgians make a habit of chatting to their neighbours or starting a conversation in a supermarket queue. It's simply not part of the culture. The easiest way to get talking to the locals is often to join an organised activity, such as a language class, a cookery course or a walking group.

Food and drink

Eating Out in Brussels

Anyone who enjoys eating should feel at home in Brussels. This is a city of excellent restaurants, superb bakeries and impeccable food shops. As you walk around the streets, the smells of cooking constantly distract you from your business. There are waffle vans oozing sticky sweetness, frites stands leaking the smell of sizzling potatoes and chocolate shops adding a hint of decadence to the air.

You can eat well in other cities, but Brussels is one of the few places with consistently good cooking (apart from the Rue des Bouchers quarter, which locals avoid). It's partly long tradition and partly due to fierce competition, which means that a bad restaurant soon goes out of business. There are good eating places in every neighbourhood, but the biggest concentrations are in the Marolles and Ixelles.

This is a city where you can eat ridiculously cheap meals, especially at lunchtime, when even the best restaurants offer special menus at outlandishly low prices. You can easily find a restaurant serving a main course, dessert and coffee for under €10. Try finding the same in London or Paris.

Most restaurants have a fairly traditional approach to dining. They have one sitting, with customers arriving at about 7–8pm and leaving before midnight. Some restaurants have websites where they post their menus. Booking is usually done by phone, not email. Always remember to cancel a booking if you can't make it. Restaurants in Brussels have a hard time making ends meet, and need to use every table they have.

Authentic Belgian

L'Achepot A perfect little bistro with wood panelling and small tables for two facing the crumbling Eglise Saint Catherine. The chef produces delicious Brussels-style dishes like grilled prawns and a wintry *pot au feu*. Place Sainte-Catherine 1, central Brussels; ☎ 02.511.62.21. Closed Sunday.

Au Vieux Bruxelles Authentic Brussels restaurants are hard to find these days. But Au Vieux Bruxelles is the real thing. It has been serving mussels and chips since 1882 in a wood-panelled interior close to the Porte de Namur. The interior is warm and grandmotherly, with red-and-white checked tablecloths and odd little objects decorating the place. The kitchen serves mussels in ten different ways, accompanied by superb frites. Those who prefer to avoid molluscs can order a good Belgian steak. Rue Saint-Boniface 35, Ixelles; ☎ 02.503.31.11. Closed Mondays.

Belga Queen Antoine Pinto has created a fabulous restaurant in a vast interior formerly occupied by a bank. The dining room sits under a magnificent leaded glass cupola, while the food is classic Belgian with a modern twist. The €15 business lunch is exceptional value. Check the week's menu on the website www.belgaqueen.be. Rue Fossé aux Loups 32, central Brussels; ☎ 02.217.21.87.

Belgo Belge A lively modern Belgian restaurant in the fashionable St Boniface quarter. The kitchen produces classic Belgian dishes such as *moules-frites* and *stoemp*. Rue de la Paix 20, Ixelles; ☎ 02.511.11.21.

Les Brigittines *Aux Marches de la Chapelle* A classic Belgian brasserie facing the Gothic church where Pieter Bruegel the Elder is buried. The interior is decorated with wood panelling and mirrors to create a Parisian mood. The menu, in keeping with the setting, features long-forgotten products from the French kitchen, like shin of veal and beef cheeks. Place de la Chapelle 5, Marolles; ☎ 02.512.41.30.

Chez Patrick An old Brussels restaurant dating from 1931 just off Grand'Place. It used to be called Chez Jean, but changed its name when Patrick Materne took over the business. The tiled floor and regimented rows of tables have stayed exactly the same. The food, too, is as hearty as Jean's. Count on generous portions of *waterzooi*, *steak frites* or *carbonnade flamande*, leaving little room for dessert. Good beer list. Rue des Chapeliers 6, Brussels centre; ☎ 02.511.98.15.

Comme Chez Soi Belgians were briefly stunned when this famous three-star restaurant was stripped of one star by the 2007 Guide Michelin. The French argued that they had to demote it when chef Pierre Wynants was replaced by Lionel Rigolet. Belgians were not put off, and bookings in fact increased after the guide came out. It's therefore still next to impossible to secure the privileged table in the kitchen. Comme Chez Soi earned its three-star rating for creative dishes such as pigeon stuffed with truffles and little slices of fried udder served as an amuse gueule. The final bill is not that shocking given that this is one of the best restaurants in Belgium if not the world. The four-course lunchtime menu is almost a snip at €68. Even the most expensive dish – *Le moelleux de plates de Florenville au crabe, aux crevettes grises et au Royal Belgian caviar, beurre blanc d'huîtres à la ciboulette* – is, at €169,00, inexpensive by London or Paris standards. Place Rouppe 23; ☎ 02.512.29.21.

De Hoef This old Belgian restaurant is located in a 1627 post inn. It's an immensely popular place with blazing wood fires, wood panelled walls and checked tablecloths. The €25 menu is exceptional value – if in doubt choose the wood-grilled steak and the *beignets aux pommes* (apple fritters traditionally served at Belgian fairgrounds). You can eat out in the summer in a courtyard shaded by an ancient lime tree. But be sure to book several days in advance. Rue Edith Cavell 218, Uccle; ☎ 02.374.34.17.

Friture René A simple Belgian restaurant and *friterie* on the main square in Anderlecht that has been around for over 70 years. You can order *frites* to take away, or sit down at one of the long tables covered with checked cloths. The menu isn't fancy. It's just a matter of plain Belgian dishes like *croquettes aux crevettes*, *américain frites* or a pot of perfect mussels. But that's all it takes to make a Brussels institution. Place de la Résistance 14, Anderlecht; ☎ 02.523.28.76. Closed Monday.

't Kelderke A flight of ancient stone steps on Grand'Place leads down to a 17th-century vaulted cellar called 't Kelderke (The Little Cellar). Despite the location, this is an authentic Brussels restaurant serving old favourites like *moules frites* and *carbonnade*. You can't book, so it's best to arrive early. Open daily from noon to 2am. Grand'Place 15; ☎ 02.513.73.44.

La Taverne du Passage A popular brasserie located in the beautiful St Hubert arcade. The crisp tablecloths and smart waiters create the ambience of the 1930s and the menu sticks resolutely to old favourites like *tomates aux crevettes* (tomatoes stuffed with North Sea shrimps) and pepper steaks. Galerie de la Reine 30, Brussels centre; ☎ 02.512.37.31.

La Roue d'Or A genuine Brussels brasserie near Grand'Place decorated with Surrealist murals. Locals come here to eat Belgian classics such as Flemish *waterzooi* and rabbit stewed in beer. Rue des Chapeliers 26, Brussels centre; ☎ 02.514.25.54.

In 't Spinnekopke A secret place you'll possibly want to keep to yourself. The *Spinnekopke* (Spider's Head) occupies an ancient coaching inn that has survived from the 18th century. The interior is dark and snug, with old paintings and checked table cloths. The food, to everyone's relief, is traditional Brussels fare. Mussels come in almost a dozen different varieties and there are more than 100 types of beer on the shelves. There's also *stoemp*, *carbonnade* and rabbit simmered in *Gueuze* beer. The portions are generous, so you may have to skip the chef's special dessert: pancake served with caramelised apple slices and a scoop of ice cream. Place du Jardin aux Fleurs 1, central Brussels; ☎ 02.511.86.95 ; www.spinnekopke.be. Closed Sundays.

Le Variétés Diners sit in long straight rows in this nostalgic 1930s-style brasserie. Located in the renovated Flagey building, where Belgian radio broadcasts began, Les Variétés is a loving homage to the wireless age, complete with shiny zebrano wood walls. Belgians just love this sort of décor, making Le Variétés an instant success. The menu offers a sensible list of brasserie favourites, from knuckle of ham to a simple chicken and chips for the kids. Place Sainte Croix, Ixelles; ☎ 02.647. 04.36; www.levarietes.be.

Volle Gas A Brussels brasserie next to Ixelles town hall where you can eat large portions of *waterzooi* or stoemp among a noisy crowd of artists, amorous couples and expatriates. Place Fernand Cocq 21; ☎ 02.502. 89.17.

Spanish Cooking

Les Asturiennes A modern Spanish restaurant located in an old Socialist printing works that was restored by the region of Asturias. The kitchen produces sublime contemporary cooking from Spain's wild northern region. Rue Saint Laurent 36; ☎ 02.218 84.54.

Le Fils de Jules The name suggests a French restaurant, but this is a fashionable Basque restaurant with unusual regional dishes served by the tallest waitresses in Brussels. The *chipirones* (fried squid) are exquisite. Rue du Page 35, Ixelles; ☎ 02.534.00.57.

Fish

The old fish market used to stand next to Place Sainte Catherine in the heart of Brussels. The market has long vanished, but the fish wholesalers and restaurants are still concentrated in this part of town. You can watch battered white fish vans from Zeebrugge bumping along the cobblestones every morning, and, in the mussels season, Dutch trucks unloading huge sacks of Zeeland *mosselen* for the hungry stomachs of those in Brussels.

Bij den Boer A wonderfully authentic Brussels eating place with a tiled floor, hard wooden chairs and scuffed wood-panelling. The restaurant stands bang in the heart of the fishmongers' quarter, so the fish you are about to eat were probably swimming in the North Sea the night before. The people who run this restaurant are friendly and relaxed. Everything is perfect. Booking essential. Quai aux Briques 60, central Brussels; ☎ 02.512.61.22. Closed Sunday.

Ecailler du Palais Royal A serious fish restaurant on the Sablon with a traditional interior. It soon fills up at lunchtime with politicians from the federal parliament, antique dealers and diplomats. The atmosphere is hushed as the diners enjoy oysters, eels and champagne. Expect to pay around €100 a head. Rue Bodenbroek 18, Sablon; ☎ 02.512.87.51. Closed Sunday.

Jacques Locals cram into this old-fashioned fish restaurant to eat Belgian classics like sole fried in butter, mussels, and turbot served in a mousseline sauce. The décor is as plain as a station waiting room, with wood-panelled walls, a bare tiled floor and huge windows looking out on to the square. It's the kind of place that makes you glad to be in Brussels. Quai aux Briques 44, central Brussels; ☎ 02.513.27.62. Closed Sunday.

Vismet Chef Tom Decroos takes a modern approach to fish in this minimalist restaurant located in a red-brick 17th-century house. The open plan kitchen allows you to watch him as he prepares dishes like *croquettes aux crevettes* and poached Ostend sole. Place Sainte-Catherine, central Brussels; ☎ 02.218.85.45. Closed Sunday and Monday.

Romantic

La Cuisine A friendly restaurant with intimate little tables located in a tiled former butcher's shop. The chef produces exceptional dishes using the freshest of fish and vegetables and rounds off the meal with decadent deserts like cheesecake and crumble. The tiny back garden is a romantic spot for summer dining. Rue Lesbroussart 85, Ixelles; ☎ 02.644.2921.

Le Fruit Défendu This relatively new restaurant in Ixelles has two tiny rooms decorated in a dark contemporary style. The menu fits snugly on one side of a blackboard, so you don't have much choice, but that leaves more time for smooching. Everything is cooked to perfection. Rue Tenbosch 108, Ixelles; ☎ 02.347.42.47. Closed Sunday.

Le Grain de Sel Gregory Yarm has been running this snug restaurant close to Place Flagey for several decades. He produces exceptional cooking using the freshest ingredients he can find at the dawn food market. His lunch menu costs just €15 and the dinner menu is only a few euro dearer. Once everyone has been served, he emerges from the kitchen to chat with his customers. Chaussée de Vleurgat 9, Ixelles; ☎ 02.648.18.58. Closed Sunday and Monday.

L'Idiot du Village A restaurant called 'The Village Idiot' could only exist in Belgium. You have to hunt down a narrow cobbled lane in the Marolles to find this place, but it's worth a little bit of effort. The interior is filled with a wonderfully eclectic collection of old stuff salvaged from flea markets. The cooking on the other hand is superior French style. Only open on weekdays and often difficult to book a table. Rue Notre-Seigneur 19, Marolles; ☎ 02.502.55.82. Closed Saturday and Sunday.

Millésime This restaurant is a bit off the beaten track. Don't let that put you off. It's worth crossing Brussels just to taste the vongole (clams). The restaurant occupies a lofty interior with bare brick walls and an open kitchen looking out on a quiet Ixelles street. The people who serve are totally dedicated and the bill is unexpectedly low. What more can be said? Book it this minute. Rue E. Cattoir, Ixelles; ☎ 02.649.82.62; www.millesimerestaurant.be

French Cooking

Aux Beaumes de Venise As soon as you step inside, you know you are going to be treated well. The name refers to a type of wine produced on the banks of the Rhone, and the cooking is solidly French in style. Not the most fashionable place in town, but steadily reliable over the years. Rue Darwin 62, Ixelles; ☎ 02.343.82.93.

La Canne en Ville A charming local restaurant with some tables on the pavement for those rare days when the sky isn't slate grey. The wall tiles, mosaic floor and scales survive from the days when this was a butcher's shop. The waitresses are friendly and the kitchen produces some fine cooking, including hefty steaks made with Irish beef. The €13 lunch menu is worth grabbing. Rue de la Réforme 22, Ixelles; ☎ 02.347.29.26.

Chez Marie This tiny restaurant behind the church on Place Flagey has a snug interior decorated with wood panelling and vintage photographs. It could almost be Paris in the 1920s. The cooking is creative bistro style, and the €50 menu offers excellent value. The chef is a French woman called Lilian Devaux so the restaurant name is a bit of a mystery. It used to be called *Mieux boire ici qu'en face* (Better to drink here than across the road), which was even more puzzling (at least until you noticed the police station on the other side of the street). Rue Alphonse de Witte 40, Ixelles; ☎ 02.644.30.31.

De la Vigne à l'Assiette A corner bistro that thrills locals with its combination of serious French cooking and an outstanding wine list selected by sommelier Eddy Dandrimont. Not a place to ask for a glass of Rosé. Rue de la Longue Haie 51, Ixelles; ☎ 02.647.68.03.

Le Coin des Artistes A romantic corner restaurant with little tables for two, an ancient tiled floor and red velvet banquettes. The chef likes to cooks heavy food from south-west France including an acclaimed cassoulet. Rue du Couloir 5, Ixelles; ☎ 02.647.34.32.

Greek Cooking

L'Ouzerie Large groups of Greeks congregate at big tables in this warm Ixelles restaurant to taste some of the best Mediterranean cooking in town. The menu lists specialities such as *saganaki* sausage, fried squid, grilled octopus and Catalan vegetables. Diners order two or three dishes each and then wait as the table slowly fills with small dishes of tasty food. It doesn't get any more Greek that this. Chaussée d'Ixelles 235, Ixelles; ☎ 02.646.44.49.

Strofilia Greeks rave about this stunning restaurant close to Place Saint Cathérine. It's located in an old 17th century brick warehouse once used for storing wine. The walls have been stripped back to bare brick to create the feel of a New York loft interior and then decorated with old tiled floors and two ancient wine presses (strofilia in Greek). The menu features small dishes of tasty Byzantine-inspired mezes made from meat, seafood and vegetables. The vaulted cellar offers a spectacular location for a private party. Rue du Marché aux Porcs 11, Brussels centre; ☎ 02.512.32.93.

Italian Cooking

Au Bon Enfants A snug restaurant in a 17th-century Sablon house with a menu that includes Italian pizzas and Belgian steaks. Place du Grand Sablon 49, Sablon; ☎ 02.512.40.95.

Cosi A romantic Italian restaurant in a lively corner of Ixelles. The long interior is decorated with velvet curtains, old bookshelves and endless candles. The waiters are friendly, and the food comes on stylish plates. Good desserts. Rue Américaine 95, Ixelles; ☎ 02.534.85.86.

Intermezzo A smart and efficient Italian restaurant on a cobbled lane facing the Monnaie theatre. Good for a quick bite before the opera begins. Rue des Princes 16, Brussels centre; ☎ 02.218.03.11.

La Main dans la Poêle A small Italian restaurant close to Avenue Louise with a lively Neapolitan owner. The chef knows how to cook Italian food. Rue Lesbroussart 122, Ixelles; ☎ 02.648.90.32.

Asian Cooking

Le Deuxième Elément A fiercely modern Thai restaurant with brushed steel tables and contemporary art. Local artists bang elbows with business people at the cramped tables, while cool waitresses deliver earthenware pots of green curry, accompanied by vividly coloured cocktails. Rue St Boniface 7, Ixelles; ☎ 02.502.00.28.

Gallery Resto Bar An elegant Asian restaurant that produces delicious dim sum and poulet au curry vert. Convenient for a quick bite after a film. Rue du Grand Cerf 7; ☎ 02.511.80.35.

Japanese Cooking

Kushi-Tei of Tokyo An austere Japanese grill restaurant off Avenue Louise with a simple lunch menu. It starts with green tea, then a bowl of noodles, then soup, then more tea, then a bowl of salad, a bowl of rice and a plate of grilled meat, then more tea, all for €9. Excellent value and all the tea you can possibly drink. Rue Lesbroussart 118, Ixelles; ☎ 02.646.48.15. Closed Sunday.

Eccentric

Cook & Book Cook & Book is a combination of bookshop and restaurant. In fact, it combines nine bookshop/restaurants, each in a different style, serving a different cuisine. Travel books are found in a mock American Winnebago, French novels fill an interior in the style of a Left Bank café, and comic books occupy a mock old library. The cookbook section has a Fiat Uno parked in the middle of a sober Italian trattoria, while the English bookshop resembles a London club - thick carpets, eccentric sofas and Union Jack flags. It's like nothing you've ever seen before. Go before it changes. Woluwe-St-Lambert; ☎ 02.761.26.00. Take the metro to Rodebeek.

Le Mess This was once an army barracks. It's now a fashionable restaurant where the chefs juggle recipes from Belgium, Thailand and Italy, leading to eclectic results like curried Thai duck. The dining takes place in a handsome 19th-century room and a light-drenched glass conservatory. Avenue Louis Schmitt 1, Etterbeek; ☎ 02.734.03.36, www.lemess.be.

La Quincaillerie Impress your visitors by booking a table at this immensely popular Ixelles brasserie located in a vast old hardware shop. Diners sit at small tables amid rows of wooden drawers that once held screws and nails. The kitchen produces reliable Belgian cooking, including seafood dishes, though the labyrinthine layout makes service a bit chaotic. A fun experience, all the same. Rue du Page 45, Ixelles; ☎ 02.538.25.53.

Eating with Children

Chez Léon Léon has been serving *moules* in the Rue des Bouchers since 1903. Belgian customers stopped going there a few years ago when standards declined, but Léon is now trying to improve. Children eat free and the place is so big that you can nearly always find a table in one of the rooms. Try it once just for the experience. Rue des Bouchers 18, central Brussels; ☎ 02.511.14.15.

Cheap Eats

BHV A diminutive snack bar opposite the Saint-Gilles town hall (the initials stand for Buffet de l'Hôtel de Ville). Nothing much to look at from the outside, but those in the know fight for a perch in this fashionable lunchtime eatery. The reason is that the food is fresh, healthy and cheap. You can eat here for under €12, but only from 11am–3pm on weekdays. Place Van Meenen 33, Saint-Gilles; No phone, no credit cards.

Quick Lunch

Au Suisse It gets pretty hectic at Au Suisse as office workers pile in at midday and hunt for a perch at the counter. Founded by a Swiss couple in 1873, this is the oldest sandwich shop in Brussels. The choice of filling is bewildering: do you want Dutch *maatjes* (raw herring), Maredsous cheese, cooked mussels or Hungarian goulash? Come on, hurry up. Boulevard Anspach 73-75, central Brussels; ☎ 02.512.95.89.

Chaochow City A basic Cantonese snack bar attached to a more sophisticated restaurant popular with Chinese tour parties. You order, wait 12 seconds, and the food appears. You have a choice of two different dishes at lunchtime, and two in the evening, for just €3.40. That converts into €2.15 - amazing value for a downtown location. Boulevard Anspach 89; ☎ 02.512.82.83.

Exki Exki cafés have a cool Scandinavian look, a bright logo and plain wooden furniture. The company has opened several smart modern cafés in various Brussels locations selling soups, wholesome sandwiches and good coffee. The branch on Place Stéphanie has a tiny garden where the sun barely shines and a secretive upstairs lounge. Branches at Chaussée de Charleroi 7 (Place Stéphanie), Porte de Namur and Rue Neuve. Open 8am-7pm.

Natural Caffè A modern coffee bar that combines quirky Italian design with creamy espresso coffee. Avenue Louise 196; ☎ 02.646.72.14.

Mer du Nord A fishmongers shop near Place Sainte Catherine has a curved pavement bar where locals stop at lunch to grab six oysters, two Dutch *maatjes* or a tiny bowl of soup made from *escargots de mer* (whelks). They wash it down with a glass of chilled *Muscadet* wine, pay the bill and head off back to work. Rue Sainte-Catherine 1; ☎ 02.513.11.92.

Pain Quotidien A spacious café on the Sablon with a big communal table, old-style pots of jam and newspapers to read. The back garden provides a shady retreat on summer days. One of more than a dozen branches in Brussels. Place du Sablon 11; ☎ 02.513.51.54.

Tout Bon This spacious café used to be a branch of Pain Quotidien. It is now under new owners, but it still has all the attributes of a Pain Quotidien, including a big farmhouse-style table, generous pots of jam and excellent croissants. Its location on the Place du Luxembourg makes it popular with staff from the European Parliament, who sit down, flip open their laptops and begin working on a new directive that will affect the lives of 500 million Europeans. Rue de Luxembourg 68; ☎ 02.230.42.44.

Sunday Brunch

Brunch is now the thing to do on a Sunday morning in Brussels. Every branch of Pain Quotidien is packed, but there are other places that are a bit less frantic.

Les Halles des Tanneurs A former wine warehouse in the Marolles is the latest place for Sunday brunch. The restaurant occupies a vast industrial space where wine was once stored. There's a childrens play area and bookshop. Rue des Tanneurs 60, Marolles; ☎ 02.548.70.40; www.hallesdestanneurs.be; email info@hallesdestanneurs.be. Open Sunday 11am-4pm.

Le Pain Quotidien

Brussels has a café culture that dates back to the late 19th century. A few old institutions are still in business, like Cirio and Metropole, but most expatriate café life happens in places that have only been around since the 1990s. It began with Alain Coumont, a former chef who set out to bake the perfect daily bread. The result was a hand-crafted 2kg round sourdough loaf. He then created the perfect café/bakery when he opened the first Pain Quotidien on the fashionable Rue Dansaert in 1990. The rustic interior played a large part in PQ's success. It was like France in the Fifties, with a bare wood floor, distressed ochre walls and a big farmhouse table surrounded by rickety metal chairs. You drank the coffee out of a bowl, dipped your spoon in a big pot of homemade jam, and ate a flaky croissant on a small marble tray. It was exactly the sort of dated rustic French dream that Belgians love to live.

The idea spread throughout Brussels, then expanded to Wallonia and Flanders. Coumont had a knack of finding sublimely romantic locations in downtown neighbourhoods, often on squares with designer shops and a few trees. As a result, anyone who wants to do a tour of chic Belgian locations, only needs to pick up a list of PQ branches.

Soon there were dozens of branches in Belgium. But would the idea take root anywhere else? It worked in France, likewise the United States. A branch opened on Madison Avenue in 1997. There are now PQs in 20 countries, each with a big farmhouse table and an old dresser stocked with jams and olive oil. Coumont even has plans to open in Kuwait and Dubai.

The PQ concept is now familiar to world travellers, yet the cafés have not lost any of their original charm. The coffee is still as good. The croissants are still as flaky. There are now more than a dozen branches in Brussels. They are perfect places for meeting friends, reading Le Soir, talking business (but not too loudly) or just dipping a croissant in your coffee.

Good Taste: A Guide to Belgian Specialities

Carbonade Flamande The Flemish call it *vlaamse stoverij*, while the Walloons call it *carbonade flamande*. It's a dish that has been around since the Middle Ages, made with stewed beef simmered in a dark Belgian beer. Served with frites. Of course. Perfect for a winter day.

Chaudfontaine Bottled mineral water from a little town near Liège. Less commercial than Spa water, and therefore much more Belgian.

Chicons A Flemish farmer invented a new type of vegetable during the Belgian Revolution when he hid some chicory roots under a heap of earth in a dark basement. He returned to find that they had sprouted white shoots. It was called *witloof* in Dutch (*chicons* in French) and became the rage in Paris in the 1870s. You can buy Flemish *witloof* in the supermarket and add it to salads, or bake it in the oven with a creamy cheese sauce to make *chicons au gratin*.

Chocotoff A mysterious Belgian national obsession involving apparently nothing more than a caramel sweet wrapped in dark Côte d'Or chocolate.

Croquettes aux Crevettes Grises A day at the Belgian beach would be considered incomplete without a plate of *croquettes aux crevettes grises*. Served in Flemish taverns along the coast, these tasty little fritters are made with tiny North Sea shrimp known as *crevettes grises*. The shrimps are cooked in bechamel sauce, deep fried in oil and served with a wedge of lemon and a sprig of deep-fried parsley. The dish is found in most taverns and restaurants, but the most sublime version is served in the James tavern in Ostend.

Steak Américain Tourists sometimes order this dish expecting to get a plump juicy American steak. Their jaws drop when they are presented with a plate of raw ground beef and a raw egg sitting in a half eggshell. Served with frites, it's a classic Belgian dish.

Frites No one knows who invented French fries, but it probably wasn't the French. Some people claim that frites were discovered in Wallonia in the 16th century, but no one really knows when they were first made. The one thing that's certain is that Belgians make the best frites in the world. They use yellowish Bintje potatoes from the muddy fields of Flanders and fry them twice in sizzling oil – once to soften the potato and a second time to turns the frites golden brown. You can pick up delicious frites at stands on every market square in Belgium, served in a paper cone with a blob of mayonnaise on top. One of the best addresses is Maison Antoine on Place Jourdan, just down the hill from the Berlaymont.

Gaufres When Belgians return home from abroad, the first thing they notice at the railway station is the sweet smell of steaming sugar waffles. You find waffle stands in almost every station in Belgium. You also find them at funfairs, shopping centres and zoos. The plump hot waffles – made using a Medieval waffle iron – originated in Liège, but you now find them almost everywhere.

Gueuze A traditional beer from Brussels and the villages of the Pajottenland to the west of the city. It is made by a process of spontaneous fermentation caused by yeasts that originate in the Zenne valley (and nowhere else in the world). Several local breweries produce *Gueuze*, but the most authentic version is lovingly brewed in the Cantillon brewery near the Gare du Midi.

Mitraillette A favourite student sandwich, comprising a baguette sliced in two and filled with chips, hamburger and mayonnaise. Popular with European school students, but possibly not with dieticians.

Mussels You find bustling mussels restaurants in the centre of Brussels and the resorts along the coast. This is as much part of the Belgian identity as cartoon books and dogs. Every year Belgians eagerly anticipate the day when the first batch of new mussels arrives from the shallow breeding beds of Zeeland. Then they start to grumble when they realise that the Dutch have raised the price yet again. Mussels are served in dozens of different ways, including raw (*moules parquées*). They come in big black iron pots with heavy lids that are used as bowls for the empty shells.

Paling in 't Groen Plump chopped eels cooked in a mixture of sorrel, tarragon and mint. Popular in Ghent and the villages close to the Donkmeer lake in East Flanders. Often listed on Brussels menus as *anguilles au vert*.

Stoemp An old Flemish peasant dish made from mashed potatoes mixed with leeks or carrots and a dash of nutmeg. Normally served with sausages, it's found in traditional Belgian restaurants such as 't Kelderke on Grand'Place.

Le Vraie Sirop de Liège Belgians have been buying *Le vrai Sirop de Liège* for more than a century. Sold in a distinctive blue pot decorated with blossoming pear trees, the syrup appears on the table at breakfast, lunch, and when children come home from school.

Waterzooi A delicious creamy broth made from chicken or fish simmered for several hours in a pot of vegetables.

Smoking or Not Smoking

The Belgian government has introduced legislation that bans smoking in public spaces such as offices, railway stations and on trains. The ban was extended in 2007 to restaurants, but not bars and clubs (unless more than 30% of turnover is food). Smoking has been banned for many years in Pain Quotidien bakeries.

Bars to Meet

Brussels has bars of all types, from old Flemish hostelries hidden down cobbled lanes to cool lounge bars in upmarket hotels. Drinking places are scattered across all 19 communes, but the most popular addresses are concentrated in a few buzzing districts, such as Place St Géry, Place St Boniface, Grand'Place, Parvis Saint-Gilles, the Sablon and the Ixelles Cemetery neighbourhood. If you're looking for a traditional Belgian beer in a quiet setting, go for one of the Belgian bars, but if you are out for a noisy yak with a bunch of fellow expats you might be better off trying one of the city's Irish bars. Then again, you might want to impress a visiting friend by taking them to one of the cool bars that have sprung up in the Rue Dansaert district.

Traditional Belgian Bars

The population of Brussels is changing, and older cafés are struggling to compete against new bars and cafés. The beautiful Art Nouveau Falstaff next to the Bourse has been badly managed for years, and now attracts only tourists. The Metropole has also lost its allure, but Cirio in the lee of the Bourse remains one of the best cafés in Europe, a favourite of everyone who lives in this city.

A la Bécasse This ancient bar lies down a narrow cobbled lane near the St Nicholas church. Inside it is suitably gloomy, with long wooden tables, waiters in aprons and a mellow Rembrandtesque light. This is a place to take visitors who want to see old Brussels in the flesh. The beer is *Gueuze*. The sandwiches contain *pottekeis* (white cream cheese). The year is 1560. Rue de Tabora 11, central Brussels; ☎ 02.511.00.06.

Le Cercueil A bar furnished with coffins isn't anyone's idea of tasteful décor. But this gloomy place has a certain morbid appeal. Somewhere to take visitors when they tire of tasteful Flemish bars. Rue des Harengs 10-12; ☎ 02.512.30.77.

Delirium A specialist beer café located in an 18th-century cellar on a narrow cobbled lane. More than 2,000 beers are listed in a menu as thick as the Brussels phone book, along with 500 *genevers* and a smattering of great malt whiskies. The brick walls are decorated with old enamel beer signs, while small pink elephants hang from the ceiling. Turn left when you leave to note the female version of the Manneken Pis, Jeanneke Pis, at the end of the lane. Impasse de la Fidelité 4A; ☎ 02.514.44.34; www. deliriumcafe.be

Le Paon Royal A plain Belgian café on two levels in the fashionable heart of the city. The terrace under the trees is perfect on a summer afternoon. Rue du Vieux Marché aux Grains 6; ☎ 02.513.08.68.

Brasserie Verschueren This handsome Art Deco bar in the shadow of Saint-Gilles church offers a grand setting for a lingering beer or two. Recently restored to its original shiny elegance, Verschueren offers customers the pleasures of stained glass windows, period light fittings and an enormous clock. Good list of beers and decent home-made soup. Parvis de Saint-Gilles 11-13; ☎ 02.539.40.68.

Poechenellekelder A dark Brussels bar next to the Manneken Pis that once had a puppet theatre (*poechenelle*) in the cellar. It's now a lively bar with more than 90 beers on the menu, including some rarities. Despite the touristy location, it remains an authentic Brussels bar, used for meetings of the Brussels Pipe Club and the Order of the Friends of the Manneken Pis. Rue du Chêne 5; ☎ 02.511.92.62.

Le Roi d'Espagne You might find this bar on Grand'Place a bit touristy, but it offers a snug Belgian interior, a blazing fire and view of the square from the upstairs windows. Not the cheapest beers in town. Grand'Place 1; ☎ 02.513.08.07.

Cool Bars

Bar Recyclart A former station buffet under a railway viaduct has been turned into a funky bar. The furniture comes from old Belgian train compartments and the bar is a recycled escalator. Hence the name. Locals come here to read the newspapers, drink coffee and write gloomy plays. Conversation stops every time a train rumbles overhead. Gare de la Chapelle, Rue des Ursulines 25, Marolles; ☎ 02.205.57.34.

Mappa Mundo A hip bar in the heart of the St Géry district with a distinctly old-fashioned interior. With cool music and beautiful staff, this place is normally packed. Rue du Pont de la Carpe 2; ☎ 02.514.35.55.

PP Café A new Brussels café with a retro look reminiscent of a Belgian railway station bar circa 1935. A good spot to catch Belgian jazz bands. Concerts are free and the doors don't close until 2am. Rue Jules Van Praet 28; ☎ 02.513.5116.

Au Soleil A handsome bar located in a former clothes shop that still has its traditional advertising signs outside. A wonderful spot for a quiet beer, with tables outside on long summer evenings. Rue du Marché au Charbon 86; ☎ 02.513.34.30.

L'Ultime Atome A plain modern bar/brasserie on a corner of Place Boniface that somehow manages to hit the right note with fashionable young Belgians. The staff can be a bit picky about how quickly they serve you, but the list of beers is impressive, and includes such rare gems as Poperings Homelbier from the far reaches of West Flanders. Rue St Boniface 14; ☎ 02.511.13.67.

Expat Bars

The Bank An upmarket Irish bar mercifully free of Celtic memorabilia. Located in a former bank in the sophisticated Châtelain district, the decor mainly consists of antique safe deposit boxes. Offers decent live music and a screen devoted to international rugby matches. Rue du Bailli 79; ☎ 02.537.52.65.

Conway's This used to be an American bar, but local demographics have shifted, and it is now a more cosmopolitan place. The food is still US-style burgers and the customers generally fall into the twentysomething-looking-for-a-wild-time bracket. But if you're wanting to hook up, there's apparently no better place. Avenue de la Toison d'Or 10; ☎ 02.511.26.68.

Fabian O'Farrell's A big friendly bar that is Irish in name but international in character. Located opposite the European Parliament, it provides a cosy melting pot for journalists, MEPs and lobbyists. The bar staff know how to pour a good Guinness and the people in the kitchen can cook a decent stew. Place du Luxembourg 7; ☎ 02.230.18.87.

Fat Boys The best bar in town for watching live football in a crush of hooting fans. Not a place for a quiet conversation, but excellent for those in search of noise, friendly faces and basic food. Ten screens cover a multitude of sports, while big summer games are shown on a giant screen set up on the cobblestones. The perfect spot to bag a perch when football fever descends upon Brussels. Place du Luxembourg 6; ☎ 02.511.32.66.

The Old Hack A well-run little bar in the shadow of the Berlaymont building, popular with journalists looking for hot gossip from the European Commission. The bar used to be a British hangout, but a friendly Dutch couple took it over and added some sophisticated touches such as De Koninck on tap and smiling service. But the nostalgic photographs of London news offices are still up there on the walls to reassure the older hacks that nothing has changed. Rue Joseph II 176; ☎ 02.230.81.18.

James Joyce The oldest Irish bar in Brussels, and not one for the fake Irish trappings. You come here to knock back a Guinness, munch a decent sandwich and maybe strike up a conversation with someone from DG AGRI. Open until the small hours on Saturday and Sunday mornings, but keep the noise down as you leave. Rue Archimède 34; ☎ 02.230.98.94.

Macsweeny's An Irish bar with dusty Celtic memorabilia located in the heart of the Avenue Louise shopping quarter. The staff are friendly and the pavement terrace makes a pleasant spot to catch any late afternoon sunshine that falls on this quarter. Rue Jean Stas 24; ☎ 02.534.47.41.

Monkey Business An old address on the expat scene, this American sports bar recently changed hands. The interior has been spruced up, but attention remains focused on televised sport, darts and food, a formula that makes this a favourite with the shrinking American community in Brussels. Rue Defacqz 30; ☎ 02.538.69.34.

O'Reilly's A cavernous Irish bar in the heart of downtown Brussels that draws an international crowd of sports fans, stag parties and students. The décor is low-key Irish, but with thick smoke added (until Belgian smoking laws catch up with Ireland). Place de la Bourse 1; ☎ 02.552.04.81

Ralph's Bar A new kid on the block, this bar on the Place du Luxembourg attracts a young and chic crowd. Located opposite the European Parliament, it's the perfect place for a chilled glass of wine on a summer evening. Place du Luxembourg 13; ☎ 02.230.16.13.

The Wild Geese Hugely successful Irish bar in the heart of the European Quarter that caters to a cosmopolitan mixture of secretaries, interns, translators and lobbyists. The staff are friendly and the atmosphere is relaxed until the *stagiaires* and au pairs arrive for their traditional Thursday evening bash. Avenue Livingstone 2; ☎ 02.230.19.90.

Wine Bar

La Piola This authentic Italian wine bar in the heart of Ixelles gets very crowded in the early evening when locals stop for a glass on their way to a restaurant. Some don't ever leave. Rue du Page 2, Ixelles.

Café Terraces

Where do you sit when the sun warms the cobblestones of Brussels? The café terraces on Grand'Place soon fill up with tourists, so you may have to look elsewhere. The fashionable place to soak up the sun is on one of the terraces on Place St Géry. But every last table is soon occupied. The Rue du Vieux Marché aux Grains isn't far away. Maybe you will find one last unoccupied table under the trees. It's then just a matter of working out whether your table falls in the territory of the beautiful but severe waitress from De Markten or the more cheerful waiter serving Le Paon Royal. Still found nowhere? You might decide to head south to the Place du Luxembourg, where the terraces catch the sun for much of the day, or further south still to Flagey, where wobbly metal tables catch the last of the sun.

Marché au Charbon

The Rue du Marché au Charbon meanders gently from Grand'Place to Place Fontainas, passing some seductive bars on the way. The street runs through the heart of the city's gay quarter, where old 17th-century houses with brick cellars have been converted into bars and clubs. Further on, the street develops a village atmosphere, with quirky shops next to little bars. The terrace of Au Soleil at No.86 is a good spot to catch the last rays of sunshine, while Fontinas at No.91 is another bar with a late-night summer terrace.

Best Brussels Cafes

Belga A new bar on Place Flagey decorated in a sober style that matches the 1930s ambience of the neighbourhood. No table service here; you just go up to the bar and hope that someone will eventually take notice. The chairs are uncomfortable, the music loud and the light gloomy, yet the place is always mobbed. Artists come here in search of warmth, businessmen tap away on laptops and local ladies sit with poodles on their lap wondering when the waiter will arrive. Place Flagey 18; ☎ 02.640.25.69.

Cirio This old Brussels café has barely changed since it was founded in 1896 by the Italian owner of a tomato canning business. The cabinets in the back room are filled with silver trophies, the walls covered with embossed wallpaper, and the toilets have elegant but defunct machines for dispensing eau de cologne. The atmosphere is particularly Belgian in the afternoon, when elderly women arrive with their fluffy miniature poodles, settle into the striped banquettes and ask the waiter for a half-en-half. This is Cirio's speciality. The waiter arrives with two bottles and proceeds to pour out half a glass of white wine, followed by half a glass of Italian Spumante. Rue de la Bourse 18-20; ☎ 02.512.13.95.

Le Greenwich This old Brussels bar hasn't changed a detail since the days when René Magritte used to come here to win chess and sell his paintings (failing on both counts). The faded décor, elegant fittings and professional staff make this one of the best bars in the city, especially if you feel like challenging a Belgian to a game of chess. Be sure to visit the toilets, which have a faded Art Nouveau grandeur. Rue des Chartreux 7; ☎ 02.511.41.67.

L'Image de Nostre-Dame A tiny corner of old Brussels has miraculously survived down a cobbled lane, resisting both the 1695 French bombardment and the 1960s property developers. The interior is a Flemish fest of old oak beams, glinting brass pots and stained glass windows. The attentive owners pour some rare Belgian ales, including the sublime *Brugse Witte*. Rue du Marché-aux-Herbes 5, central Brussels; ☎ 02.512.13.95.

A la Mort Subite This cavernous Brussels institution added an upper floor a few years ago, but the best atmosphere is on the lower level, where melancholy locals rub shoulders with boisterous Dutch tourists. The interior is a stupendous blend of mirrors and columns dating from sometime before the First World War. The café serves its own Gueuze, a tart local beer which you either love or hate. Order a plattekaas (a sandwich with cream cheese and radishes) for an authentic Brussels experience. Rue Montagne aux Herbes Potagères 7; ☎ 02.513.13.18.l

Some Belgian Beers to Taste

Cantillon A classic sour Brussels *Gueuze* brewed in a historic brewery close to Midi Station. The first sip can be a shock to drinkers used to artificially sweetened beers. Hard to find in Brussels bars but you can taste it in the Cantillon brewery.

Trappistes Rochefort 10 A potent beer brewed by Trappist monks, with a complex and spicy taste. Considered Belgium's finest Trappist ale, on a par with an expensive Burgundy wine.

Saison Dupont An amber-tinted beer with a generous head and a mysterious earthy taste. '*The best beer in the world. Period,*' claims one seasoned beer connoisseur.

Duvel A favourite of former prime minister Jean-Luc Dehaene, this strong golden ale is rated by beer writer Michael Jackson as '*one of the five best beers in the world*'.

La Chouffe A sublime amber beer with a spicy taste, brewed in a small village in the Ardennes.

Westvleteren 12° A dark and malty ale brewed by monks in West Flanders and sold by the crate at the abbey gatehouse. But you have to phone ahead to reserve an order. The line gets very busy in the brewing season.

De Koninck A classic Belgian ale from Antwerp, sold in virtually every café in its home town. Simply ask for a *bolleke* and the waiter will bring you a 33cl round glass. Found in The Old Hack, opposite the Berlaymont.

Poperings Hommel Bier A subtly-flavoured hop beer brewed in the village of Watou in West Flanders. Ask for a glass in L'Ultieme Atome.

Rodenbach Grand Cru A Belgian summer classic, this red-brown beer is fermented in huge oak casks to give it a distinctive sour flavour.

Nights

Brussels changes after dark. The centre is taken over by a younger, wilder crowd. They come from all over Europe to party. There are multilingual teenagers from the European Schools, interns from the international institutions, Londoners who have hopped across on the Eurostar without bothering to book a hotel, young professionals, older professionals, and couples from France who wouldn't dare go out in their own town.

Brussels used to be quiet after dark, but it has changed completely in recent years. *'Brussels now leads the way on the European party scene,' The Guardian* recently said. It's cheaper than London and safer than most big cities. It has a relaxed atmosphere that means you can get into just about any venue as long as you don't look too threatening or drunk. Bouncers are generally friendly, drinks don't cost much more than €5 and some places don't even bother about an entrance charge. Visiting bands like Brussels because they can go out into an ordinary bar without being swamped by adoring fans. In fact, they are more likely to be utterly ignored. Madonna once went cycling through the streets of Brussels and no one noticed.

Lighting up the City

Pascal Smet is a minister with a mission. He wants to put bicycles on the streets and lights on landmark buildings. His 'light plan' has already turned the TV broadcasting tower in Schaerbeek into a nocturnal monument lit in 22 different hues. Smet still has a €2.5m budget in pocket to illuminate further buildings such as the Cinquantenaire arch, the Basilique de Koekelberg, the Porte de Hal and the Wiels art centre. Private companies are also contributing to the night glow – Electrabel's Drogenbos cooling

Brussels at night

tower shimmers with millions of lights after dark, while the Dexia bank tower on Place Rogier is illuminated by 4,800 light installations placed on the window ledges. The glowing tower is reflected on nearby skyscrapers, including the dull Sheraton Hotel, transforming the entire neighbourhood from sinister to scintillating. But perhaps the most impressive sight – at least for those driving into town – is the double 'light wall' on the Rue de la Loi created by the French light artist Patrick Rimoux using 102 vertical lights. *'This is a unique street that for me symbolises the heart of Brussels and Europe,'* Rimoux says.

Clubs

Bazaar This venue isn't the easiest to find. It's down a lane in the Marolles, in a building painted black and white. The site was once occupied by a Capucin monastery. The cellars are still intact, providing a striking setting for late-night partying. A hot air balloon adds to the exotic atmosphere. But don't arrive too early. The clubbing only gets going after midnight. Rue des Capucins 63; ☎ 02.511.26.00; www.bazaarresto.be

Fuse A techno venue in the Marolles that has been going for more than a decade. The two-floor building draws crowds of up to 2,000 from as far off as Paris and Amsterdam. Entry is a mere €5 if you arrive before midnight. Rue Blaes 208; ☎ 02.511.97.89; www.fuse.be

Havana In the shadow of the Palais de Justice, Havana is an upmarket restaurant-bar that attracts a bronzed European crowd. Rue de l'Epée 4; ☎ 02.502.12.24; www.havana-brussels.com

Le You A favourite stop for anyone tramping the Brussels streets after midnight. Located near Grand'Place, this was once the Sparrow, and before that, Le Garage. It has been revamped in 1980s disco style by the designer of the Buddha Bar in Paris and offers free entry and a welcome drink. Rue Duquesnoy 18; www.leyou.be

Recyclart A throbbing venue in a disused railway station where every wall is covered with graffiti art. The DJs play the latest electronic sounds. Gare de la Chapelle, Rue des Ursulines 25, Marolles; ☎ 02. 02.205.57.34; www.recyclart.be

Belgian Bands

Some may argue that Belgian pop music reached its apex in 1978 with the release of Plastic Bertrand's *Ca Plane Pour Moi*, which made number eight in the UK charts, and that it rapidly went downhill, reaching rock bottom with the band Front 242, which the BBC likened to '*music which sounds like someone dropping a piano down a laundry chute*'. But Jacques Brel, Vaya Con Dios, Hooverphonic, Axelle Red and dEUS are all products of the Belgian music scene, and Ghent is currently considered a hotspot for club culture.

Out of Town

Despite its image as a somewhat dull country, Belgium has one of the best clubbing scenes in Europe. The only problem is that much of the action takes place in Antwerp and Ghent. Not that the location need put you off. The distances are hardly huge in Belgium, and trains start early in the morning. So all you need to do is to find out what's happening by turning to the site www. noctis.com, which helpfully gives full information in English on festivals, summer raves and the biggest parties. It's also a useful source for night owls in search of food, radio stations and funky shops.

Shopping

Brussels is dotted with shops that stock the very best vellum writing paper, the rarest sheet music, the most elusive perfumes. You can also find wooden dolls houses, leather handbags, Illy coffee machines, West Flanders beers, Italian fabrics, artist's supplies and exclusive art books. The shops in Brussels may stock almost anything you might need, but they are often hard to find. Some of the best places in Brussels lie off the beaten track, down narrow cobbled lanes, away from the crowds.

Shop Opening Hours

Shops in Brussels are normally open Monday to Saturday 9.30am to 6.30pm, but small boutiques may only open at 10am. Some supermarkets are open longer hours (8.30am to 8pm or 9pm), but most are closed on Sundays. Other shops are also closed on Sundays, except for bakers, pastry shops, newsagents, flower shops, shops at petrol stations and small supermarkets. The city has a good range of night shops, especially in the urban areas of central Brussels and Ixelles.

Where to shop

Dansaert No one went shopping in Rue Dansaert until Sonia Noel opened Stijl in the early 1980s. It's now the fashion hub of Brussels. Wander down this street and you

Mural in the Marolles

find some of the most stylish Antwerp and Brussels fashions displayed in minimalist interiors with bare brick walls and severe lighting. The district has gradually expanded into neighbouring streets such as Rue des Chartreux and the Rue de Flandre, but attempts to extend the fashion quarter to the canal zone have so far failed.

Rue Neuve Brussels main shopping street was recently redesigned, but it still looks miserable. The main chain stores are all located here, including Inno, C&A, Media Markt and H&M, but the atmosphere is grim, especially on Saturday afternoons. Pause for a coffee and cake in Exki (Rue Neuve 78).

Sablon This is the city's most elegant and expensive shopping quarter, where the city's antique dealers sell Flemish tapestries, French furniture and African masks. It's also a district of upmarket Belgian chocolate shops, like Wittamer, Neuhaus and Pierre Marcolini. Yet the restaurants and cafes are not particularly pricey. You can eat a simple Belgian meal of *moules-frites* in Cafe Leffe (Place du Grand Sablon 46) for under €30.

Antique shop in Marolles

Marolles The Marolles district has two main shopping streets and several steep cobbled lanes. Some of the shops are unexpectedly upmarket – Michiels at Rue Haute 195 has been selling sharp men's suits since 1859. Others are simply weird. You come to the Marolles to hunt for things sold nowhere else in Brussels. You can find Oriental furniture, oak refectory tables and Victorian bathtubs. The best place to begin is New De Wolf, an enchanting place stuffed with furniture and accessories. The shop (which has, despite the name, been around for nearly 50 years) has two entrances (91 Rue Haute and 40 Rue Blaes), several floors and countless small rooms furnished like Belgian family homes. Other intriguing shops are found on the steep Rue de Renards. You pass a violin workshop, a shop selling Tintin memorabilia and a Belgian fashion shop. Then you come to Het Warm Water, one of the friendliest cafes in the Marolles.

Louise Belgian royalty can occasionally be spotted darting out of one of the Belgian designer shops on Avenue Louise, close to Place Stéphanie. They may well be carrying a bag from Nathan at No. 158, where Edouard Vermeulen has been selling his particular brand of stylish yet sober clothes since 1984. A few blocks away, Olivier Strelli (at No. 72) offers clothes in rich colours made from the smoothest fabrics. Stop for coffee at Pain Quotidien (No. 124).

Boulevard de Waterloo International designers like Gucci and Chanel have gradually taken over a row of neo-classical townhouses on the Boulevard de Waterloo (opposite the more garish Avenue de la Toison d'Or). The houses have been smartly renovated to create a stylish shopping area conveniently close to the Hilton Hotel. Other shops are located in former coach houses hidden at the back of the mansions. Upmarket Belgian companies such as the handbag maker Delvaux and Scapa of Scotland (which has no Scottish connection apart from a vaguely Balmoral style). Stop for coffee in the white Iselp gallery café located in a former stable block at Boulevard de Waterloo 31.

Châtelain A relaxed neighbourhood with creative boutiques, art bookshops and quirky cafés. Begin on the square and look down the side streets running towards Rue du Bailly. Stop for coffee at Passiflore (Rue du Bailly 97).

St Boniface The quarter around the Eglise St Boniface has recently blossomed into a fashionable shopping area. The willowy Art Nouveau houses signed by Ernest Blérot are now occupied by various eclectic shops and cool restaurants. The nearby Rue de la Paix has a more funky mood, with clothes from the 1950s on sale at Look 50 (Rue de la Paix 8) and more funky stuff next door at Pax Clothes. Place Saint Boniface also has an excellent camera shop, Campion, at No. 13, while a workshop on Rue de la Paix creates unique Art Nouveau stained glass windows. The square appeals to the acclaimed Belgian designer Nina Meert, who sells smart clothes with a elegant Art Deco touch in a large shop at Rue Saint Boniface 1-5. Meert chose to settle here because *'it's an area where artists and intellectuals have always settled, a place where, whatever the hour of day or night, there's always a table for you'*. She is almost certainly thinking of the Café L'Ultime Atome at Place St Boniface 14, where you can sit on the pavement reading the newspaper while the square slowly comes to life.

Suburbs Some of the city's most attractive shops are located in the quiet suburbs. The main clusters in Brussels are on Place Dumont in Woluwe St Pierre and Rue Xavier de Bué in Uccle. The Woluwe Shopping Centre is a modern shopping mall with chain stores including Habitat and Inno.

Supermarkets

Belgian supermarkets are beginning to take the environment seriously. In a bid to cut down on waste, shoppers now have to pay a few cents for a plastic bag. Some supermarkets such as Delhaize sell sturdy bags which can be reused. Once they have reached the end of their life, the bags are replaced free of charge.

Delhaize Delhaize opened the first supermarket in Belgium on Place Flagey back in 1957. The company now has supermarkets in almost every Belgian town, including branches dotted around Brussels. Most are in populated urban areas, where they generally have an underground or rooftop car park. Delhaize supermarkets generally have excellent meat, though their fish counter can be disappointing. Their wine departments are stocked with some of the best bottles from France and Spain, though New World wines get only limited shelf space. You can also find a good selection of Chinese, Italian and Thai specialities, and even a few British products. www.delhaizegroup.com

Carrefour The French supermarket chain Carrefour recently took over Belgium's GB group and began to transform the somewhat jaded supermarket chain. There are now several Carrefour hypermarkets in the Brussels suburbs, where much of the floor space is taken up with TVs and clothes. Carrefour generally has a good fish counter and a wide choice of French wines. But they make less effort than Delhaize to attract expatriates. www.carrefourbelgium.be

Colruyt This is the place to go for cheap food, but it's not the most relaxed of shopping experiences. The car parks are cramped, the trolleys wobbly and the interiors have an austere wartime look. The meat is good quality, but ordering is a challenging bureaucratic procedure and the system of packing groceries takes time to master. Yet Colruyt is a friendly place where you might well strike up a conversation with an elderly Belgian looking for the tinned dog food. www.colruyt.be

Cool Capital

Brussels can no longer be ignored by anyone looking for the latest trends. Much of the credit for the Brussels style revolution lies with La Cambre School in Ixelles, which in recent years has turned out a steady stream of exciting young designers.

While some graduates have opened their own shops in Brussels, others have been snapped up by chic Parisian couture houses. One young Brussels designer, Olivier Theyskens, shot to fame in 1998 when Madonna wore one of his creations to the Academy Awards. He has subsequently dressed Nicole Kidman and Gwyneth Paltrow, and now designs the couture collection of Rochas.

The big international designers are based on Avenue Louise and the Boulevard de Waterloo, while avant-garde designers prefer the downtown edge of Rue Dansaert. The Rue Dansaert has gradually evolved into the most stylish street in the city, with the latest fashion collections displayed in beautiful restored interiors. Other downtown streets in the neighbourhood like the Rue de Flandre and the Rue des Chartreux have recently gone through a similar transformation. Since the neighbourhood changes constantly, it is worth picking up a copy of the *Downtown* guide to track down the most fashionable addresses for shopping and eating.

Set up to promote the fashion industry in Brussels, the organisation Modo Bruxellae (www.modobruxellae.be) provides information on shops and designers. It also organises a fashion sale every May in the Beursschouwburg, allowing people to pick up designer clothes at big discounts. But the main fashion event in the city is Modo Bruxellae's biannual Fashion Designers' Trail, when prominent Belgian designers are invited to display their latest designs in unusual locations in downtown Brussels.

It's not just the streets of Brussels that are becoming more fashionable. In 2004, the Royal Windsor Hotel near Grand'Place commissioned four Belgian designers, including Gérard Watelet and Marina Yee, to create exclusive fashion rooms. The idea was a success and the hotel went on to add six more rooms in 2005, including a striking white room by Kaat Tilley, with stylised female figures surrounding the bed, and a romantic room by Nicolas Woit that evokes a night under the desert stars.

Books

Cook & Book Eat lunch and then buy a book in a series of nine themed bookshops opposite the Woluwe arts centre Wolubilis. The topics include children, travel and cookbooks. Most books are in French but one of the shops is dedicated to English books. The atmosphere is relaxed, but don't read the books before you have paid for them. Take the metro to Rodebeek. Woluwe-St-Lambert; ☎ 02.761.26.00.

La Librairie Bookshop on the first floor of a restored wine warehouse in the Marolles. Good for French novels, children's books and new English fiction. It's also an upmarket restaurant. Open Monday to Friday and Sunday. Rue des Tanneurs 60, Marolles; ☎ 02.548.70.40; email info@hallesdestanneurs.be; www.hallesdestanneurs.be

Nicola's Bookshop This intimate English-language bookshop hides from the crowds in a street near Place Stéphanie. Nicola Lennon is an Irish woman who is determined to sell nothing but the best in contemporary fiction. She stocks some English and Irish writers, but her real passion is for translated foreign writers like Joseph Roth. Rue de Stassart 106, Ixelles; ☎ 02.513.94.00; www.nicolasbookshop.com

Sterling Well-stocked English bookshop offering customers books at a significantly lower price than Waterstone's. Friendly staff and a reading corner for children. Rue Fossé aux Loups 38, central Brussels; ☎ 02.223.62.23 ; www.sterlingbooks.be. Opens Sundays noon-6.30pm.

Tropismes The most beautiful bookshop in Brussels, located in a former restaurant in the Galerie des Princes. The books are displayed amid classical columns, mirrors and gilt details. The emphasis is on gorgeous French art books and elegant novels by Parisian writers, but you might find a small collection of recent English fiction lurking in a corner. Galerie des Princes 11; ☎ 02.512.88.52; www.tropismes.be

Waterstone's The oldest English bookshop in Belgium has been on Boulevard Adolphe Max for as long as anyone can remember. Unlike Waterstone's in Britain, this outpost remains a highbrow place, where Brits come for their copies of Chris Patten's memoirs and the latest edition of Private Eye. Boulevard Adolphe Max 71, central Brussels; ☎ 02.219.27.08; www.waterstones.be

Books, Books, Books

The quarter around Place Anneessens has a slight bohemian feel. This is where you find specialised guitar shops, record stores selling old Supertramp LPs, and cluttered stores filled with Jurassic Age computers. But the main attraction is a second-hand bookstore called Pêle-Mêle at Boulevard Lemonnier 55–59. It doesn't look much from the outside, but the inside is a warren of rooms, passages and bookshelves. There's a small English section where you find unexpected books, nothing costing more than a few euro, even novels that won last year's Whitebread prize. It attracts an eclectic mix of people, from university professors to Brussels *ketjes*.

DAILY LIFE

Bread

Pain Quotidien Bakeries across Brussels stocked with delicious sourdough breads, crisp rolls, buttery croissants and sweet lemon tarts. Branches listed at www.painquotidien.com

Cakes

Wittamer A sophisticated pastry shop and chocolatier founded in 1910 with an upstairs tea room. Pierre Marcolini learnt the trade here. Place du Grand Sablon 6 and 12; ☎ 02.512.37.42; www.wittamer.com

Children

Baby 2000 Baby on the way? The hunt for a good pushchair is far from easy in Brussels. Most parents end up trekking off to Baby 2000 in Zaventem. The choice is huge and prices are reasonable, but customer service is minimal. Weiveldlaan 35F, Zaventem (leave the E40 motorway at the Sterrebeek exit); ☎ 02.725.20.13.

Petit Bateau This is the place for babywear to give as a present. The shop sells beautiful clothes for newborns. Avenue de la Toison d'Or, Ixelles; ☎ 02.545.76.50.

Tinök Look out for the big window displays filled with children's toys. This is where chic parents dress their offspring. Expensive but fun. Avenue Louise 165; ☎ 02.646.35.87.

Chocolates

Brussels has some distinguished chocolate shops that use the very best ingredients. No expatriate living in Brussels should go back home without a few small boxes (*ballotins*) packed in their suitcase.

Galler Galler's rich dark chocolates pack more punch than most. The high note comes from the 70% cocoa content. Rue au Beurre 44, off Grand'Place; ☎ 02.502.02.66; www.galler.com

Godiva Famous Belgian chocolates sold across the world. Grand'Place 22 and other branches; ☎ 02.511.25.37; www.godiva.be

Leonidas Founded by a Greek immigrant in 1910, Leonidas sells delicious chocolates straight from the factory at about half the price of the chic brands. Sold at the shop window. Boulevard Anspach 46 and other branches; ☎ 20.218.03.63; www.leonidas.be

Neuhaus Neuhaus was a Swiss confectioner who opened a beautiful shop in the Galeries St Hubert in 1857. His grandson is credited with inventing the filled chocolate known as the praline. Galerie de la Reine 25-27; ☎ 02.512.63.59; www.neuhaus.be

Pierre Marcolini Each Marcolini chocolate is a work of art. The distinctive square chocolates are made using unexpected ingredients like Earl Grey tea, ginger and thyme. Sold in a chic shop on the Sablon. Rue des Minimes 1, Sablon; ☎ 02.514.12.06; www.marcolini.be

Belgian Chocolate

Belgium is famous for its rich, dark chocolate. It produces 172,000 tons every year, sold in 2,000 shops. The busy time of year is just before Valentine's Day, when shop windows are filled with chocolate hearts sitting on red cushions. Easter is another busy time, and Christmas provides a further excuse for extravagant creations. The best chocolate is brut grand cru made from at least 70% cocoa, after which a bar of Cadbury's or Hershey's simply won't do. Several Belgian brands have developed into international names, like Godiva, now 75 years old, which uses a naked woman riding a horse as its trade mark. Neuhaus is even older, founded in 1857 in the glass-roofed Galeries Royale St Hubert by an emigrant Swiss pharmacist who began by selling liquorice and chocolate as medicines. The Neuhaus family went on to invent the filled chocolate known as the praline and the distinctive gilt-coloured box called the *ballotin*. Several large companies now dominate the chocolate business, the biggest being Leonidas, which has 1,400 shops worldwide. Their chocolates are perfectly made, but many Belgians prefer to buy one of the more classy brands to take as a gift. The big names dominate the main squares of Belgium, but every town and village has its own local chocolatier offering a unique experience. Pierre Marcolini on the Place du Grand Sablon is one of the most distinctive chocolate makers in Brussels, flavouring his neat little chocolates with rare flavours of tea and fruit. Mary on the Rue Royale is another address worth knowing about. But every Belgian has their own favourite shop and no one minds at all driving two hours to a remote village in the Ardennes to satisfy their craving.

Clothes for Men

Crossword Men looking for something suitable for the office should take a look at the three Crossword shops in the Louise quarter. They sell classic suits, casual clothes, shirts and shoes. Avenue Louise 79, Galerie de la Toison d'Or 504 and Galerie Espace Louise; ☎ 02.537.42.26; www.crosswordbrussels.be

Massimo Dutti Smart men's clothes from Spain that fit the Brussels office code. Avenue de la Toison d'Or 22; ☎ 02.289.10.50.

Clothes for Women

Kaat Tilley A romantic Brussels designer who creates unique white dresses featuring multiple layers of fabric. Galaries St Hubert 4; ☎ 02.514.07.63; www.kaatilley.com

Mais il est où le soleil? 'So where is the sun?' asks this likeable Belgian boutique. It sells summer clothes in flowing styles for the odd days when le soleil makes an appearance. Place du Châtelain 38, Ixelles; ☎ 02.538.82.77.

Olivier Strelli Beautifully styled clothes made from flowing fabrics in a range of rich colours. Avenue Louise 72; ☎ 02.512.56.07.

Stijl Sonja Noel began by selling early creations of the Antwerp Six, including Ann Demeulemeester and Dries van Noten, but now gives space to local designers such as Olivier Theyskens and Xavier Delcour. New names appear on the rails at regular intervals, but nothing is cheap. Rue Antoine Dansaert 74; ☎ 02.512.03.13.

Flowers

Daniël Ost Daniël Ost's sublime flower shop occupies a stunning Art Nouveau building designed by Paul Hankar. His contemporary creations use unexpected elements like twigs, grass and fruit. He has provided floral arrangements for two Belgian royal weddings, Christie's auction house in New York and Sophie Coppola's film Marie Antoinette. Rue Royale 13, central Brussels; ☎ 02.217.29.17; email info@danielost.be; www.danielost.be

Hairdressers

Olivier Dachkin A Belgian chain with 85 branches in main cities, offering fast service and cheap prices. Branches are conveniently located in urban shopping districts, including Avenue Louise, Rue de Tongres and Bascule. A basic wash, cut and blow-dry costs €25. www.olivierdachkin.com

Guillaume Sénéchal A traditional men's salon, not far from the Hotel Conrad. Superb haircuts and shaves. Avenue Louise 85a; ☎ 02.534.33.36.

Tony & Guy Friendly hair stylists who regularly work on fashion shoots and local theatre productions. Expect to pay at least €47 for a wash, cut and gossip. Avenue de la Toison d'Or 12, Ixelles; ☎ 02.515.11.11.

Interior Design

Dille & Kamille Attractive Dutch design shop selling inexpensive household items like tablecloths, plants, toys, cookbooks and cutlery. Rue Jean Stas 16 (off Avenue Louise); ☎ 02.538.81.25.

Espace 161 An endless rambling place stuffed with Ardennes cupboards and garden statues. Rue Haute 161; ☎ 02.502.31.64; www.espace161.com

Flamant Home Interiors A beautiful shop on the Sablon with snug rooms furnished in the style of a Belgian country house. The shop has a stylish restaurant called Flamand Kitchen serving brunch and lunch. Place du Grand Sablon 36; www.flamant.com

New de Wolf A Brussels institution that has been around for decades. It stocks every type of home decoration in a warren of little rooms furnished in every imaginable style. Wonderful at Christmas, when people squeeze inside to hunt for candles and tree decoration. Nothing is too expensive, making this the perfect place to take children when they want to buy a gift for a mother or grandmother. A five euro note will do nicely. Entrances at Rue Haute 91 and Rue Blaes 40, Marolles; ☎ 02.511.10.18.

Rambagh Asian Lifestyle A striking shop in the Marolles with exposed brick walls, a clanging metal staircase and antique carved windows set in the walls. Worth a look, especially if you are hunting for an Indonesian coffee table, a Cantonese wok or an antique door salvaged from the Far East. They also have a courtyard filled with old statues and stone fountains. Branches at Rue Haute 64 and 100, Marolles; ☎ 02.502.25.20.

Multimedia

Fnac Huge French electronics store on the top floor of City 2 shopping centre with extensive range of DVDs, CDs, computers and MP3 players. The staff are sometimes helpful, sometimes not. Stylish café at the entrance sells coffee and brownies. www.fnac.be

Media Markt Giant store on the top floor of the Inno department store selling computers, TVs, DVDs, CDs and games. It looks cheap, but prices are not always that different from other outlets. Customer service is minimal. www.mediamarkt.be

Vandenborre Belgian chain selling TVs, DVD players, cameras and computers. Forced to bring down prices to compete with foreign chains, but customer service remains a weakness. www.vandenborre.be

Postcards

Plaizier An appealing shop whose Dutch owners sell quirky postcards, including a range of Brussels cards. You can find an unusual view of the Atomium, an Art Nouveau house interior, or a moody 1930s streetscape by Leonard Missonne. They also sell art books and posters. Rue des Eperonniers 50, central Brussels; www.plaizier.be

Wine

Mig's Wine Shop Miguel Saelens runs a wonderfully eclectic wine shop in a rambling shop with moulded stucco, exposed brick walls and globes hanging from the ceiling. Mig is a charming and inquisitive wine seller who likes to introduce his customers to new wines at his Saturday tasting sessions. He sells 700-800 different wines from all over the world, but Australian wines are his special passion. He has some exceptional wines bearing names of distant vineyards, like Forgotten Field and Bird in Hand. Some of his picks are as cheap as €4, but he also stocks top wines from the Leeuwin Estate. Chaussée de Charleroi 43, Saint-Gilles; ☎ 02.534.77.03; email mig@migsworldwines.be; www.migsworldwines.be

Brussels Markets

More than 100 markets are held regularly in Brussels, along with the occasional brocante where locals try to get rid of useless junk that has been cluttering up their basement for the past 10 years.

Grand'Place A flower market is held every day in the middle of the cobbled Grand'Place. The sellers are mainly Flemish market gardeners from the countryside around Brussels. Prices are only slightly higher than elsewhere in the city. Daily 8am-6pm.

Jeu de Balle You visit the Jeu de Balle to hunt for old tin toys, an antique brass door handle or two silver candlestick holders. This ancient Brussels market (close to the house where Pieter Bruegel the Elder spent much of his life) is one of Europe's last genuine flea markets. You can find anything here if you hunt long enough: a box of rusty nails, a stuffed bear, one ski boot, a framed photograph of King Albert, a broken telephone. The best stuff is snapped up by professional dealers, leaving nothing but dross by 1pm. The dealers used to be Belgians, whereas most are now North Africans. But they're just as sharp. End with a bowl of soup in De Skieven Architek, an artistic cafe located in an old fire station. Daily 7am-2pm.

Marché du Midi A huge street market held every Sunday morning next to the railway viaduct running into the Gare du Midi. It has the atmosphere of an Italian or Moroccan market, with stallholders selling vast quantities of oranges, olives, artichokes and melons. They also sell CDs, socks, cooking equipment, and flowers from Flanders. Prices are cheap, but it can be a crush. Hang onto your wallet, say regulars. Sunday 8am-1pm.

Place du Châtelain An amiable little market in the middle of a pretty square in Ixelles. Foodies gather here after work to taste cheeses, buy bread and chat with friends. Wednesday 2pm-7pm.

Place Flagey A popular Sunday market where you can buy French cheeses, Italian salamis, organic wines and plants for your small Ixelles back garden.

Post

The Belgian postal system (www.post.be) has been gradually modernising its services since it was privatised in 2000. Now managed by the Danish company Post Danmark, *La Poste/De Post* has set itself the target of becoming the most efficient postal service in Europe.

Some progress has already been made. The Post is improving its delivery service and opening up new outlets in supermarkets and hotels. It also sells stamps at its online shop www.depost.be/eshop.

Post Offices

Many Belgian post offices remain antiquated relics of an older Belgium, but some have been completely restyled, including the main post office in the European Quarter at 16 Avenue de Cortenbergh. La Poste is currently trying to tackle the problem of long queues, but it is also slashing the number of staff and outlets.

Many branches now have a Post Shop, which sells padded envelopes, PostPac boxes, stationery and cards. The post office also has its own bank, the Banque de la Poste/Postbank, which offers a wide range of services, sometimes with lower charges than other banks. But you should bear in mind that you might have a long wait in a post office queue to carry out a transaction.

Most post offices are open Monday to Friday from 9am to 5pm, but some close as early as 4pm. The main Brussels post office is in the Monnaie shopping centre, on Place de la Monnaie (open Monday to Friday 8am-6pm, Saturday 9.30am-3pm). The branch at Gare du Midi is open the longest; Monday to Friday 7am-10pm, Saturday 10am-7pm, Sunday 11am-7pm.

Fiscal Stamps

Napoleon invented them because he didn't trust local administrations to deal with cash, and they are still being used in Belgium more than two centuries later. Fiscal stamps (*timbres fiscaux/fiscale zegels*) are one of the more bizarre anachronisms of Belgian life. They are bought at post office counters to pay for administrative fees such as registering a car or paying a parking fine. The government wants to abolish the system and replace it with electronic payment, but fiscal stamps worth more than €1m are still sold every year.

Mail

The post office has simplified mail delivery by abolishing second-class post. Under the new system, the post office guarantees to deliver any letter to a Belgian address by the following day.

The price of a stamp depends on the size of the envelope and the destination. A normal-sized letter (*normalisée*) is much cheaper than one that exceeds the limit, even by 1mm. Postal employees are equipped with complicated measuring devices to ensure that letters conform to the guidelines. Most cards and envelopes sold in Belgium are correctly sized, but cards sold in Britain (or in English shops in Belgium) often fall foul of the rules.

The price of a stamp will also depend on whether the destination is Belgium, Europe or the rest of the world. A normal letter for Belgium costs €0.52, a normal letter for Europe costs €0.80 and a letter to anywhere else costs €0.90.

The rate rises steeply for letters that fall outside the normal range: €1.04 for Belgium, and €2.40 for Europe. The rate also goes up progressively for letters weighing over 100g.

The rate for parcel post depends on the weight of the package, the destination and the speed of delivery. A parcel sent by the basic Kilopost service should arrive within four days, but you can speed things up by paying for the premium Taxipost service, which will get your parcel delivered the next working day (or even on the same day). Call the customer line on 022.012345 for more information in French or Dutch (or possibly English) or work it out for yourself on the website www.post.be by clicking 'parcels' and then 'International Service'.

Under a new agreement, stamps can be sold in some 2,000 outlets in Belgium, including Delhaize and Match supermarkets, Q8 petrol stations, hotels, campsites and some corner shops. You can also order stamps online, or even stock up on stamps illustrated with your own photograph (www.montimbre.be).

The distinctive red mailboxes are found outside post offices and on street corners. The last collection time is given on the mailbox. This can be surprisingly early in the day at some locations, though mailboxes outside main post offices generally have later collection times.

Mail is delivered once a day from Monday to Friday. Parcels are delivered separately. If you are not at home, a delivery notice is left in you letterbox. You can collect the parcel at the post office indicated on the form, or ask for the parcel to be delivered a second time. Uncollected parcels are returned to the sender after just 15 days, so take care not to order anything from Amazon just before you take a three-week holiday.

Import Duty

Import duty is not normally paid on goods from another EU country, but you may have to pay import duty and VAT on goods ordered from outside the EU. The duty is normally paid to the postman or delivery company when the parcel is delivered.

You may, for example, have to pay import duty on books, CDs and DVDs ordered from US websites such as Amazon.com. It is often cheaper and simpler to order from a European website such as Amazon.co.uk or Amazon.fr.

You should not have to pay duty on gifts sent from outside the EU that are below €45. The sender has to attach a green customs sticker to the package with the value of the contents and the word 'gift'.

Complaints

Despite recent improvements, many people are still unhappy with their postal service. You can complain by contacting the customer service department, ☎ 022.012345. You can also register a complaint online. The form (in French or Dutch) can be found on the web page www.post.be/site/en under 'customer service'.

DAILY LIFE

Waste

Rubbish is collected in plastic bags that are put out the evening before the collection day. Bags normally have to be put out after 6pm. Don't put them out any earlier or you could be fined.

Most Belgian authorities have introduced a system of waste sorting. General waste is collected twice a week in Brussels, while sorted waste is normally picked up once weekly. Different rules apply in different municipalities, while towns in Flanders and Wallonia have their own procedures. The system used in Brussels Region is based on four types of plastic bag, coloured yellow, blue, green and white.

Yellow bags are for paper and cardboard; blue bags take a range of recyclable materials including tin cans, drink cartons, water bottles and plastic cartons; green bags are used for garden waste (but only in the more leafy municipalities); and white bags are used for everything else.

Many supermarkets charge a small deposit on wine and beer bottles. Take them back and they will be used again. Other glass bottles should be taken a local bottle bank for recycling, and separated into green and clear glass. Some supermarkets will take non-deposit bottles for recycling.

Take care to clean containers before putting them in a recycling bin, as everything is hand sorted before recycling. Unsorted rubbish is taken to a vast incinerator plant near the canal in Neder-over-Heembeek.

You can dispose of large household items by calling your local commune and asking for a collection (*collection objets encombrants/grofvuil*). Each household has a limit of two cubic metres every six months. They will collect household goods such as mattresses and old furniture, but not building rubble or old sinks.

Another option is to take old items to your municipal container park. You should phone in advance to check out opening times and find out what sort of rubbish they will accept. You have to show your Belgian identity card to prove you live in the municipality and may have to pay a small fee.

You can also take large items by car to the Brussels Region container park (next to the incinerator plant). You have to show your ID card to prove you live in Brussels Region. The rubbish is sorted into different skips. But the staff won't let you dump all your waste. The rejected junk has to be taken to a commercial dump further along the canal, where you pay for rubbish by weight.

The Flemish municipalities are generally stricter than in Brussels. Householders have to buy official rubbish bags, so don't buy bags in Overijse if your live in Kraainem. The bags are expensive compared to Brussels and often break. Take care to sort the rubbish carefully, as collectors often refuse to pick up a bag because of a single misplaced yoghurt pot.

Health

Belgium has one of the best health services in the world. But it isn't the cheapest. You have to pay about 13% of your income into a compulsory healthcare fund and then pay a certain amount for every visit to a doctor, dentist or hospital. But most Belgians are extremely satisfied with the standard of care on offer.

EU nationals who move to Belgium should ask their national health service for a European Health Insurance Card. This covers most health bills during the first six months in another EU country. British residents should obtain the Department of Health leaflet T7.1 Health Advice for Travellers. This leaflet should be available from any post office or doctor's surgery. Alternatively you can request a free copy on the Health Literature Line (☎ 0870.155.5455 or read it online at www.dh.gov.uk).

The old E111 certificate of entitlement to medical treatment within Europe has been superseded by the European Health Insurance Card (EHIC). In the first phase of introduction, the new card will cover health care for short stays. By 2008, the electronic card will take the place of the current E128 and E119 which cover longer stays. This reciprocal cover is extended only to emergency treatment. Application forms can be obtained at post offices. The EHIC can also be ordered by telephone at 0845.606.2030 or online at www.dh.gov.uk.

Other nationalities should arrange for temporary private health insurance to cover the first six months. Don't panic if you have not arranged health cover when you arrive; most doctors and dentists in Belgium are relaxed about formalities. You simply turn up and pay the fee in cash (normally €25-€35). You can then claim repayment from your national health service or simply pay the whole amount yourself.

One advantage of the Belgian system is that you are free to choose any doctor, dentist, specialist or hospital. The country has 40,000 doctors and 80,000 hospital beds, and most types of treatment are provided without a long wait.

Private Medical Insurance

Those who are going to Belgium seeking work, or who spend a few weeks or months there each year, will require private medical insurance to cover the balance of the cost not covered by the E111/EHIC (see above). If you already hold private health insurance you will find that most companies will switch this for European cover once you are in Belgium. With the increase of British and foreign insurance companies offering this kind of cover, it is worth shopping around as cover and costs vary considerably.

Useful Addresses

AXA PPP Healthcare: ☎ 01892 612 080 (UK); www.axappphealthcare.co.uk.

British United Provident Association (BUPA): BUPA International offers a range of worldwide schemes for individuals and companies of three or more employees based outside the UK for six or more months. ☎ 01273 208181 (UK); email info@bupa-intl.com; www.bupa-int.com

Centers for Disease Control and Prevention: General travel health advice for US citizens. ☎ 404 639 3534/800 311 3435 (US); www.cdc.gov

Community Insurance Agency Inc: International health coverage agency. ☎ 847 897 5120 (US); email info@ciainsagency.com; www.ciainsagency.com

Europ-Assistance: The world's largest assistance organisation with doctors, air ambulances, agents and vehicle rescue services. ☎ 02.533.75.75 (Belgium); email front office@europ-assistance.be; www.europ-assistance.be

Exeter Friendly Society: ☎ 01392 353535; email sales@exeterfriendly.co.uk; www.exeterfriendly.co.uk

Expacare: Specialists in expatriate healthcare offering high quality health insurance cover for individuals and their families, including group cover for five or more employees. Cover is available for expatriates of all nationalities worldwide. ☎ 01344 381650; email: info@expacare.com; www.expacare.net

Goodhealth Worldwide (Europe): ☎ 0870 460 9923 (UK); email enquiries@goodhealth.co.uk; www.goodhealth.co.uk

Healthcare International: ☎ 020 7590 8800 (UK); email enquiries@healthcareinternational.com; www.healthcareinternational.com

HIFAC Health Insurance: Provides access to all the top private medical insurance providers. ☎ 0870 112.8239; email enquiries@insurancewide.co.uk; www.insurancewide.com

Health Insurance

Anyone who has lived in France will immediately understand the Belgian health service, which has a similar structure. But someone familiar with the UK's health service may find the Belgian system confusing, bureaucratic and expensive. Yet the Belgian system has its advantages. You can normally book a consultation very easily and arrange for an operation without having to wait.

The Belgian health system is financed by taxes and social contributions. Everyone in Belgium has to register with a health insurance fund (*mutuelle/ziekenfonds*). If you are employed by a Belgian company, your contributions are automatically deducted from your salary by the National Office for Social Security. Self-employed people can join any mutual fund they want. They will then have to decide whether to take out the minimal insurance cover or add insurance for small risks (*petits risks/kleine risico's*). You have to wait six months after joining a fund before you can enjoy any of the benefits.

You are free to choose which fund to join. The choice is bewildering for those not used to the system. Some are run by political parties, while others have a religious slant, but all offer a similar package of benefits. The main choice is between Christian, Socialist, Liberal and Neutral health funds. You might ask someone familiar with the system to recommend a fund, or simply drop into the local *mutuelle* office to ask about their services.

EU civil servants are not covered by Belgian sickness insurance, but insured by the EU's own health insurance fund.

Who Pays for Treatment?

The main role of health insurance funds is to refund a percentage of the costs of medical expenses, such as visits to the doctor or dentist, prescription medicines and hospital care. The patient then pays the balance, usually 30-50% of the cost.

Doctors and dentists will usually advise you on the percentage that is refunded before carrying out expensive treatment. Some people take out additional insurance (*aanvullende verzekering/assurance complémentaire*) or a hospital insurance (*assurance hospitalisation/hospitalisatieverzekering*) to cover additional costs.

You will need to take cash with you when you visit a doctor or dentist, as most are not equipped for electronic payment. A simple visit to the doctor is likely to cost about €22, while a basic trip to the dentist can easily cost €50-€100.

The health fund issues you with a social security identity card (SIS). The cards contain limited information about the holders' health insurance fund, date of birth and level of cover. You should take this with you when you visit a pharmacist or hospital, as the refund can then be deducted automatically, leaving you to pay the balance.

The SIS system will eventually be extended to doctors and dentists, but this is a slow process. At present, you will probably need to follow a somewhat antiquated system of green invoices and stickers (*vignettes*) containing your personal details. The *vignettes* are issued by your mutual fund. You attach one at the top of the doctor's or dentist's bill and post the bill to your health fund to obtain the refund.

Doctors

Most doctors in Belgium work in private practice, but some are attached to clinics and hospitals. They can choose to work for the public sector (*conventionné/geconventioneerd*) or the private sector (*non-conventionné/niet-geconventioneerd*). It is important to check in advance about their status. Those who work for the public sector charge standard prices set by the mutual funds, whereas doctors in private practice can set their own charges. The patient in each case receives the same refund from the mutual fund, so it pays to check your doctor's status before agreeing to expensive treatment.

The price difference doesn't guarantee any better standard of care. Many Belgian doctors do both public and private work, charging different rates in each case. Specialists normally charge higher fees, especially if they are in demand.

It's always worth checking fees before you book an appointment. If you have private insurance, or are uninsured, you pay the whole lot there and then.

Dentists

Belgium has more dentists than any other country in the world. Most work in the private sector, though some work for the state sector. The difference in fees can be enormous, so it pays to check in advance. Dentists will normally outline the costs involved before carrying out major treatment, and offer a range of alternatives at different rates. If you have trouble finding a dentist in your area, try posting a question on the Q&A forum at www.xpats.com.

Hospitals

Patients have the right to visit any hospital they choose in Belgium. Brussels has about 30 different hospitals, including three excellent university hospitals. The Cliniques Universitaires Erasme is attached to the French language ULB; the AZ-VUB Jette is linked to the Flemish university VUB; and the Cliniques Universitaires St-Luc is connected to the Catholic University of Leuven. Most hospitals have staff who can speak English as well as other major European languages. The standard of care is generally excellent. Certain hospitals have a particular area of expertise and attract patients from all over Europe. The Institut Jules Bordet specialises in cancer treatment, while the Hôpital Universitaire des Enfants Reine Fabiola treats seriously sick children.

Most hospitals belong to the state system, but there are some private hospitals, including the Clinique Edith Cavell. Private hospitals do not offer any better healthcare than a Belgian state hospital, but they can charge as much as they want. They should be avoided if you want to keep costs low. Remember to take along your SIS card and relevant medical details, along with clothes, towels, soap and bottled water.

Alternative Medicine

The Belgian health ministry recognises certain types of alternative treatment, including homeopathy, acupuncture and osteopathy. The costs are partly reimbursed by health insurance funds, but only if the treatment is carried out by a qualified doctor. Otherwise, you pay the full cost.

Emergency Treatment

The number to call in an emergency is 112. This number can be used in all EU countries to contact emergency services. But you can also call the Belgian emergency number 100. The ambulance normally arrives very quickly. They will take you to the nearest emergency centre, or to a specialised centre such as the burns unit. It helps if you have your SIS card, or a credit card to pay for treatment, but no one is ever turned away from a Belgian hospital because they are uninsured.

Pharmacies

You are never far from a chemist in Belgium. Their flashing green neon crosses are a familiar sight in Belgian towns. Most chemists are open normal shopping hours, while duty chemists stay open throughout the night. A list of night chemists is posted in pharmacy windows and published in local newspapers such as Le Soir. The current list of late-night chemists is also available online (www.fpb.be/fr/dutychemist.html).

Most medicines in Belgium are only available with a doctor's prescription. Your heath insurance fund repays part of the cost. This is deducted by the chemist at the time of sale, as long as you have an SIS card.

Childbirth

Many expatriates end up having children in Brussels. For most mothers, giving birth in Belgium is a positive experience. It isn't necessary to choose a private hospital, but, if your finances allow, the Edith Cavell private hospital in Uccle has an excellent reputation among expatriates. It is worth booking a single room to ensure that the mother gets some rest after birth.

How to Find a Doctor or Dentist

It's not difficult to find a doctor or dentist in Belgium. Walk down almost any residential street and you are likely to find a name on a shiny brass plate. For a longer term relationship, you can ask for recommendations from neighbours, friends or work colleagues. You can also ask your embassy for a list of English-speaking doctors, though you may be told bluntly that every doctor in Belgium speaks English. For a more sympathetic response, call the Community Help Service's Help Line for their list of English-speaking doctors (☎ 02.648.40.14; www.chsbelgium.org). Another popular method is to post a question on the Q&A forum of www.xpats.com asking for recommended doctors, dentists or specialists in a particular neighbourhood.

24 Hour Casualty Departments

Brugmann Hospital: Place van Gehuchten 4; ☎ 02.477.21.11

St Luc University Hospital: Avenue d'Hippocrate 10; ☎ 02.764.11.11

St Pierre Hospital: Rue Haute 322; ☎ 02.535.31.11

Edith Cavell Institute: Rue Edith Cavell 32; ☎ 02.340.40.40

Schools

Choosing a School

Choosing a school is a difficult decision for foreign parents. Children enrolled in a local Belgian school will eventually become integrated into the neighbourhood and learn the two main national languages, but they may find the transition very difficult, especially if they don't speak the local language when they arrive. Parents should be prepared for their children coming home in tears because they don't understand what anyone is saying. Many decide to avoid the trauma of moving by finding an international school, where their children are taught in their own language, and can often follow the national curriculum. But the fees charged are often beyond families on average salaries.

The Belgian Education System

The Belgian school system is free for everyone, though parents have to pay a sizeable sum each year for books and materials. The state sets national standards, but the language communities run the schools. The schools in Wallonia are the responsibility of the French Community, while those in Flanders are controlled by the Flemish Region. Within Brussels, parents can choose between the French and Dutch sectors.

The language situation sometimes leads to problems. Many schools in the Flemish suburbs of Brussels have an overwhelming number of students from French-speaking or expatriate families. Some schools have introduced rules banning students from speaking any language except Dutch within the school grounds. Certain Flemish suburbs have French as well as Dutch schools, including Kraainem, Sint-Genesius Rode and Wezembeek-Oppem, but this is a politically sensitive issue, and the French schools may eventually be abolished.

Parents can also choose one of the religious schools run by the Catholic, Protestant and Jewish churches. They teach the same basic curriculum as normal schools, but provide a certain amount of religious education. Most religious schools are Catholic, but they generally allow children from non-Catholic backgrounds.

Parents registering a child have to produce the child's ID card and a certificate from the commune listing the members of the household (*composition de ménage/gezinssamenstelling*). The certificate costs €3.75.

Education is compulsory from six to 18, but students can sometimes drop their hours after 16. All schools are mixed. Most are closed on Wednesday afternoon. Childcare facilities are available for working parents, allowing them to drop off children before school begins and collect them after school is over. There is also childcare offered on Wednesday afternoons. Schools charge a modest amount for this service.

Primary Schools

Belgian children start primary school (*école primaire/basis school*) when they are six, though most will already have attended nursery and crèche for several years. They stay at primary school for six years and learn a variety of subjects, with particular emphasis on mathematics and languages. All children learn a second language (French or Dutch) from an early age. Standards are generally tough compared to British or American schools, and children are regularly held back a year if they fail to get the minimum grades. Most teachers set a small amount of homework from an early age, yet there is also time for craft activities, and younger children spend enormous amounts of time constructing elaborate presents for the *Fête de Maman* (*Moedersdag* in Flanders) and the *Fête de Papa* (*Vadersdag*).

Secondary Schools

Children attend secondary school (*école secondaire/secundair onderwijs*) from 12 to 18. Most state secondary schools follow a reformed system called Type I, introduced in 1978 as a flexible alternative to the more rigidly traditional Type II schools.

Type II schools introduce specialisation at 12, forcing children to choose between technical, vocational, artistic and general studies. Type I schools provide a general curriculum for children aged 12 to 14, then allow children to choose a more specialised timetable. The aim of the reformed system is to allow students more time studying a wide range of subjects.

Students taking general studies follow the most academic timetable. The vocational studies option is aimed at students who want to work in areas such as commerce, printing, graphic arts and agriculture. The technical studies course provides basic theory and practical training, while the artistic studies option involves a choice between music and visual arts.

Teachers carry out regular assessments in both systems. Students sit exams in their fourth year, leading to the Certificate of Lower Secondary Education, and in their final year, giving them a Certificate of Higher Education.

Montessori Schools

Montessori schools are based on a progressive educational system devised by a 19th-century Italian doctor, Maria Montessori. These schools encourage children to develop their own potential in a relaxed setting. There are several Montessori schools in Brussels, almost all offering bilingual teaching in French and English, with additional languages such as Dutch and Spanish added as the children become older.

International Schools

Brussels has a wide variety of international schools, which are mainly located in the green suburbs. They charge high fees in return for excellent teaching, superb sport facilities and outstanding science labs. There are international schools offering British, American, French, German and Scandinavian teaching. Many parents on short-term contracts choose these schools to ensure that their children get educated in a language they understand and can easily reintegrate into their national system.

BEPS - Brussels A friendly primary school that takes children up to 11 years. Classes are small and children learn French as a second language from the age of four. ☎ 02.648.43.11; email Brussels@beps.com; www.beps.com

BEPS Waterloo International School Well-equipped primary school located south of Brussels. Offers high-quality teaching in international classes, with French taught as a foreign language from pre-school. ☎ 02.358.56.06; email waterloo@besp.com; www.beps.com

British Junior Academy of Brussels Primary school for children aged three to 11 with teaching based on the Briitsh curriculum. ☎ 02.732.53.76; email bjabrussels@yahoo.com; www.bjab.org

British School of Brussels The BSB is the main international school teaching the British curriculum. The school is located 20km from Brussels, in the leafy Flemish town of Tervuren. It has 1,200 students from 65 countries, but 70% of students are British. Set on a large campus on the edge of the forest, the school offers the International Baccalaureate programme to older students as well as GCSE and A levels. The school has outstanding sports facilities and an extensive arts programme. It also has a playgroup for children aged one to three. ☎ 02.766.04.30; email admissions@britishschool.be; www.britishschool.be

Brussels American School Based in Sterrebeek, the Brussels American School is run by the US government for the children of US governmental staff and Nato officials. ☎ 02.717.95.52; www.brus-ehs.eu.dodea.edu

International School of Brussels The ISB is located on a beautiful 40-acre wooded site on the southern edge of the city. The school provides education in English for students aged three to 18 in a relaxed environment. The students come from 60 different countries, including 42% from Europe and 30% from America. Teaching follows the American curriculum, but the school also offers the increasingly popular International Baccalaureate. The school has an excellent theatre that is often used by amateur companies, along with superb sports facilities. ☎ 02.661.42.25; www.isb.be

St John's International School St John's is a Christian school that takes pride in the number of students it gets into prestigious universities such as Cambridge, Oxford, Yale and Harvard. Located on a campus in Waterloo, the school was founded in 1964 to provide a broad education, including excellent language teaching. Students have French lessons every day from the age of three, and can take up German and Spanish after 13. The school recently added a 400-seat theatre. ☎ 02.352.06.14; email admissions@stjohns.be; www.stjohns.be

Scandinavian School of Brussels Founded in 1973, the Scandinavian School admits children aged two to 19. Based near Waterloo, the school follows a Scandinavian curriculum, with emphasis on European studies and modern languages. Some classes are taught in English and French. ☎ 02.357.06.70; email Scandinavian.school@ssb.be; www.ssb.be

Lycée Français Established in 1907, the French Lycée in Uccle offers a traditional French curriculum. Some 2,000 students are enrolled, with 71% coming from French families and 8% from a Belgian background. ☎ 02.374.58.78; www.lyceefrancais-jmonnet.be

The Bac Explained

The International Baccalaureate (IB) is becoming an increasingly popular choice among international schools. Its supporters argue that it provides a broader and more enriching education for students than national certificates, and prepares them better for higher education and the workplace. Students who take the IB study six main subjects over two years, selecting from literature, a second language, social studies, experimental sciences, mathematics and computer sciences, and the arts. The final exam includes a 4,000-word essay on a topic selected by the student.

The European Baccalaureate (EB) is a similar certificate awarded by the EU's highly academic European schools. The main difference is that students must take several core subjects in their second language. The final assessment is based on written and oral exams, some taken in the student's second language.

Universities in Britain used to be suspicious of the IB and EB, but these certificates are now officially recognised by the admissions authority UCAS. Some independent schools in Britain have even begun to offer the option of sitting the IB, arguing that it offers a better education than traditional A levels.

DAILY LIFE

School Holidays

Schools in Belgium begin in early September and run until early July. They usually have a one-week holiday in early November, a week-long break in early February and two weeks at Easter. The Christmas holiday begins a few days before Christmas and runs until early January. European Schools do not reopen in the New Year until after January 6. They remain open on November 11, but take Europe Day (May 9) as a holiday, along with a week in late May.

Crisis in the European Schools

The European School system was created more than 50 years ago to provide children of Europe's civil servants with education in their own language. But there was also a determination to create schools that would produce model citizens. *'They shall be Europeans in spirit,'* reads the mission statement, *'while preserving their love and pride for their own countries, and shall be well-prepared to complete and consolidate the work undertaken by their fathers, towards the creation of a united and prosperous Europe'.*

The European Schools still make a stab at the higher aims. They produce children fluent in four or even five EU languages and mix classes so that children learn to get along with different nationalities. Children learn a second language in primary and a third language from the second year of secondary school. Many take a fourth language and all students are required to follow certain courses in their second language. The end result is that almost all students emerge from the system perfectly bilingual.

Yet student numbers keep growing. The Belgian government, which is responsible for building the schools, struggles to keep up with the demand. The first European School in Brussels opened in Uccle in 1958. A second school opened in Woluwe in 1974 and a third was built next to the university campus in Ixelles in 2000. They all suffer from overcrowding.

The European Schools initially took some children from non-EU backgrounds, though parents had to pay school fees and transport costs. Now they are much more severe in their admissions policy, only admitting children with a parent working for the European Commission, the European Parliament, the European Council or Eurocontrol. No one else gets a place, apart from children of European school teachers and some senior diplomats.

The schools have to be tough because of chronic overcrowding. The three existing Brussels schools were designed to accommodate 2,500 pupils each. But the parents' organisation APEEE claims that Uccle currently has about 3,100 pupils, Woluwe 3,050 and Ixelles 2,600. That's 1,250 too many. And it's going to get worse. The school administration believes that the number of students will rise to at least 10,300 by 2010 – so where will they put the extra 2,800 students? The answer lies in Laeken, where the Belgian government is building a fourth school on the site of a disused army barracks. But it won't open until September 2009. Even then, it will only provide 1,000 places initially, rising to 2,500 in 2010. Until the new school is built, the Belgian government plans to open a temporary school in Rue Berckendael in September 2007 for 750 students. Parents are unhappy because the school is close to two prisons, including one for sexual offenders, and it is a long way from Laeken, where the students will eventually have to move. The parents have unanimously rejected the school, but the Belgian government insists there is no alternative.

The schools have also had to rethink their original goal of providing teaching in each of the official EU languages. That ideal was attainable in the 1950s, when there were just four official languages, but it has become an administrative nightmare in a Europe of 23 official languages. All schools still provide teaching in French, German and English, but other languages are only taught at some of the schools. The various problems are starting to look insurmountable, yet most students are blissfully unaware of any crisis. They enjoy the excitement, pick up half a dozen languages and perhaps even emerge as model Europeans.

Childcare

Belgium has one of the best systems of childcare in Europe, providing a range of facilities mainly aimed at working parents. Children can attend a crèche from six months to three years, while kindergartens take children from three until they enter school at six years old. More than 50% of Belgian children under the age of six are enrolled in some form of organised daycare.

Crèches

Belgium has an extensive network of crèches for young children from six months to three years old. They are usually open long hours (normally 7am-6pm) to allow parents to continue working full-time. Some crèches are private, but most are run by the state. The state crèches are heavily subsidised and employ fully trained staff. They have to respect strict guidelines on hygiene, staff/child ratios and charges. Mainly aimed at working parents, they charge fees based on the household income, up to a maximum of €28 per day (part of which can be deducted from tax). A private crèche can set its own fees, but it is still subject to the same strict controls as state childcare institutions. Places are increasingly scarce, and parents often start looking for a suitable crèche in the fourth month of pregnancy, hoping to have a place booked well before the birth.

The Office de la Naissance et de l'Enfance (ONE) is responsible for crèches in the French language sector, while Kind en Gezin runs crèches for Dutch-speaking children. The two organisations have lists of approved babysitters, libraries of books on bringing up children, and extensive information on childcare in Belgium. They also employ nurses who can carry out routine checks and give injections.

Several international schools have their own crèches which employ English-speaking staff. Employees of the European Commission and European Parliament can choose to put their children into one the official crèches reserved for staff.

Childminders

Some parents prefer to arrange for a child minder to look after their child, often in a small group of three to five children. Some childminders work independently and charge their own rates, while others (*gardinennes encadrées*) are employed by a local authority. The ONE and Kind en Gezin have lists of approved independent child minders who are regularly checked to ensure that they provide a safe and healthy environment.

Playgroups

Many expatriate parents prefer to find an informal playgroup or mother and baby group. The best sources for contact details are international women's clubs or online sites such as www.xpats.com. The organisation La Farandoline (www.lafarandoline.be) organises creative playgroups for children aged one to three years in several locations in suburban Brussels.

Kindergartens

Most Belgian children move from crèche to kindergarten (*écoles maternelles/ kleuterscholen*) at about two and a half years. The kindergartens are usually attached to primary schools and remain open long hours for working parents. Children move from kindergarten to primary school at the age of six.

Occasional Help

Parents sometimes need to find a childminder for a few hours while they visit a doctor or meet their bank manager. There is an easy solution in Belgium. You can drop off your child at a *halte garderie* for a short period. The kids are looked after by professional staff and provided with toys and books. The centres are run by parent groups, family associations and local authorities.

Babysitters

The Ligue des Familles provides members with contact details of registered babysitters in their area. The Gezinsbond offers the same service for families in Flanders. Babysitters also put up notices in local supermarkets and shops. Or you can look on websites such as www.xpats.com and www.quefaire.be. The European School in Uccle has a network of student babysitters (www.eeb1.com; contact details under 'Student Help Network'). Rates for babysitters vary. Members of the Gezinsbond pay €3 per hour for a babysitter during the day and €2,50 in the evening. Rates for private babysitters are considerably higher. A fair rate for a teenager is currently about €5 an hour, while older babysitters should be paid about €6-€10 per hour.

Childcare Contacts

Ligue des Familles Family association for French-speaking parents in Belgium. Rue du Trône 127; ☎ 02.507.72.11; www.liguedesfamilles.be

Gezinsbond Family association for Dutch-speaking parents. Rue du Trône 125; ☎ 02.507.88.11; www.gezinsbond.be

Office de la Naissance et de l'Enfance (O.N.E) Organises French-speaking crèches in Belgium. Chaussée de Charleroi 95; ☎ 02.542.12.11; www.one.be

Kind en Gezin Organises Dutch-speaking crèches in Belgium. Avenue de la Porte de Hal 27, central Brussels; ☎ 02.533.12.11; www.kindengezin.be

Brussels Childbirth Trust English-speaking organisation offering advice on having a baby in Brussels. Organises regular meeting groups for parents with small children in Brussels and surrounding towns. ☎ 02.215. 33.77; email info@bctbelgium.com; www.bctbelgium.com

Studying in Brussels

Brussels offers a wide range of courses for anyone who wants to gain a new qualification. The city has two universities and several international business schools. You have to pay fees, of course, but these are significantly lower than most other countries charge. In addition, many classes are taught in English and often involve visiting specialists from European and US universities.

Belgian Universities

ULB The Université Libre de Bruxelles, based on a campus in Ixelles off Avenue F.D. Roosevelt, mainly teaches in French, but offers some courses in English. It has a strong reputation for research and attracts students from all over the world. ☎ 02.650.20.27; www.ulb.ac.be

VUB The Vrije Universiteit Brussel, located on a modern campus in Ixelles, is the Dutch-speaking university of Brussels. It offers a range of postgraduate degrees in English, including management, international law and human ecology. ☎ 02.629.21.11; email infovub@vub.ac.be; www.vub.ac.be

Other Universities

Boston University US style teaching in English with a strong emphasis on discussion and critical thinking. Evening classes are organised for working professionals. ☎ 02.640.65.15; email Brussels@bu.edu; www.bu.edu/brussels

Brussels School of International Studies The University of Kent in southern England teaches courses in international studies in Brussels. Classes are organized jointly with the ULB and VUB. www.kent.ac.uk/brussels

The Open University About 500 students in Belgium follow part-time courses with the UK's Open University. Students are expected to spend about 6-16 hours a week studying at home, combined with regular tutorials. ☎ 02.644.33.72; email Belgium@ open.ac.uk; www.open.ac.uk.

Business Schools

OU Business School The Open University's business school offers part-time management courses to executives. www.oubs.open.ac.uk/belgium

Solvay Business School One of the oldest business schools in Europe, the Solvay school was founded by the Belgian industrial chemist Ernest Solvay in 1903. Now part of the ULB, the school has set itself the goal of being 'the most European of European business schools'. ☎ 02.650.41.67; www.solvay.edu/mba

Vesalius College Linked to the VUB, Vesalius teaches business classes in English and takes advantage of its location in Brussels by inviting guest lecturers from international companies based in the city. ☎ 02.629.28.21; email vesalius@vub.ac.be; www.vesalius.edu

Vlerick Management School You need to travel to Ghent or Leuven to study at the Vlerick Management School. But it's worth the 30-minute train journey. This is one of the world's top business schools, with many of the country's most successful company directors among its alumni. ☎ 09.210.97.11; email info@vlerick.be; www.vlerick.be

DAILY LIFE

There are many enjoyable ways of getting around Brussels that avoid using a car.

Public Transport

The Brussels public transport system is operated by Stib/Mivb (www.stib.irisnet.be). It is not the easiest system in the world to use, but provides a reasonably efficient service. Many services begin running at 5.30am and continue until shortly after midnight, but certain routes close down early in the evening and on Sundays. The main complaints from passengers involve overcrowding on the metro and poor bus and tram services after 6pm and on Sundays. Many people therefore use public transport during the day, but rely on their cars to get around in the evenings and on Sundays.

The network is based on two intersecting metro lines, 18 tram routes and 47 bus routes. This makes for complicated journeys, especially if you have to change from one type of transport to another.

Metro The metro is the simplest system to use. Stations are indicated by a white M on a blue background and named in French and Dutch. The names are generally taken from the nearest street or square. Most important places can be reached by metro including the Gare du Midi, Gare Centrale, Schuman (for the European institutions) and Heysel (for the exhibition centre). But large areas of Brussels are a long way from the nearest metro station, including much of Uccle and Forest.

Five Best Metro Stations

Porte de Hal Imaginary cityscapes above the escalators, created by the cartoon book illustrator François Schuiten.

Maelbeek Cartoon figures by Benoît van Innes.

Stockel Long mural featuring figures from Tintin comic books.

Parvis de Saint-Gilles Metro station in Saint-Gilles decorated by the artist Françoise Schein with blue tiles spelling out the Declaration of Human Rights in French and Dutch.

Horta Cast iron railings from Victor Horta's Maison du Peuple decorate this metro station in Saint-Gilles.

DAILY LIFE

The main disadvantage of the metro is that it is chronically overcrowded during rush hour, especially on line one between Schuman and Gare Centrale. At times it is simply impossible to get on board. The transport authority has introduced more spacious French-style BOA metro trains, but more fundamental changes may be needed.

Trams

Trams have been part of the Brussels streetscape for more than a century. While other cities abandoned this form of transport in the 1960s, Brussels maintained its network, although certain lines were replaced by metros and others were put underground. Yet investment in new trams is only now beginning to happen. The antiquated trams dating from the 1950s are gradually being replaced by stylish new models with wide doors and low floors.

One of the main tram routes passes through the city centre. Five tram lines (52, 55, 56, 81 and 90) run through a tunnel that links Gare du Midi and Gare du Nord. The tunnel, known as the pré metro, connects with the metro at several stations, including Midi, Porte de Hal Bronckére and Rogier.

Another important tram route runs on the surface between Botanique and Louise, following the Rue Royale and Rue de la Régence axis. Some trams continue down Avenue Louise to Boitsfort, while others take the Chaussée de Charleroi to serve Uccle.

The old models of tram are virtually inaccessible for bicycles and buggies. The door is opened from the outside by pushing a green plastic strip that runs between the doors. The new models are far better designed, with large areas for parking buggies, bicycles and wheelchairs.

Buses

The bus network covers most parts of the city. Bus 71 is the most important route, providing a vital link between the university quarter, Flagey and the city centre. This bus runs at short intervals, and includes a night service. But buses in Brussels rarely have dedicated lanes, so that they often get caught in traffic, especially in the rush hours.

Night Buses

The transport authority recently decided to create a network of night buses called Noctis. The buses operate on 20 different routes on Friday and Saturday nights until 3am. Most routes begin at Place de Brouckère, serving destinations such as Flagey, Schuman and the main railway stations. A single ticket costs a flat rate of €3.

Timetables

Timetables for metro, tram and bus services are available online (www.stib.be). You can also phone for information, but only during the day from Monday to Saturday (☎ 0900.10.310). Many public transport stops now have illuminated signs which indicate the exact arrival time of the next tram or bus. You can also find out the exact waiting time at a particular stop by using a mobile phone. You simply send a text message to the number 3883 with a message giving the route number followed by a space followed by first three letters of the name of the stop. So someone waiting at Louise for tram 93 would send the message *93 LOU*. The reply comes within seconds, based on the actual position of the bus or tram.

Tickets

The simplest way to travel is to buy a single Jump ticket from the driver as you board a tram or bus. But the public transport authority doesn't want too many people to do this because it slows everything down. They therefore decided in 2007 to make it an expensive option. It now costs €2 to buy a single ticket from a driver, but just €1.50 if you buy it in a machine or ticket office.

A cheaper option is to buy a five-journey (€7) or 10-journey (€11) Jump ticket in advance. These are sold at most metro stations and railway stations. You can also buy them at large supermarkets and some newsagents (where you see the Stib/Mivb sign in the window). Some metro stations now have automatic ticket machines which accept coins, notes and Mister Cash cards.

Other tickets are useful if you want to spend a whole day exploring Brussels by public transport. A one-day public transport ticket costs €4 and a three-day ticket costs €9.

The Jump ticket allows you to travel for one hour on the entire Brussels public transport network. The ticket is also valid on trains, TEC buses and De Lijn buses, but only within the city limits. Be careful when you take tram 44 to Tervuren, as you will need to buy a separate ticket if you travel beyond Brussels Region.

Tickets must be validated every time you enter a bus, tram or metro station. This is done by inserting the card in one of the orange machines at the metro station entrance or inside the tram or bus. The machine reads the magnetic strip and, if the ticket is still valid, displays the message Transit. Otherwise, it will stamp it again for one hour of travel.

Take care that you have a valid ticket at all time. Those caught without a ticket must show ID (a Belgian identity card or a passport) and pay a hefty fine. The basic fine is €76, but if you don't pay within three days the bill rises to €84. Anyone caught a second time is fined €190, while third-time offenders are hit with a €380 invoice.

Regular commuters can buy a monthly or annual season ticket for the transport network. You will need to get a travel card with photo from a public transport sales office, then buy the season ticket. Monthly tickets are sold at Stib sales offices, train stations in Brussels Region and some supermarkets. Annual tickets can also be ordered online at the public transport website.

Children can travel free on Brussels public transport up to 12 years. There are no formalities for children under six, but older children have to carry a special travel pass with a passport photograph (*Abonnement J*). Parents can pick up the pass at public transport sales office.

The transport authority also issues free travel passes to everyone over 65 who is officially resident in Brussels Region. You simply have to fill in an application and include a passport photograph. The passes are not valid for travel on the network before 9am.

The main public transport office, recently named Bootiek, is at 15 Avenue de la Toison d'Or, near Louise metro station. There are other smaller offices in Rogier and Port de Namur metro stations. The shops sell tickets and provide free maps of the Brussels public transport network. Time your visit carefully, as there are often very long queues at the start of the school terms.

Improvements

The transport authority is currently working on various projects to improve the network and deal with overcrowding. The metro is currently being extended to create a new loop line and longer trains are being introduced. In addition, modern trams are being introduced on certain lines, including the T4000 supertram, which is air conditioned and carries 258 passengers. The authority is also changing its livery from a jaunty blue and yellow to a more muted silver and grey.

Tram to Tervuren

You can experience one of the world's most beautiful tram rides by riding tram 44 to Tervuren. The tram starts in a dark undergound station, but soon surfaces in the middle of Leopold II's beloved Avenue de Tervuren. Look right for a glimpse of the Palais Stocklet, a Wiener Werkstätte masterpiece, then admire the sweeping lawns of the Parc de Woluwé. Beyond the park, look left to spot a former tram depot which is now home to the Tram Museum. The nostalgic collection includes trams even more ancient than the ones that run to Tervuren. The tram soon rumbles through the Forest de Soignes, swinging wildly as it follows a meandering route through the beech trees. The ride ends at a wistful 19th-century tram station, just a few paces from the spectacular museum built by Leopold II to display his Congo spoils.

DAILY LIFE

Taxis

Brussels has a reasonably well regulated taxi system compared to some capital cities, though its drivers are sometimes surprisingly clueless about the city. Make sure you use an official taxi with a distinctive yellow and blue Brussels Region sign on the roof. New Yorkers may be annoyed that taxis cannot be hailed in the street – they have to be ordered by phone. The taxi usually arrives within five or ten minutes, except at busy times of the year such as New Year's Eve. All taxis are equipped with a taximeter linked to a printer. The driver has to print out a receipt at the end of the journey and give it to the customer. The price covers a maximum of four passengers and includes a tip, though most people round up the fare to the nearest euro. Some drivers do not carry much change, so you should always try to have roughly the right sum.

There are inevitably a few rogue drivers who take unsuspecting tourists on unnecessary detours, but a phone call to the Brussels Region's taxi ombudsman might get results if you feel you have been badly treated. Call the phone number 0800.14.795 to talk to the taxi licensing authority, or register an online complaint at the website www.brusselstaxi.be.

The main Brussels companies are: Taxis Verts (☎ 02.349.4949), Taxis Bleus (☎ 02.268.0000), Taxi Oranges (☎ 02.349.4343) and Autolux (☎ 02.512.3123). Autolux provides a taxi service to and from Brussels Airport. The other firms are only allowed to take people to the airport and pick up passengers from outside the departures hall after they have dropped customers off.

Belgian Railways is working on an ambitious €1.6 billion plan to upgrade commuter rail links into Brussels. A total of eight lines within a 30km radius of the city are being improved to create a Brussels Regional Express Network, similar to the nippy RER network in Paris. The plan, which is being carried out by the rail authority Infrabel, aims to offer commuters one train every 15 minutes during rush hours. It also plans to develop a new ticketing system that will allow train passengers to use Brussels public transport without having to buy an extra ticket. Under the plan, some 120 stations in the Brussels commuter zone will be upgraded. But the project has become bogged down with planning procedures, and may not run properly until 2015.

Car-Sharing

Cambio The newest idea to solve traffic congestion in Brussels is a car-sharing scheme called Cambio (www.cambio.be). This system allows you to use any car from the Cambio fleet for a fixed membership fee and variable additional charge (depending on the length of time you use the car and the distance covered). Once you have joined, you simply book a car at any one of 16 locations across the city, either by phone or online. The scheme is a cheap and easy option for anyone who uses a car occasionally. The promoters say that it is particularly worthwhile for anyone who drives less than 10,000km a year. You are also saved the chores of insurance, maintenance and hunting for a parking place. In addition, Cambio drivers enjoy a few little perks, such as free parking in Evere commune. There are now Cambio projects in all main Belgian cities, but Brussels is by far the most popular, with some 1,200 subscribers out of a national membership of 1,600.

Taxistop Taxistop (www.taxistop.be) combines cheap travel with the chance to meet interesting people. Taxistop charges a small fee to put drivers in touch with people who need a lift. The driver pays for the petrol while the passenger pays a set rate per km (and a small fee to Taxistop). The Taxistop office is at Rue Fossé aux Loups 28 in downtown Brussels.

Cycling

Brussels is a surprisingly good city for cycling. It is relatively compact, with pleasant green avenues and quiet suburban streets. Even in the city centre, cyclists can easily get around without too many problems. It can, of course, suddenly rain, which makes cycling miserable in any city. Some enlightened Brussels employers have taken account of their cycling employees by installing changing rooms and showers.

Most cyclists in Brussels are fit young professionals with smart city bikes. Many work for the European institutions and come from countries with a strong cycling culture, like The Netherlands and Denmark. Only a small number of children cycle to school.

Brussels Region wants more people to cycle in the city and is currently working on a plan to create a network of cycle routes throughout the city. The Region is also trying to convince people to leave their cars at home or even sell them. Anyone who sells a car in Brussels and hands back their Belgian licence plates is offered free public transport and Cambio membership for a year.

Cyclists should try to get hold of the useful waterproof cycle map of Brussels Region showing recommended cycle routes and bike repair shops. The map can be ordered from Gracq for just one euro, or downloaded free from the Brussels Region website at www.fiets.irisnet.be.

Those who prefer quiet weekend cycling can head with their bikes to the Bois de la Cambre. Most of the roads through the park are closed to traffic on Saturday and Sunday, leaving the broad avenues safe for cyclists, roller bladers and walkers. Adventurous cyclists can head off into the Forêt de Soignes, following the network of cycling trails that cut across the ancient woodlands.

Bikes can be taken on metros and some trams, but not during the rush hours.

Cycling Contacts

Cyclists' House: Three Brussels cycling organisations are based at the Maison des Cyclists, 15 Rue de Londres in Ixelles.

Pro Vélo: An energetic cycling lobby group that has been monitoring bike use in Brussels for over a decade. Offers guided tours of Brussels on Sundays and organises annual Dring Dring bike day. ☎ 02.502.73.55; email info@provelo.org; www.provelo.org;

Gracq Campaigns for cycle-friendly policies in Brussels and Wallonia. Currently celebrating new legislation that allows cyclists to use flashing lights at night. ☎ 02.502.61.30; email info@gracq.org; www.gracq.org

Fietsersbond Brussel: Flemish cycling lobby group closely linked to GRACQ. www.fietsersbond.be/brussel

European Union Cyclists Group: Cycling lobby group for EU staff. www.eu-cg.info

Bike Repair Shop: The Ateliers de la Rue Voot is a friendly bike repair workshop where experts teach you the basics for a nominal charge. www.voot.be

Bike Hire: The Maison des Cyclists at 15 Rue de Londres in Ixelles has more than 100 bikes for rent. www.provelo.org

Getting around Brussels: Brussels Region has sponsored the publication of a laminated bike map of the city. It marks official bike routes as well as bike repair shops and cycle parking. Available from the Maison des Cyclists.

City Bikes

Brussels now has a system of Cyclocity public bikes operating in the central districts. Some 250 bikes are available at 23 bike parks within the inner ring road. There's a certain amount of minor bureaucracy involved before you can use a bike. This is done at the machine located next to the bike racks by following some simple instructions in French, Dutch and English. You need to have a Belgian Mastercard or Visa card to pay (or a foreign bankcard with Maestro). This is used to pay a €150 deposit, which is temporarily taken off your card. You then get a seven-day pass, which costs €1,50.

It is now simple. You insert the pass, type in your four-digit code and remove a bike. You are charged 50 cents for the first half hour, followed by €1 for each additional hour. The final amount due is taken off your credit card at the end of seven days.

Is it Safe to Cycle in Brussels?

Cycling in Brussels isn't as dangerous as it looks. Traffic generally moves slowly around the city, and streets are well lit at night. There are almost no fatal accidents involving cyclists, but a lot of minor scrapes. The main hazards that catch out cyclists are tram rails and car doors opening suddenly. Aware of the potential benefits of cycling, Brussels Region now wants to persuade more people to use bicycles rather than cars. Its policies are slowly having an impact. The number of journeys done by bicycle was four times higher in 2006 compared with 2001 and Pro Vélo estimates that 5,000 people cycle to work in Brussels every day. Yet this is still just 4% of all journeys, compared to 14% in Flanders and 30% in Amsterdam.

The city recently appointed a bicycle manager to boost the image of cycling. But he is realistic and accepts that Brussels has too many hills to make it an ideal cycling city. He estimates that 15 percent of journeys could be done by bike. Some improvements have already been made to the infrastructure. The most ambitious (and costly) was the creation of two dedicated cycle lanes down the busy Rue de la Loi. The city now aims to create a network of 19 cycle routes by 2009. The authorities are also carrying out more modest improvements by creating reservoirs for cyclists at many traffic lights, allowing bikes to move off ahead of cars. Traffic rules have also been modified to allow bikes to travel in both directions on one-way streets (as long as there is a contraflow bicycle lane painted on the road). Cyclists can also use some bus lanes, mainly in the city centre.

The public transport authority has relaxed its rules so that cyclists can now take bikes on the metro or the new range of trams at any time except for weekdays 7–9am and 4–6.30pm. You must stamp the ticket twice (once for you and once for the bike) and use the open areas reserved for bikes.

The European Commission has also made an effort to encourage its staff to cycle in Brussels. As well as providing bike racks and showers, it has about 150 service bicycles available for staff to travel between buildings.

Yet the city streets are still unsafe for young children. There are too many unexpected hazards and not enough cycle lanes. You can let them cycle in the Bois de la Cambre at weekends, but it's still not really a good idea to allow them on the roads by themselves.

There is the cheaper option of a one-year pass, which costs €10. This has to be ordered online at the site www.cyclocity.be, and can take several weeks to arrive by post. Once you have the pass, you pay a rental charge of 50 cents an hour deducted automatically from your bank account every month. ☎ 0900.11.000; www.cyclocity.be

Driving

Driving In Belgium

Driving a car in Brussels is not particularly easy or enjoyable. A British journalist once described the city as *'the world capital of the motorised insane'*. Some roads have traffic moving at near motorway speeds. Others are narrow cobbled lanes with bicycles squeezing past cars. The city is a mixture of cultures, which means a variety of driving styles. There are safe North American and Scandinavian drivers and more reckless Mediterranean drivers. This creates aggression on the roads and countless minor accidents.

Traffic often comes to a standstill on the main roads into Brussels, especially during rush hours, which last from 7am to 10am and 5pm to 7pm. Another traffic peak occurs during the lunch period, noon to 2pm. Other random problems occur because of accidents, demonstrations and road works. Parking is almost always a problem, especially during weekdays, when 30,000 cars are driven into the city from the suburbs. Many areas simply don't have enough parking spaces available, such as the inner city and Ixelles.

Drivers in Belgium have to be 18 years old with a valid driving licence (*permis de conduire/rijbewijs*). The licence is granted by the local town hall after the candidate has passed a theoretical and practical test. Drivers with a valid licence from an EU state can drive in Belgium without any further formalities. Drivers from countries outside the EU face a certain amount of bureaucracy depending on their nationality. They can initially drive with an international licence, but should go to the town hall

Priority from the Right

Foreign drivers are often caught out by the rule of priority from the right, which was once common throughout Europe, but is gradually being abolished. The rule still applies on many Belgian roads, meaning that drivers must give way to cars joining the road from the right, even when the road on the right is nothing more than a cobbled lane leading to a farmhouse.

The rule does not apply on priority roads (identified by small orange lozenge signs placed just beyond a junction) or on roundabouts with a give-way sign. The law was recently amended so that cars coming from the right have priority even when they stop for pedestrians or bicycles. In the past, drivers coming from the right lost their priority if they stopped at a junction. Some Belgians argue that the priority rule helps to slow down traffic, yet it is the cause of thousands of minor accidents, leaving pools of broken glass at countless crossroads.

once they have received a Belgian ID card and apply for a Belgian driving licence. Canadians can sometimes be caught out if they come from a province that has not signed an agreement with Belgium. They will then have to sit a Belgian test. Check with the town hall about the documents required (usually a current national driving licence, two passport photographs, your residents permit and a translation of the licence into Dutch or French.) Join the queue at the counter marked *Service Permis de Conduire/Dienst Rijbewijzen*.

Traffic Information

The Brussels Ring is notorious for long delays and accidents, especially during the rush hours. You can check the traffic situation before you set off by looking at the *camerabeelden* (camera images) on the Flanders traffic control centre website (www.verkeerscentrum.be). This relays images from 14 traffic cameras on the Brussels Ring. It also shows traffic flow on Antwerp and Ghent Rings.

The Belgian motoring organisation Touring provides further useful information on driving conditions in Belgium. You can call Touring Mobilis on 0900.10.280 (premium rate) for details of traffic conditions on Belgian and European roads, every day from 7am-9pm (operators answer in French or Dutch). You can also find out about traffic jams and road works on the organisation's website www.touring.be.

Buying a Car

It's worth checking out a few dealers in Brussels before you buy a new car, as outlets often have special deals, especially in December and January. Once you have chosen a car, ask your dealer to explain the procedure for getting it registered and insured.

The first step is to insure the car (see below). You will be sent a pink registration certificate (*demande d'immatriculation*) by the insurance company. Take this to the Vehicle Registration Department (DIV) to get a number plate. The DIV office is close to Schuman metro station in the heart of the European Quarter. You can, if you prefer, apply by post and wait for the number plate to arrive by post. Or you can ask your insurance company to apply online. The DIV issues you with a car registration number and hands you a new Belgian licence plate. The registration fee is about €62.

Now for a strangely Belgian detail. You only receive the rear licence plate. You then have to go to a Mister Minute key-cutting shop to get a copy made. There is a convenient shop in Schuman metro station where the job is done in two minutes. You then attach the original plate to the back of the vehicle and the copy to the front. Or you can ask your dealer to do it. The licence plates belong to the car owner. When you buy a new car, you simply transfer the plates and notify the vehicle registration office. This explains why some of the smartest new cars in Belgium have old dented plates.

You now have to pay various road taxes. Anyone buying a new car has to pay a one-off *taxe de mise en circulation/taks van ingebruiksstelling* which is based on the engine size. The bill is sent to you automatically by the local tax office (*Administration des contributions directes*). You also have to pay an annual road tax determined by the engine size.

If you leave the country permanently, you should return the number plates to the Vehicle Registration Department. Don't take too long to do so, as you remain liable for Belgian road tax as long as you have the plates.

Road Regulations

Super fines

The government recently introduced tough new penalties known as 'super fines' for many road traffic offences. The traffic authorities have also placed speed cameras on many routes to cut down on accidents. It is well worth respecting the traffic laws if you want to avoid a receiving a hefty fine through the post.

Speed limits

- Motorways: 120km/hour, but cut to 90km/hour during smog alerts
- Major routes: 90km/hour or 70 km/hour
- Major urban roads: 50 km/hour
- Other urban roads: 30 km/hour
- Outside schools: 30 km/hour

Traffic safety:

- Drivers must be 18.
- Maximum permitted blood alcohol level: 50 micrograms of alcohol per 100ml of blood.
- Seat belts have to be worn at all times in front and back seats.
- Children's safety seats must be correctly installed, following the instructions on the seat.
- Drivers must give way to cars coming from the right, except on priority roads (marked by an orange lozenge sign).
- Cars must always give way to trams, trains and emergency vehicles.
- Never overtake a tram on the inside when it has stopped at a tram halt.
- Never block a tram line.
- Always stop for pedestrians on or approaching a zebra crossing.
- Vehicles must carry a red warning triangle.
- Motorcyclists must wear helmets and use headlights at all times.
- Keep out of bus lanes, cycle lanes and red routes (*axe rouge/ax rode*).
- Watch out for cyclists on your inside when you turn right.
- Carry at least two fluorescent yellow jackets in your car to wear if you break down. This is a legal requirement in Belgium and many other EU countries.

Parking:

- Do not park in disabled bays or bus stops.
- Never park in front of a garage.
- Do not park where the kerb is painted yellow.

DAILY LIFE

- Always look out for temporary no-parking signs placed by the local police. The times and dates are usually indicated on the sign, and arrows indicate the direction of the parking restrictions. You need to check for signs every day, or your car could be towed away without warning.
- Bear in mind that you are not allowed to park in any space for longer than 24 hours. Your car can be towed away without any warning, simply because someone has complained to the police.
- Watch out for streets where the parking changes to the opposite side every 15 days. You must move your car on the evening before the change occurs.

Importing a Car

You can drive your car into Belgium when you move without any formalities. But you will have to officially import your car if you plan to stay in the country. Do nothing until you have registered with your local town hall. You then have six months to import the car. You will not be liable for import tax if you come from another EU country and the car is more than six months old. But you have to produce the sales receipt and the car's EU certificate of conformity (*gelijkvormigheidsattest/certificat de conformité*). This is usually supplied by the car manufacturer. You also need to insure the car with a Belgian company and, if the car is over four years old, take it for a Belgian *contrôle technique*. Once you have gathered all the necessary paperwork, you can apply to the vehicle registration department (DIV) to register the car and pick up a Belgian number plate.

Car Insurance

Car insurance is expensive in Belgium due to the country's high accident rate and inflated repair bills. But you just have to accept it. The car has to be insured before you pick up your number plates and drive it away. Insurance can be arranged through your bank or (usually more cheaply) an insurance company. Most companies have websites where you can get an online quote. Make a few comparisons before you take up an offer, as rates vary considerably. The minimum insurance policy covers third-party liability. This insures you for causing death, bodily injury or physical damage to another person. It also covers anyone else in the car who causes injury (such as a passenger who injures someone or causes damage by opening a car door). The more expensive option is comprehensive coverage (*Omnium*), which covers vandalism, fire, theft or damage resulting from a collision. An Omnium policy is normally the best choice, as scrapes are almost inevitable. It's also worth adding insurance for broken car windows if you park on the street. Some companies recently introduced a reduced insurance rate for drivers who keep below a fixed number of km (normally 10,000) every year. Young people generally pay very high insurance premiums.

Premiums are calculated by the driver's age, engine size and accident record in Belgium. Your premium rises each time you have an accident that was your fault, but drops for every year of accident-free driving. Many drivers settle small accidents with a cash payment, which keeps their insurance rating positive.

Most companies do not give foreign drivers any credit for their previous driving record, but a few companies do offer expat deals. You can also get a special deal from some companies if you drive less than 10,000km a year or park the car in a garage overnight. Once you have signed up with a company, you will be sent a certificate of insurance known as a green card, which should be kept in the car.

The chaotic driving conditions in Brussels mean that you will almost inevitably have an accident at some time. The most important thing is to remain calm and courteous. Minor dents might be settled with a cash payment, but more serious accidents will have to be dealt with by your insurance companies. That means filling in a *constat d'accident* form and sending a copy to your insurance company. You will then have to arrange an appointment with the company's assessor to determine the cost of repairs.

Insurance Contacts

Most large Belgian banks offer car insurance, but their premiums are often high. The following insurance companies deal with car insurance.

Ethias: Leading insurance company with competitive rates. ☎ 02.227.99.00 (English contact centre); www.ethias.be

Actel Direct: Major insurance company offering good rates. ☎ 0800.130.30; www.actel.be

Corona Direct: ☎ 078.15.14.15; www.corona.be

All three companies provide online application forms which allow you to get an instant quote by email. The sites are only in French and Dutch.

Road Charges

The Belgian government planned to introduce a sticker (*vignette*) in 2009 for all cars driving on Belgian motorways. The *vignette* was to have cost €60 a year, but Belgian drivers would have been compensated by an equivalent reduction in road tax. The vignette system is already in use in several European countries, including Austria and Switzerland, but the Belgian plan was condemned by German and Dutch road users. It was finally scrapped, but the idea of road charging is still being debated. Brussels Region recently considered introducing a charge for cars entering the city, but the plan was fiercely opposed.

Parking Fines

Be careful where you park in Brussels as many places are illegal. You should never park in front of a garage, on a bus stop, or next to a pavement marked with a single yellow line. Some parking spaces are marked with a jagged line, which means that parking is illegal at certain times (often to allow vans to deliver to shops).

Watch out also for temporary parking restrictions, such as weekly markets. These are usually indicated by a signpost giving the times when parking is prohibited. You are usually banned from parking on the market square after 8pm on the evening before the market day.

Parking is often suspended because of road cleaning, construction work or house moving. The traffic police then put up temporary signs indicating the period when parking is banned.

If your car is towed away, contact the police station in the district where the car was parked, as soon as you find out. They will tell you where the car has been taken. You should collect it as quickly as possible, as you have to pay a large fee for each day it is held, as well as a towing charge and a fine.

Petrol Prices

Petrol in Belgium is fairly expensive. Some drivers make a point of filling up the tank in Luxembourg, where the price is significantly lower. The cheapest Belgian petrol is sold at DATS (owned by Colruyt) and Jet outlets. But you may have to join a long queue.

Road Accidents

Belgian roads are among the most dangerous in the world, with 10 road deaths per 100,000 people compared to just 4.5 in The Netherlands. While other countries have improved road safety in recent years, the accident rate in Belgium remains one of the highest in Europe. The weekends are particularly dangerous, but it is wrong to put all the blame on Belgian drivers, as one in five cars caught speeding has foreign number plates. Drivers from Britain are often involved in accidents caused by the priority from the right rule.

Accidents Happen

Forget politics and Big Brother. The topic everyone talks about in Belgium is road accidents (*accrochage/ongeluk*). Everyone has had one, normally involving the famous rule of priority from the right. Either you are the victim of a stupid law that should have been repealed. Or you are the victim of a stupid driver who shouldn't be allowed on the road. Yet something strange happens after the familiar squeal of brakes and crunch of twisted bumper. A strange silence descends on the neighbourhood. Traffic comes to a halt. People stand watching with their dogs. Everyone is expecting road rage, because that is what would happen in the United States or Britain. But the Belgian response is one of weary resignation. The drivers get out and inspect the damage. A bent bumper. A dented door. They confer and decide to settle *à l'amiable*, using the *constat d'accident*. This takes time. Being Belgian helps. They understand forms. The drivers lean the document on their car bonnet, sketching out a diagram of the accident for their insurance company. At some point, a police car will arrive, siren whooping. The forms are signed. The cars move off. Belgium once again shows the world how it solves disputes. Not with violence, but with an official form. It's all very civilised, if a little odd.

Urban Motorways

Some Belgians are proud of the city motorways in Brussels. Others argue that they have destroyed the city. The inner ring motorway provides a fast route around the old centre, following the line of the city walls and punctuated by exit ramps named after vanished city gates. Other fast routes radiate out from the inner ring, often using elevated viaducts or long tunnels. These routes were built in the 1960s and 1970s, and allowed thousands of city workers to commute from the Brabant countryside. But the urban motorway programme was suddenly halted in the late 1970s, leaving two unfinished projects at the end of the E411 to Luxembourg and the E19 to Antwerp. The city is now pursuing a different approach to traffic planning that will make it increasingly difficult to commute by car.

Tunnels

Brussels has a complex system of 31 road tunnels built in the 1950s and 1960s. Most are not marked on maps, because they run under existing avenues, and it is not always clear where they lead. The main tunnels follow Avenue Louise, Boulevard Leopold II and the inner ring. There are also tunnels linking the European Quarter with the motorway system. One tunnel runs under the Parc du Cinquantenaire, while another connects with the E40 motorway. There is even a mysterious side tunnel that leads into the Berlaymont car park. While the tunnels can be a fast route through the city, they often get blocked during the rush hours or after heavy rain storms. They are also frequently closed because of accidents, especially late on Saturday nights.

A Car-Free Future?

Brussels currently has some of the worst traffic conditions in Europe, but the authorities are working cautiously on various options to reduce the traffic. The most impressive initiative is the annual car-free day held in late September, when drivers in Brussels are forced to leave their cars at home for the day (unless they can secure a permit from their local town hall). The aim is to allow people to try out alternative forms of transport, such as public transport, cycling, walking or even roller blading.

The authorities briefly considered introducing a congestion charge modelled on London's, but finally decided against the idea. Yet there is a certain modest interest in car-sharing and urban bicycles. The city streets are also being redesigned to encourage people to walk longer distances. But it will take many more years before Brussels becomes as appealing for pedestrians as Amsterdam or Copenhagen.

Online Route Planners

Travel routes in Belgium can be planned online at various sites. Some are better than others.

Brussels Public Transport The Brussels public transport authority has a route planner on its website www.stib.be. Click on *'Meilleur itinéraire'* and indicate the departure place and destination. The planner indicates how much walking is involved as well as public transport links. It includes detailed area maps showing the recommended route.

Flanders Public Transport The Flemish transport authority De Lijn has a Dutch-language route planner that covers public transport in Flanders and Brussels at its website www.delijn.be. Click on 'reisinfo' and then 'routeplanner'.

Wallonia Public Transport The Walloon transport authority TEC has a French-language route planner that covers all public transport networks in Belgium. www.infotec.be

Belgian Roads The Mappy route planner provides detailed route descriptions and maps for journeys in Belgium and across Europe. www.mappy.be

European Roads The Michelin route planner provides a detailed travel itinerary from your home address to anywhere in Europe. www.viamichelin.com

Driving Highlights

Like it or not, you are probably going to spend some time driving in Brussels. It may not be enjoyable, but there are occasional highlights to enjoy as you cross the city.

Cinquantenaire Arch The best driving view in Brussels is obtained in the Rue Belliard tunnel, when drivers heading out of Brussels emerge for a brief glimpse of the Cinquantenaire Arch before plunging below ground again.

Citroen Garage An interesting example of automobile architecture is the Citroen garage on Place de l'Yser, built in 1934 on the edge of the Brussels canal.

Car museum For a fine collection of vintage cars, visit the Autoworld car museum in the Cinquantenaire Park.

Montgomery The Montgomery roundabout is no place for sightseeing, but look out for the statue of Field Marshall Montgomery.

Drive-in cinema A drive in cinema is set up every year under the arch in the Cinquantenaire Park. Those without cars can perch on stools.

Triumphant Arch at the Cincuentenario Park

Tax

Taxes in Belgium are among the highest in the industrialised world. A single person loses about 65% of their income in taxes and social security contributions. Belgians inevitably grumble about the high taxes, and devise complicated tax avoidance arrangements, but they are deeply unwilling to change the system. Why not vote for a party that promises lower taxes? The reason is simple. High taxes bring a high quality of life. Belgians have access to an excellent health system, a good education system, excellent motorways, an efficient rail network, extensive childcare and a generous retirement system. Take away the high taxes and Belgium would be a much less comfortable society.

Foreign companies based in Belgium often complain about the punitive tax regime. For a single executive on a fixed three-year contract, it may seem unfair that they are contributing heavily to a system that will provide them with few benefits. The Belgian government keeps promising to cut personal income tax, but never this year. Many US companies are beginning to get impatient, though the predicted exodus has still not happened.

Belgians may accept high taxes as inevitable, but they are keen to avoid paying them. There is a widespread commitment to tax avoidance schemes. Companies often offer employees fringe benefits, instead of a salary increase, because it avoids tax. You might be offered a company car, lunch vouchers or a lobster at Christmas - anything to avoid paying more to the state.

Those on high incomes with private property tend to do well under the Belgian system, as there is no wealth tax or capital gains tax. This has turned Belgium into an unexpected tax haven, attracting rich tax exiles from the Netherlands and France. The Dutch tend to settle in the rich suburbs north of Antwerp, close to the Dutch border, whereas the French prefer the urban Parisian charms of Ixelles and Uccle.

Tax Returns

Tax forms (*declaration/aangifte*) are normally sent out every year in May and relate to income earned the previous calendar year. The forms have to be returned by mid June. If you don't receive a form, you should contact the Ministry of Finance.

Everyone is entitled to a basic exemption of €6,040 regardless of their status, with further exemptions granted to married employees and those with children. A family with four dependent children qualifies for a total exemption of €11,980. The taxable income is calculated by taking total worldwide earnings and deducting social security contributions and a percentage of private pension contributions. Professionals can deduct expenses up to a maximum of €3,290 and working parents can deduct 80% of crèche costs. The tax authorities also allow 69% of restaurant expenses to be deducted, which sometimes leads to an unseemly scramble to grab the bill at the end of a meal.

The basic tax rate begins at 25%, rising to 30% on incomes above €6,950 and reaching 50% for anyone earning more than €30,200. Residents also pay a municipal tax, which is normally calculated at 6% of total taxable income.

About one million Belgians filled in an online tax return in 2006. This is done using a special registration number that comes with their digital ID card. Most foreign residents have not yet been issued with a digital ID card, and so have to submit an old-fashioned tax form by post.

The government tax website has extensive information on taxation (www.minfin. fgov.be), but only in French and Dutch.

Other Taxes

Home owners pay a local property tax (the *précompte immobilier/onroerende voorheffing*) which is calculated on the property's estimated rental value (*revenue cadastral/kadastral inkomen*). The tax varies by municipality, from 20% to 50%. Home owners are also charged an annual regional tax, although families with three children or more can apply for an exemption. The regional tax in Brussels was cut by 50% in 2007 to €89 per household. The self employed pay an additional regional tax.

Most goods and services are taxed at 21%, but a lower rate of 6% applies to basic necessities, such as food, transport, children's clothes and renovation work on older houses.

Tax Advice

You may need help from a tax adviser if you are working freelance or setting up a small company. Several tax advisers offer specialised advice to expatriates.

Ernst & Young: A dynamic company with experts in every area of tax. The company deals with small and large companies. ☎ 02.774.91.11; www.ey.be

Fidum: A small and friendly company that specialises in tax advice and bookkeeping for small and medium-sized companies in Brussels. Its advisers are fluent English speakers. www.bvbafidum.com

PricewaterhouseCoopers Europe: Global firm offering tax and legal advice. ☎ 02.710.42.11; www.pwc.com

Tax Offices

Ministry of Finance: (Ministère des Finances/Ministerie van Financien) Central Administration of Direct Contributions, CAE Tour des Finances, Boîte 32, Boulevard du Jardin Botanique 50, 1000 Brussels; ☎ 02.210.22.11; www.minfin.fgov.be

Tax Contact Centre: Useful helpdesk for resolving simple tax question. ☎ 0257.257.57.

Local Tax Offices: your main contact as a tax payer is with the local tax office in your commune. The offices are listed in the white phone book. Turn to the section 'Ministères/Ministeries', then look under 'Finances/Financien', and finally search for the section 'Contributions Directes/Directe Blastingen'. The offices are listed by commune.

Crime

For a city of one million people, Brussels is a relatively safe place to live. Yet, like any big city, it has black spots for crime. Watch out in the Gare du Midi, where pickpockets frequently rob tourists. Keep hold of your suitcase at all times, and be particularly careful with laptops and cameras.

The streets around the Gare du Midi can be rough, so it is best to take a taxi or tram into town. The metro is reasonably safe at all times, though you should take care in deserted stations late at night.

Be on your guard in the European Quarter and other international office districts, as thieves often target these areas. Handbag snatching is the main problem, but people are also robbed at cash machines. The area around the European Parliament is a desolate district where crimes can happen.

Parents should warn their kids to take care with expensive electronic items, such as iPods or mobile phones. Car owners should also remove valuables when they park, and hide all evidence of mobile phones and satellite navigation equipment.

The city has a considerable number of homeless people and beggars. Begging is not a crime, and an estimated 250 people regularly ask for money on the streets of Brussels. One third of these people are Belgian, while the others are mainly Roma gypsies.

Drunken behaviour is not a big problem in Brussels. You may come across a few noisy revellers on a Saturday night in downtown Brussels, but the mood is normally relaxed compared to an average provincial town in Britain. The one dangerous street in Brussels is the Rue de la Longue Vie in the Matonge district of Ixelles. This neighbourhood is used by drug dealers and has a violent reputation.

Despite living in a relatively safe society, Belgians are extremely worried about urban violence and meaningless murders. The country remains haunted by the case of Marc Dutroux, who murdered four young girls and kidnapped two others in 1996. While other countries have experienced similar horrors, the Dutroux case was exacerbated by police incompetence and bureaucratic indifference. The abduction and murder of two more girls in Liege in 2006 revived uncomfortable memories of the Dutroux case, though the police response was far more efficient this time. As soon as a child goes missing in Belgium, parents can contact Child Focus (www.childfocus.be) as well as the police. This ensures that the authorities act efficiently and posters of the missing child are displayed throughout the country.

Palais de Justice

The Charlemagne building

Working in Brussels

- Brussels is one of best cities in Europe for English-speaking job seekers.
- The EU and Nato are of course large employers, but there are also over 2,000 international companies representing sectors such as telecommunications, high tech, banking, legal services and pharmaceuticals.
- The Belgian economy is currently booming and many employers are finding it hard to fill posts, especially in sectors like banking.
- Salary levels in Brussels are relatively modest compared to other capital cities, but rents are much lower.
- Work found through an employment agency is often poorly paid, but it can sometimes lead to an interesting permanent job.
- Brussels is full of people who want to learn English; if you have a TEFL certificate you can easily pick up a job teaching English in a language school.
- Setting up a company used to be a long procedure that took many weeks to complete, but a company founder can now do almost everything in three to four days.
- Taxes in Belgium are among the highest in the industrialised world; a single person loses about 65% of their income in taxes and social security contributions.
- Business in Brussels is generally conducted in English, though companies in Flanders often use Dutch as their working language, while Walloon firms will almost always use French.

Finding a job

For all its quaint charm and cobblestone squares, Brussels is a city of international business and politics. Home to Nato and the European Union, it has a booming economy with more than 2,000 international companies representing sectors such as telecommunications, high-tech, banking, legal services and pharmaceuticals.

A Guide to the Market

Brussels is one of the most promising cities in Continental Europe for English-speaking job seekers. As capital of Europe, the city is home to thousands of international companies and organisations, most of them using English as their main language. Many expatriate jobs require serious qualifications, ideally a university degree and at least one foreign language. English is widely spoken in business, but French is still used extensively in the European institutions and a certain fluency in Dutch is a useful asset. About 40% of Brussels jobs need candidates who speak both French and Dutch.

You can find some exciting opportunities in Brussels if you are a graphic designer, IT specialist or qualified lawyer. There are also plenty of jobs for anyone with a talent for drafting corporate press releases or translating company reports from French to English. Brussels job adverts tend to contain a daunting list of requirements, including, almost inevitably, several years of experience. But it is worth applying even if you do not have all the talents sought. One organisation recently advertised in Brussels for a communications manager, specifying that the candidate was expected to *'speak English on at least mother tongue level.'*

The internet is probably the best place to begin a job search. You can find several hundred jobs in international organisations listed on websites such as Eurobrussels and Jobs in Brussels. Some international jobs are also listed in the weekly *The Bulletin* and posted on the website www.bulletin.be. You can also find some interesting jobs, including temporary posts and unskilled work, in the classified section of the Belgian website www.xpats.com.

You have to bear in mind that thousands of people across the world are looking online at the same sites, so these jobs will inevitably receive a huge number of applicants. It's necessary therefore to develop some strategies for finding the jobs that others don't know about.

Many jobs in Brussels don't ever get advertised in the media, particularly in small companies, think tanks and research organisations. It is worth sending off a CV to organisations in your field of interest, even if there are no vacancies advertised. Check organisations' websites regularly, as jobs are often announced there. Make a phone call to the company's HR department and ask for the email address of the person in charge of recruitment. That way your application is more likely to be noticed. It's even worth asking to speak to the head of HR to find out if there are any job opportunities. Most HR departments welcome unsolicited CVs and file away promising candidates in case a job suddenly comes vacant. Always send a covering letter explaining why you are interested in the organisation, or your CV will probably get binned. It may be worth sending your CV by post, rather than email, as many emails are deleted unread or lost in a junk file. A letter is also quite a rarity these days, so it might be given more than a cursory glance.

The Belgian economy is currently booming and many employers are finding it hard to fill posts, especially in sectors like banking. The situation is expected to become worse in the next five years, as many baby boomers are due to retire, and there are not going to be enough younger Belgians to fill the gap. But the vacant jobs often require very precise skills and qualifications. If you have what is wanted, you should be able to negotiate a very attractive contract.

What to Expect

Salary levels in Brussels are relatively modest compared to other capital cities, but rents are much lower. The average Belgian takes home about €1,400 a month, while salaries in international companies start at around €1,800 a month. Belgium's high rate of taxation is the main reason for the low salaries. But many companies offer various perks, such as a company car, transport allowance or meal vouchers. Nine out of 10 Belgian employees receive some form of perk on top of their basic salary. Those in large companies generally get better benefits than employees in small firms. For the average employee, the tax-free benefit represents about 20% of their total income. A company car boosts income by about 5%, while meal vouchers - worth about €6 a day - represent a further 4%. Most Belgian employers also offer a Christmas and summer bonus of about one month's salary, which makes the annual salary worth about 14 times the basic monthly salary. Hospital insurance is another frequent perk.

The biggest shock for many expatriates is that they may have to work in their first Belgian job for an entire year without any holiday, as entitlement is based on the previous working year. It's worth talking this over with your future employer before taking up a new post. Most jobs also have a probationary period of six months. Once the trial period is ended, employees are normally offered a permanent contract (*durée indeterminée*).

WORKING IN BRUSSELS

Who's better off?

Many expatriates from Britain and the US are shocked at the high rates of tax and health insurance in Belgium, combined with relatively low salaries. Yet people in Belgium seem to be better off than those on similar salaries in Britain. So what's the explanation? One important factor is the cost of housing, which is much lower in Belgium. Many other costs are lower, such as a new car, wine, public transport, the opera, childcare, a drink in a night club. The end result is that many Belgians enjoy a higher standard of living while working shorter hours and earning lower salaries.

Not everyone does equally well under the Belgian system. It works well if you can take advantages of all the benefits, such as childcare, healthcare and a pension. It is much less favourable if you are a single self-employed person who plans to leave Belgium in a few years.

Parental leave in Belgium is not particularly generous compared to other European countries. Both parents are entitled to three months paid leave per child, which has to be taken within the child's first three years. The state pays just over €78 a month in child benefit for the first child, while the average cost of raising a child in Belgium is estimated at €400 a month.

Job Search Sites

Computer Futures Specialised site for IT jobs in Belgium. www.computerfutures.be

Eures New EU-funded job search site listing unfilled vacancies across the European Union plus Norway and Iceland. The focus is on employers who are looking for foreign staff. Most jobs listed in Belgium are in the public sector. www.europa.eu/eures

Jobs in Brussels Well-designed site with extensive list of jobs for English-speaking professionals in sectors such as IT, marketing, law and science. www.jobsinbrussels.com

Jobs-Brussels Specialised site with extensive list of jobs in EU institutions, international organisations, lobbying companies and law firms. www.jobs-brussels.com

Euro Brussels Extensive list of jobs in EU institutions and international organisations. The best site to track down a job with one of the many small international organisations based in Brussels. www.eurobrussels.com

Actiris Official employment centre for Brussels Region with three offices in the city. Its website lists job offers in Brussels, mainly in catering and retailing. Residents of Brussels Region can post CVs online and get advice on finding work, including part-time jobs. Actiris also issues language cheques, which can be used to pay for language lessons. The cheques are only issued once you have been offered a job that requires fluency in a language you don't speak. www.actiris.be

References Belgian site aimed at professionals. Most jobs require candidates to speak French and possibly also Dutch. But there are occasional jobs aimed at English native speakers that don't require another language. You can track them down by going to the *'recherche approfondie'* page and ticking the box 'anglais' in the 'langue de l'annonce' section. www.references.be

StepStone Extensive online job site in four languages (including English). Worth posting your CV here as Belgian companies needing staff urgently often search StepStone for suitable candidates. www.stepstone.be

Vacature Weekly jobs supplement published on Saturday by *De Morgen*. Filled with job adverts posted by Flemish employers. Mainly technical, sales, marketing and banking jobs. Most require good spoken Dutch, but the occasional job is aimed at fluent English speakers. www.vacature.com

LinkedIn Join this free US networking site to post your profile online, find out about job offers and get the inside information on potential employers. www.linkedin.com

Xing German business networking site that allows members to post a profile online, search for job offers and contact other members. Similar to LinkedIn, but with a more European membership. Organises occasional events in Brussels and Antwerp where you can build up a network of professional contacts. www.xing.com

Employment Agencies

Working for a job agency is often poorly paid, but it can sometimes lead to an interesting permanent job. Many employment agencies have offices in Brussels. Those in the Avenue Louise and Avenue des Arts districts serve the international companies based in Brussels.

You can simply wander around looking at the job offers posted in the windows, which cover areas such as IT, secretarial, call centres and warehouse work. The job offers usually specify the different languages required. It is not uncommon in Belgium for a fairly low-paid job to require fluency in three or four languages.

Employment agencies also put job offers in newspapers and magazines. *The Bulletin* regularly carries lists of vacancies in Brussels from local agencies. They normally involve secretarial or administrative jobs. The ads give the office location and salary, but don't mention the employer. This is to avoid candidates approaching the company directly, and depriving the agency of its fee. But you should check the office location before you begin, as some places are hard to reach without a car.

The agency charges the employer a hefty fee for providing a suitable candidate, while the job applicant normally pays nothing.

Temp Agencies

Daoust Friendly agency based in the Galerie de la Porte Louise with all types of temp work. ☎ 02.513.87.55; email louise@daoust.be; www.daoust.be

Manpower Large group with job centres across Brussels, some specialising in a particular sector. ☎ 02.639.10.70; www.manpower.be

Rainbow Careers Recruits multilingual secretaries and administrative staff for major Belgian companies. ☎ 02.735.41.54; email jobs@rainbow-careers.be; www.rainbow-careers.be

Randstad The largest employment agency in the country, with some jobs for English speakers, mainly involving secretarial or call centre work. ☎ 02.229.14.00; www.randstad.be

Secretary Plus Agency specialising in highly qualified secretarial staff and administrative assistants. ☎ 02.346.44.64; email brussel@secretary-plus.be; www.secretary-plus.be

Startpeople Large Belgian agency with nearly 100 offices across the country, formerly called Creyff's. ☎ 02.218.83.70; email Brussels@startpeople.be; www.startpeople.be

Unique Friendly Belgian employment agency handling a wide range of office jobs. ☎ 02.227.10.66; email info@unique.be; www.unique.be

Interim Management

Brussels has a number of interim management (IM) agencies specialising in short-term contracts for skilled professionals. These offer challenging positions for people with substantial experience in areas such as IT, management, finance and human resources. You might be called upon to replace a department head on maternity leave, or supervise the setting up of a new warehouse. Contracts are likely to run from three to nine months. IM jobs generally call for flexibility, confidence and many years of experience.

Contacts

Artemis Network: ☎ 02.640.89.49; email info@artemisnetwork.be; www.artemisnetwork.be

Robert Half: ☎ 02.626.11.11; email Brussels-im@roberthalf.be; www.roberthalf.be

Robert Walters: ☎ 02.511.66.88; www.robertwalters.com

Employment Opportunities

Working for the EU

Many thousands of Europeans want to work for the European institutions in Brussels. An EU job offers many tempting benefits, including a generous salary, low tax rate, job security, steady promotion, free international schooling and perhaps the opportunity to travel. Yet these are not always dream jobs. You may have to work in a dull office, frustrated by petty bureaucratic rules. Anyone who thrives on creativity and challenge may find the atmosphere stifling.

All European Commission jobs, including temporary contracts, are posted by the European Personnel Selection Office on the EU website (www.europa.eu/epso). All candidates for EU permanent posts have to sit a public examination known as the *concours*. The first step is to take a written multiple-choice exam, sometimes partly in a second language.

Many candidates fail to get past the first hurdle because of lack of preparation. You really need to have excellent knowledge of EU institutions and history to pass the procedure. It's worth taking time to read the *European Voice* or an EU news website such as www.euobserver.com to keep in touch with EU issues. You can also find much of the information you need in the official EU publications available free at one of the EU Info Points in Britain or Ireland (or any other EU country). The most useful publications are 'Europe in 12 lessons' and 'How the EU works'. The information can also be found on the internet at the EU's official website (www.europa.eu).

Some determined candidates go further and buy one of the many books that provide advice on passing the entry exam. The Europa Bookshop at Rue de l'Orme 1, close to Mérode metro station, has a large selection of books devoted to EU exam techniques (www.libeurop.be). Another approach is to subscribe to an online tutoring package such as www.eu-careers.com. You might find it equally useful to look at the sample tests from previous years published on the Europa website. The free 45-minute audio tour of the European Parliament is another useful source of information for anyone cramming for the *concours*.

Those who pass the first hurdle then go on to an interview. Candidates are likely to be tested on their knowledge of EU procedures or asked for their views on Turkey's accession or the EU Constitution. Successful candidates are put on a reserve list, and offered posts as they become available.

Many candidates at this stage simply wait patiently to hear from the Commission, but applicants from countries like France, Belgium and Italy understand better how the system works. They start phoning contacts in the relevant department, hoping to improve their chances of selection. Bear in mind that some candidates never get offered a job even though they have passed the *concours*. The reserve list expires after one or two years and those who have not been successful have to apply again.

Working for the European Parliament

The European Parliament provides a steady stream of jobs for people who want to work in European politics. Some jobs involve working as an assistant to a European Member of Parliament (MEP), possibly doing fairly routine office management, or perhaps in a more demanding position as a political adviser or speechwriter. Some MEPs occasionally offer temporary intern posts to young people, lasting a few months.

These jobs are normally based in Brussels, but they almost inevitably involve some travel to Strasbourg, since MEPs have to spend one week every month attending parliamentary sessions in Strasbourg. You will normally be expected have the same political outlook as the MEP and speak their language fluently. Since you are working in a small office, you need to be very flexible about working hours and duties.

Other jobs in the European Parliament involve working for one of the political parties. You might find yourself working in an international team as a research assistant, policy adviser or press officer.

Working for Nato

The 26-member North Atlantic Treaty Organisation, Nato, has its headquarters in eastern Brussels and employs some 5,500 people. Many are military personnel and diplomats, but Nato also employs secretaries, interpreters, translators and web designers. Jobs are advertised on the Nato website (www.nato.int) under 'recruitment'. The headquarters occupy a grim functional building on the edge of the city, behind a high-security fence. Public transport connections are poor, so that about 80% of staff drive to work every day. Most choose to live in the eastern suburbs to avoid a long daily commute. The Belgian government plans to begin work on a new Nato headquarters in 2008. This futuristic glass building, designed by the Chicago firm Skidmore, Owings and Merrill (SOM), will contain a swimming pool and crèche. But it won't be completed until at least 2012. Until then, staff will have to put up with the existing gloomy offices.

Temporary Contracts

The EU institutions often need temporary staff to work on a particular project. The jobs are listed as Temporary Agents (TA) or Contractual Agents (CA). These posts are limited in duration, although the contracts can be renewed. The salary is generally much lower than an EU official's. Candidates have to pass a preliminary test to qualify, but this is simpler than the *concours*.

Industry Lobbying

Now that Brussels has become a legislator in areas such as finance, pharmaceuticals and environmental law, international companies are beginning to realise the need to keep in touch with EU policy. This has led to an explosion in the number of professional lobbyists based in the European Quarter. It's impossible to give precise figures, but some experts believe that there may be as many as 15,000 lobbyists, compared to some 22,000 EU civil servants. Yet lobbying in Brussels is not the aggressive game that is played in Washington. The job of a Washington lobbyist is to influence legislation, whereas those that work in Brussels are more likely to spend their days gathering information on EU developments.

Some of the lobbying is carried out by law firms that have developed an expertise in this area. There are also specialised consultancies that lobby on behalf of particular companies. A few of the world's largest corporations have opened their own office in Brussels to protect their interests. Many European industrial associations also have offices in Brussels. You could find yourself working in Brussels on behalf of an organisation like the paper industry, the chemical sector or European trade unions.

Lobbying jobs require excellent communication skills and a close understanding of the EU legislative process. They tend to go to people who have already worked in EU institutions, know how to argue coherently and have a Blackberry laden with contact names.

NGO Lobbying

Businesses aren't the only bodies that lobby in Brussels. Many international charities and campaigning organisations have set up an office in the Capital of Europe. Their aim - like business lobbyists - is to keep track of EU policies in their area of concern and to add their voice to the EU legislative process. These offices are generally small and friendly places to work. The pay might be relatively modest, but they offer a chance to work for a worthwhile cause.

Mostly, these jobs are not advertised. They tend to go to people who already work for the organisation and are enthusiastic about the cause. The first step might be to work as a volunteer in an organisation you admire. Within a short time, you could have the expertise needed to take on a position in Brussels.

Regional and City Offices

More than 200 regions and cities have an office in Brussels. Some are small offices employing a single person, but others are much larger. The work involves monitoring EU policies and providing information for local authorities, companies and universities on EU policy and subsidies. Some 30 offices represent British regions and cities, including London, Thames Valley and Scotland. Seven people work for London's European Office in Brussels, while Scotland House has a staff of 11. Ireland is represented by the Irish Regions Office (www.iro.ie). Most jobs in these offices are taken up by local government staff, but you might be considered for a post if you can show EU work experience, enthusiasm for the organisation and an ability to speak foreign languages.

Think Tanks

Several think tanks are based in Brussels close to the EU institutions. Their role is to carry out political research, organise conferences and nudge EU policy in a particular direction. They include Friends of Europe, the European Policy Centre and BRUEGEL. They tend to need researchers with qualifications in an area related to EU policy, but they also have occasional openings for interns.

Banks

Most international banks have a large office in Brussels. They often require in-house English speakers to translate documents. You can sometimes find these jobs listed on the bank's website. The Bank of New York frequently advertises for English-speaking staff to work in its Brussels office. The bank provides training and offers the possibility of working a four-day week. Other major banks to approach include Fortis, ING, Dexia and Citibank.

Embassies

Brussels is full of embassies. Almost every country in the world has at least one embassy to Belgium, but many have a second embassy working with the EU and even a third embassy to Nato. The embassies need a range of staff, including secretaries, drivers and managers. Some embassies only employ their own citizens or require candidates to be fluent in the national language. Jobs are often posted on the embassy website.

Teaching English

Brussels is full of people who want to learn English. You can easily pick up a job teaching English teacher in a language school as long as you have a TEFL certificate. Most schools take on freelance teachers and offer €20-€25 for one hour of teaching. Begin by approaching the large schools such as Berlitz, The English Academy and Fondation 9. Some schools such as Berlitz (www.berlitz.be) have job offers online. Working as an English teacher in a Belgian school is more difficult, as you must have a teaching diploma recognised by the Belgian education ministries. But you can give private English lessons without any qualifications. Your chances of finding students are better if you can offer specialised tuition in an area such as business English or legal English. The easiest way to find students is to put up a notice in a local supermarket or advertise in the classified section of www.xpats.com under 'lessons and languages'. Bear in mind that most students are looking for teachers to work in the evenings or on Saturday mornings. The rate for freelance teachers ranges from €10 to €25 an hour.

Tutoring

Students at international schools often need extra tutoring in subjects like English, maths and science. You might be able to find work by putting a free classified ad on www.xpats.com under 'lessons and languages'. The rate is about €30 to €35 an hour.

Editing

Most companies and international organisations in Brussels produce large volumes of material in English, including newsletters, press releases and websites. You can often find a full-time job with a large Belgian company working as an English language specialist in their communication department. Many banks and Belgian legal firms have at least one English speaker on their staff. Or you can work as a freelance editor, taking on projects for several organisations. The current rate for freelancing ranges from €30-€50, depending on the type of work.

Translating

Brussels is full of translators who spend their lives translating documents, websites and company reports. Many are employed by translation agencies, but some work as freelance translators. Rates vary depending on the type of document, with legal texts and marketing brochures costing much more than literary translations. Translators in Brussels normally charge €0.10-€0.14 per word of original text. Some prefer to set an hourly rate of €30-€40.

Journalism

More than 1,000 foreign journalists work in Brussels. They mainly report on the European Union, but occasionally have to cover major Belgian news stories. In recent years, as the EU has expanded, some newspapers and TV stations have increased their coverage of EU news. The main news outlets are international newspapers, TV stations, news agencies and websites. Some journalists have a salaried position as a Brussels correspondent, while others work freelance for several media. But the market is becoming more difficult: newspapers are cutting back on foreign correspondents because of the high costs and the internet is starting to have an impact on journalism jobs, since people can now find free news online.

Journalists who want access to the EU institutions have to get an EU press card. This is granted to anyone who can provide a national press card, a letter signed by their editor and a photocopy of their passport or ID card. The EU press card allows you to attend daily EU press briefings in the Breydel building. It also gives journalists access to the press bar, where the Commission's press officers give informal interviews.

English is the main working language for journalists based in Brussels. It is also useful to speak French if you are dealing with the EU. Anyone reporting on Belgian politics should try to speak some Dutch, or they will end up with a distorted impression of the country filtered through the French language media.

It is almost impossible to find a job working for a major newspaper in Brussels without previous experience and good contacts. But you might be able to write for various specialised publications as a freelance Brussels correspondent.

IT

Brussels has millions of computers that need to be serviced, repaired and upgraded. Anyone with IT skills should be able to find a good job with a company or freelance work as an IT specialist. The growth areas include web design, telecommunications,

PC support and IT consulting. Begin the search by looking at the specialist recruitment sites Computer Futures (www.computerfutures.be) or ICT Vacatures (www.ictvacatures.be).

Childcare

Brussels is full of expatriate working couples and single parents looking for someone to look after their children. Some require a nanny with professional qualifications, while others are looking for an au pair who will live as part of the family. Other child-minding work involves picking up children after school, looking after sick children or babysitting. You can advertise your services or look for childcare opportunities in the classified ads pages of www.xpats.com under 'children'. It helps if you drive a car, as many expatriate families live in leafy suburbs outside Brussels where public transport is limited.

Multinationals

Many of the world's multinationals have their European headquarters in Brussels, including Microsoft and Intel. Some of these offices are small, employing just a few people, but Toyota has a large European headquarters in eastern Brussels which employs 1,600 people from 52 countries in a range of departments, from sales to research (www.toyotajobs.com).

Hotel Work

Brussels has a large number of international hotels with a steady turnover of staff. Some jobs such as chambermaid or kitchen help require very little training, but a post as receptionist will call for fluency in at least four languages (French, Dutch, English and German). The large international hotels frequently need staff - try the Crowne Plaza Brussels City Centre, NH Hoteles group, Renaissance Brussels Hotel, Sheraton Brussels, Radisson SAS Royal Hotel, Radisson SAS EU Hotel and Marriott Brussels. Begin by calling the hotel and asking for the email address of the head of human resources. Then send a CV and covering letter, either by email or post. Follow this with a phone call. You may impress the HR head with your determination.

Bed and Breakfast

Brussels has an oversupply of business style hotels, but an acute shortage of bed and breakfast accommodation. The Region is currently trying to meet demand by encouraging locals with large houses to offer B&Bs to tourists. Anyone with a large house can apply to go on the register, but no more than three rooms can be let under current legislation.

Running a Restaurant

New restaurants open in Brussels every week, but some close down within a few months. You need to provide consistently good food in a popular area of town to be guaranteed a steady income. The investment is high, regulations are fierce and competition pushes prices down, especially at lunchtime. Yet some expatriates have succeeded, such as Irish chef Mary Fehily, who opened the gourmet lunch restaurant Mary's on Rue Lesbroussart in the 1990s. She quickly built up a reputation for serving imaginative dishes using the freshest ingredients, bought at the daily market in Laeken. The restaurant continues to thrive, now under the name Fresh Company, while Fehily also runs a highly successful catering business (www.fresh-company.be). As well as catering for several events a week, she sometimes cooks private meals for MEPs. But this is not a job for softies. Her working day begin at 6.15am and ends at 8pm or even later. "The phone never stops ringing," she says. "It's madness."

Artists

Belgium is a highly cultured country with an extensive network of art galleries and art fairs. An artist can work as a self-employed person, or work for a series of individual clients on temporary employment contracts.

Cultural Jobs

Brussels has several large cultural institutions that employ a range of creative people, including stage designers, graphic designers and web page designers. The arts organisations are often looking for talented freelancers to join their teams. Information on vacancies and application procedures at the Palais des Beaux-Arts can be found on the Bozar website (www.bozar.be) under 'jobs'.

Airport Jobs

Brussels Airport is currently booming as new low-cost airlines arrive and freight services increase. You can often find a temporary job handling baggage or cargo, though you may have to work at awkward hours. Job offers are posted on the Brussels Airport website, www.brusselsairport.be/en/jobs.

Freelancing

Belgium employment law is not particularly favourable to freelancing. Those who choose to work as an independent have to pay high medical insurance costs and income tax and receive fewer benefits than those with job contracts. Yet many people in Belgium are self employed, including most doctors and dentists. The main opportunities for foreigners are in the knowledge sector, such as editing, translating and teaching English. You face a certain amount of bureaucracy before you can start working, but Brussels is a relatively good city for establishing contacts and networking. Once you have done some work, you may find that your telephone never stops ringing.

Letting Property

Many Belgians and some expatriates invest in property as a way of generating income. But is a Belgian buy to let a good idea? The market is currently oversupplied with rental accommodation (as is clear from the bright orange *A Louer/Te Huur* signs in every neighbourhood). This means that a lot of people are making nothing from their investment. Yet there are many people looking for quality rented accommodation in attractive neighbourhoods. You may need to upgrade an apartment to attract tenants, but you will not have to worry about income tax if you rent an unfurnished apartment in Belgium. Your only cost is an annual propery tax (*précompte immobilier*) based on the assessed rental value.

Interns

Working for Nothing? Many young people come to Brussels to work as an intern (stagiaire) in an international organisation. The pay is minimal (or even nil), but these positions offer work experience and an opportunity to make useful professional contacts. Interns normally receive a monthly allowance which barely covers their monthly rent, though some organisations are more generous. The internship normally lasts three to six months.

Most international organisations in Brussels have a system of internships. Some of the vacant posts are listed on the job website www.eurobrussels.be. The European Commission runs the world's largest internship programme (www.ec.europa.eu/stages). Since it was set up in 1960, it has recruited more than 25,000 *stagiaires* from 65 countries. Every year some 1,200 people get taken on for a five-month internship. Applicants have to be university graduates with a good command of at least two EU languages. The Commission offers interns a basic allowance and travel expenses. As well as gaining work experience, interns are taken to visit other EU institutions such as the Parliament. The internships run twice yearly - in the early summer (March to July) and the winter months (October to February). But it's not easy to get a place. Competition is ferocious, and nine out of ten applicants end up with a rejection letter.

The European Parliament is another big source of intern posts. The parliamentary programme offers young people the chance to get an insight into European politics and perhaps secure a permenent position as a political assistant. The parliament offers about 600 internships every year. Most involve working as assistants for European political parties or individual MEPs. Not all posts are paid and only one in ten applicants is successful. Full details of training schemes are given on the European Parliament website (www.europarl.europa.eu). Go to the English homepage and click on 'quick links' and then 'traineeships'.

About 20-25 graduates are taken on twice a year to work as interns at Nato headquarters in Brussels. The interns have to be nationals of one of the Nato member countries. These posts offer citizens of Canada and the United States an opportunity to work in Europe. Full details are given on the Nato website (www.nato.int) under 'internship programme'.

Internships can also be found working for one of the non-governmental organisations (NGOs) in Brussels. This provides invaluable work experience as well as useful contacts, and could eventually lead to a permanent position in the organisation. The British Council often has openings for interns advertised on its website (www.britishcouncil.org/brussels).

Over the years, interns have built up their own network of contacts in Brussels. New arrivals can sometimes take over a rented room from a departing intern.

Unskilled

Brussels does not have a wide choice of work for unskilled people. Most jobs require a basic knowledge of French and Dutch. But many Irish pubs need people to work behind the bar or wash dishes in the kitchen. If you have a good phone manner, and can put up with a certain degree of tedium, you might find a job working as an English speaker in a call centre. Begin your search by looking in the windows of the temp agencies on Avenue Louise.

Voluntary Work

There are plenty of opportunities for voluntary work in Brussels. Most campaigning agencies have an office in the city, including Greenpeace, Amnesty and UNICEF. Look up their websites for details of opportunities for volunteers.

Studying

Brussels is an ideal city for anyone who wants to study a new language or take a degree. It's a relatively cheap city for students, with an enormous range of courses on offer, many of them taught in English. With its cosmopolitan population, you can make contacts easily and get in touch with people who work in the EU institutions and Nato.

Business districts

Who Works Where

The gleaming offices of the EU institutions are concentrated in the European Quarter around Rond Point Schuman, while many of the big legal and insurance firms occupy offices on Avenue Louise. Another cluster of skyscrapers rises above Place Rogier and the Gare du Nord, including the landmark Belgacom tower and the World Trade Centre. Further out of town, computer companies and other service industries are clustered around the Nato headquarters, close to Brussels Airport.

Despite the booming economy, property developers have kept ahead of demand, so there is still a plentiful supply of high-quality office space at a fraction of the cost of London, Paris or Amsterdam.

Schuman Most of the important EU institutions are located around Rond Point Schuman, as are many regional offices and lobby groups. The quarter has every type of restaurant and bar, but food shops are scarce. The metro provides a fast link to the city centre and trains run out to some suburban stations.

Madou The European Commission has moved into a tower at Madou metro station. Other organisations may soon open offices in the neighbourhood, which has good restaurants and public transport.

Midi A business district has grown around the Gare du Midi, but the area has a bad reputation and many companies are still reluctant to lease buildings here. Transport connections are excellent but the streets around the station can be grim after dark.

Nord This modern office district was planned in the early 1970s on the site of the red light district close to the Gare du Nord, but abandoned after the oil crisis, with just two isolated towers completed. For many years, this was a dismal area of abandoned buildings, brothels and offices where no one wanted to work. The district was finally finished in the 1990s, but it is far from an ideal work neighbourhood. Most offices are occupied by the regional governments of Flanders and Brussels, but the Belgacom tower brings some corporate flair to the neighbourhood.

Tour et Taxis The industrial zone around the port of Brussels is being rapidly turned into a vibrant new office district. The main development is the conversion of a bonded warehouse on the Tour et Taxis site known as the Royal Depot. This vast industrial space where imported coffee and tea was once stored has been converted into 100 loft-style offices. The result is a stylish complex that includes two restaurants, six shops, two crèches and a bank. But the area suffers from a total lack of public transport and can be sinister after dark.

Louise The sweeping boulevard created by Leopold II in southern Brussels is lined with large company offices in gleaming glass buildings. This is a favourite address for international law firms and advertising agencies. Access is easy for car drivers, but public transport can be slow.

Beaulieu An EU office complex on the Avenue de Beaulieu next to the E411 motorway. The six office buildings are close to Beaulieu metro station, but the neighbourhood is dull and rooms overheat in the summer. *'It's a long way from anywhere,'* says one unhappy EU civil servant.

Evere Evere became an office hub in the late 1960s when Nato moved into an abandoned hospital on a main road to the airport. The location appeals to international computer companies and accountancy firms, who like the fact that the airport is ten minutes away. The European Commission is now moving into the neighbourhood in a bid to ease pressure on the European Quarter. More than 1,000 translators and secretarial staff now work in three modern office buildings on the Rue de Gèneve, but most are far from happy with the location. Public transport links are bad and the neighbourhood is dull. Yet the Commission is stubbornly pressing ahead with plans to acquire other offices in the neighbourhood.

Cité Administrative A huge office development near the city centre that took 25 years to build. Typical of the period when it was planned (1958), it features long monotonous office blocks built on a windswept concrete plaza above a depressing car park. The offices were once occupied by Belgian civil servants, but now lie empty. The Region wants to revitalise the area, with a mix of offices, apartments and shops. But the work won't begin until 2012.

Diegem An important office cluster outside Brussels, close to the airport, and popular with freight companies. It's a bleak area, with poor public transport and nowhere interesting for lunch.

Career advice

Focus Volunteers offer career advice and networking opportunities for English-speaking expatriates in Belgium. Much of the effort goes into helping trailing spouses find work in Brussels. Members pay €95 a year. www.focusbelgium.org

Landmark Office Buildings

Berlaymont The European Commission's headquarters, constructed in 1969, stands on the site of a 17th-century convent. Renovated at the turn of the 20th century, it remains the architectural symbol of the EU.

Charlemagne The American architect Helmut Jahn transformed a dull European office building by wrapping it in a high glass screen. Several EU DGs are based here.

Madou Plaza A 1965 concrete tower on Place Madou, transformed by the architects Assar and Archi 2000 into a sleek 33-floor glass building for 1,200 European officials. It takes its name from the 19th century Belgian artist Jean-Baptiste Madou.

Stephanie Square Two identical office buildings provide a monumental gate on the Avenue Louise. Designed in 1973 and 1986 in a style influenced by the Vienna Secession.

Central Plaza A beautiful place to work next to Central Station. The pleasing curved tower was designed by the Brussels firm Art + Build in 1998. It replaces the 1962 'Lotto Tower', torn down despite protests from architectural historians. The new tower had to be eight floors lower than its predecessor because of the city's tough new policy on building height. A consortium of three international law firms – Stibbe, Herbert Smith and Gleiss Lutz – occupies the top seven floors of the 15-floor complex.

Dexia Tower The Dexia bank has its headquarters in a stylish glass tower with a jagged profile overlooking Place Rogier. Designed by Jean-Michel Jaspers, it replaces the 1958 'Martini Tower,' which some considered a landmark of modern Belgian architecture.

WORKING IN BRUSSELS

Employment regulations: how to get legal

Work Permits

No work permit is needed if you come from one of the 18 countries belonging to the European Economic Area (see *Setting Up Home*). But it's more difficult for people outside the EEA to get legal employment. They first have to find a job in Belgium and then ask the employer to apply for employment authorisation from the regional employment office.

The employment office will only grant a permit if there are no suitable EU nationals for the position. If the job is a senior management position or a research and development post, the permit is normally issued without too many problems. Other jobs are harder to get approved. The application process can take anything from four to 12 weeks to complete. Three different types of work permit are issued.

Permit A This allows someone to work for any employer in Belgium for an unlimited period of time. But it is hard to obtain. You can get one if you are married to someone who holds a work permit A, or married to an EU national resident in Belgium. Otherwise you must have lived and worked legally in Belgium for five years without any interruption.

Permit B This is the standard work permit issued to non EU citizens. It is valid for one year for one employer. If you change jobs, your new employer has to apply for a new B permit and you may have to return to your home country to apply again for a residence visa. The permit can be renewed four times, after which you should qualify for an unlimited A permit.

Permit C Seasonal agricultural workers and domestic staff often get issued with a work permit C, allowing them to work for several employers for one year. This type of permit is normally not renewable.

Work Regulations

Once you have found a job, there is usually a probationary period of two weeks for blue collar workers and anything between one and 12 months for white collar workers, depending on the salary level. Someone earning less than €32,200 a year will normally have a trial period lasting one to six months, whereas those on higher salaries might be on trial for six to 12 months. During this period either side can terminate the employment contract by giving seven days notice.

The average working week is 38.5 hours, although longer working hours are common, particularly in international institutions. Many organisations expect staff to work longer hours without paying overtime.

In Belgium, employees have to work for one year before any holiday entitlement is granted. The amount is calculated on the basis of the number of months you worked in the preceding year. If you worked a full calendar year, you are then entitled to a minimum of 20 days of holiday.

Every employee is entitled to take off the ten official holidays. Many of these are Catholic holidays, shared with France, Italy and Germany. They rarely coincide with legal holidays in Britain. If an official holiday falls on a Saturday or Sunday, employees are entitled to one day off at another time.

Qualifications

Many professions in Belgium are strictly regulated so that you can only practise if you have a qualification or certificate. Some professions such as medicine have been harmonised across the EU, so that qualifications are automatically accepted in every country. Most EU university degrees and diplomas are accepted in Belgium. You can contact one of the National Academic Recognition Information Centres if you experience problems.

Some professionals find it difficult to transfer to Belgium. You may have to sit a test, or prove to the authorities that you have the proper level of training. You may also be required to sit a language text in the official language of the region.

Most professions have a national professional body which can advise you about the situation in Belgium. They can also put you in touch with the appropriate professional body in Belgium.

Belgium has a surprising number of regulated professions that require you to have a certificate or professional qualification. They include photographers, second-hand car dealers, plumbers, electricians and bricklayers. Anyone who plans to run a café, restaurant or food shop is required to provide a professional qualification. Before you start work in a regulated profession, you have to register your qualifications with the Brussels Chamber of Commerce. This may involve contacting a certified translator to translate your qualifications into French or Dutch.

Self-Employed

Belgium employment law is not particularly favourable to freelancing. Those who choose to work as an independent face high medical insurance costs and taxes. Yet this is becoming an increasingly popular option for people because it avoids commuting, allows flexible hours and makes it easier to raise children.

EU citizens have the right to be self employed in Belgium. The procedure for registering has been simplified, so that you just need to register as a self-employed person at a business one-stop shop (*guichet d'entreprise unique*). You may have to prove that you are capable of managing a business, but can normally satisfy this requirement by producing a university degree or professional qualification. You then get a VAT number (unless you are in an exempted profession, such as journalism). All that remains is to register as a self-employed person with a Belgian health insurance fund.

You can work as a fully self-employed person, or run your business as a complimentary occupation. Many Belgian couples work as a self-employed partnership, with one spouse assisting the other.

The procedure is naturally not as easy for people from a non-EU country. You have to begin by applying to the Belgian consulate in your home country for a professional card (*carte professionale/beroepskaart*). You also have to provide a passport, medical certificate and police certificate (*certificat de bonne vie et moeurs/bewijs van goed gedrag en zeden*). You will also have to provide some sort of evidence of a business plan, previous experience and professional qualifications relating to the activity. If, for example, you want to work as a freelance writer, you will be expected to produce copies of published work and proof of income over several years. The professional card is valid for up to five years. Once you have it, you can apply to the consulate for a visa.

Payments made to the health insurance fund as a freelance worker cover health care, family allowances and pension. But the system is not particularly generous towards self-employed people. The basic insurance package only covers major health expenses (*grandes risques/grote risico's*), so many self-employed people take out a second insurance for minor health problems (*petites risques/kleine risico's*). The state pension is also lower for the self employed, so it is worth taking out a complimentary pension (*pension complémentaire/aanvullend pensioen*), which can be deducted from tax. Many self-employed people call on a Belgian accountant for help with tax, VAT and deductions.

Au Pairs

An au pair's role is to provide help with childcare in return for accommodation, meals and a small allowance. The aim is to give a young person the opportunity to live in a foreign country, learn a new language and develop their social skills. It is not meant to be a simple job contract.

Anyone from an EU country aged 18-26 can work in Belgium as an au pair. All that is required is a valid passport. The host family is obliged to pay a minimum monthly wage of €450 in return for a maximum of 20 hours a week.

The regulations for people outside Europe are tougher and more costly. The au pair has to apply to the Belgian Embassy for a visa (Schengen Type B) before they can take up a post. Meanwhile, the host family has to apply to the local authorities for an employment authorisation and a work permit (Type B). The au pair also has to register for a language course in Belgium.

Investing in Belgium

Belgium is one of the world's most popular countries for investment, particularly for US companies. This is proved by the most recent figures compiled by the American Chamber of Commerce in Belgium (AmCham), which puts Belgium in fifth position worldwide as a recipient of US investment. Some $6.5 billion was invested in 2005, accounting for almost 160,000 jobs. 'Belgium is a wonderful place to live and work,' says the 2007 AmCham report. *'Its excellent location, skilled work force, solid infrastructure, and open and vivid culture make it a superb destination for companies and families alike.'* Potential investors can obtain advice from the federal government or one of the three regional investment offices covering Brussels, Flanders and Wallonia. The offices employ skilled staff who speak fluent English and can explain the incentives available as well as the tax implications of investment.

Starting a Business in Brussels

Anyone from an EU country is free to start up a business in Brussels. But budding entrepreneurs from non-EU countries face more obstacles. They have to apply for a professional card, which is only granted if the applicant can prove to the authorities that they have a sound business plan and clients in Belgium.

The first step for anyone starting a business is to find a good Belgian notary who can guide you through the legal procedures. You will also need an accountant to ensure that you keep your tax payments and VAT in order.

Several different types of company can be created under Belgian law. The main entities are public limited companies (*société anonyme, SA*), private limited companies (*société privée à responsabilité limitée, SPRL*) and various forms of cooperative companies (*société cooperative*). You require a minimum start up capital of €61,500 to set up an SA and at least €18,550 in the bank to set up an SPRL. The notary fees will add at least €1,000 to your costs.

Setting up a company used to be a long procedure that took many weeks to complete. It isn't any more. The company founder can now do almost everything in three to four days. The first step is to contact a notary, who will advise on the best form of company structure and draw up the title deeds. You then go to a bank and open an account. The final step involves a visit to one of the 21 business one-stop shops (*guichets d'entreprises*) in Brussels, where you will get a company number and help with tax registration and other formalities.

Many startups begin by renting space in one of several business centres in Brussels. These centres are often located in converted industrial buildings shared by a range of young companies. The centres get subsidies from the Belgian authorities and the EU, allowing them to offer cheap rents and free consultation services. There are about six centres in Brussels, including an industrial building in the Dansaert district (www.dansaert.be) and a former wine warehouse in the Marolles (www.ateliersdutanneurs.be).

Now for the question that every entrepreneur dreads. How much will the government claw back at the end of the tax year? The answer is, unfortunately, a lot. You will have to pay direct tax as an individual, which takes away about 50% of your income, company tax rated at 33.99% (which is one of the highest rates in Europe), 21% VAT, and various regional and municipal taxes.

You need to be sure that your business plan will produce enough income to cover all these costs, along with rent, equipment and health insurance. Many Belgian businesses end up defeated by the relentless orange bills, but seven out of 10 startups are still running after five years.

Setting Up a Subsidiary in Brussels

Most companies setting up in Brussels (or elsewhere in Belgium) create a Belgian subsidiary rather than a branch. The main legal difference is that a branch is controlled by the parent company whereas a subsidiary is considered as a separate Belgian legal entity. That means the parent company is liable for the debts of a branch, but not for those of a subsidiary. Subsidiaries also benefit from various tax advantages, such as the right in most cases to repatriate profits without paying withholding tax and exemption from capital duties.

Useful Government Contacts

Federal Public Service Economy - SMEs, Self-Employed and Energy:
Federal government agency offering general advice on investing in Belgium.
www.investinbelgium.fgov.be

Brussels Enterprise Agency: Advice and consultation for companies that want to invest in Brussels. www.investinbrussels.com

Flanders Investment & Trade: Flemish government office offering advice to companies wanting to invest in northern Belgium. www.investinflanders.com

Wallonia Export and Investment Agency: Walloon government office advising companies on investment opportunities in southern Belgium. www.investinwallonia.be

Other Contacts

American Chamber of Commerce in Belgium: Advice and networking opportunities for US companies based in Belgium. www.amcham.be

British Chamber of Commerce in Belgium: Advises British companies based in Belgium and offers excellent networking opportunities. www.britcham.be

European Business Centre: Furnished offices for rent in an attractive building close to the European institutions. www.ebc-youroffice.com

Focus Career Services: Volunteer-run advice centre for anyone planning to start their own business in Belgium. Organises regular seminars, workshops and an annual one-day seminar on setting up your own business in Belgium. Rue Lesbroussart 23, Ixelles; ☎ 02.646.6530; www.focusbelgium.org

Solvit: European businesses can turn to the EU for help if they find themselves caught in a bureaucratic nightmare. The Solvit network is a free online service that helps European entrepreneurs who face administrative problems within the EU market. www.ec.europa.eu/solvit

Enterprising Brussels

Brussels Region is currently encouraging innovative people to set up new companies in the city, especially in areas such as information technology and life sciences. There is, inevitably, a certain amount of bureaucracy involved in setting up a business, but not as much has you might expect. According to the latest Belgian government figures, an entrepreneur can set up a company in Belgium in just under a week. The Brussels Enterprise Agency (BEA) is a government-funded office with a team of clued-up advisers who can guide you though the whole procedure in fluent English. They will also point you in the direction of various subsidies available from Belgian or European funds. The offices are located in Tour et Taxis, a spectacular industrial colossus in the Brussels canal zone. For those still unsure about investing in Brussels, the BEA offers free use of their business centre, consultants and secretarial services for a three-month trial. www.investinbrussels.be.

Five Hot Brussels Companies

Delhaize International supermarket chain founded in Ixelles in 1867. Delhaize continues to supply many Belgians with plump rump steaks and fine Bordeaux wines. Respected for the quality of its food, the group has built up a global network of 2,565 shops in eight countries, including the US.

Kinepolis The Kinepolis story began with the opening of a 24-screen megaplex in Brussels in 1989. The company now has 22 cinemas complexes in five countries across Europe and sells almost 25 million tickets a year.

Delvaux One year older than the Belgian nation, Delvaux started in 1829 as a downtown Brussels shop selling travel luggage. It later turned to leather goods and launched a classic handbag called the brillant at the 1958 Brussels World Fair. It is now based in a former arsenal in Etterbeek and has shops in New York and Tokio. Several Belgian designers have been brought in recently to revamp the collection. www.delvaux.com

Le Pain Quotidien This fashionable bakery and café chain was founded in 1990 by Alain Coumont in a shop in downtown Brussels. It now has branches in almost every Belgian city, as well as outposts in Paris, London, New York and LA.

Leonidas Belgian chocolate company with 1,400 shops worldwide founded by a Greek immigrant who settled in Brussels in 1913.

Is Belgian Bureaucracy Inefficient?

Belgian bureaucrats, like their Italian counterparts, have a reputation for being lazy and obstructive. But the government has made a huge effort in recent years to streamline official procedures and replace form filling with online administration. The results are already impressive. It used to take several months to set up a company in Belgium. It now takes just three days. Many administrative formalities can now be carried out online. There are still problems, but the system normally works with impressive efficiency.

Business etiquette

- Show respect. Be prepared to adjust to a different social and business environment.
- Belgian formality. Belgian society is rather formal and respectful behaviour is the norm.
- Learn the language. Make every effort to learn to speak at least some Dutch or French. It may not be essential for business success, but it helps to make friends.
- Meeting and Greeting. Learn how to address people, and when to shake hands or kiss.
- Negotiations. Prepare your arguments carefully but be prepared to be flexible. Compromise is the key to Belgian life.
- Conversation. Keep your criticisms to yourself unless asked, and don't joke too much.
- Chauvinism. Try to understand Belgian history and the roots of Flemish nationalism – and resist the urge to make anti-Belgian jokes.

Belgians are serious about business, but they like to relax over lunch and get home to their families at a decent time in the evenings. Most Belgians deal with many different nationalities, and they are reasonably tolerant of alternative forms of social interaction. Here are a few basic tips on how to behave in formal business situations.

How to Say Hello Most business encounters begin with a handshake. But Belgians who know each other reasonably well often kiss one another on the cheek in the morning. This ritual can take some time in a large office.

Which Language? Business in Brussels is generally conducted in English, though companies in Flanders often use Dutch as their working language, while Walloon firms will almost always use French.

What to Wear? Brussels is a fairly relaxed environment. Most men wear a jacket and tie to a meeting or job interview, but formal suits are less common. Men looking for the right clothes to wear should visit shops like Maximo Dutti and Crossword. Legal firms and multinationals often have smarter dress codes, but people in translating and the media can wear casual clothes without eyebrows being raised.

Business Cards It's worth ordering some business cards to hand out to people you meet.

Business Style Be careful not to offend Belgians by adopting an aggressive business style. This is a country that has suffered humiliation at the hands of foreign occupiers for centuries. If you appear domineering, a Belgian will immediately adopt strategies to undermine you.

Names Belgians are usually quite formal in business meetings. It's normal to call someone *Monsieur* or *Madame* (*Mijnheer* or *Mevrouw* in Flanders) rather than use their first name.

Respect People from Anglo-American backgrounds are often highly critical of Belgium and Belgian businesses. This is arrogant and will earn you enemies. Belgium has some highly successful companies, and its state services are second to none. Rather than criticise, it's more useful to find out all you can about the positive features of the Belgian system.

Dismissal Companies in Belgium are required to take account of the views of trade unions and works councils. Hiring and firing are relatively complicated processes compared to the Anglo-American system.

Deference Belgian companies are hierarchical structures. The person at the top takes the decisions, while those below follow instructions to the letter. There is often not much room for creativity or criticism.

Compromise Belgium is an extremely complicated country. Even Belgians find it hard to understand. Don't expect things to happen instantly. And be prepared to compromise, just like Belgians have been doing for centuries.

Lunch Business meetings are often held over lunch in a good restaurant. It is perfectly acceptable to drink a glass of wine or a Belgian beer during a working lunch. This is one of the few opportunities you have to meet colleagues informally. The conversation is rarely work related. Belgians prefer to talk about their families, their home town, or their favourite restaurant on the coast.

Holidays Belgians like to work hard, but they are also fond of holidays. You may need to adapt your working methods to fit in with Belgian routines. Most Belgian offices work hardest in the winter months, but become more relaxed around Easter. May is a difficult month to get any serious work done, as the month is dotted with one-day holidays. The months of July and August are also quiet, as most Belgians take three or four weeks off in the summer, leaving the streets of Brussels relatively empty. You also need to be aware that the Belgians, like the French, tend to make a pont (bridge) when a public holiday falls close to a weekend, by taking an extra day off. They also like to leave the office early on a Friday to beat the traffic.

Etiquette in the EU

Working for the EU implies a certain commitment to European values. You should avoid boasting about your own country's achievements or criticising other EU countries. The dress code is relaxed in most EU institutions, but it can vary from one office to another. Scandinavians tend to have a more laid back style, while French, Italians and Spanish are more formal. It makes sense to dress fairly formally for interviews. Once you are in a job, take your cue from your boss and colleagues.

Meeting Venues

As well as 20 or so business hotels with conference facilities, the city has a range of inspiring venues for meetings and dinners, including the vaulted cellars under the Anderlecht slaughterhouse, the Art Deco Plaza cinema, the car museum Autoworld, the Atomium and the Belgian Centre for Comic Strips. But perhaps the oddest venue for holding a business meeting is amid the 250-million-year-old dinosaur skeletons in the Natural Sciences Museum. Some 350 venues in Brussels are listed on the website www.idj.be/catalogue/salles.lasso. Click on *'Consulter ce guide en ligne'* to find addresses and contact details.

Claridge A former Art Deco cinema close to the Madou Tower has been restyled as a venue for parties and product launches. The design features something called digital wallpaper which can turn your digital images into a surprising background décor. www.claridge.be

Cureghem Cellars An impressive complex of vaulted brick cellars below the Anderlecht abattoir. The space can be rented for conferences, receptions and Bruegelian feasts. ☎ 02.521.54.19; www.abatan.be

Hôtel Wielemans A beautiful townhouse off Avenue Louise with a tiled courtyard modelled on the Alhambra. The courtyard can be rented for conferences and receptions for up to 250 people. ☎ 02.403.85.85; email info@art-media.org; www.art-media.org

Plaza Theatre The handsome Plaza Hotel on Boulevard Adolphe Max has restored a spectacular 1930s cinema as a conference venue. The setting is a sumptuous mix of Spanish and Moroccan motifs from the 'Golden Age' of cinema. ☎ 02.278.01.00; email reservations@leplaza-brussels.be; www.leplaza-brussels.be

Résidence Palace The International Press Centre occupies a grand Art Deco apartment complex in the European district. Conferences can be organised in several meeting rooms, while drinks are served around a fountain in a Moorish courtyard. ☎ 02.235.21.11; email info@presscenter.org; www.presscenter.org

Tour et Taxis The Tour et Taxis complex includes some impressive 19th-century industrial spaces for holding meetings and events. Four large sheds can be rented, the cheapest costing just over €2,500 a day. Parking is easy. ☎ 02.420.60.69; email events@tour-taxis.com; www.tourtaxis.com

Directory of major employers

Accountancy

Accenture: ☎ 02.226.72.07; www.accenture.com

Arthur D. Little: ☎ 02.761.72.00; www.adlittle.be; email adlittle.brussels@adlittle.com

Ernst & Young: ☎ 02.774.91.11; www.ey.be

Moores Rowland Europe: ☎ 02.541.07.50; www.mrieurope.com

KPMG: ☎ 02.708.43.00; www.kpmg.be

PriceWaterhouse Coopers: ☎ 02.710.42.11; www.pwc.com

Airport

Brussels Airport: www.brusselsairport.be/en/jobs

Car Manufacture and Heavy Industry

Alcan Europe: ☎ 02.234.39.90; www.alcan.com

Belgian Shell: ☎ 02.508.91.11; www.shell.be

Caterpillar Logistics Services: Vilvoorde ☎ 02.263.46.11; www.catlogistics.com

Toyota: ☎ 02.745.20.11; www.toyotajobs.com

Banking and Insurance

Bank of New York: ☎ 02.545.81.11; www.bankofny.com

Citibank Belgium: ☎ 02.626.51.11; www.citibank.com

Deutsche Bank: ☎ 02.551.65.11; www.deutschebank.be

Fortis AG: ☎ 02.220.86.06; www.fortisag.be

ING Bank: ☎ 02.547.23.92; www.ing.be

JPMorgan Chase: ☎ 02.208.88.11; www.jpmorganchase.com

KBC Bank: ☎ 02.429.17.60; www.kbc.be

Chemical and Pharmaceutical Companies

3M NV: (Diegem) ☎ 02.722.51.11; www.3M.com; info@mmm.be

Eli Lilly Benelux: ☎ 02.548.86.86 ; www.lilly.be

GlaxoSmithKline: (Rixensart) ☎ 02.656.81.11 ; www.gsk.com

Monsanto Europe SA: ☎ 02.776.76.00 ; www.monsanto.com

Pfizer: ☎ 02.554.62.11; www.pfizer.be

Solvay: ☎ 02.509.61.11 ; www.solvay.com

UCB: ☎ 02.559.99.99; email contactucb@ucb-group.com; www.ucb-group.com

Computers and IT

Getronics Belgium: ☎ 02.229.91.11 ; www.getronics.be

Hewlett-Packard Belgium: ☎ 02.729.71.11 ; www.hp.be

Honeywell: ☎ 02.728.26.11; email communications.europe@honeywell.com; www.honeywell.com/europe

IBM Belgium: ☎ 02.225.21.11; www.ibm.com/be

Logica CMG: ☎ 02.708.61.00; email recruitment.be@logicacmg.com; www.logicacmg.com/be/careers

Microsoft: (Diegem): ☎ 02.704.30.00; www.microsoft.com/belux

Oracle Belgium: (Diegem) ☎ 02.719.12.11; www.oracle.be

Siemens: ☎ 02 536.21.11; www.siemens.be

Unisys Belgium: ☎ 02.728.07.11; www.unisys.com

Food and Drink

Colgate-Palmolive Belgium: ☎ 02.674.92.11; www.colgate.com

Nestle Belgilux: ☎ 02.529.52.52; www.nestle.be

Clothing and Furniture

Ikea: ☎ 02.712.15.00; www.ikea.com

Levi Strauss & Co Europe: ☎ 02.641.60.11; www.levistrauss.com

Nike Europe: ☎ 02.646.44.05; www.nike.com

Law Firms

Baker & McKenzie: ☎ 02.639.36.11; www.bakernet.com

Berwin Leighton Paisner: ☎ 02.792.20.11; www.blplaw.com; email info@blplaw.com

Cleary Gottlieb Steen & Hamilton: ☎ 02.287.20.00 ; www.cgsh.com

Clifford Chance: ☎ 02.533.59.11; www.cliffordchance.com

DLA Piper Rudnick Gray Cary: ☎ 02.500.15.00; www.dlapiper.be

Eversheds: ☎ 02.737.93.40; www.eversheds.com

Freshfields Bruckhaus Deringer: ☎ 02.504.70.00; email brussels@freshfields.com; www.freshfields.com

Hammonds: ☎ 02.627.76.76; www.hammonds.com.

Herbert Smith SA: ☎ 02.511.74.50; www.herbertsmith.com.

Leboeuf Lamb Greene & MacRae: ☎ 02.227.09.00; www.llgm.com.

Linklaters & De Bandt: ☎ 02.501.94.11; email europe.info@linklaters.com; www.linklaters.com

Loyens: ☎ 02.743.43.43 ; www.loyens.com

Lovells: ☎ 02.647.06.60 ; www.lovells.com

Norton Rose: ☎ 02.237.61.11; email info@nortonrose.com; www.nortonrose.com

Slaughter & May: ☎ 02.737.94.00; www.slaughterandmay.com

Squire Sanders & Dempsey: ☎ 02.627.11.11; www.ssd.com

McDermott Will & Emery/Stanbrook: ☎ 02.230.50.59; www.mwe.com

Taylor Wessing: ☎ 02.289.60.60; email brussels@taylorwessing.com

Thompson Hine: ☎ 02.626.32.80; www.thompsonhine.com

Management Consultants and Accountants

Accenture: ☎ 02.226.72.07 ; www.accenture.com

Berkley Associates: ☎ 02.219.04.98; email berkleyassociates@skynet.be; www.berkleyassociates.be

Boston Consulting Group: ☎ 02.289.02.02 ; www.bcg.com

Deloitte & Touche Consultants: (Diegem): ☎ 02.800.29.16 ; email beinfo@deloitte.com; www.deloitte.com

Egon Zehnder International SA: ☎ 02.648.00.83; www.egonzehnder.com

Ernst & Young: ☎ 02.774.91.11; info@be.ey.com; www.ey.com/be

KPMG: ☎ 02.708.43.00; www.kpmg.be

Mercer Human Resource: ☎ 02.674.89.11 ; www.mercerhr.be

McKinsey & Company: ☎ 02.645.42.11; www.mckinsey.com

PriceWaterhouseCoopers: ☎ 02.710.46.42; www.pwc.com/epa

Towers Perrin: ☎ 02.749.30.00; www.towersperrin.com

Public Relations

Burson-Marsteller Brussels: ☎ 02.743.66.11; www.bmbrussels.be

European Communication Strategies: ☎ 02.674.22.50; email mail@cs-brussels.com; www.cs-brussels.com

DDB Group Belgium: ☎ 02.761.19.00; www.ddb.be; email info-ddb@ddb.be

Hill & Knowlton Belgium: ☎ 02.737.95.00; www.hillandknowlton.com

Media+: ☎ 02.678.24.24; email info.belgium@mindshare.com; www.mindshareworld.com

Ogilvy Public Relations Worldwide: ☎ 02.545.65.00; www.ogilvy.be

Weber Shandwick Worldwide: ☎ 02.282.16.21; www.webershandwick-eu.com

NGOs

Amnesty International EU Office: ☎ 02.502.14.99; email amnesty-eu@aieu.be; www.amnesty-eu.org

Friends of the Earth Europe: ☎ 02.542.01.80; email info@foeeurope.org; www.foeeurope.org

Greenpeace European Unit: ☎ 02.274.19.00; email European.unit@diala. greenpeace.org; www.greenpeace.eu

WWF European Policy Office: ☎ 02.743.88.00; email wwf-epo@wwfepo.org; www.panda.org

City and Regional European Offices

London European Office: ☎ 02.650.08.00; email europeanoffice@london.gov.uk; www.london.gov.uk

East Midlands European Office: ☎ 02.735.99.38; email info@ eastmidlandseurope.org; www.eastmidlandseurope.org

East of England European Partnership: ☎ 02.289.12.00; email brusselsoffice@ eastofengland.be; www.eastofengland.be

Scotland Europa: ☎ 02.282.83.02; email information.desk@scotent.co.uk; www.scotlandeuropa.com

West Midlands in Europe: ☎ 02.740.27.10; www.westmidlandsineurope.org

International Estate Agents

Cushman & Wakefield: ☎ 02.514.40.00; www.cushmanwakefield.com

DTZ: ☎ 02.629.02.68; www.dtz.com

Jones Lang LaSalle: ☎ 02.550.25.25; email receptionbru@eu.jll.com; www.joneslanglasalle.com

Knight Frank: ☎ 02.548.05.48; www.knightfrank.com/belgium

CB Richard Ellis: ☎ 02.643.33.33; email cbre.brussels@cbre.com; www.cbre.be

Telecommunications

Base: ☎ 0484.006.200; www.base.be

Belgacom: ☎ 02.202.41.11; www.belgacom.be

BT Worldwide Ltd: (Zaventem) ☎ 02.700.22.11; email info.belgium@bt.com; www.bt.com

International Health Clubs

Aspria: ☎ 02.542.46.66; email hr@aspria.be; www.aspria.be

John Harris Fitness: ☎ 02.219.82.54; email office@johnharrisfitness.be; www.johnharrisfitness.be

World Class Fitness Belgium: ☎ 02.551.59.90; email info@worldclass.be; www.worldclass.be

Press

Ackroyd Publications: ☎ 02.373.99.09; email info@ackroyd.be; www.ackroyd.be

Bloomberg News: ☎ 02.285.43.00; email belgium@bloomberg.net; www.bloomberg.com

Euractiv: email recruitment@euractiv.com; www.euractiv.com

Reuters Ltd: ☎ 02 287 66 11; www.reuters.com

Language Schools and International Schools

BEPS International Schools: ☎ 02.648.43.11; email info@beps.com; www.beps.com

Berlitz: ☎ 02.649.61.75; www.berlitz.com

British School of Brussels: ☎ 02.766.04.30; email reception@britishschool.be; www.britishschool.be

International School of Brussels: ☎ 02.661.42.11; email web@isb.be; www.isb.be

Distribution Centres

DHL: ☎ 02.715.50.50; www.dhl.be

Federal Express Europe: ☎ 02.752.71.11; www.fedex.com

Hotels

Hilton Brussels: ☎ 02.504.11.11; www.hilton.com

Marriott Brussels: ☎ 02.516.90.90; www.marriott.com/brudt

Sheraton Brussels: ☎ 02.224.31.11; email reservations.brussels@sheraton.com; www.sheratonbrussels.be

Thon Hotels: Norwegian group with four large hotels in Brussels. ☎ 02.506.91.11 (Stanhope Hotel); email info@stanhope.be (www.thonhotels.be for general information on the group)

Think Tanks

European Policy Centre: ☎ 02.231.03.40; info@theepc.be; www.theepc.be

Friends of Europe: ☎ 02.737.91.45; info@friendsofeurope.org; www.friendsofeurope.org

The Centre: ☎ 02.548.02.60; www.thecentre.eu

Company searches

US Companies

The American Chamber of Commerce in Brussels publishes a yearly list of its 1,700 members and all American firms operating in Belgium at €160 (surface mail within Benelux); additional postage is payable outside Belgium. Order from: American Chamber of Commerce, Rue du Commerce 41, 1000 Brussels; ☎ 02.513.67.70; www.amcham.be

Belgian Companies

The Belgian Employers' Federation issues a free list of member organisations. Obtainable from: *Verbond van Belgische Ondernemingen-Federation des Entreprises Belges*, Rue Ravenstein 4, 1000 Brussels; ☎ 02.515.08.11; email info@vbo-feb.be. The VBO-FEB website (www.vbo-feb.be) gives internet addresses of member organisations.

All Companies

A detailed list of all businesses in Belgium can be found using the Kompass business to business search engine (www.kompass.com).

WORKING IN BRUSSELS

Time off

- Brussels is a city best discovered on foot since only then do you notice the architectural details, odd shops and little corners that look like Bruges.
- Foreign films are always shown in the original language, usually with subtitles in French and sometimes also in Dutch.
- Brussels has in the Palais des Beaux-Arts one of the world's oldest multifunctional cultural centres, which contains one of the best concert halls in the country.
- The acclaimed Théâtre de la Monnaie is considered one of the great opera houses of Europe.
- The city also has much to offer lovers of contemporary dance, jazz, art galleries and museums.
- Comic books are regarded as a serious art form in Brussels: the first thing to greet tourists when they step off the Eurostar at Gare du Midi is a huge Tintin mural.
- Children will find plenty to amuse themselves including parks with playgrounds, dedicated skateboarding rinks, bowling alleys and nearby theme parks.

Where to take visitors

You can find just about anything you want in this city of one million people. There are Cuban bars, Japanese movies, Asian supermarkets, market stalls selling organic wine, city farms, Moroccan pastry shops, Art Nouveau tours, gay tea dances, cartoon murals, city bikes and children's drama groups.

> **Plamena Mangova, Bulgarian pianist, interviewed in *The Bulletin***
> Brussels is a little paradise, not too hectic and impossibly noisy like other capitals, yet at the same time with fantastic cultural traditions. There's something quite bohemian about its atmosphere, which I think is why so many truly great musicians choose to stay here.

Sights

When friends come to stay, you need to show them the main sights and museums of Brussels. A coffee on the Grand'Place sets the right tone for the start of the visit. Then stroll in the Galeries St Hubert looking at the shops. Now head uphill to the Musical Instruments Museum to listen to painted harpsichords and *krummhorns* before eating lunch on the roof terrace. Then, time permitting, cross the street to the Fine Arts Museum for a quiet look at the Bruegels and Magrittes.

Yet there's more to discover in this city if you have the time to explore. There are about 80 museums for rainy days, ranging from the stunning to the downright odd. The city is also generously provided with parks, some of them formal while others invite romantic rambles.

What to do with Visitors

Late Breakfast Impress your visitors with the rustic farmhouse interior of a Pain Quotidien café-bakery. Any branch will do, but the one on Rue Dansaert is perhaps the most fashionable. The branch on the Sablon has ample space and a sunny conservatory.

Street Market Show your visitors one of Europe's last authentic flea markets on the Place du Jeu de Balle. You can find every imaginable category of useless item, including fax machines that will never work again, damp copies of the 1977 Brussels telephone directory and wedding photographs of Belgian couples taken when Leopold II was still on the throne.

Flemish Art If visitors are keen to look at Belgian art, propose a trip to the Museum of Fine Art (www.fine-arts-museum.be), which has a superb collection of paintings by Bruegel, Rubens and Magritte. Watch out for lunchtime closing times, with the old art section closing from 12-1pm, while the modern art rooms are shut from 1-2pm.

Brasserie Lunch Consider lunch in Brasserie Horta, next to the Comic Strip Museum, for traditional Belgian cooking served in an airy Art Nouveau brasserie. Or book a table at 't Kelderke on Grand'Place for plain Belgian steaks, large black pots of mussels and possibly the best frites in town.

Cool Shops The St Géry Quarter is the place to take someone with an eye for clothes. Wander down Rue Dansaert to look at the Belgian design shops and take a look at Rue des Chartreux for more quirky boutiques. Don't miss the hats in Christophe Coppens window at 2 Rue Léon Lepage.

Belgian Style Dazzle guests with a stroll in one of the most beautiful shopping arcades in Europe. The Galeries St Hubert is lined with elegant shops selling books, chocolates and clothes. There are also cafés, a cinema, a restaurant and a theatre.

Urban Walk Take a stroll through the quiet streets behind Grand'Place, avoiding the impossibly busy Rue de l'Etuve and heading instead down the sinuous Rue du Marché au Charbon. Pause where it crosses Rue du Lombard to point out the supersize comic strip murals painted on nearby walls. Continue down Rue du Marché au Charbon to discover the lovingly restored St Jacques Quarter.

Frites Introduce your visitors to the art of the frite by taking them to Friterie de St Josse under the church on Place St Josse. As you wait in the queue, explain that the secret of perfect Belgian frites lies in the choice of potato and the technique of double frying. Don't forget to ask for mayonnaise.

Secret Museum Hardly anyone knows about the Charlier Museum in St Josse (www. charliermuseum.be). This strangely seductive house was built in the late 19th century for a Belgian art collector. It's filled with *fin de siècle* paintings, and occasionally stages small but intriguing exhibitions. Closed at weekends.

History Lesson Take visitors to the edge of Waterloo battlefield and explain how the course of world history changed in these empty fields on a damp June day in 1815.

Eccentric Art Try taking visitors to the eccentric Wiertz Museum in Ixelles. The museum occupies the former studio of Antoine Wiertz, a 19th-century Belgian artist who saw himself as a second Rubens. One gruesome work represents an impoverished Belgian mother cooking her baby in a pot. Another shows Napoleon in Hell.

When it Rains Pass a rainy day wandering through spectacular rooms at the Cinquantenaire Museum, where you will find reconstructed Gothic interiors, an Art Nouveau shop, Roman temple, Egyptian burial chamber, and, lurking in a dark corner, an immense Easter Island statue.

Rue de Flandre

The Rue de Flandre used to be one of the busiest streets in Brussels, leading from the Porte de Flandre, the old city gate, to Grand'Place. Everyone who came from Britain – including Wellington, Byron and Brontë – passed this way. Some of the houses have hardly changed in the past three centuries, especially those down the narrow Medieval side alleys. The street is now almost free of traffic, and feels slightly forgotten. People visit Rue Dansaert and Place Sainte Catherine, but they often miss the Rue de Flandre. Yet it's worth taking a look at this typical old Brussels street before the inevitable gentrification happens. You find a little shop where they mend broken zips, a place where they sell traditional wedding dresses, and a shop that mends bicycles. But how long will they survive? The old buildings are already being taken over by art galleries, cool restaurants and Flemish bars.

Secret Brussels

Place des Martyrs This 18th-century cobbled square was shamelessly left to rot for many decades. Now the buildings have been restored as government offices and luxury apartments, leaving just one crumbling house occupied by a stubborn Belgian woman. A sunken crypt in the middle of the square, surrounded by four statues of weeping women, commemorates the Belgians who died in the 1830 Revolution. A volunteer guard can sometimes be seen watching over the monument. He'll tell you the secret history of the square if you ask.

Musée Magritte The modest Brussels townhouse where René Magritte painted some of his most famous Surrealist canvases. The rooms contain furniture and other items that once belonged to the Magrittes. Rue Esseghem 135, Jette; tel: 02.428.2626; www.magrittemuseum.be

Saint-Gilles Town Hall Brussels has some impressive town halls, but none more so than the Hôtel de Ville in Saint-Gilles, which is modeled on a French Renaissance château. Go in one of the side doors and climb the monumental staircase. The building is filled with paintings and sculpture by artists who once lived in Saint-Gilles. You will find Symbolist murals, Art Nouveau sculpture and a fragment of a painting of the 'Battle of Waterloo'. Open Monday to Friday 9am-5pm.

Cercle des Voyageurs It's just a dozen footsteps from the Manneken Pis, yet this café somehow remains a secret place. Push open the heavy front door and you enter the lofty front room of an old Brussels townhouse dating from just after the 1695 bombardment. It feels like a private club more than a café, with big armchairs, bare wood floors and a vaguely tropical mood. Its aim is to serve as a meeting place for international travellers – hence the row of clocks showing the time in different cities and the long table in the library spread with world maps. Excellent Lavazza coffee, but watch out for the odd opening hours. Rue des Grands Carmes 18, central Brussls; ☎ 02.514.39.49; www.lecercledesvoyageurs.com

Vuylbeek An ancient stream flows through the Forêt de Soignes, just to the south of Brussels. It's just 15 minutes on foot from the nearest tram stop, yet it feels as if you are walking in the deep Ardennes. Take tram 94 to Coccinelles and turn down the cobbled lane.

Sculpture in Place des Martyrs

Magritte in Brussels

Bored in Brussels? Why not spend a day tracking down the haunts of René Magritte. The Belgian artist was born in a Walloon industrial town in 1898, but, apart from a brief spell in Paris, he spent most of his life in Brussels. Magritte struggled for many years to make a living, first as a wallpaper designer and later as an artist. Money was in short supply, and he and his wife Georgette rented a modest apartment in the quiet suburb of Jette. Georgette filled the house with cheap imitation Louis XV furniture, while René set up an easel in the tiny dining room. They lived here for 23 years before moving to a larger house in Schaerbeek.

The house in Jette was bought by two Antwerp art dealers in the 1990s and restored to its original state. You won't find any original paintings here, but you can admire the room where Magritte painted a train coming out of a fireplace, and the staircase that appears in 'The Forbidden Reading'. The upstairs rooms contain a little museum filled with odd mementoes (including the pipe that inspired Magritte's classic 'Ceci n'est pas une pipe').

Some of Magritte's Brussels haunts are still standing. The Café Greenwich has barely changed since Magritte went there to play chess and sell paintings (unsuccessfully, on both counts). The Fleur en Papier Doré was another favourite café. A new Magritte Museum is due to open in autumn 2008 in a restored neo-classical townhouse on Place Royale. It will display more than 200 paintings, many of them bequeathed to the Musée des Beaux-Arts by Georgette. René and Georgette are buried in Schaerbeek cemetery, not far from the Nato headquarters. A street near the cemetery is called Rue René Magritte, though it has no links with the artist.

Urban rambles

Brussels is best discovered on foot. It's only then that you notice the architectural details, odd shops and little corners that look like Bruges. Several organisations offer guided tours through different areas of the city. Arau (www.arau.org) is one of the best. Their guides tell you about the history, the stylish Art Nouveau architecture and the political blunders. The Brussels Art Nouveau bus tour in English on Saturday mornings immerses you in the fabulous architectural style of *fin-de-siècle* Brussels. But there are other groups that do different things. Itinéraires (www.itineraires.be) offers tours, mainly in French, on themes like Gay Brusssels, Tintin and Jewish Brussels. Brukselbinnenstebuiten (www.brukselbinnenstebuiten.be) takes people on Dutch language tours into hidden corners of the Marolles, Molenbeek and St Géry. You can even take a boat tour through the Port of Brussels organised by Brussels by Water Rivertours (www.rivertours.be).

The Brussels Card

Tour the city's sights over a long weekend with a Brussels Card tucked in your pocket. With this €30 card, you have free entry to the city's main museums, along with discounts in shops and restaurants. But the best part of the deal is that you have free use of public transport for 72 hours. It's the perfect opportunity to take a look at some of those secret corners of Brussels that no one ever talks about, like the overgrown cemetery on the Dieweg in Uccle and the wild northern edge of Jette. There are also cheaper versions of the card valid for 24 or 48 hours.

TIME OFF

Cinema

Brussels has some good cinemas where they screen films from every country you can name. The foreign films are always shown in the original language, usually with French subtitles, sometimes also with Dutch. Most Hollywood films get shown on Brussels screens, but the bad ones are quickly dropped. Cinema audiences in Brussels are a sophisticated lot, and they happily watch experimental films from far-off regions, or classics from the early days of the movies. Hollywood films usually get screened in Brussels a few months after they premiered in London and New York, but alternative European films are often shown in Brussels long before they reach the art cinemas of London.

Brussels used to have cinemas in every quarter, but most were wiped out by the arrival of television, including the giant Metropole on Rue Neuve (now a branch of Zara). Some of the former cinemas are still standing, often converted into supermarkets or clothes shops, but a few can still be identified by the concrete awning above the entrance (where queuing audiences once sheltered from the rain).

The cinema sector suffered a new assault in 1988 when the Bert Claeys group built the world's first megaplex on the northern edge of the city. The 24-screen complex offered the public free parking in a giant car park, comfortable seats and the best sound quality in Europe.

The small city cinemas soon began to shut down, leaving just a handful of survivors. But the old cinemas then began to fight back. The UGC refurbished two complexes on Place de Brouckère and Avenue de la Toison d'Or, while the independent Vendôme made a few improvements to its interior. Many cinemas screen films throughout the day, beginning as early as 11am.

Downtown Cinemas

Actor's Studio A small two-screen arts cinema hidden in a bland shopping arcade. A cosy place to catch reruns of highbrow movies by Spanish and Iranian directors. Petite Rue des Bouchers 16 and Rue de la Fourche; ☎ 0900.27.854.

Arenberg A sublime Art Deco cinema located in the elegant Galeries St Hubert. They like to show obscure films in Farsi and Serbo-Croat, but they may have to revise their policy as the cinema teeters ever closer to bankruptcy. Galerie de la Reine 26; ☎ 02.512.80.63; www.arenberg.be

Aventure A run down cinema in a shopping arcade. The equipment is ancient, but they continue to show some serious films. Galerie du Centre 57; ☎ 02.219.92.02.

Nova No one thought that this alternative cinema, housed in a former theatre, would last more than a season. Yet it has survived more than ten years, bringing a steady diet of edgy alternative movies to Brussels. This is the kind of cinema where they will show a Lithuanian film from the 1970s that was last screened in Berlin when the Wall was still standing. Rue d'Arenberg 3; ☎ 02.511 27.77; www.nova-cinema.org

UGC De Brouckère This is the last big cinema in downtown Brussels, where they show the latest films from Hollywood and France. It was built in the 1930s as a giant 3,000-seat cinema, but the UGC group split it up in 1982 into 12 smaller cinemas. They kept part of the old cinema, which is now named Grand Salle Eldorado. This is the place to watch the big blockbusters, surrounded by gilded Congo-style frescoes. Place de Brouckère 30; ☎ 0900.10.440; www.ugc.be

Uptown Cinemas

Film Museum The Brussels Film Museum has one of the largest film archives in the world. Founded by the Belgian director Henri Storck in 1938, it nurtures more than 100,000 copies of feature films and documentaries from the earliest days of cinema. The museum screens several films every day in two tiny rooms inside the Palais des Beaux-Arts. Silent movies are normally shown with live piano accompaniment. Tickets are cheap, but the limited seats sell out fast. Rue Baron Horta 9; ☎ 02.507.83.70; www.cinematheque.be

Flagey The old radio broadcasting building on Place Flagey has become the place to catch edgy European arthouse movies by directors whose names barely register on the Hollywood radar. Several annual film festivals have moved to Flagey, including Anima and the European Film Festival. Watch out for summer screenings on the roof. Place Ste-Croix; ☎ 02.641.10.20; www.flagey.be

Styx This tiny neighbourhood cinema in a back street of Ixelles screens quality films in an auditorium that barely holds 30 people. You can sometimes be the only person in the room. Rue de l'Arbre Bénit 72, Ixelles; ☎ 0900.27.854.

UGC Toison d'Or A large cinema complex in two separate locations on the Avenue de la Toison d'Or. The cinema received a complete facelift in 2000, making it more comfortable but no less of a warren. They tend to show French and American hits, but the occasional offbeat film gets a brief showing. Avenue de la Toison d'Or 8; ☎ 0900.10.440; www.ugc.be.

Vendôme A small cinema with five screens in the heart of the African quarter. It tends to show highbrow French and Spanish films, and has a weakness for Woody Allen. Chaussée de Wavre 18, Ixelles; ☎ 02.502.37.00 (after 2pm).

Suburban Cinemas

Movy Club A neighbourhood cinema in a residential suburb that should have closed down decades ago. It's kept going by an eccentric owner who sells tickets and then disappears into the projection room to start the film. Heating bills are something he can't afford and regulars know to wear woolly sweaters. Rue des Moines 21; ☎ 02.537.69.54.

Stockel A small local cinema that puts on a programme aimed mainly at French-speaking audiences. Avenue de Hinnisdael 17; ☎ 02.779.10.79.

Kinepolis The luxurious 24-screen complex on the northern edge of Brussels mainly screens mainstream Hollywood movies, but it shows the occasional Flemish or Walloon film in one of the small theatres. The car park is vast, yet often totally full. Heysel; ☎ 0900.00.555; www.kinepolis.be

Film Festivals and Events

Brussels has several small-scale film festivals every year featuring the rare, the forgotten and the weird.

Anima A serious film festival at Flagey devoted to cartoon films from all over the world. www.folioscope.awn.com

Brussels International Festival of Fantasy, Thriller and Science Fiction Not for the nervous, this festival laps up some of the goriest movies ever made. As well as screening more than 100 films, they organise a body painting competition and a Vampire's Ball. Held in various venues including Tour et Taxis and Cinema Nova. www.bifff.org

Gay and Lesbian Film Festival A serious selection of gay-themed films that rarely get screened on the commercial circuit. www.fglb.org

Court Métrage Inspiring festival devoted to new short films by young directors. www.courtmetrage.be

Brussels European Film Festival An inspiring festival at Flagey cultural centre featuring new European films and talks by acclaimed directors. Don't be surprised if you spot Scorsese in the corridor. www.fffb.be

Festival of Spanish and Latin American Film An affectionate homage to Spanish language films held at Flagey in dampest November. www.intercommunication.be

Ladies@The Movies Kinepolis holds a women-only night on the first Wednesday of the month. Men are politely turned away. www.kinepolis.be

Free information

It's not always easy to find out what's happening in Brussels, but there are several free publications that point you in the right direction. You can pick up *Metro* in the morning for a full list of the day's TV programmes, or read the *Agenda* magazine that comes with *Brussel Deze Week* for full coverage of films, concerts, exhibitions dance and theatre.

Cultural centres

Bozar The Palais des Beaux-Arts is one of the world's oldest multifunctional cultural centres. It was planned by the architect Victor Horta before the First World War, but delayed for many years, due partly to war and partly to a government cash freeze. The final building had to be sunk below ground (to protect the view from the royal palace) and surrounded by small shops. Victor Horta was not pleased with the result. *'Palace? I hardly think so,'* he muttered. It grew into an elite institution with the best concert hall in the country, home to both the National Orchestra and the Philharmonic Society. But it was also a deeply conservative place with an increasingly shabby look. Then Paul Dujardian took over as director in 2002 and transformed the institution into a vibrant arts centre that was as much interested in children's activities as in gala performances. The buildings have been totally renovated, returning the glass-roofed exhibition halls to their original state. Even the name has been tidied up to become simply Bozar. Main entrance at Rue Ravenstein 23. Second entrance (not always open) on Rue Royale; ☎ 02.507.82.00; www.bozar.be

Cultural posters

Flagey The new Flagey arts centre opened in 2002 in a 1930s building in Ixelles. Older Belgians remember it as the National Institute for Radio Broadcasting, where the country's earliest radio broadcasts were made. It was eventually split, as in a messy divorce settlement, between the Flemish and French language communities, and left to rot for many years. The authorities were finally roused from torpor when it appeared on a list of the world's 100 most threatened buildings. Now restored, it is still jointly owned by the bickering communities, but manages, in spit of the occasional tiff, to put on a superb programme of art films, contemporary music and talks. A young art and architecture crowd hang out in Café Belga, in the same building, enjoying the 1930s aura of the place. Place Sainte Croix; ☎ 02.641.10.20; www.flagey.be

Tour et Taxis A new cultural complex is being shaped in a vast complex of bonded warehouses and train sheds close to the canal. One building known as the Sheds is the setting for more than 100 exhibitions and festivals every year, including the Brussels Antiques Fair, the Brussels Book Fair and the Couleur Café music festival. The Brussels Circus School rehearses in a tent next to the Sheds. Avenue du Port 86c; ☎ 02.420.60.69; www.tour-taxis.com.

Wolubilis Wolubilis is the unlovely name for a striking new cultural centre in Woluwe-St-Lambert. The setting may be dull suburbia, but the city's newest cultural centre is determined to show exciting drama, dance and film. Eat something simple in one of the Cook & Book restaurants before the performance begins. Avenue Paul Hymans 251; ☎ 02.761.60.30; www.wolubilis.be

TIME OFF

| 239

Classical music and opera

Théâtre de la Monnaie The acclaimed Monnaie (www.lamonnaie.be) stands on the site of the theatre where the Belgian Revolution broke out in the summer of 1830. This is considered one of the great opera houses of Europe, staging an impressive programme of classic and contemporary opera in a lavish mid 19th-century interior. Many of La Monnaie's works are bought by other opera houses once they finish their Brussels run, but audiences in Brussels get to see them at a fraction of the price. The cheapest tickets are deliberately priced to match the cost of a cinema ticket (about €8), whereas most opera houses wouldn't dream of selling a ticket for less than €50. But you have to book early as the best performances sell out months in advance. Place de la Monnaie; ☎ 070.23.39.39 (box office); www.lamonnaie.be

Conservatoire The Conservatoire was designed by the Dutch architect J.P. Cluysenaar almost 30 years after he built the Galeries de Saint Hubert. It's an intimate, slightly shabby building that has hints of fading empire. Yet musicians and audiences love the place for its excellent acoustics and serious dedication to classical music. Rue de la Régence 30; ☎ 02.511.04.27; www.conservatoire.be

Live music

Ancienne Belgique The Ancienne Belgique (AB to its fans) is an old Brussels concert hall dating back to 1857. Jacques Brel used to perform on its stage, but it closed down in the 1970s. The Flemish government saved the building in the 1980s, creating a stylish venue for bands like Oasis, Nadiya and Belgium's Zita Swoon. Boulevard Anspach 110; ☎ 02.548.24.24; www.abconcerts.be

Beursschouwburg The stylishly renovated Beursschouwburg theatre draws rave reviews with its eclectic programme of concerts, club nights and jam sessions. The bare brick-walled bar is a relaxed place for hanging out, while the rooftop terrace is stunning on warm summer nights. Rue A. Orts 20-28; ☎ 02.550.03.50; www.beursschouwburg.be

Forest National All the big names in rock pass through Forest National at some stage in their careers. It's the biggest indoor venue in Brussels, with seats for 11,000. Public transport is lousy, so most people drive here, hunting desperately for a parking place in the residential streets. ☎ 02.340.22.11; www.forestnational.be

Brel's Brussels

Most people think Jacques Brel was French, but he was in fact born in 1929 at 138 Avenue du Diamant in the Brussels suburb of Schaerbeek. Brel attended a Catholic school opposite the botanical gardens and almost ended up working for the rest of his life in his Flemish father's cardboard box factory. *'There were two things I could do in life,'* he once told a journalist. *'I could breed chickens, or I could become a singer. To breed chickens, you need capital, whereas to become a singer, all you need is a guitar. That's why I became a singer.'*

Brel began his career in Brussels, hanging around bars like the Metropole and A la Morte Subite (which still has a photograph of Brel on the wall) and made his breakthrough in 1952 singing in the Rose Noire cabaret next to the restaurant Aux Armes de Bruxelles. But he didn't stay long in Brussels. In 1953, he moved to Paris, where he became one of the great chanson performers of the Fifties, thrilling audiences in smoky cabarets with his songs about love, death and the Belgian bourgeoisie. *'Each line hits you in the face and leaves you dazed,'* Edith Piaf once said.

Brel went on to write some of the classic songs of the period, like the plaintive 'Ne Me Quitte Pas,' the gritty 'Amsterdam' and the mournful 'Le Plat Pays.' He made occasional return visits to *le plat pays* to give concerts at the Ancienne Belgique, but most of the time was spent on tour, separated from his wife and three children.

Brel was proud of his Flemish roots (his father's family originated in West Flanders), but disliked extreme Flemish nationalism. '*If I were King,*' Brel once said, '*I would send all the Flemings to Wallonia and all the Walloons to Flanders for six months. Like military service. They would live with a family and that would soon solve all our ethnic and linguistic problems. Because everybody's tooth aches in the same way, everybody loves their mother, everybody loves or hates spinach. And those are the things that really count.*'

Brel gave his final concert in the French industrial town of Roubaix in 1966 and then gave it all up. He left his wife and children and fans and sailed off in his yacht. He finally settled down on Hiva Oa island in the middle of the Pacific, not far from Gauguin's bordello, the House of the Orgasm, and lived with a young woman named Madly Baty. He died of cancer in a Paris clinic in 1978.

For many years after his death, there was hardly anything of Brel in Brussels, apart from a gloomy metro station with his name not far from the cardboard factory owned by his father (still standing at 18 Rue Verheyden). His daughter, France, finally set up a small museum in the Place Vieux Halle aux Blés where fans can now see a few mementoes and hang around to catch the hourly screening of Brel's concert at the Olympia stadium in Paris.

Brussels celebrated the 25th anniversary of Brel's death in 2003 with a major exhibition. A city square was named after Brel's fictional Place St Justine in the same year.

Jazz

Sounds A small jazz club in the depths of Ixelles where some of the best Belgian bands perform modern jazz on a tiny stage. It was founded more than 20 years ago by an Italian couple. Rue de la Tulipe 28; ☎ 02.512.92.50 (after 6pm).

The Music Village A serious jazz bar in a 17th-century building near Grand'Place. Tickets are more expensive than at other Brussels venues. Look out for the free Broodje Brussel jazz concerts every second Thursday. Rue des Pierres 50; ☎ 02.513.13.45; www.themusicvillage.com

Dance and theatre

Chapelle des Brigittines A neat 1663 baroque chapel in a desolate area of the Marolles once used as a prison and now transformed into a dance venue. Some exciting productions take place in the bare brick interior. The modern extension on the north side is the work of the Italian architect Andrea Bruno. Petite Rue des Brigittines; ☎ 02.506.43.00 ; www.brigittines.be

Halles de Schaerbeek A former 19th-century covered market provides a spectacular setting for contemporary dance, theatre and circus. Rue Royale Sainte Marie 22; ☎ 02.227.59.60; www.halles.be

Kaaitheater Exciting contemporary dance in a 1930s theatre close to the canal. Smaller productions are staged in a former gueuze brewery. Look out for works by Belgian choreographer Anne-Teresa de Keersmaeker. Square Sainctelette 20; ☎ 02.201.59.59 ; www.kaaitheater.be

KVS Lavishly restored 19th-century theatre with an exciting programme of contemporary drama. Most plays are in Dutch, but English groups occasionally perform. Quai aux Pierres de Taille 7; ☎ 02.210.11.00; www.kvs.be

Théâtre National Smart new theatre in central Brussels where the French Community of Belgium puts on some serious drama, mostly in French. Boulevard Jacqmain 111; ☎ 02.203.53.03; www.theatrenational.be.

TIME OFF

Belgian Cultural Classics

Landscape with the Fall of Icarus Painting by Pieter Bruegel the Elder showing Icarus falling unobserved into the sea. W.H. Auden's 1938 poem 'Musée des Beaux-Arts' was inspired by the painting. 'About suffering they were never wrong,/The Old Masters,' he wrote. 'How well, they understood/Its human position.'

Ceci n'est pas une pipe Classic of Belgian Surrealism painted by René Magritte in 1929 in which a painting of a pipe is labelled 'This is not a pipe.'

Horta House Beautiful Art Nouveau house and studio designed by Victor Horta at 25 Rue Américaine in Saint-Gilles.

The Secret of the Unicorn One of the best Tintin comic books, published by Hergé in 1949. A personal favourite of Hergé, who published 24 adventures featuring Tintin and his dog Snowy.

Ne me Quitte Pas The plaintive love song that in 1959 marked Jacques Brel's breakthrough as a chanson singer.

Atomium Extraordinary building in northern Brussels put up for the 1958 World Fair and representing an atom of iron magnified some 160 billion times.

The Sorrow of Belgium Classic Flemish novel by Hugo Claus on growing up in Belgium in the 1930s.

Art galleries

Brussels art has always been quietly subversive. It often happens in unexpected places, like the dull suburban street in Jette where Magritte produced many of his greatest works, or the front living room in Ixelles where Marcel Broodthaers created his famous 'museum of art'. Those who want to find what contemporary Belgian artists are doing have to be prepared to drive to distant parts of town, park in dodgy neighbourhoods and hope that the gallery owner is not out for lunch.

The municipal authorities occasionally offer some pointers. Under mayor Charles Picqué, Saint-Gilles nosed ahead of other communes with the launch of *Parcours d'Artistes* in 1988. In the first year, some 90 artists opened their galleries to the public, and by 2004 the programme had grown to include more than 300 artists scattered across 173 studios and seven exhibitions.

The commercial galleries in Brussels have never managed to create anything resembling an art quarter. Some galleries are in classical townhouses in quiet Ixelles streets, others are located in industrial spaces in the Sainte Catherine district. The best approach is to pick up the free *Agenda* cultural supplement (available in tourist offices and cultural centres), or the monthly *Contemporary Art in Brussels* leaflet to be found lying around art galleries.

The Avenue Louise axis is where you find galleries dealing in big international names. The downtown district is where the art of the moment is found, often displayed in reclaimed industrial spaces in the Rue Dansaert neighbourhood. Some of these galleries have a short life span, but several have become established names.

With so much happening in the arts scene, some people have started to mull over the idea of a Brussels art fair like the Venice Biennale or Kassel's Dokumenta. Until that happens, the city depends for its annual injection of contemporary art on the *Artbrussels* art fair in April. Held in two echoing exhibition halls at Brussels Expo, the fair assembles the newest art trends from almost 170 contemporary galleries across the world. *'Brussels is fast becoming an exciting creative laboratory,'* the organisers claim.

Louise Quarter

Aeroplastics Gallery located in a grand Ixelles townhouse on Rue Blanche. The focus is on heretical modern artists, many of them part of the current London scene. Rue Blanche 32, Saint-Gilles; ☎ 02.537.22.02; www.aeroplastics.net

Galerie Rodolphe Janssen Cool contemporary gallery in a white industrial space featuring international artists that set out to surprise. Rue de Livourne 35, Ixelles; ☎ 02.538.08.18; www.galerierodolphejanssen.com

Galerie Xavier Hufkens Exhibits established artists such as Antony Gormley and Louise Bourgeois in a luminous Ixelles townhouse, yet also pays attention to emerging artists such as the British photographer Adam Fuss, who recently exhibited works from his Ark series based on techniques used by the earliest photographers. Rue Saint-Georges 6-8, Ixelles; ☎ 02.639.67.30; www.xavierhufkens.com

Sorry We're Closed Rudolphe Janssen has a tiny white space gallery in a shop window close to the Palais de Justice where he exhibits odd and witty installations. And, yes, if you were wondering, they are closed. Rue de la Régence 65a; ☎ 02.538.08.18; www.sorrywereclosed.com

City Centre

Aliceday A small art space featuring some interesting contemporary artists. Rue des Fabriques 1b; ☎ 02.646.31.53; www.aliceday.be.

Argos An exciting centre for video and audio-visual art located in a brutal industrial warehouse close to the canal zone. Rue du Chantier 13; ☎ 02.229.00.03; www.argosarts.org

Other Art Spaces

Bains: Connective The Art Deco swimming pool in Forest took 40 years to build and was obsolete before it opened. It only served as a swimming pool for 25 years and then became a disco for a time until local residents had it closed down. It's now an intriguing 'arts laboratory' where young artists create experimental works in brown tiled spaces. The bar hosts occasional film screenings and art events, while a monthly tango evening is held in the drained pool. Rue Berthelotstraat 34, Forest; ☎ 02.534.48.55; www.bains.be; info@bains.be

Flemish Parliament The Flemish government recently opened a new exhibition space in the entrance hall of the parliament building on Rue de la Croix de Fer. Known as De Loketten, this vast open space has already featured exhibitions by Flemish artists such as Panamarenko and Jan Fabre.

Comic City

Brussels is a city where comic books are regarded as a serious art form, just like paintings and sculpture. The first thing to greet tourists when they step off the Eurostar at Gare du Midi is a huge Tintin mural.

The Centre Belge de la Bande Dessinnée is the high temple of the *'ninth art'*, as fans loftily describe their passion. Located in a striking Art Nouveau department store designed by Victor Horta, it exhibits original drawings and full-scale models of cartoon scenes. The bookshops sell cartoon books, while the museum's Brasserie Horta gives you a place to read them while waiting for the food to arrive.

The city has dozens of bookshops devoted to cartoon books. Some are located on Boulevard Anspach, while others huddle together in low-rent shops on the Chaussée de Wavre. Don't make the mistake of thinking that these are places to take children. They are serious bookshops aimed at specialised collectors. *'Children can look at comic books in Fnac'*, says one grumpy owner.

You may not notice at first, but the city is awash with cartoons. There's a statue of Gaston Lagaffe, André Franquin's lovable rogue, at the top of the steps leading to the comic strip museum, on Boulevard de Pacheco. Other figures decorate the walls of houses, metro stations and even the snub nose of one of the Thalys trains from Paris.

Hergé In Brussels

Most comic fans think of Tintin as a classic French icon, but he's as Belgian as mussels and frites. Georges Remy, the Belgian creator of Tintin, was born in 1907 at 33 Rue Philippe Baucq in the Brussels municipality of Etterbeek (the house is marked with a plaque). He later changed his name to Hergé (his two initials reversed and pronounced with a French accent).

Tintin's creator had a typical Belgian upbringing, attending the strict Catholic Collège St Boniface in the Rue de la Paix and joining the Boy Scout movement. Some of his earliest drawings were published in a Boy Scout magazine. He created the first Tintin adventure in 1929, introducing readers to the Belgian boy detective (apparently modelled on Hergé's brother) and the typical fluffy white Brussels dog Snowy.

Hergé went on to produce 24 Tintin adventures at the rate of about one a year. He introduced new characters, such as Professor Calculus, the Thompson twins and the drunken Captain Haddock, famous for his wild outbursts ('*blistering barnacles*') and obscure scientific curses ('*Cyclotron*' and '*Anthropithecus!*').

Tintin slowly evolved over the years from an almost featureless drawing in the earliest strips to the familiar boy reporter of later volumes. His famous quiff was acquired in 1929 after a fast ride in an open-topped car in 'The Land of the Soviets'. Hergé added Captain Haddock just before the Second World War, the name apparently based on his wife's irritated reply when asked what was for dinner. (His wife also served as the model for the screeching opera singer Bianca Castafiore).

Tintin's adventures took him all over the world, yet several episodes occur in recognisable Brussels settings. Tintin finds a model galleon containing a map of buried treasure at the flea market on Place du Jeu de Balle in the 1943 adventure 'The Secret of the Unicorn'. The home of Professor Tarregon in the 'Seven Crystal Balls' can be found virtually as it appears in the comic book, at Avenue Delleur 6 in Watermael-Boitsfort.

In 2007 Belgium celebrated the 100th anniversary of Hergé's birth by unveiling a Tintin mural at Gare du Midi based on a frame from 'Tintin in America'. Other Tintin images appeared on a Thalys train, the fuselage of a Brussels Airline plane and a commemorative €20 coin.

The city is full of places to warm the hearts of Tintinologists. The perfect place to begin is the Belgian Centre for Comic Strips (www.comicscenter.net), a sublime Art Nouveau building dedicated to Tintin, The Smurfs, Lucky Luke and other Belgian cartoon figures. The Tintin Boutique (13 Rue de la Colline) is the place to buy Tintin collectables, but the prices are enough to make you utter a Captain Haddock oath. Elderly Tintin memorabilia can be found in the Marolles, but prices here are also high.

Hergé's former studio is still standing at 162 Avenue Louise. It is now home to Moulinsart, the company that fiercely protects the Tintin brand name. Hergé is buried among the ancient tombs in Dieweg Cemetery in Uccle. Characters from his comic books decorate a 135m mural at Stockel metro station. Tintin and Captain Haddock also appear on a mural in the Rue de l'Etuve, not far from Grand'Place, while Quick and Flupke decorate a wall in the Rue Haute.

Children in the city

Anyone with children has to make sure that they are happy with their new country, or the foreign adventure will probably fall apart within a few months. According to a recent survey, 90% of expatriates who return home early put the failure down to family problems. But Brussels is perhaps a city where expatriate families have a good chance of settling down happily. The city is crammed with attractions that will keep the whole family entertained, including parks for little ones, bowling alleys for older kids and exciting nightlife for when they are old enough to go out on their own.

Out of town attractions include the Sealife Centre in Zeebrugge (www.sealife.be), where you can crawl through the belly of a Russian sub, the atmospheric Medieval castle in Ghent, or a race to the top of the Belfry in Bruges.

Your biggest worry is perhaps what to do with teenage children on winter weekends. Well, relax. Teenage girls can be let loose on the stylish shops in Antwerp and Ghent, and boys can check out the skateboard ramps at Recyclart, next to Bruxelles-Chapelle railway station. If you are still stuck for something to do, turn to the website www.quefaire.be for some inspiring and unusual ideas.

City Parks Brussels has dozens of parks with good playgrounds, such as the little Tenbosch Park in Ixelles, the Parc du Cinquantaenaire or the Parc du Bruxelles. But the best equipped park is Rouge Cloître in eastern Brussels, where kids can run amok on a pirate ship, hurtle down a rope runway or build up their muscles on a fitness course. The playground is a 10-minute walk from Herrmann-Debroux metro station.

Puppet Theatres Brussels has several traditional puppet theatres where resident companies put on performances at weekends. One of the best summer events for children is the puppet festival in the Parc de Bruxelles, where marionette companies put on shows in a traditional open-air theatre near the children's playground. The dialogue is usually in French, but plots are easy to follow.

Cycling The Bois de la Cambre is closed to traffic every weekend, giving children wide tarmac roads where they can ride their bikes. For cycle trails in the countryside, follow the marked cycle routes in the Forêt de Soignes, or take a look at the Ravel website (www.ravel.wallonie.be), which has extensive information on the network of cycle routes created by Walloon Region along canals and disused railway lines in the south of the country.

Kessel-Lo The Flemish provincial park at Kessel-Lo, east of Leuven, recently opened a new paddling pool for small children. The water is just one metre deep, and there's a separate pool for very small children. Older kids can play on high rope bridges, slides, rowing boats, tennis courts, skateboard ramps and a cycling course. It is not the easiest park to find. Take the E40 from Brussels to Leuven, then turn off onto the E314 to Hasselt, leaving at the Kessel-Lo exit, then look for the small brown signs pointing to Provinciedomein.

Huizingen The provincial park at Huizingen, south of Brussels, has several excellent playgrounds with rope bridges and slides. There are also rowing boats for rent, a climbing area and an open-air pool. Take the E19 motorway to Paris and leave at the Huizingen exit.

Museums

Army Museum The Army Museum in the Cinquantenare Park is filled with swords, armour and guns from almost every conflict in European history. With large sections devoted to the Middle Ages, the Battle of Waterloo and the First World War, this is the perfect place to take small boys on a rainy day. Entrance is free, but the museum closes over lunchtime. www.klm-mra.be

Atomium The landmark Atomium in northern Brussels reopened in February 2006 following a five-year renovation. As well as offering your children the chance to see a molecule of iron expanded 165 billion times, the building includes a new children's sphere designed by the Barcelona artist Alicia Framis, where kids can spend the night in strange suspended pods. www.atomium.be

Musée des Enfants Everything is designed to appeal to children in this rambling Ixelles townhouse. They can do face painting, dress up in costumes, crawl through tunnels and open secret drawers. But it gets hot and hectic, especially on rainy Sundays. Only 250 children are allowed in at a time, so you may find yourself making a journey for nothing. email: childrenmuseum.brussels@skynet.be; www.museedesenfants.be

Musée du Jouet A big townhouse filled with an enormous collection of old toys. The place is totally chaotic, with toys spilling out of cardboard boxes and teddy bears losing their stuffing, but it has a certain nostalgic Belgian charm. email: info@museedujouet.be; www.museedujouet.be

Natural History Museum For dinosaur-crazy kids, the Natural History Museum is a must. The museum has the world's largest collection of dinosaur relics - 29 complete dinosaur skeletons that drowned in a bog 250 million years ago. There are also model dinosaurs that roar, a reconstructed prehistoric cave and a staircase modelled on a strand of DNA. The museum organises excellent children's workshops during Belgian school holidays. www.kbinirsnb.be

Planckendael Planckendael estate near Mechelen is home to bisons, zebras, rhinos, lions and antelopes. There is also an African village, a stork colony, a raft ride and some spectacular rope bridges high in the trees. www.planckendael.be

Scientastic A chaotic but fun science museum located in the Bourse underground tram station. Hardly the most appealing of locations, but this private museum is run on a tight budget. It is, in spite of everything, an inspiring place for kids, packed with quirky experiments for kids to try out. Beurs underground tram station; tel: 02.732.13.36; email info@scientastic.be; www.scientastic.com

Technopolis Technopolis was recently voted one of the three best science centres in Europe. Located in a bright modern building outside Mechelen, the centre has 261 hands-on experiments for children to try out. They can fly a plane, blow a giant soap bubble, lie on a bed of nails, ride a bike across a high wire or launch a hot air balloon. The staff are brilliant at explaining things in English and the café has decent food. www.technopolis.be

Theme Parks

Mini Europe The Mini Europe theme park, located in northern Brussels, has models of more than 300 famous buildings from the 27 countries of the European Union. Kids can stand next to the Eiffel Tower, peer down on the canals of Venice, and watch a scale model of Vesuvius erupting. www.minieurope.com

Walibi Your heart may sink when you see the long line of cars edging into the Walibi car park, 20km south of Brussels. This is just the beginning of a long day spent queuing, getting soaked, eating junk food, and posing for a photograph beside a large furry animal. Why do we do it? Well, it's for the kids, stupid. Four years ago, Walibi was rebranded Six Flags Belgium by an American company, but Belgians didn't like it, and the old name has been restored. New rides are being added every year. Look out for the Nocturnes in the summer when the park stays open until 23.00. It's quite magical after dark. www.walibi.be

Swimming Pools

Aqualibi Exciting water park next to Walibi theme park, 20km south of Brussels, with slides, rapid rivers, waterfalls and jacuzzis. Tickets for Walibi include entry to Aqualibi, but the water park is open all year, whereas Walibi is closed during the winter months. Make sure that boys wear speedo swimming trunks and not shorts. ☎ 010.42.15.00; www.walibi.be

Océade Subtropical water park near the Atomium with 11 slides, a waterfall and a tropical beach. Can be crowded during the summer holidays. ☎ 02.478.43.20; email: info@oceade.be; www.oceade.be

Sport

Bowling Crosly This large bowling alley in central Brussels is open to parents with kids up until 18.00. The building is located near the Sablon, next to a stretch of old city wall. Another branch is close to the old fish market. ☎ 02.512.08.74; email empereur@crosly.be; www.crosly.be

Cricket The Royal Brussels Cricket Club has several junior teams that train on Sunday afternoons in the winter months at the British School in Tervuren. Matches are played in the summer at the club's ground at Ohain. Everyone is welcome to turn up for the free training sessions, which brings together kids from Britain, Belgium and India. www.rbcc.be

Ice Skating The Poseidon ice skating rink in Brussels is next to a big swimming pool in Woluwe-St-Lambert. It's open from September to April, and attracts a huge crowd of teenagers to its Friday night discos. www.patinoireposeidon.be

Kid's Factory Vast indoor space in Waterloo with climbing frames, bouncy castles and play houses. Kids love coming here for birthday parties, but it can get hot and frantic. ☎ 02.351.23.45; www.kidsfactory.be

Roller Blading Paris was the first to hold a roller parade, but Brussels soon caught up. Every Friday in the summer, young people on roller blades set off from Place Poelaert at 8pm. Escorted by cool police officers on roller blades, they head down the main avenues before ending up in the city centre bars. www.belgiumrollers.com

Roller Skating Children can try out roller skating at an open-air rink in the Bois de la Cambre. It's located next to the Chalet de la Gymnase at the Avenue Louise end of the park, close to the Legrand tram stop. Only open in the summer.

Rugby Brussels has several junior rugby clubs where boys can play a modified version of the game. Brussels Celtic (www.brusselsceltic.com) is a friendly junior club that runs training sessions and organises matches in the winter months. The coaching is in French and English.

Skateboarding The area around the Gare de la Chapelle is a skateboarder's paradise. They can practise on the Place de la Gare in front of the station and on the nearby Squares des Ursulines above the railway tunnel. But skateboarding is strictly banned on the broad concrete plaza next to the Berlaymont building.

Swimming Pools Most Brussels communes have a swimming pool, but some are better than others for children. The Calypso pool in Watermael-Boitsfort and the Poseidon pool in Woluwe-St-Lambert are friendly pools to take young children.

Trampeasy Trampeasy is an English-speaking trampolining club that meets every Sunday in the main gym at the British School in Tervuren. Open to children from seven to 16 years. www.trampeasy.com

Other Ideas

Cartoon Trail One of the best urban rambles for kids is to follow the cartoon mural trail through downtown Brussels. The tourist office sells an inexpensive map that pinpoints more than 30 walls in the city that have been brightened up with huge murals based on Belgian cartoon figures. The full 6km route might be a bit far for small feet, but you can set them a simple task - like finding the three murals in the Rue Marché au Charbon.

Shopping in Antwerp All the style magazines agree that Antwerp is one of the coolest cities on the planet. The Flemish city is perfectly designed for teenage girls who like to mooch around clothes shops and hang out in cafés. The chain stores are located on the Meir, while the hip designer boutiques are not far off in Kammenstraat, Sint Antoniusstraat and Nationalestraat. Call in at the Antwerp tourist office on Grote Markt for a copy of the free booklet Shopping@Antwerpen.be, which guides the fashion-seeker to the best addresses in eight urban zones.

Urban Details Most kids are less than impressed by the Manneken Pis, but they might be amused by the little statue of a Brussels dog relieving itself on a bollard. The statue is located in the lovely Rue des Chartreux, not far from the Bourse.

Events

Le Sortilège du Rouge-Cloître The forests and meadows close to the Rouge-Cloître abbey are turned in the summer into an adventure playground known as Le Sortilège du Rouge-Cloître. Kids can take part in an elaborate treasure hunt that involves crossing rope bridges, hauling a wooden raft across a lake and swinging on ropes. Along the way, they are met by various people dressed as witches, knights and beggars. www.sortilege.be

Eating out with Children

Restaurants You can usually find somewhere friendly to stop for a bite to eat in Belgium. Belgian restaurant owners tend to have a relaxed attitude towards children, with many offering special children's menus that end with a small lollipop.

Ice Cream You can find Italian ice cream vans parked outside most parks, but the best addresses for ice cream are elsewhere in town. Some discerning kids insist on a cone from Il Gelato (168 Rue Vanderkindere), while others are fiercely loyal to Zizi, just a few steps away (57 Rue de la Mutualité). There are also those who claim that no one in Brussels makes better ice cream than Capoue, which has branches at 36 Avenue des Celtes and 395 Chaussée de Boondael. For those who are too lazy to leave the park, Il Gelato serves ice cream in the summer at a stall in the Bois de la Cambre.

School Holidays

Expatriate families often have a difficult time during school holidays. Belgian families normally have grandparents with a house in the Ardennes or an apartment at the coast. But expatriates are more likely to be on their own in Brussels. It's important then to have a strategy for dealing with school breaks, especially if both parents work.

Carnival Belgian schools close for one week in February around Mardi Gras. The weather is usually bleak, making trips to parks difficult. But there are Carnival festivities in several small towns, including a spectacular Mardi Gras procession in Binche (which can be reached by train from Brussels). Otherwise, you might use the week to explore some of the city's museums, such as the Natural History Museum or the Museum of Musical Instruments. Check the website www.quefaire.be (in French) for other ideas.

Easter The weather has perhaps improved by Easter, making it possible to visit a park. The park at Rouge Cloître has excellent climbing equipment and can be reached by metro. The provincial parks at Kessel-Lo and Huizingen are superbly equipped, but most easily reached by car.

Summer The summer holidays normally last about two months in Belgium. Working parents who can only take off a few weeks will probably need to find activities for their children. Many organisations offer summer courses covering activities like athletics, languages, art and music. But most courses in Belgium are run for children who can speak French or Dutch. Expatriate children will perhaps feel left out if they can't communicate. It might be better in that case to find an au pair for a month.

November Schools close for one week in November around Armistice Day (November 11). This is a difficult time of year to keep children amused. You might consider visiting Ghent (which has a castle), or Paris (which is just 90 minutes by train). Or take them out for a meal in a child-friendly restaurant. But bear in mind that all museums in Belgium are closed on November 11.

Christmas Most expatriate families leave Brussels over Christmas. Those who stay behind can take their children to look at the lights on Grand'Place, the big wheel on Place Ste-Catherine and the Christmas market in the streets around the Bourse.

Organised Activities

Working parents often sign their children up for courses and activities on Wednesday afternoons, Saturday mornings and during the school holidays. There is a huge choice of activities on offer. Some are run by official organisations such as communes and museums, while others are private initiatives. The official courses are generally cheap but may be fairly basic in terms of care. The more expensive private organisations often have a more welcoming attitude towards expatriate children. Outdoor activities and sports are best for children who are fairly confident. Shy children might prefer attending a music course run by the Museum of Modern Instruments. Children who don't speak French or Dutch might feel isolated in activities aimed at Belgian children. Most will feel more comfortable if they have siblings or friends doing the same activity.

Languages

Kiddy and Junior Language Classes It might sound a strange idea for a holiday activity, but Kiddy and Junior Language Classes are immensely popular in Brussels. Founded in 1980, they offer courses for children aged three to 18 in 10 major languages, including Chinese and Russian. For expatriate children who are struggling with French or Dutch, a week of lessons will boost their chances of integrating into multilingual Brussels. Classes are organised in nine locations, including central Brussels, Etterbeek, Woluwe Saint-Pierre and Waterloo. ☎ 02.218.39.20; email: info@kiddyclasses.net; www.kiddyclasses.net

Kid's Computer Club A friendly place where children aged four to 18 can spend a week learning a foreign language along with the basics of computing. Avenue René Gobert 31; ☎ 02.374.27.08; email secretariat@kidscomputer.be; www.kidscomputer.be

Sport and Gyms

The Little Gym Based on a concept developed in the United States in the 1970s, Little Gyms offer fun activities for kids aged up to 12, including music, dance and craft workshops. There are two branches just outside Brussels, in Wezembeek-Oppem and Waterloo. www.thelittlegym.be

St John's Sports Camps St John's International School in Waterloo organises sports camps during school holidays for kids from St John's and other schools. The programme includes basketball, tennis, hockey and gymnastics. Children who only speak English should find it easy to integrate. The camps are listed on the school's website under 'Our Community/Athletics'. www.stjohns.be

Sport City A modern sports centre in Woluwe-St-Pierre with a range of courses for children that combine sport and culture. The programme includes football, tennis, photography and dance. All ages from three to 16 can sign up, though small children might find it overwhelming. Avenue Salomé, Woluwe-St-Pierre; 010.22.94.93; www.sportcity-woluwe.be

Toboggan A Belgian association set up by parents 20 years ago to organise fun activities for children in the holidays. Toboggan now offers a wide choice of activities aimed at children aged three to 14. Activities are held at more than a dozen different centres in Brussels and the surrounding suburbs. Most courses run from 8am to 6pm for the benefit of working parents. On offer are dance, painting, horse riding and cooking, with a one-week course starting at €82. ☎ 02.731.11.96; www.tobogganasbl.be

Cooking

Toquetoc Line Couvreur is a friendly young Belgian mother who runs cookery courses for kids during the school holidays. The budding chefs work in a bright loft apartment near the Porte de Hal in Saint-Gilles. The classes are in French, but kids are welcome no matter what they speak. ☎ 0495.22.57.66; email info@toquetoc.be; www.toquetoc.be

Art and Music

Contraste A serious photography workshop in Etterbeek that organises holiday courses for children over 12. Rue Général Capiaumont 45, Etterbeek; ☎ 02.640.94.40; www.photo-contraste.com

Musical Instuments Museum The museum organises a range of courses for children, allowing them to play instruments like drums and guitars. Courses are usually in French or Dutch. www.mim.fgov.be

Pantalone A magical art house for kids on the Place des Martyrs where they can let their imaginations run wild for a day. Check the website for information on activities and book in advance to be sure of a place. The art house is a Flemish initiative, but it's open to kids of all languages. Most activities cost about €5. Place des Martyrs 10, central Brussels; ☎ 02.223.00.84; www.pantalone.be

Turtle Wings A creative art studio run by an inspiring American designer (see the *Case Histories*), where younger kids can make things using recycled material and found objects. Organises holiday courses and birthday parties in English. Rue de l'Abbaye 55, Ixelles; ☎ 0475.35.55.04; email: jverbeelen@turtlewings.be; www. turtlewings.be

Circus

L'Ecole de Cirque de Bruxelles A Brussels institution, the Circus School teaches children how to do tightrope walking, juggling and acrobatics. The school recently moved to the Tour et Taxis complex in northern Brussels. Courses are aimed at children aged three to 12. www.ecoledecirquedebruxelles.be

Birthday Parties

Organising a birthday party in Brussels needn't be too stressful. You can book various child-friendly venues where they will take care of the food and organise activities. Most small kids adore the Musée des Enfants in Ixelles, where they can mess around with face paints and rampage around an old townhouse. The Toy Museum is another popular place where smaller children can have a party in a room filled with old toys. For older children, Bowling Crosly will organise a morning or afternoon birthday party combined with bowling and Q-Zar at two venues in Brussels. The Scientastic science museum regularly caters for birthday parties, though the place can be chaotic. For older children with energy to burn, a birthday party at the Océade water park in northern Brussels could be perfect. Or (if you can organise the transport), you might opt for a birthday party at Aqualibi near Wavre.

Cartoons in the City

The walls in Brussels are mostly grey. But some of the blank gable ends have been decorated with large cartoons. More than 30 murals are dotted around the streets in the centre, the oldest dating from the early 1990s. These cheeky Belgian images can cheer you up immensely on a wet November day, particularly in the dingy back streets of the Marolles. Several murals appear on walls along the meandering Rue Marché aux Charbon. Others are tough to find without guidance. Visit the tourist office to pick up a book listing all the cartoon murals.

SEVEN MURALS TO FIND

Tintin and Captain Haddock Hergé's hero is shown climbing a fire escape on a wall next to the Hôtel La Légende in Rue de l'Etuve. Painted to mark Tintin's 75th anniversary in 2004.

Lucky Luke Morris' nonchalant cowboy appears with the Dalton brothers on a house wall in the Rue de la Buanderie.

Quick & Flupke Hergé's two roguish street urchins taunt a plump Belgian policeman on a mural on Rue Haute, in the Marolles.

Cartoon mural on Place St Géry

Blake & Mortimer Edgar P. Jacobs' English detectives appear in a mural on the Rue du Petit Rampart.

Boule et Bill Roba's gloriously chaotic street scene from his *Boule et Bill* series brightens up a wall at Rue du Chevreuil 25.

Rik Hochet Duchateau's Rik Hochet appears on a house wall in the narrow Rue du Bon Secours.

Nero A mural on Place Saint Géry is illustrated with characters from Marc Sleen's long-running *Nero* comic books.

Blondie and Blinkie Characters from Jijé's *Blondie and Blinkie* books appear on a wall at Rue des Capucins 15, in the Marolles.

Rik Hochet mural

Events

A Year in Belgium

The Belgian year is crowded out with festivals, fairs and parades. Live like a Belgian and immerse yourself in the friendly crush of a street market or the noisy reenactment of a historical battle.

Autumn

Beer Weekend As *la rentrée* approaches, some of the best brewers in the land present their ales to the public in tents on Grand'Place.

Open Monument Days A unique chance to see inside historical buildings that are normally closed to the public. Held on different dates in Brussels, Wallonia and Flanders.

Car-Free Sunday The streets of Brussels are car free on one Sunday in late September, allowing city dwellers to discover the joys of cycling, roller blading or even horse riding.

Winter

Christmas Market Stylish Christmas market held in the Grand'Place, featuring Christmas tree, crib with live animals and superb lighting effects. Stalls selling mulled wine and gifts fill the streets around the Bourse, while an artificial ice rink is set up in Place Sainte Catherine.

Carnival Towns and villages throughout Belgium celebrate Carnival with street parades, masked balls and music. The most famous Carnival is held every year in Binche, featuring flamboyant costumes, masks and hats with ostrich plumes, but there are other spectacular Carnival processions in Malmédy, Aalst and Ostend. Most parades are held on Mardi Gras or the preceding two days.

Spring

Royal Greenhouses Open to the public for a few weeks, beginning at the end of April, allows garden enthusiasts a chance to see inside the extraordinary glass buildings constructed by King Leopold II to cultivate his collection of tropical plants.

Les Nuits Botaniques A relaxed festival at the end of April devoted to European and American alternative and indie music.

Holy Blood Procession This spectacular annual procession has been held in Bruges almost without a break since the Middle Ages. Held on Ascension Day, it has its roots in the Crusades, when Flemish Knights brought back a holy relic believed to contain drops of Christ's blood. The relic is paraded through the streets of the city in a dazzling procession that includes musicians, dancers, soldiers and even a flock of sheep.

Queen Elisabeth Competition For more than 50 years, young musicians have been coming to Brussels to take part in one of the world's most important and demanding musical competitions. It culminates in a final competition in the Palais des Beaux-Arts which is shown on Belgian television.

Zinneke Parade Held every second year in May, this is a contemporary procession with an eccentric multicultural twist, featuring musicians and dancers who converge on downtown Brussels.

Brussels Jazz Marathon A convivial festival in May featuring more than 100 concerts in cafés, clubs and city squares.

Belgian Lesbian and Gay Pride Downtown traffic is halted as an estimated 25,000 participants parade along the central boulevards, watched by hundreds of tolerant if bemused Belgian shoppers.

Brussels 20K The city comes to a standstill on a Sunday in late May as more than 20,000 runners pound the boulevards for the annual Brussels 20K. The race takes runners down Avenue Louise and through the Bois de la Cambre before ending in front of cheering crowds in the Parc du Cinquantenaire.

Sinksefoor Antwerp's sprawling five-week fun fair is held on a vast open space in southern Antwerp (beginning on Whit Saturday). The attractions include wild rides, ghost trains and gaudy stalls selling sticky Flemish *smoutebollen* (apple fritters).

Namur en Mai An engaging festival of traditional street theatre held in Wallonia's beautiful capital in late May and early June.

Summer

City Parade A free street party in Ghent featuring dance music, floats and late-night parties.

Ducasse de Mons This event in Mons is one of Belgium's greatest festivals, ending with a spectacular battle on the main square between St George and a dragon affectionately known as *Doudou*.

Beer Passion Weekend A friendly festival in Antwerp during which more than 100 of Belgium's small brewers offer samples of their ales.

Couleur Café The summer festival season takes off in Brussels with everyone heading along the canal to take part in three scintillating days of world music amid the impressive industrial architecture of Tour et Taxis.

Rock Werchter The biggest rock festival in Belgium, which manages to secure big names like Franz Ferdinand, Red Hot Chili Peppers and Hooverphonic, but rarely succeeds in picking a dry weekend.

Brussels European Film Festival This 10-day film festival is back on a sound footing after a few wobbly years. Now held in the summer in the Flagey building, the festival selects new feature films and shorts by young European directors.

Opera in the Grand'Place One night every year, the Grand'Place provides a unique setting for an open-air opera.

Ommegang A spectacular procession held on the Grand'Place. It features thousands of participants in flamboyant costumes, flag waving displays and a battle on stilts.

Foire du Midi A noisy funfair takes over the boulevards near the Gare du Midi for more than a month.

Festival of Flanders A large-scale classical music festival with performances across Flanders and Brussels, some held in concert halls while others take place in historic houses and castles.

Festival Midis-Minimes An off beat summer festival offering concerts in the Eglise du Minimes every weekday throughout July and August.

Dour Festival Thousands of music fans camp out in a muddy field close to the French border for one of the best alternative festivals in Europe.

Belgian National Day Held on 21 July, this marks the accession of King Leopold I to the Belgian throne in 1831. The day begins with a military parade in front of the royal palace in Brussels and ends with fireworks in the park. The royal palace is open to the public for the summer, allowing the curious to nose around the glittering ballrooms and admire the ceiling of irridescent green beetles recently added by Belgian artist Jan Fabré.

Bruxelles-les-Bains A stretch of Brussels canal is transformed every summer into a beach; complete with sand, umbrellas and deck chairs. Inspired by Paris, Brussels launched this idea a few years ago, providing city dwellers with a place to sunbathe, play beach volleyball or simply sip a cocktail under a palm tree. Place Sainctelette; www.bruxelleslesbains.be

Cactus Festival An acclaimed summer event in Bruges that brings Flemish bands to the beautiful Minnewaterpark.

Gentse Feesten A spectacular 10-day street festival that draws a crowd of more than a million revellers to the streets of Ghent. Having begun in the 19th century as a workers' festival, the event was relaunched by a local folk singer in the 1970s. The exhausting programme includes a glitzy ball, street theatre, parades, open-air cinema, free entry to city museums, rock concerts in city squares, a blues festival and jazz performances. For those who have any energy left, Ghent also hosts Ten Days Off, a major festival of club music featuring some of Europe's top DJs, running at the same time as the Feesten.

Zomer van Antwerpen Antwerp keeps its streets lively in the summer with an international festival that runs throughout July and August. It features a huge programme of events in unusual locations, including street theatre, open-air cinema and jazz concerts.

Meiboom August is a quiet month in Brussels, with the main festivals taking place in the Ardennes or along the coast. The big events of the month are the Planting of the Meiboom on 9 August, and a flower carpet on the cobbles of Grand'Place.

Memorial Van Damme Towards the end of summer, many of the world's best athletes arrive in Brussels to take part in the annual Memorial Van Damme at the King Baudouin Stadium in northern Brussels.

Belgian public holidays

New Year's Day, January 1

Easter Monday, (date varies)

Labour Day, May 1

Ascension Day

Whit Sunday (Pentecost)

Whit Monday (Pentecost Monday)

National Day, July 21

Assumption of the Blessed Virgin Mary, August 15

All Saints' Day, November 1

Armistice Day, November 11. European institutions remain open.

Christmas Day, December 25

Boxing Day, December 26

Regional Holidays

Flemish Community Holiday, June 11. Only in Flanders.

French Community Holiday, September 27. Only in Wallonia.

Major Festivals

Epiphany, January 6

St Valentine's, February 14. Look out for red hearts on traffic lights close to the day.

Carnival, Belgians celebrate Carnival on Shrove Tuesday, 47 days before Easter Sunday. Belgian schools close for a week around Carnival.

Europe Day, May 9. European institutions and EU schools closed.

St Nicholas, December 6

Newspapers and magazines

The main source for local news and listings in English is *The Bulletin* magazine, founded in 1962, which comes out every Thursday. The weekly *European Voice* contains in-depth news on the European Union, but little of interest on Brussels or Belgium.

Mural of man reading newspaper on the Chaussée de Wavre

The Belgian press is divided into French and Dutch newspapers. The main French newspapers are *Le Soir* (www.lesoir.be), which has good coverage of Brussels and Walloon Brabant news, but little serious reporting on Flanders, and *La Libre Belgique* (www.lalibrebelgique.be), a more conservative Catholic newpaper with good reporting on business and finance. The *Dernière Heure* is the main tabloid newspaper. Its reporting of breaking news is particularly robust.

The main Flemish newspapers are *De Morgen* (www.demorgen.be) and *De Standaard* (www.destandaard.be). *De Morgen* has a strong tradition of investigative reporting and fearless exposure of Belgian corruption. Its editor was recently rebuked by Prince Philippe, next in line to the throne, for critical reporting of the monarchy. *De Standaard* is a more respectful Catholic newspaper that would never offend someone of Philippe's rank.

The Belgian press is good on foreign news stories, but less reliable on reporting events across the language divide. The French press creates an impression of a Flanders that is deeply racist, while the Flemish press provides an image of a Wallonia mired in corruption. The best reporting on Brussels is provided by *Le Soir* (www.lesoir.be), or, for Dutch readers, the free *Brussel Deze Week*.

Newsagents

Most major foreign newspapers are available in Brussels newsagents, but some shops also stock an impressive range of magazines from all over the world.

Librairie de Rome The polyglot owner stocks almost all the important international newspapers and magazines. Rue Jean Stas 16, off Avenue Louise; ☎ 02.511.79.37. Open daily 8.30am-8pm.

Press Line Sablon Business travellers and residents are drawn here because of the vast stock of daily newspapers displayed outside, including Cologne's *Kölner Stadt Unzeiger*, Turkey's *Milliyet*, Slovakia's *Pravda* and even the UK's *Racing Post*. The magazine section is equally diverse, with Russian *Elle*, *Californian Homes* and every possible version of *Cosmopolitan*, along with specialised antique magazines for the dealers who work in this quarter. The *Gazette de l'Hôtel Drouot* is the one they like to read over coffee. Rue de la Régence 9, Sablon; ☎ 02.503.23.07. Open Tuesday to Friday 6am-7.30pm; Monday 6.30am-7.30pm; Saturday 7.30am-7.30pm; Sunday 8.30am-7.30pm.

Socialising in the city

You can sometimes feel alone and homesick in Brussels, as in any other big city. Yet there are many different ways to connect with other people in Brussels, including social clubs, expat bars and online sites.

How to Meet Singles

More than one quarter of Brussels residents are single, according to a 2007 survey. But that doesn't mean they are sad. The singles lifestyle has taken off in Brussels in recent years, fuelled by a growing population of expats on temporary contracts. Some singles choose to party until the small hours, while others find a quiet niche reading a new novel in a book group.

@Seven Young single professionals get together every Thursday at the Mirano Continental on the Chaussée de Louvain. The idea is to meet after work in a relaxed setting and exchange small talk as well as business cards. Doors open just before seven and most people leave before midnight, so they can be at their desks fresh the next morning. There's no particular dress code, but it possibly helps to take along a business card to hand the doorman. www.at7.be

Eat & Speak Monthly dinners in a Saint-Gilles café for small groups of sophisticated Belgian and expat singles. Applicants are strictly vetted to ensure that no one is married. www.eatandspeak.be

Eurolunch Organises lunch dates between members who share compatible profiles. Aimed at successful professionals who want everything done for them. But is love like that? www.eurolunch.be

Expatica Large European online dating site with some Belgian members. www.expatica.com

Xpats.com Belgian expat website with free personal ads in the classified section and an online dating service. www.xpats.com

How to Meet Belgians

Every expatriate will tell you the same story. It isn't easy to meet Belgians unless you marry one or work in a Belgian company. Most Belgians like to have a quiet family life rather than meet new people. They also tend to leave Brussels on a Friday evening to spend the weekend in the family apartment at the coast or to visit family in the Ardennes. But younger Belgians in big cities are becoming more open towards outsiders. In addition, some groups have started organising events aimed at making the city more welcoming.

Apéros Urbains/Stads Aperos A new idea for getting people to meet in the summer over a glass of wine. Events are organised in inspiring urban locations around the city,

TIME OFF

The Miracle of St Géry

St Géry is where the city began. The oldest settlement stood here on an island in the marshes. There was once a church on the spot, but it vanished long ago, leaving an empty square with an obelisk in the middle. The 19th-century Marché St Géry was built in the middle of the square, enclosing the obelisk. Then the market closed and the neighbourhood went into slow decline. Someone tried to revitalise the old building in the style of Covent Garden in London, but it didn't work. Then Brussels Region moved its environmental offices into the building and turned the rest into an exhibition centre and café. It has now taken off, sort of. But Place St Géry was truly turned around by the entrepreneur Fred Nicolay, who opened fashionable bars like Mappa Mundo, Zebra and Le Roi des Belges. With their terraces spilling out into the Brussels night, this has become the epicentre of youthful cool. The urban rot has been halted, and wealthy young professionals (many on EU salaries) are moving into the old apartments and warehouses. A film shown in the Halles charts the history of Brussels from the earliest days.

such as the Place Guy d'Arezzo and the Mont des Arts. You simply turn up and start up a conversation with the first person you meet. www.aperos.be.

Cooking Courses Several organisations in Brussels organise cooking courses where you can chat with Belgians while learning to make stylish meals.

Pain Quotidien The Pain Quotidien cafés have large farmhouse tables to encourage conviviality. Sit down with a book and see what happens.

How to Meet Expatriates

It's easy to strike up a conversation in one of the many Irish pubs in the city. But if you are not wild about spending a night in the noise and smoke, take a look at the network of expat clubs and associations that have developed in Brussels.

Book Clubs Brussels has a growing number of book clubs run by expatriates. Members mainly meet over a glass of wine in a private house or café. Nicola Lennon of Nicola's Bookshop organises one of the best. www.nicolasbookshop.com.

Churches Brussels has a large number of churches offering social contacts for expatriates. The main churches are listed on www.xpats.com under 'community.'

Sport The expatriate sports scene is particularly active in Brussels. You can easily track down fellow players for a game of rugby, football or golf. For those who don't like team games, several groups organise running and country walks every weekend.

Drama Groups Brussels has several expatriate drama groups, including the English Comedy Club, which first performed in Brussels in 1909. Other groups include the American Theatre Company (www.atc-brussels.com), the Irish Theatre Group (www.irishtheatregroup.com) and the Brussels Shakespeare Society (www.shaksoc.com). Several companies share a rehearsal space in Schaerbeek and put on plays in venues throughout Brussels. The standard of acting is high.

Gays and Lesbians

Brussels is not famous as a gay or lesbian destination, yet the city has a quietly tolerant approach to alternative lifestyles. In 2003, Belgium became the second country in the world to recognise gay marriage. Three years later, the government passed a law allowing gay couples to adopt children.

The city's main gay and lesbian district is located around the Rue du Marché au Charbon in the heart of the city. Yet this is far from being a gay ghetto. The gay bar The Slave is next door to the Palais au Thé, which has been a bourgeois institution for more than a century, and opposite Le Palais au Pantouffles, where older people buy their carpet slippers. Gay tea dances are held on Sunday afternoons at Le You (www.leyou.be).

Cartoon mural in the Rue du Marché au Charbon

Fitness and wellness

Brussels has excellent facilities for most sports. You can swim, cycle, run, play golf, or just walk in the woods. There are expatriate clubs for most sports, but joining a Belgian club is a good way to integrate in the local community.

School Grounds

British School of Brussels The British School at Tervuren has a range of excellent sports facilities that can be used by the public after 6pm and at weekends. The campus has three astroturf football pitches, hockey and rugby pitches, tennis courts, squash courts and a large indoor sports hall. Visitors can book a single session or a block of 10 sessions by filling in a form and paying by bank transfer or cash. ☎ 02.766.04.42; email community@britishschool.be

Sports

Bowling The city centre bowling crowd tends to hang out at the 20-lane Crosly bowling alley. It occupies a modern building next to a stretch of old city wall, not far from the Sablon (Boulevard de l'Empereur 36). A second Crosly centre is located close to the old fish market at Quai du Foin 43. It can get noisy when all 20 lanes are in use. www.crosly.be

Cricket British soldiers are believed to have played cricket on the eve of the Battle of Waterloo on a patch of grass known as the *Pélouse des Anglais*. The Royal Brussels Cricket Club was founded about 70 years later and originally played games on the site of the first match. The club now has a ground in the lovely Walloon Brabant village of Ohain, south of Waterloo. In the summer, the club has a busy schedule playing against teams from Belgium, Paris and Kent. www.rbcc.be

Football Brussels has three expatriate football clubs. They organise training sessions during the week and play games at the weekend. The oldest club is the Royal Brussels British Football Club (www.rbbfc.be), which has been organising matches in Belgium since 1933. It has six teams that train on the astroturf pitches at the British School of Brussels. Its main rival is the British United Football Club (www.bufc.org), formed in 1972, which trains at the British School in Tervuren and drinks at the Bok and Dragon. A third club, FC Irlande (www.fcirlande.be), has five teams that train at a ground in Overijse and drink in the Wild Geese.

Golf There are several golf courses in the green countryside around Brussels. Most are exclusive organisations with steep membership fees. The Royal Belgian Golf Federation has full details. ☎ 02.672.23.89; email info@golfbelgium.be; www.golfbelgium.be

Horse Riding Brussels has several riding stables located on the fringes of the Forêt de Soignes, including two centres in Uccle. Riders sign up for lessons and set off on the marked bridlepaths that cut across the ancient beech forest. Other riding clubs are located in the countryside south of Brussels, mainly around Waterloo and La Hulpe.

Hurling The Irish have introduced the ancient Celtic game of hurling to Brussels. Not the gentlest of sports. www.hurling.be

Rugby Brussels has two rugby clubs that play on winter weekends regardless of mud and rain. The Brussels Barbarians (www.brusselsbarbarians.com) train at the British School in Tervuren and play games on Sundays. A second expatriate club, Brussels Celtic (www.brusselsceltic.com), was founded in 1998. It trains at the British School and meets for drinks in the Old Oak.

Swimming Pools The city has a number of swimming pools, but not all are good for training. The most serious pools are Poseidon in Woluwe-St-Lambert and Calypso in Watermael-Boitsfort.

Tennis Belgian tennis clubs have produced some exceptional players in recent years. For information on tennis clubs, contact the Fédération Royale Belge de Tennis, Galerie de la Porte de Louise 203/3, Ixelles; ☎ 02.548.03.04; www.rbtf.be

Health Clubs

Brussels has a large number of health clubs, many of them aimed at expatriates. Some are very expensive, especially in the European Quarter and Avenue Louise district, where annual membership can easily cost over €1,000. But competition is fierce, and you can often negotiate a discount, especially in the summer months.

Aspria A sublime light-filled gym in the heart of the European Quarter with a luxurious 21-metre pool and stylish lounge bar. The gym equipment incorporates computers to keep track of your personal training record. The membership fees may seem daunting if you are not on an EU salary. A second Aspria gym is located at the Conrad Hotel on Avenue Louise. Rue de l'Industrie 26; ☎ 02.508.08.00; www.aspria.be

B Fitness A bright modern gym located above the Bascule shopping centre in Uccle. Relaxed and friendly, the club has all the equipment you might want. Galerie de la Bascule, Chaussée de Waterloo 715; ☎ 02.346.21.96 ; www.bfitness.be

Corpus Pilates A centre for alternative fitness located in a traditional Ixelles terraced house close to Place Flagey. The instructors are trained in the Pilates method and the even newer Gyrotronics system. Three rooms contain a range of sophisticated exercise machines. Less flashy than the big gyms, the centre has a warm family feel. You leave your shoes at the door and change in the main room. Rue Borrens 33, Ixelles; ☎ 02.513.07.66; www.corpuspilates.com

David Lloyd Uccle The UK's David Lloyd gyms have found a niche in Belgium at the upper end of the market. This gym is out of town, set in beautiful grounds, best reached by car. It has 11 tennis courts, squash courts, two swimming pools and several fitness rooms. Drève de Lorraine 41, Uccle; ☎ 02.534.90.00; www.davidlloyd.be

La Pavillon A small functional gym located in a pavilion saved from the 1958 Brussels World Fair. The exercise room is bright and sunny, with potted plants dotted among the machines. The fees are well below the price of a European Quarter gym, the atmosphere friendly. Rue de Verrewinkel 97; ☎ 02.375.18.52; www.pavillon58.be

Physical Golden Club Everyone knows that Jean-Claude Van Damme started out in this gym before becoming 'muscles from Brussels'. This is therefore a serious gym for

TIME OFF

people interested in tough workouts. Annual fees are about half the rate of a European Quarter gym, but facilities are basic. Place du Châtelain 33, Ixelles; ☎ 02.538.19.06.

Royal La Rasante La Rasante opened a few years ago in an old Belgian sports club. Word quickly spread about its excellent facilities, including two swimming pools, a hammam, fitness areas, three exercise studios, bar, restaurant, conference area and underground car park. It also has seven outdoor tennis courts and a hockey pitch. It is aimed at families who can spend the whole day here, working out in the gym while babies spend time in the crèche. It belongs to the Aspria group. Rue Sombre 56; ☎ 02.609.19.02; www.royallarasante.be

Sportcity You can use an Olympic size swimming pool, tennis and squash courts, along with saunas, baths and steam rooms, all for a few euro. Avenue Salomé 2, Woluwe St Pierre; ☎ 02.773.18.20; www.sportcity-woluwe.be

World Class Health Academy A spacious fitness centre close to the European Parliament with rooms on four levels. The complex includes a swimming pool, gyms, saunas and jacuzzis. Membership doesn't come cheap, but you will be training among Europe's elite politicians. Rue du Parnasse 19; ☎ 02.551.59.90; www.worldclassfitness.net

Outdoor Fitness

Friskis & Svettis Brisk Swedish-style outdoor aerobics to the beat of pop music in quiet corners of Brussels parks. www.friskissvettis.be

Jogging Trails Several jogging trails have been created in the Forêt de Soignes, ranging from five to 20km. The trails begin at the Forêt de Soignes sports centre, off the E411 motorway on the edge of Brussels. The website of Brussels Environment (www.ibgebim.be) has a map showing the routes (look under: parcours jogging).

Nordic Walking Scandinavians and Belgians stride off on high energy walks through the woods around Brussels. Walks are regularly organised by Friskis & Svettis. www.friskissvettis.be

Running Brussels has two branches of the international running group Hash House Harriers. Runners follow trails laid down in various locations across Belgium and end up with a beer or a family picnic. The Brussels Hash (users.skynet.be/bruh3) meets every Saturday afternoon, while the Manneken Pis Hash (www.bmph3.com) runs on Sunday afternoons and Monday evenings.

Wellness

Bikram Yoga Centre A new Indian yoga centre on Avenue Louise was opened in 2006 by the British EU Commissioner and yoga enthusiast Peter Mandelson. The centre teaches basic postures and breathing exercises designed to strengthen the spine and eliminate toxins. Classes cost €180 for 10 sessions. Avenue Louise 207; ☎ 02.644.12.24; email info@bikramyogabrussels.com; www.bikramyogabrussels.com

Spasiba A restful white-walled Zen space located down a passage near the Hilton Hotel. Every type of massage is available, including Moroccan, Thai and Indian. Not the cheapest way to relax. Boulevard de Waterloo 47, central Brussels; ☎ 02.514.15.33; www.spasiba.be

Parks

Brussels is a surprisingly green city. Although many areas are densely developed, more than half of the city is green space, including large areas of beech forest and patches of marshy wilderness that have not been touched since Bruegel's day. While the centre is fairly urban, it takes no time at all to hop on a tram and get out to the green fringes to the south. Much of the woodland lies close to business districts, making Brussels one of the few capital cities in the world where you can go for a forest walk during your lunch hour. There are indeed areas of woodland near the Avenue Louise office district that have remained untouched since the last ice age.

Parc de Bruxelles The city's oldest park, forming a green space between the parliament and the palace. A favourite of 19th-century visitors, it still has a quiet formal charm, with classical statues overlooking fountains. People from the American Embassy use the dusty trails for lunchtime jogging, children crowd into the little playground and office workers catch the sun on the café terraces.

Bois de la Cambre A huge area of rolling park and woodland in the south of the city, designed in mid 19th-century romantic style by the German landscape architect Keiler. It has winding paths, a lake, a playground and a roller skating rink. Everything the city needs. But it has a neglected appearance. The playgrounds are falling apart, buildings are dilapidated and the main avenues are used by fast traffic. Worst of all, the romantic Chalet Robinson, a restaurant on an island, has been left in ruins following a fire many years ago. The city recently announced a plan to curb traffic in the park and restore it to its former grandeur, but progress has been slow. Even so, it's an immensely popular park, especially at the weekend when some of the roads are closed to traffic, creating a circuit around the lake for cyclists and roller bladers.

Secret Parks

Many of the city's parks and gardens are hidden away, concealed behind houses or reached by narrow lanes.

Parc d'Egmont A little park hidden behind the Hilton Hotel, reached by an old cobbled lane. It has a café located in an old orangerie, a statue of Peter Pan and some mysterious ruins.

Parc Tenbosch A lovely sloping park in Ixelles reached by an almost invisible gate on the Chaussée de Vleurgat. A favourite spot for local parents with little children, who come for the sandpit, the playground and the chance to chat in the sun.

Walks in the country

Forest Walks

The area of woodland closest to the city lies at the end of a cobbled lane off Boulevard du Souverain. Take tram 94 to the Coccinelles stop, follow the footpath down to the lake, Etang des Enfants Noyés, then take the meandering trail that skirts the left side. The path follows a tiny stream for about 20 minutes, after which you will begin to hear the distant sound of traffic. Turn back and follow the path on the other side of the valley.

Country Walks near Brussels

Tervuren Woods The woods in Tervuren have been a favourite escape for Brussels residents since at least the 16th century. To enjoy this vast area of forest, take tram 44 from Montgomery underground station to the Tervuren terminus and cross the road to the Africa Museum. Walk past the pond behind the museum and follow the path straight ahead to reach the canal. Cross by the bridge and turn left along the Spaans Huisdreef. This brings you to a historic red brick building, 't Spaans Huis. Follow the lakeside path beyond here and turn right along the Vaartdreef, another canal. This leads to a broad avenue, the Duisburgsedreef, where you turn right to reach a spot where seven paths cross. Follow the meandering trail marked with blue posts to reach the old town of Tervuren, which has several cafés.

Zoet Water The woods and low hills south of Leuven are crossed by various walking trails. One of the best begins at *Zoute Water*, near the university campus at Heverlee. The *Zoet Water wandeling*, marked by small hexagonal signs, takes about one hour. It begins in the woods on the south side of the ponds and continues along farm tracks and sunken forest trails. The walk ends at a cluster of lakeside cafés and taverns where you can join Belgians eating *stoemp* and drinking *Westmalle Tripel*. Try to get a table in the tavern Brasserie Saint Jean for the best cooking or just sit at a wobbly table in the garden.

Meerdalbos The Meerdaalbos is a large area of woods to the south of Leuven. There are endless trails through the woods, including one for children with rope bridges and old-fashioned Flemish games along the way.

Solvay Estate The Solvay Estate lies south of Brussels in the rolling Walloon Brabant countryside. The estate once belonged to Ernest Solvay, the famous Belgian chemist, but is now tended by the Walloon Region. It offers lakeside walks, rhododendron glades, woods with wild deer, an obelisk and a belvedere. The café is a friendly place located in a whitewashed building on a cobbled courtyard. Across the way, the Fondation Folon exhibits works by a Belgian graphic artist who worked for organisations like Unesco and the Italian Socialist Party.

Lakeside Walks

The little lakeside town of Genval, just south of Brussels, looks like somewhere in Switzerland. It even has a copy of William Tell's mountain chapel. The artificial lake was created in 1904 by an entrepreneur who hoped to turn Genval into a spa town. One hundred years later, it is still a picturesque spot, with several excellent hotels, including the luxurious Château du Lac, built in 1904 as part of the spa development and later used by Schweppes as a water bottling plant. People come from Brussels to walk around the lake and eat in one of the restaurants, as they have been doing for more than a century.

Foret de Soignes

Courses

Brussels is a good city for picking up a new skill. There are workshops and courses in every neighbourhood. Most are cheap by international standards.

Art Courses

Contraste A photography workshop in Etterbeek with a range of courses taught by professionals. Rue Général Capiaumont 45, Etterbeek; ☎ 02.640.94.40; www.photo-contraste.com

Cookery Courses

With some of the best chefs in Europe, Brussels is the ideal place to learn the art of cooking. This is a good way to meet people and understand the Belgian lifestyle. You can sign up for courses in many different venues, from serious culinary schools to quirky loft apartments.

Mmmmh! Cookery courses and wine appreciation in a smart contemporary kitchen close to Place Stéphanie. Organises evening courses and courses for kids. The latest idea is speed cooking at lunchtime where participants cook a meal and eat it in the space of a lunch hour. Costs €15. Booking essential.

Toquetoc A young Belgian mother runs cookery courses in her bright loft apartment near the Porte de Hal. Popular with young city people who appreciate the convivial atmosphere as much as the delicious food. ☎ 0495.22.57.66; email info@toquetoc.be; www.toquetoc.be

Salsa

La Tentation Take salsa lessons in a striking cultural venue carved out of an old department store by the city's Galician community. The centre also hosts Galician bagpipe lessons. Rue de Laeken 28, central Brussels; ☎ 02.223.22.75; email info@latentation.org; www.latentation.be

Los Romanticos Salsa lessons are organised on Mondays, Thursdays and Fridays above a romantic restaurant near Place Sainte Catherine. Quai aux Bois à Brûler 5, central Brussels; www.salsabruxelles.be

Weekends away

Exploring the Heart of Europe

Belgium is a small country, but it offers an amazing variety of experiences. You can go for a walk along a North Sea beach, spot wild boar in the Ardennes forests (or on your dinner plate in the evening), retreat to a stone cottage with a blazing fire, or stand on the spot just outside Waterloo where Napoleon saw his Empire collapse.

Flanders

Flanders is the flat Dutch-speaking region to the north of Brussels extending as far as the North Sea beaches. This is an area famous for ancient cities like Ghent, Bruges and Antwerp, but also for the battlefields and war cemeteries of the First World War around Ypres. The flat landscape may seem dull at first, but it is crossed by tidal creeks and old canals, and dotted with ancient abbeys famous for their beer and cheese.

Bruges

Some of Europe's great historic cities are close to Brussels, including the Flemish city of Bruges (www.brugge.be). The town is visited by three million tourists every year, but most go in the summer months, so that autumn and winter weekends are normally quiet. Even if it is bitterly cold outside, you can dive into the Onze-Lieve-Vrouwe church to look at Michelangelo's tiny statue of the Madonna and Child, admire Flemish masters in the Groeningemuseum, and marvel at the Memling paintings in the Medieval St Jan's hospital. Bruges can easily be done as a day trip, but it is worth booking a hotel for the night, so that you can wander the deserted canals after dark and wake up to the sound of church bells. The best time to book a trip is in December, when a Christmas market is held on the Simon Stevinplein and hotels offer special winter deals.

Antwerp

Some cities seduce. Others don't. Antwerp (www.antwerpen.be) has the gift. It's not the most beautiful of cities, but it regularly gets a mention in style magazines as one of the planet's coolest cities. It's the perfect place for aimlessly wandering around. Almost every street has something of interest - a crumbling townhouse, an open doorway leading to an overgrown courtyard, a shop window filled with junk. But it also has superb museums, an invigorating waterfront and some striking modern architecture. It's easy to visit Antwerp in a day, but worth booking a night in a bed and breakfast so that you can eat a leisurely meal, wander around the old streets after dark and soak up the vitality of this maritime city.

Ghent

Bruges may attract more tourists, but Ghent (www.gent.be) has a subtle charm that is hard to resist. Just half an hour from Brussels by train or car, this small town has some exceptional art and architecture. The main attraction is Jan and Hubert van Eyck's 'Altarpiece of the Mystic Lamb', which has hung in Ghent Cathedral since its completion in 1432 (although one panel was stolen). Once you have seen that, you can explore the cobbled streets of the restored Patershol district, possibly fitting in a visit to the enchanting Museum of Folklore. The Fine Art Museum reopened in 2007, and the city has an acclaimed contemporary art museum, Smak, located in the romantic Citadelpark. The town has some stylish boutiques around the Kouter square and countless seductive restaurants where you might try local specialities such as waterzooi (a stew made from fish or chicken).

In Flanders Fields

The main event every year in Ypres is the 11 November ceremony under the Menin Gate to mark the end of the First World War. Destroyed in the First World War, Ypres was totally rebuilt in its original style. The main sights include the Menin Gate war memorial, the Medieval cloth hall and the outstanding war museum In Flanders Fields (www.inflandersfields.be). The town is surrounded by more than 150 war cemeteries, including the burial place of John McCrae, a Canadian doctor who wrote the poem 'In Flanders Fields'. Ypres can be reached by car or train in about one hour.

Contacts

Tourist information: Flanders and Brussels Tourist Office covers Brussels and the northern part of the country, including Antwerp, Bruges, Ghent and the coast. Office close to Grand'Place. Rue Marché aux Herbes 61, central Brussels. ☎ 02.504.03.90; email info@visitflanders.co.uk (for information in English); www.visitflanders. co.uk

Cycling: Flanders Region has created an extensive network of signed bike routes. There are beer cycle routes, a 100km circuit around Brussels and a strawberry route. www.fietsroute.org

Wallonia

Wallonia is the French-speaking region extending south from Brussels to the French and German borders. This is an area of old cities such as Namur, Mons and Liège, which have been battered by war and industrialisation. The countryside is hilly and forested, with sheer cliffs rising above meandering rivers. The region is dotted with castles and abbeys, picturesque villages and wayside shrines. It takes time to discover the secrets, but there are exceptional places barely more than an hour from Brussels.

Spa

The small Ardennes town of Spa (www.spa-info.be), which gave its name to health resorts all over the world, is the perfect place to book a winter break. Famous since the 16th century for its mineral-rich waters, the town grew into one of the most fashionable resorts in Europe. It lost much of its edge after the Second World War, but new investment has recently transformed the place, providing it with a state-of-the-art thermal centre (www.thermesdespa.com) and a stylish new Radisson Palace Hotel offering a range of spa treatments (www.radissonsas.com). Allow two hours to get there by car or train.

Namur

Just 40 minutes from Brussels by car or train, Namur (www.namur.be) is an ancient town with a relaxed charm. Since becoming the capital of Wallonia Region, the town has invested heavily in urban renovation, bringing a fresh feel to the streets. Climb the hill to visit the ancient fortress, then stroll through the attractive streets of the lower town, stopping for lunch in a traditional Belgian restaurant such as Temps des Cerises. For a romantic weekend, book Les Tanneurs de Namur (www.tanneurs. com), a beautiful hotel located in a renovated tannery close to the river.

Ski Slopes

As soon as temperatures dip below zero, skiing enthusiasts start to listen to weather reports from the Ardennes. The uplands of southern Belgium have several dozen ski centres, mainly in the eastern Ardennes. Most are suited to cross-country skiing, but there are a few downhill runs and sledging slopes. While no one pretends that the skiing is as good as the Alps, the Belgian resorts have the advantage of being just a couple of hours away by car or train.

Walking in the Ardennes

Active winter weekends in Belgium are easy to organise with the help of map shops, tourist offices and internet sites. You can take a hike on one of the many marked trails laid out by local tourist offices, or go for a more serious ramble on one of the Sentiers de Grandes Randonnées - a network of hiking trails that cross Flanders and the Ardennes (www. grsentiers.org).

Cycling in Wallonia

The Walloon Region has recently invested in a network of trails that follow old railway lines, forest paths and canals in the south of the country. These routes are destined for walkers, horse riders, skaters and cyclists. Detailed maps can be downloaded from the Ravel website (www.ravel.wallonie.be).

A Cottage in the Ardennes

The Ardennes region in the south of Belgium is ideally situated for an autumn break away from the city. You can book a room in a country inn with gastronomic cooking (www.logis.be) or opt for the simple life in a rented stone farmhouse (www.gitesdewallonie.net). The region offers a range of distractions, including forest walks, spectacular caves and ancient castles.

Contacts

Tourist information The Wallonia and Brussels Tourist Office covers Brussels and the southern part of the country, including Waterloo, Namur, Liège and the Ardennes. ☎ 02.504.03.90; email info@belgiumtheplacetobe.be (for information in English); www.belgiumtheplaceto.be

The Netherlands

Domburg

The small resorts on the Zeeland coast can be reached in a couple of hours from Brussels. They get crowded in the summer, but are perfect for an impulsive autumn break. Domburg is the main resort, a jaunty seaside town with several grand 19th-century buildings, including an old Kurhaus that is currently being restored. The young artist Piet Mondriaan came to Domburg to paint the lighthouse. Now it's a place where Dutch and German families come to play on the beach, eat fried fish in beach bars and turn gently pink in the sun. It takes under two hours to get there by car from Brussels, though the traffic can be slow at the weekend.

Kröller-Müller Museum

One of the most outstanding modern art museums in Europe is just two hours by car from Brussels (or a little longer if you hit a traffic jam). The Kröller-Müller Museum (www.kmm.nl) contains the private art collection of Hélène Kröller-Müller, including some astonishing works by Vincent van Gogh. The museum occupies a striking modern building in the middle of a national park. You can drive to the museum, but it's more fun (and more Dutch) to leave your car at the park entrance and borrow one of the 1,700 free white bicycles. You can then set off to explore the strangely wild landscape of heath, pine woods and drifting sand, ending up at the museum for lunch. The park is surrounded by rustic pancake houses and friendly Dutch hotels. The Bilderberg Hotel de Buunderkamp at Wolfheze (www.bilderberg.be) is a comfortable modern hotel buried deep in the pine woods with an attractive indoor swimming pool and an upscale restaurant. The breakfast is sublime.

Contact

Dutch Tourist Board: ☎ 02.543.08.00; www.holland.com/uk; email info-be@holland.com

Northern France

Lille

Lille (www.lilletourism.com) was a run-down industrial town until the Eurostar project was announced. With the coming of the high-speed train, it turned into a vibrant northern city with a high-tech business quarter and a beautifully restored old town. The architectural style is an enticing combination of French and Flemish influences, while the museums contain some surprising works. Thalys trains from Brussels to Lille take less than 40 minutes, while driving on the relatively quiet A8 motorway will take about an hour. Lille has a smart fully automated metro. It's fun to take a ride, though hardly essential, since most places are within walking distance.

Le Crotoy

Le Crotoy is a sleepy French seaside town overlooking the tidal wastes of the Baie de Somme, about two hours by car from Brussels. It's not a place for a wild weekend, but it has an old-fashioned Gallic charm. You come here to fly a kite on the sand, take an old steam train around the bay and look for rare birds in the marshes. The red-hued Hotel des Tourelles (www.lestourelles.com) on the seafront is the place to stay for anyone looking for romance. A group of Belgians fell in love with this hotel and turned it from a turreted ruin into a chic design hotel. Bedrooms are small but tasteful, while dorms are available for kids. The restaurant serves impeccable fresh fish and local salt marsh lamb. A simple double room costs €57 without breakfast.

Contact

Maison de la France: Avenue de la Toison d'Or 21; ☎ 0902.880.25; email info.be@ franceguide.com; www.franceguide.com

Germany

Monschau

Monschau is an old German town in the Eiffel hills, just a few kilometres from the Belgian border, and about two hours by car from Brussels. You can leave Brussels after work on a Friday and arrive in Monschau in time for a late dinner in a snug German restaurant. The town has attractive cobbled streets with old half-timbered houses that once belonged to merchants. It can be crowded, but not impossibly so. The Carat Hotel (www.carathotel.de) is a comfortable hotel in the heart of the town with a swimming pool and wellness programme. Double rooms start at about €98.

Contact

German Tourist Board: ☎ 02.245.97.00; email info@d-z-t.com; www.germany-tourism.de

Tourist Information

Belgium

Tourist offices have all the information you need on museums, restaurants, shops, concerts, cafés and walks. The large city tourist offices have the most information, but some of the smaller offices are run by passionate locals who can provide unexpected tips.

Brussels International Information on tourism and congresses in Brussels. Hôtel de Ville, Grand'Place; ☎ 02.513.89.40; email tourism@brusselsinternational.be; www. brusselsinternational.be

Online Hotel Reservations

The simplest way to book a hotel for the weekend is via an online booking site. But you need to look carefully to avoid ending up in a dismal chain hotel.

Hotels.nl A simple site for booking hotel rooms in The Netherlands. www.hotels.nl

Weekendcompany.be Dutch online booking service with a range of weekend breaks in the Netherlands, Belgium and Germany. The site is in Dutch only. www. weekendcompany.be

Weekendhotel.nl An inspiring Dutch site that lists the most charming hotels and B&Bs in the Netherlands and Belgium. www.weekendhotel.nl

Hotels

Most visitors to Brussels are there for business rather than sightseeing, and hotels tend to be dull modern places with little character. But there are some attractive small hotels dotted around the city, especially in the neighbourhood of Grand Place and Place Stéphanie. Hotel rates in Brussels are average for a European capital, though considerably lower than London or Amsterdam. But there are good deals at weekends, when many large business hotels struggle to find guests. A few minutes on the internet will get you some astonishing deals, though the hotel might be in a dull business district close to the airport. Smaller hotels don't normally cut rates at weekends, with the result that you can pay more on Saturday night for a plain room in a modest hotel than you pay for a luxury room in an upmarket hotel. During the week, such anomalies disappear, and business hotels charge top prices.

Upmarket

Amigo It's hard to find fault with this splendid hotel located in a narrow lane just off Grand'Place. It was built for the 1958 Brussels Expo, and filled with costly antiques to suggest a much older pedigree. Rocco Forte bought the place in 2000 and employed his sister to give a more contemporary designer look to the interior. The result is close to perfection. Doubles from €175. Rue de l'Amigo 1-3; ☎ 02.547.47.47; email reservations.amigo@roccofortehotels.com; www.hotelamigo.com

Le Dixseptième A gorgeous little hotel located in an unassuming spot close to Grand'Place. The house was built in the 17th century by a Spanish ambassador and retains many old features like a wooden staircase and a cobbled courtyard. The bedrooms are sublimely decorated in different styles, with quirky touches alluding to European artists like Magritte and Jordaens. Hunt on the internet and you might find a double room during the week for €220, dropping to as low a €99 at weekends. Rue de la Madeleine 25; ☎ 02.517.17.17; www.ledixseptieme.be

Manos Stephanie A discreet luxurious hotel near Avenue Louise filled with antiques, old paintings and chandeliers. Guests can rent a Smart car to nip around town for €49. Chaussée de Charleroi 28; ☎ 02.539.02.50; email: manos@manoshotel.com; www.manoshotel.com

Plaza The Plaza opened in the 1930s as one of the grand hotels of Europe, but it eventually went bust. It might have been torn down, but a Belgian aristocrat intervened in 1996 and restored the building to its former splendour, complete with crystal chandeliers and Gobelins tapestries. The bedrooms are suitably grand and the service is faultless. The only disadvantage is its location in a slightly sleazy district. Doubles from €109. Boulevard Adolphe Max 118; ☎ 02.227.67.00; email reservations@leplaza-brussels.be; www.leplaza-brussels.be

Mid Range

Melia Avenue Louise A comfortable hotel off Avenue Louise with an attractive library bar. Doubles for €79 at the weekend. More expensive during weekdays, but doubles sometimes available for as little as €120. Rue Blanche 4; ☎ 02.535.95.00; email melia.avenue.louise@solmelia.com; www.solmelia.com

Orts A newly opened hotel in a 19th-century corner building in the heart of the fashionable Dansaert quarter. The location is perfect for Brussels nightlife, but light sleepers could find it a bit noisy. Doubles start at €150 and prices don't drop at weekends. Rue Auguste Orts; ☎ 02.517.07.17; www.hotelorts.be

Sofitel Quartier Europe A new hotel located on the lively Place Jourdan, within walking distance of the European institutions. A double can be secured on a weekday night for €185, dropping to €110 at weekends. Place Jourdan 1, ☎ 02.235.51.00; www.sofitel.com

The White Hotel A cool boutique hotel on Avenue Louise with white rooms decorated with objects by Belgian designers. Guest can rent a Honda bike for €18 a day to zoom around the designer shops and cool cafés. Doubles for less than €100. Avenue Louise 212; ☎ 02.644.29.29; email info@thewhitehotel.be; www.thewhitehotel.be

Budget

Noga A charming little hotel in a quiet street close to the fish restaurants on Place Sainte Catherine. Rooms are furnished with antiques and odd ornaments, while old family portraits decorate the staircase. The owners offer little extras you won't find in the bigger hotels, like a library, games, a snooker room and a piano. Truly special. Doubles for €110 during the week and €85 at weekends. Rue du Béguinage 38; ☎ 02.218.67.63; email info@nogahotel.com; www.nogahotel.com

Rembrandt The Rembrandt is located in a corner house in a quiet street near Avenue Louise. You have to ring the bell and then tip toe around to avoid knocking over one of the China vases. Some might find it all a bit old fashioned, but this 13-room hotel has its devoted fans; the corner room at the top is particularly in demand. Rates are low, with singles from €45 and doubles from €65. Rue de la Concorde 42; ☎ 02.512.71.39; email rembrandt@brutele.be; www.hotel-rembrandt.be

Welcome This little hotel stands among the fish restaurants on Place Saint Catherine. It is (as the name suggests) friendly and rooms are decorated in individual styles. You can stay in an exotic Indian room or choose a minimalist Japanese interior. Quai aux Bois à Brûler 23; ☎ 02.219.95.46; email info@hotelwelcome.com; www. hotelwelcome.com

B&B

Phileas Fogg A warm and friendly guest house in a beautiful old Brussels townhouse close to the botanical gardens. It's run by Karin Dhadamus, who speaks seven languages and chats endlessly with her guests. The rooms are spacious and decorated in a quirky personal style. There are some wonderful details, like old oak floors and fluffy red feathers hung from the door handles. Rue van Bemmel 6; ☎ 02.217.83.38; email phileas.fogg@belgacom.net; www.phileasfogg.be

Online Reservations

The simplest and cheapest way to book a hotel in Brussels is by using an online booking site.

Bed & Brussels Online reservation of B&Bs in Brussels with rooms ranging from basic to luxurious. Useful sections for business executives and interns looking for longer-term accommodation. www.bnb-brussels.be

Booking.com A Dutch company that has some exceptional hotel deals in Brussels. The site includes hotel reviews posted by guests. www.bookings.com

Otel.com Hotel booking site with deals at business hotels in Brussels and a customer loyalty scheme. www.otel.com

Weekendhotel.nl A Dutch site that lists some charming hotels and B&Bs in Brussels (with English pages). No business hotels and no special deals. The site doesn't handle bookings but indicates availability and provides an email enquiry form to send to the hotel or B&B. www.weekendhotel.nl

Antwerp waterfront

About Belgium

- The Hapsburg Emperor Charles V made Brussels the capital of the Netherlands.
- The Belgians rebelled against the Dutch in 1830 and it was recognised as an independent state in 1831.
- Belgium was one of the six founding members of the European Economic Community in 1957, and Brussels became its provisional headquarters.
- In the 1960s Brussels the city grew in international importance, gaining the headquarters of NATO in 1967.
- The gently anarchic spirit of the Belgians can be seen around Brussels in sights from the Manneken Pis to the murals of cartoon characters.
- In 2001 Brussels became the official capital of the European Union under the Treaty of Nice.
- Brussels is a highly cosmopolitan city with a Chinatown, Moroccan and African quarters and even French and Irish areas.
- The European Quarter is notorious for its uninspired architecture and failed urban planning, but the Brussels authorities are now committed to making it more appealing.
- The presence of the international community has raised the average income to the second highest in Europe, but this wealth is unevenly distributed round the city.
- The European Parliament is not based exclusively in Brussels: ten times a year it moves to Strasbourg, and it has a Secretariat in Luxembourg.
- The European Parliament building is the largest EU complex in the city and is known locally as the Caprice des Dieux because it resembles a certain French cheese.
- The main work of the European Commission in Brussels consists of drafting new legislation that will apply to all 27 member countries and ensuring that they implement it.
- The EU employs around 25,000 staff in Brussels, and there are also some 15,000 lobbyists working there.

The Belgians

Who are the Belgians?

The Belgians have been trying to create a national identity since the revolution of 1830. Yet this is a country with many different identities. It lies at the hub of land routes leading to Paris, the Channel ports, Germany and the Alps. The inhabitants of this region are constantly borrowing ideas from other countries. So Belgium can seem like Britain, or France, or Germany, or America, or nowhere.

More than anything, Belgians love food. This is something that everyone agrees about, whether they are Walloon or Flemish. The average Belgian is probably happiest sitting in a plain restaurant with a large pot of mussels, or *steak-frites*, drinking a glass of beer, surrounded by family.

Belgians are also fond of festivals. The Dutch envy the Belgians for their Burgundian spirit, their *joie de vivre*. Every town and village has its local festival, complete with brass bands and beer. Some are ancient religious festivals. Others are just an excuse to dress up in a Napoleonic uniform and fire off blank cartridges in a field.

Royal Pride and Shame

Belgians are rather proud of their monarchy and there are statues of former kings all over the city. King Leopold I stands on top of the Colonne du Congrès on Rue Royale, holding the Belgian Constitution. King Leopold sits on a horse on a grassy square next to the royal palace, while King Albert I, again on horseback, occupies a position at the bottom of the Mont des Arts, facing Queen Elisabeth on the other side of the road. A more modest bust of King Baudouin stands on the square in front of the Cathedral. But where is King Leopold III? The country never forgave him for collaborating with the enemy in the Second World War. His only memorial is a boulevard with his name running out to the airport.

One Nation or Two: is Belgium about to Split?

For several decades, political commentators have being asking whether Belgium will eventually disappear, to be replaced by the separate states of Flanders and Wallonia. Many have considered a split impossible or undesirable, but public opinion in Flanders is gradually moving in favour of divorce, with recent polls showing 51% of Flemish citizens in favour of an independent Flanders. The Flemish call for independence is fuelled by a belief that the booming economy of the north is being dragged down by the high level of unemployment in Wallonia.

The debate was rekindled in 2005 by a think tank called the Warande Group, which published a manifesto calling for two separate states, arguing that both regions would benefit from the dissolution of Belgium. The group also called for Brussels to be made into a 'District of Europe' under EU control. The King reacted angrily to these proposals.

The topic returned to the news in December 2006 when the RTBF, the main French language TV station, broadcast a fake news report claiming that Flanders had broken away from Belgium to form a separate state. The story was accompanied by live interviews, shots of a tram halted at the Flemish border and a report that King Albert and Queen Paola had fled the country on a military plane. Ninety percent of RTBF viewers said that they believed the story. Half an hour into the report, the TV channel was forced to display a message at the bottom of the screen reading 'This is Fiction'. The producer argued that the programme was intended to stimulate debate. But many people, including the prime minister, were not amused.

The Identity of Brussels

The people of Brussels have a gently anarchic temperament that comes from centuries of foreign domination. The spirit of the city is best seen in the statues dotted around the streets, like the policeman tripping over (on a corner of the Place Sainctelette) or the stray city dog raising its leg to urinate (on the corner of Rue des Chartreux). *The Manneken Pis*, dating back to the early Middle Ages, is the city's oldest and most famous symbol. It seems a rather unexpected emblem for a capital city. One would expect a national leader on horseback to take pride of place, rather than this diminutive bronze figure of a small boy peeing into a fountain. Yet it captures the spirit of a city that has defied authority for centuries. Many of the cartoon figures created in Brussels have a similar defiant character. The best loved is Gaston Lagaffe, whose statue stands at the top of the steps leading down to the Comic Strip Centre. Lagaffe spends much of his time coming up with elaborate schemes to avoid paying money for parking meters. It is difficult to imagine a more Belgian hero.

Office façade on Rue des Deux Eglises

Writers on Brussels

For a relatively small city, Brussels has a distinguished literary history. Some of the great works of European literature were written here, including part of Karl Marx's *Communist Manifesto*, several chapters of Victor Hugo's Les Misérables and Multatuli's anti-colonial Dutch classic *Max Havelaar*.

The literary past of Brussels is still relatively uncharted, so few people are aware that the Palais des Beaux-Arts stands on the site of the Pensionnat Heger, the boarding school where Charlotte Brontë spent two unhappy years (providing material for her novels *The Professor* and *Villette*). Nor do many people know that W.H. Auden stayed in Brussels in 1938 and wrote several of his most famous poems here, including *Musée des Beaux-Arts* and *Brussels in Winter*.

History of Brussels

How Brussels Grew from a Village in a Bog to the Washington DC of Europe

Stand in the middle of the Halles St Géry and you are close to the spot where Brussels began. The official foundation date is 979, when the Duke of Lorraine built a castle on an island in the River Senne. But there was already a settlement in this marshy region known in Old Dutch as Broucsella, the village in the marshes.

Brussels was shaped by its location. It stands in the valley below a ridge of sand left by the retreating sea. The marshy Flemish plain lies to the north, the forested Walloon uplands to the south. The Franks conquered the north, but they were stopped by the forests south of the River Senne, leaving the uphill region in the hands of the Gauls. The Forêt de Soignes, where Brussels residents now walk their dogs on Sunday mornings, marks the boundary of two civilisations. The language changes just south of Brussels, from Dutch to French, and the culture shifts from Germanic to Latin. This gives Brussels its unique identity. Or, some would say, no identity at all.

The city was surrounded in the 11th century by a 4km wall with seven gates and 40 towers, fragments of which are still standing. A trading economy developed based on the city's strategic location on the road from Cologne to Flanders. Much of the wealth came from luxury cloth produced by the weavers of Brussels using English wool and sold to wealthy nobles in Paris and Venice. The city's craftsmen expressed their wealth and power by building tall guild houses on the Grand'Place - forerunners of the gilt-laden buildings that now glint in the sunlight.

The city grew rapidly in the 14th century, pushing beyond the old city walls into the rolling Brabant fields. The authorities built a new wall, three kilometres longer than the first, which enclosed the high ground to the south of the old town. The rich merchants chose to settle here, away from the smell and noise of the city, building large houses with Flemish gables on the ancient geological sandbank known as the Sablon.

A New Elite

The city's craftsmen were kept busy in the 15th century producing high-value goods like cloth, tapestries and silverware for the nobility. Brussels was then under the rule of the Dukes of Burgundy, a French royal family that acquired the Low Countries through marriage. The language shift began at this time, as French became the language of the ruling class of the upper town, while Dutch remained the language of the craftsmen in the lower town.

In 1477, the Burgundian Netherlands passed by marriage into the hands of the Hapsburgs. As the most important city in the Low Countries, Brussels grew in importance, particularly under Emperor Charles V, who came to power on his nineteenth birthday in 1519 and chose Brussels as capital of the Netherlands in 1531.

The city continued to produce luxury goods for the upper end of the market. Its tapestries, woven with the initials B.B.B., kept out the chill in castles and palaces throughout Europe, and many of the richest people went to sleep on Brussels 'pillow lace'.

Under Charles, who was taught by Erasmus, the spirit of the Renaissance reached Brussels. The city attracted a growing number of painters, scholars and philosophers. But it also attracted free-thinking Protestants who challenged the dogmas of the Catholic church. Charles was tolerant of many things, but he drew the line at religious heresy, and executed some of the leading dissidents.

By 1555, Charles had grown weary of ruling his vast empire and came to Brussels to abdicate. The vast hall called the Aula Magna where Charles took leave of his empire was destroyed by fire in the 18th century, but the vast cellars have survived below the cobblestones on Place Royale.

The relatively mild rule of Charles was followed by a cruel period under his son Philip. Initially, Brussels continued to prosper at the heart of an Empire that stretched from the Netherlands to America. In 1561, Brussels became an inland port, linked to Antwerp by the Willebroeck Canal. The new waterway, which still flows along the northern edge of the old town, brought ships to the heart of the city. The Sainte Catherine Quarter became an inland port, with ships moored next to the stone walls of the Ste Catherine church until well into the 19th century.

Intolerance

The golden age ended abruptly in 1567 when Philip sent the Duke of Alva to the Low Countries to crush the heretics. The Duke set up a commission known as the 'Council of Blood', which tried and executed hundreds of religious dissidents, including some of the aristocrats who lived around the Sablon. Even the mildest critics were ruthlessly punished, including Counts Egmont and Hoorn, who were beheaded in 1568 on Grand'Place. A statue was put up on the site of their execution in the 19th century, but later moved to the little park in the Place du Petit Sablon, within view of the palace where Egmont once lived.

The Spanish didn't stay in Brussels for long. William of Orange captured the city in 1578 and held onto it for the next seven years. But Spanish troops finally pushed the Dutch out of Flanders in 1585. A new frontier was drawn across the region, separating the Protestant Dutch Republic from the Catholic Spanish Netherlands. Many skilled Protestants fled north, leaving the Spanish cities to decline. Yet the culture was far from moribund in the early 17th century; the energetic Antwerp artist Peter Paul Rubens ran a painting workshop that ensured a plentiful supply of vigorous baroque paintings for the churches and palaces of Europe.

The Spanish signed a truce with the Dutch in 1648, but the region was regularly revisited by war in the late 17th and early 18th century. In 1695, the French artillery of Louis XIV aimed at the spire on Grand'Place and pounded the city for two days and nights. Most of the old town was reduced to rubble, including almost every building on Grand'Place (though the spire used as a target miraculously survived). The late 17th-century economy was strong enough to recover, and the entire city was rebuilt in less than five years. Look at the façades on Grand'Place and you will see stones marking the reconstruction year, most of them dated between 1596 and 1599.

The wars came to an end in 1713 with the signing of the Treaty of Utrecht, which brought the Spanish Netherlands under Austrian control. Brussels became the capital of the Austrian Netherlands, but its citizens had little say in the running of the city. At first, the Austrians brought prosperity, introducing new industries and opening up export markets, but the guilds finally rebelled against their loss of political power. The Austrians regained control and executed the leader of the local guilds, a man called François Anneessens, who lost his head but gave his name to a city square and metro station.

Napoleon

The Austrian peace did not last long. Napoleon's troops arrived in the city in 1792, bringing revolutionary ideas to this strongly Catholic country. The French occupied the city for 23 years and introduced many administrative reforms that persist to this day. They also founded a stock exchange and an art museum.

Napoleon fought his final battle in the rye fields south of Brussels. The city waited nervously on June 18, 1815, to learn the outcome. For a time it seemed as if the French had won, and British residents in Brussels began packing their bags and getting ready to flee the country. But then news arrived that Wellington's troops had, with the help of Blücher's Prussians, defeated the French, and Napoleon was fleeing towards Paris without his hat.

The victory brought British battlefield tourists to Brussels, including Lord Byron, who stayed in a house overlooking the park and wrote a poem describing the Duchess of Richmond's ball on the eve of the battle. *'There was a sound of revelry by night/And Belgium's capital had gathered then/Her beauty and her chivalry'*, it begins.

The Allies met to debate the fate of Belgium at the 1815 Congress of Vienna. Their main aim was to keep France in check, and so they decided to join Belgium with the Netherlands and Luxembourg to create a buffer zone. The new country, named the United Netherlands, was led by King William I of the Netherlands. This arrangement looked promising to those who knew their Medieval history - was it not simply a resurrection of the Low Countries of the Dukes of Burgundy? But the regions had grown apart over the centuries - the north was Dutch speaking, mercantile and Protestant, while the south was mainly French-speaking, bureaucratic and Catholic.

Initially, the arrangement seemed to work. The Dutch injected capital and a spirit of enterprise into the southern economy, and granted Brussels a measure of political power. But unrest continued to grow in the south, fuelled by high unemployment and a harsh winter in 1829. Finally, riots broke out in the streets of Brussels on August 25th, 1830, following a performance of a popular patriotic opera, *La Muette de Portici*. King William sent 10,000 Dutch troops to put down the rebellion. The two forces clashed in the area round the park, and the Belgians drove out the Dutch after four days of street-to-street and tree-to-tree fighting.

A New Beginning

A provisional government was rapidly formed and a National Assembly met in November 1830, the first form of self government in Brussels since the Middle Ages. By January 1831, the European powers recognised Belgium as an independent state, though the Dutch continued to claim the territory for the next eight years.

The young rebels drafted a progressive Constitution that was a model of liberal ideals. Yet they were careful not to go as far as the French Revolution; they wanted Belgium to be a monarchy, and found their new king, Leopold I, in the German house of Saxe-Coburg. He was an uncle of Queen Victoria, which pleased the British.

Under its liberal government, the new country rapidly turned into an industrial powerhouse. Five years after independence, the first trains in Continental Europe ran on a line built from Brussels to Mechelen. Steelworks and coal mines were opened along the valley of the River Meuse, and Brussels was transformed into one of the most elegant little capitals of Europe.

The city continued to boom under Leopold II, a ruthlessly ambitious monarch who insisted that Belgium needed a colony. He didn't get much support from the government, but he paid the Welsh explorer Henry Morton Stanley to travel along the largely unexplored Congo river. With Stanley's help, Leopold carved himself out a private colony that was rich in natural resources, including ivory and rubber, and Leopold's bank accounts began to swell.

The King spent his enormous profits on ambitious architectural projects in Brussels, Antwerp and Ostend. The broad Avenue de Tervuren was built with Congo money, as was the Museum of the Congo in Tervuren. But Leopold's projects helped to destroy some of the oldest quarters of the city. His plan for a railway under the city obliterated the old Putterie Quarter and his plan for a Mont des Arts virtually wiped out the old Isabella Quarter near Place Royale, including the Pensionnat Heger where Charlotte and Emily Brontë studied.

The wealth from the Congo also funded the development of Art Nouveau architecture. This elaborate style, using iron and glass, flourished in Brussels between 1893-1914, led by architects such as Victor Horta and Paul Hankar.

Statue on the Square Marie-Louise depicting "the birth of Belgium"

Occupation

Leopold died in 1909, having been condemned in the international press and stripped of his colony by the Belgian government. He was succeeded by Albert I, who was still a young monarch when the First World War broke out in 1914. The German generals had calculated that Belgium would collapse within a few days, leaving them with a free passage into France, but Albert spoiled the invasion plan by resisting. His army held on to a small corner of West Flanders, which became the northern point of a line of trenches that ran from the North Sea to Switzerland.

For four years, Brussels was under German occupation. The military regime dealt harshly with the Resistance, shooting many Belgians at a firing range in eastern Brussels. One of the victims was Edith Cavell, a British nurse who was working in a Brussels hospital when the German army entered the city. She stayed on in Brussels, helping some 200 British soldiers escape back to Britain, but was eventually arrested, sentenced as a spy and shot at 2am on 12 October 1915.

Four years of war left Belgium devastated, with several cities in rubble, 40,000 dead and the economy shattered. Yet Brussels survived the war relatively undamaged. Workmen were soon back in the streets, completing the Palais des Beaux-Arts, digging another stretch of the junction rail tunnel, and building shiny new Art Deco apartment buildings on Avenue Louise.

Construction work ground to a halt again during the Great Depression. The news got steadily worse in the 1930s, with Hitler's rise to power, followed by Albert I's death in a climbing accident, followed, barely a year later, by news that the young King Leopold III had crashed his car in Switzerland, killing his beautiful Swedish wife Astrid.

The Second World War brought further misery to Brussels. Unlike his father, Leopold III surrendered to the Germans after a brief period of fighting, raising suspicions of collaboration. To his credit, he wrote a letter to Hitler in 1942 that may have saved thousands of Belgian from deportation. But his reputation was blemished by photographs showing him clearly enjoying Hitler's company at Berchtesgarten.

The Belgian people took different sides in the war. Some risked their lives by hiding Jews in their houses, saving about 2,700 from deportation, but others collaborated with the enemy.

Apart from some villages in the Ardennes, the country did not suffer major damage in the Second World War. But it entered the post-war period with the future of the monarchy in doubt. Leopold III was forced to live in exile in Switzerland along with his second wife. A 1950 referendum on the royal question produced a small majority in support of Leopold's return, but Leopold felt uncomfortable with the slender majority, and abdicated in favour of his oldest son Baudouin.

What? sells T-shirts and bags

Optimism

Baudouin's rule began during the bright optimism of the 1950s, when Brussels began to promote itself as a modern, international and American-style city. The country was one of the six founding members of the European Economic Community in 1957 and Brussels became the temporary capital of the new organisation. One year later, the 1958 Brussels Expo launched an era of scientific progress, consumerism and optimism. But hardly two years later, the dream turned sour when the Belgian Congo gained independence.

The city continued to grow in international importance in the 1960s, and the headquarters of Nato moved to the Brussels suburbs in 1967. Since then the city has developed into a global capital where decisions are taken that affect the future of Europe. Despite its growing political power, the city that began in a bog has managed to preserve its old-fashioned charm and anarchic sense of humour.

1830

The Belgian nation was born after a brief revolution that costs about 1,000 lives. On 25 August 1830, following a performance of the minor romantic opera *La Muette de Portici,* Belgian citizens took to the streets in protest at the policies of King William of the Netherlands (who had ruled the country since 1815). After four days of street fighting in Brussels, the Dutch troops were driven out of the city. The new government drafted a Constitution that was the most progressive in Europe, guaranteeing a wide range of unprecedented liberties.

1831

Leopold of Saxe-Coburg, an uncle of Queen Victoria, was proclaimed the first King of the Belgians on 21 July. The date is now a national holiday.

1835

The first railway line in mainland Europe was built between Brussels and Mechelen, marking the beginning of Belgium's emergence as one of the leading industrial nations in Europe.

1865

Leopold I was succeeded by his son Leopold II in 1865. Twenty years later, he established a Belgian colony in the Congo, a region of Africa 80 times the size of Belgium, with enormous natural resources. The Colony brought Leopold II enormous personal gain, some of which was spent on grand architectural projects such as the Avenue de Tervuren, the royal greenhouses and the Africa Museum in Tervuren. But Leopold came under increasing fire from campaigners for his cruel treatment of the Congolese, and his colony was transferred to the Belgian state in 1908.

1880

Belgium celebrated 50 years of independence by organising a World Fair in the Parc du Cinquantenaire, or Jubilee Park. Several large exhibition halls have survived from 1880.

1909

King Leopold II died in 1909, after spending his final days living as a virtual hermit in one of his greenhouses. He was succeeded by his nephew Albert I.

1914

The German army invaded Belgium at the start of the First World War. King Albert I led the army in a heroic stand, losing Brussels and Antwerp, but holding onto a small corner of Belgian territory in West Flanders. Some of the heaviest battles of the war were fought in West Flanders around the towns of Ypres (Ieper) and Diksmuide.

1929

Hergé published the first Tintin comic strip.

1934

King Albert I died in a climbing accident on the cliffs at Marche-les-Dames, near Namur, in 1934. He was succeeded by his son Leopold III.

1935

The country was plunged into a second period of mourning when Queen Astrid died in a car crash in Switzerland while Leopold III was driving.

1940

Germany invaded Belgium on 10 May 1940. Leopold III led the army, but surrendered after just 18 days of fighting. The King remained in Belgium as a prisoner of the Germans.

1944

The country was liberated by the Allies in early September 1944, but the Germans made a final attack in the Ardennes in December 1944. The German army was halted at Bastogne by American forces in a winter campaign known as the Battle of the Bulge. Leopold III remained widely unpopular in Belgium after the Liberation because of his conduct during the war. His brother Charles was appointed regent.

1950

Leopold III finally abdicated following a referendum in which 43% of Belgians voted against his return. He was succeeded in 1951 by his eldest son, Baudouin.

ABOUT BRUSSELS

1957

Six European countries including Belgium signed the Treaty of Rome, creating the European Economic Community. Brussels was chosen as the provisional headquarters.

1958

Brussels hosted a World Fair at the Heysel which attracted 50 million visitors and gave Brussels its most striking building, the Atomium.

1960

The Belgian Congo was granted independence and became the state of Zaire.

1962

The language frontier was defined by law, splitting the country into a Dutch-speaking region in the north and a French-speaking region in the south. Brussels was officially a bilingual city, though the majority of the population was French-speaking.

1966

The Maison du Peuple, a masterpiece of Art Nouveau architecture near the Sablon, was demolished despite worldwide protests. An office block was built on the site.

Grand'Place

1967

Brussels became the headquarters of Nato after General de Gaulle ordered the organisation to leave Paris.

1993

King Baudouin died suddenly while on holiday in Spain. He was succeeded by his brother Albert, married to Paola Ruffo di Calabria. They have two sons and a daughter. First in line to the Belgian throne is Prince Philippe, who is married to Mathilde d'Udekem d'Acoz.

2001

Brussels became the official capital of the European Union under the Treaty of Nice.

2005

Belgium celebrated 175 years of independence with a series of large exhibitions.

2007

Brussels celebrated the 50th anniversary of the signing of the Treaty of Rome with a year of exhibitions and events.

Ten Myths about Belgium

Belgium is boring Belgium has two capitals, three languages, seven governments, 350 different types of beer, a museum of bird boxes and an annual bathtub regatta. It might be confusing, but it's not boring.

Belgium is a hardship posting A strange myth that has become embedded in expatriate folklore. Yet a recent United Nations survey ranked Belgium as the fifth best country to live on the planet. Hardly a tough assignment, but many companies have trouble persuading executives to move.

Belgium is flat The area in the north, called Low Belgium, is very flat with sandy beaches, polders and small hills rising to about 60m. The area in the centre known as Middle Belgium has some rolling hills and river valleys, while the area in the south referred to as High Belgium rises to 694m above sea level at the Signal de Botrange in the wild Hautes Fagnes region.

Belgians are miserable Belgians may not be constantly laughing, but they are quietly contented with their lives. A recent survey by the European Commission ranked Belgians as the third happiest nation in Europe, below the Danes and the Dutch, and on a level with the Irish and the Swedes.

It always rains The average rainfall is 852mm a year, compared with 635mm in Britain, 863mm in the Netherlands, and 812mm in Italy. So it's really only slightly wetter than Italy, even though it sometimes seems as if it never stops raining.

There are no famous Belgians Not true, although some are cartoon characters and others are frequently taken as French. Among the famous Belgians are René Magritte, Jean-Claude Van Damme, Jacques Brel, Justine Henin and Hergé.

Everyone speaks French In fact, less than half the population speaks French. The main language is Dutch, spoken by 57% of Belgians. Some 42% speak French and the other one percent are German speakers.

Brussels is French-speaking Brussels is officially bilingual, though 85% of Belgians living in Brussels speak French. Yet there are also large communities that speak other languages such as Polish, English and Spanish.

Belgium is bureaucratic Not any more. The government has been working for several years on a plan to eliminate red tape, and has already scrapped 130 petty regulations. The French government might copy the Belgian initiative, and the UK and US are also interested.

Belgium could split up tomorrow It is possible. But life would go on. Belgium would end with a peaceful revolution, like the one that split Czechoslovakia.

Social rules

Brussels is a relaxed city with an informal social life. You will generally find people welcoming if you use a few simple French words like *bonjour* (hello), *au revoir* (goodbye), *merci* (thank you) and *pardon* (sorry). Many of the social rules are common to other western countries, but a few might be unfamiliar.

Language Language can be a delicate issue, especially in the Flemish *gemeenten* on the edge of Brussels, where Dutch-speakers feel threatened by the presence of a large French-speaking population, many of them unable or unwilling to speak Dutch. The working languages in Flemish companies are Dutch and English, and French is rarely spoken. The linguistic tension is less noticeable in Brussels, where French speakers are in the majority, but English has become the language of business. In European institutions and schools, French still has the upper hand, but English is rapidly gaining ground.

Dogs Belgians are deeply attached to their dogs, which they take everywhere, even into cafés and restaurants. Asking your neighbour about their dog can be an easy way of establishing social contact. Complaining about it barking in the night is a shortcut to social exclusion.

Dinner Invitations When invited to dinner, most Belgians take along a small gift like a bunch of flowers or a box of Belgian chocolates. But you might equally take along something unexpected like an art book. The gift needn't be lavish, but it should be carefully chosen. It's not a good idea to take a random bottle of wine, as Belgians are generally serious about the wine they drink. After a formal occasion, some people send the hosts a note of thanks.

Smoking In Belgium smoking is on the decline and is now banned from most public places such as offices and restaurants (and some cafés). It is considered bad manners to light up in someone's house without asking permission. Most smokers visiting friends generally go out into in the garden or stand on a balcony to smoke.

Kissing Some Belgians kiss friends and work colleagues once on each cheek when they meet. Kissing three times is more common in France and the Netherlands.

Breastfeeding Belgians are generally relaxed about breastfeeding in public places like cafés, parks and waiting rooms. The best places are cosmopolitan cafés such as Pain Quotidien and Exki.

Children Belgian children are raised fairly strictly. They do not normally call around to play at friends' houses without their parent making a phone call in advance. Don't be surprised if a Belgian child kisses you once on the cheek when they arrive at your house.

Small Talk Most Belgians enjoy discussing restaurants, travel and culture. They are less at ease in conversations involving politics or money. It is tactful to keep negative comments about Belgium to yourself.

Shops It is polite in Belgium to say *bonjour* when you go into a small shop or boutique and *au revoir* as you leave. It's also customary to say *s'il vous plaît* (please) when you hand over money or a credit card.

Swimming Pools Most Belgian swimming pools have strict rules about what can be worn in the pool. The regulations generally insist on bathing caps for everyone and tight Speedo style trunks for men.

Tipping

How much to tip depends on the service offered. When you go to a public toilet, you should tip the lady attendant the amount indicated (usually about 30-50 cents), because tips are her only source of income. Cinema attendants also rely on tips to survive, so it is mean to refuse to pay a 50 cent tip, even if the usherette merely hands out a free magazine.

The bill in a restaurant always includes a service charge, so you need pay no more than the amount indicated. But Belgians normally leave a few euro coins, especially if the service has been attentive.

The same applies to hairdressers. You need pay no more than the amount indicated, but some customers like to add a small tip.

Taxi fares also include a service charge, so you do not need to give a large tip, though it is customary to round up the fare to the nearest euro. Of course, you may want to show your appreciation by giving a larger tip, especially if the driver has helped with suitcases or rushed you to the airport.

Various people ring doorbells at Christmas offering their best wishes. Some deserve a bonus, while others are probably working scams. Your postman should be given a tip. You may also want to reward the rubbish collectors, though you have to bear in mind that there are several different teams to pay (normally one for the white bags, one for blue and yellow bags and one representing the street sweepers). You might also be asked to buy an expensive calendar on behalf of the local firemen or police. It's hard to keep everyone happy, but perhaps the solution is to give each service a sealed envelope containing €5-€10.

The language battle

How Brussels Became a Bilingual City and Why it Matters

Belgium is officially divided into three language regions, with Dutch as the official language of Flanders, French as the language of Wallonia and German spoken in the small Ostkantone region of the eastern Ardennes. To add to the confusion, Brussels is a bilingual enclave within Flanders, with both French and Dutch given equal status.

The language issue goes back to the fall of the Roman Empire, when Germanic tribes poured across the low marshlands to the north, but the Romanised Celts held on to the forested uplands in the south. For many centuries, Brussels was a Dutch-speaking city, located just to the north of the language watershed. The French-speaking population began to emerge in the 15th century and grew significantly after 1830, when Walloons moved to Brussels to work in the new French-speaking administration. The Dutch speakers eventually became a minority, mainly concentrated in the poorer quarters of the city.

Divided by Topography

Brussels has been divided by topography since the early Middle Ages. The aristocracy settled on the slopes of the Coudenberg Hill, close to the castle, while the workers lived in the less healthy marshland around Grand'Place. As the city expanded, the rich settled in the rolling hills to the south, while the poor were crowded together in the industrials zone close to the canal. The divisions are beginning to blur, as wealthy young people move into former industrial areas such as Molenbeek and Tour et Taxis, but Brussels is still a deeply divided city. For the 50th anniversary of the Treaty of Rome, the elite attended an invitation-only performance of Beethoven's *Ninth Symphony* in the Palais des Beaux-Arts, while 30,000 queued in the rain for a free rock concert at the Heysel.

Civil Rights Inspired by the civil rights movements in America, Dutch speakers began to assert their language rights in the 1960s, leading in 1962 to the creation of a language frontier dividing the country into two main language regions. Further reforms came in 1980, when a new constitution created the three autonomous regions of Brussels, Flanders and Wallonia. As a result of the reforms, Belgium has slowly split in two, with separate television stations, newspapers, schools and libraries. It is now a deeply divided country, where readers of Dutch newspapers know little about events in Wallonia and readers of French papers are only vaguely aware of anything that happens north of Brussels and Wallonia.

Yet the language issue is far from simple. Many Belgians, especially those who move from their home town, have a complex identity, composed of different cultural influences. The Belgian singer Axelle Red sings in French, but speaks perfect Dutch with a beautiful soft Limburg accent. It turns out that her parents were Walloon, but she grew up in the Flemish town of Hasselt.

The singer Dani Klein of Vaya Con Dios has a similar mixed background. She was born in Flanders and started singing in Dutch with the band Arbeid Adelt, but now sings with Vaya Con Dios in a throaty French accent. Yet she also sings in a soulful English accent that makes you wonder if her roots might lie in the Deep South. The Flemish a capella folk group Lais are even more versatile, singing ancient songs in Dutch, French, English and Finnish.

While the language dispute provides material for regular newspaper editorials, it barely ruffles the lives of expatriates (or many Belgians, for that matter). For most foreigners living in Belgium, it merely provides occasional cultural confusion, as when someone fails to realise that Braine-le-Comte and 's Gravenbrakel are the same place.

Yet there are occasional unpleasant incidents. Someone who chooses to speak Dutch in a Brussels café can get a chilly reception. And it is not a good idea to speak French in a local café in Overijse if you want to get along with the locals.

English in Brussels The situation in Brussels is further complicated by the rise of English, which is now the second language in Brussels. Some 36% of the population speak 'good or very good' English, compared with only 30% in the case of Dutch. Meanwhile, the number of people with French as a mother tongue has dropped to below 50% in Brussels, while those with Dutch as their first language is about 10%. Some people are now arguing that English should become a third official language in Brussels, ranked equally along with Dutch and French. But such a situation will not happen overnight.

Brussels Dialect: Not Dead Yet

A handful of people in Brussels still speak the local dialect known as *Bruxellois* or *Brusseleir*. Dating back to the Middle Ages, this is a gutteral French dialect influenced by Brabant Dutch, and including the occasional stray word borrowed from Spanish or Arabic. It can still be heard in some of the cafés of the Marolles, the streets around the Eglise du Béguinage and the terraces of l'Union Saint Gilloise. Some street signs in the Marolles are in Brussels dialect, and the Toone theatre continues to perform Shakespeare and Racine in Bruxellois, proving that the city's old language is far from dead.

Going Dutch: Where to Find the Flemish

Most people think of Brussels as a French-speaking city. Yet the original language spoken in the village on the marsh was Dutch. Bruocsella only gradually became a French city in the Middle Ages, when the Dukes of Burgundy imported their language and culture to the upper town, but the main language of the lower town remained Dutch for many centuries. Look at the names on the 17th-century guild houses on Grand'Place. They are almost always in Dutch.

Arabic boucherie

The French language became dominant after Napoleon's army marched into the city in 1792, bringing French bureaucrats and French ideas. After 23 years of French rule, the Dutch language was revived, briefly, in the period after Waterloo, when King William of the Netherlands ruled over Belgium. But it only lasted for 15 years. The 1830 Revolution led to an independent Belgium in which French was the official language. Since then the Dutch speakers of Belgium have been battling to have their language recognised.

The Flemish population of Brussels has been in decline for many decades. Those who speak Dutch prefer to live in the Flemish villages just outside the city limits, rather than live in a city where they feel like an oppressed minority. Yet there are Dutch schools in most neighbourhoods, a large Flemish public library on the Place de la Monnaie and 22 Flemish cultural centres scattered across the city.

The cultural centres offer inexpensive language courses for Brussels residents who want to speak Dutch. Once the language is mastered, you can tune to FM Brussel on the car radio at 98.8 and listen to the local news read in beautiful Brabant Dutch as you drive to work. Or you can watch local news in Dutch on TV Brussel.

You can read the news in Dutch in the left-wing *De Morgen* (www.demorgen.be) or the more Catholic *De Standaard* (www.destandaard.be). But both newspapers are more focused on events in Antwerp and Ghent, and miss a great deal that happens on the streets of the capital. The best source for news on Brussels in Dutch is the free weekly *Brussel Deze Week*, which comes with a useful cultural supplement (www.brusseldezeweek.be).

You can spend a Saturday morning exploring the vibrant Flemish Quarter around the Rue Dansaert, starting with Sonia Noël's Stijl boutique at Rue Dansaert 74, which brought cool Antwerp fashion to the staid Belgian capital in the early 1980s.

The main Flemish cultural institutions lie near at hand. The Ancienne Belgique has a French name, but is firmly under the control of the Flemish minister of culture. New rock and indie bands perform on the stage where Jacques Brel once sang in French and Dutch in front of 2,000 fans. The Beursschouwburg is another Flemish institution known for its concerts and café.

A ten minute walk down Rue de Laeken brings you to the KVS, the Royal Flemish Theatre, built in 1883 on the site of a former armoury to stage Dutch language productions. The building was recently restored to its original grandeur. The programme covers theatre, film and debates, with the occasional production in English. Café Congo, located on the first floor of a new annexe at Quai aux Pierres-de-Taille is open on weekdays from 10.30am to 6pm for coffee, soup and Flemish newspapers.

You can end with a coffee in De Markten on the Vieux Marché aux Grains. The café has a cool industrial interior with wooden tables, ancient iron radiators and an open kitchen. The waitresses are sublimely beautiful, but, in the manner of Antwerp, can sometimes chill you with a look. The coffee, supplied by Cook and Boon, is worth the risk.

Flemish Contacts in Brussels

Ancienne Belgique: Concert centre with large hall seating 2,000 and intimate upstairs club. Boulevard Anspach 110; ☎ 02.548.24.24; www.abconcerts.be

Beursschouwburg: Important centre for contemporary Flemish dance and theatre. Rue A. Orts 20-28; ☎ 02.550.03.50; www.beursschouwburg.be

Op Brussel: Dynamic Flemish organisation set up to persuade Dutch-speakers to settle in Brussels. Organises 'Broodje Brussel' lunchtime activities aimed at Flemish commuters who flee the city at 6pm. www.opbrussel.be

De Markten: Exciting Flemish cultural centre and cafe. Vieux Marché aux Grains 5; ☎ 02.512.34.25; www.demarkten.be

FM Brussel: Flemish city radio. Tune to 98.8 or listen online at www.fmbrussel.be

Hoofdstedelijk Bibliotheek: Excellent Flemish public library with books in several languages, including a large English fiction section. Place de la Monnaie 6; ☎ 02.229.18.40; www.hob.be

KVS: The main Flemish theatre in Brussels. Quai aux Pierres-de-Taille, ☎ 02.210.11.12; www.kvs.be

Kaaitheater: Radical Flemish dance and theatre in a striking modernist building from the 1930s. Square Sainctelette 20, ☎ 02.201.59.59; www.kaaitheater.be

Stijl: Chic and bleak fashion from Antwerp designers. Rue Antoine Dansaert 74; ☎ 02.512.03.13.

TV Brussel: Local TV station aimed mainly at the Flemish in Brussels, but with programmes in English on Sunday evenings. www.tvbrussel.be

Vouchers for Culture Vultures

The Flemish Community wants more people to enjoy dance, theatre and exhibitions in Brussels. Its solution is to offer every Brussels resident three free culture tickets worth €6,20 each. The vouchers (*cultuurwaardebon*) can be ordered online (using a very simple Dutch form) at www.vgc.be/cultuur. They can be used to get discounts when you book tickets at some of the main venues in Brussels, including the Kaaitheater, the Museum of Musical Instruments, Bozar and the Beursschouwburg. Residents living in the Flemish suburbs can also apply.

Belgian politics

How does it Work?

Brussels has one king, six governments, 19 mayors and a third of a million foreigners. How on earth does the city work? Some would say it doesn't. They would point to the endless traffic delays, the potholes, the construction projects that drag on for years.

The politics have been shaped by the constitutional reforms of 1980 and the creation of an autonomous Brussels Region in 1989. As a result, the federal government plays only a small role in the destiny of Brussels. Most of the important urban issues are decided by the government of Brussels Region, including transport, employment, rubbish collection and the environment. A minister president heads Brussels Region, rather like a city mayor, but with a lower public profile.

The 19 local town halls remain powerful in certain areas, such as education, policing and street cleaning. The local administrations deal with residence permits, ID cards and planning permission.

The politics of the city are heavily influenced by the language tensions outside the city. For the past two centuries, Brussels has been a predominantly French-speaking city. No one knows the exact figures, but most experts reckon that 85% of people now living in Brussels are French speakers.

The cultural life of the city falls under the control of the French and Dutch language communities. This means that there are two cultural circuits in the city, one funded by Flanders and the other supported by the Walloon government in Namur. Some cultural venues manage to rise above the language issue and achieve a truly international standing, like Bozar and Flagey.

Who does What?

The Federal Government Responsible for defence, foreign policy, overseas aid, justice, law and order, currency, tax, monetary policy, social security, pensions and immigration. Some responsibilities are shared with the Regions, such as health and employment. The parliament is divided into a Chamber of Representatives with 150 members and a Senate with 71 members, of whom 40 are directly elected. The government is made up of a maximum of 15 cabinet members, with a balanced number from each of the two main language groups.

The Regions Created in 1995, the three Regions are responsible for environment, housing, planning, the economy, energy, agriculture, transport, foreign trade, and public works. The Walloon Region has its capital in Namur, while Flanders Region and Brussels Region both have their capital in Brussels.

The Communes The 589 communes (gemeenten in Flanders) are in charge of local government services such as schools, the police, fire services, some roads, town planning, water supplies, and social welfare. Each commune has a mayor and board of aldermen. These are the people to contact if you have a local problem. They can be surprisingly accessible.

Voting

Anyone who belongs to an EU country has the right to vote in Belgium in European elections and municipal elections. But they are not allowed to vote for the regional or federal governments. Residents from non-EU countries have the right to vote in municipal elections if they have lived legally in the country for five years.

Foreign voters can register at their local town hall. The procedure takes no more than a few minutes. The only document needed is a Belgian ID. You will then be sent an official convocation close to election day, which gives the date of the election and the address of your local polling station. Voting is compulsory in Belgium and you can, at least in theory, be fined for not voting.

The Belgian authorities make a great effort to inform foreigners of their rights and try to persuade them to vote. Yet the registration rate is very low. Some expatriates are deterred because of the compulsory vote, but a large number are simply indifferent. The expatriate vote could in theory have a significant impact in Brussels, where foreigners represent about one third of the electorate.

Ethnic Brussels

The World in Brussels

You can more or less see the whole world in Brussels. The city has an African Quarter close to the Porte de Namur, a quarter known to taxi drivers as the Quartier Irlandais close to Rond-Point Schuman, a Viennese-style district around the Parc de Bruxelles and a skyscraper district originally known as the Manhattan Quarter. You can meander along the Rue de Brabant to quench your desire for Morocco, make a quick tour of the Gare du Midi Quarter to satisfy your urge to eat paella, and stroll down Rue Dansaert to discover a little corner of Brussels that is almost Parisian. You will find suburbs that resemble America, loft apartments that look like London and street smells in the Bourse district that evoke Saigon.

African Brussels The Congo has always been a difficult subject for Belgians. Like most former colonial powers, Belgium prefers not to confront the darker episodes in its past. Yet the Royal Museum of Central Africa in Tervuren has recently begun to take a critical look at the history of Belgium in Africa.

The story began in 1860 when the young King Leopold II handed the Belgian finance minister a stone tablet carved with the message: *Il faut à la Belgique une colonie.* Twenty-five years later, the Welsh explorer Henry Morton Stanley provided an older Leopold with exactly what he wanted: an unclaimed and largely uncharted territory that was eighty times the size of Belgium.

Leopold was originally interested in the ivory reserves. But then he struck gold (in the form of rubber). The Congo river was the home of rubber trees. They oozed a liquid that could be used for making rubber boots, car tyres and condoms. Leopold's agents began a ruthless campaign of terror. The King, who never set foot in the Congo, was condemned for encouraging cruelty on an unprecedented scale. He was attacked by some of the most influential figures of the Victorian period, including Arthur Conan Doyle, Mark Twain and Roger Casement. His alleged crimes inspired Joseph Conrad's *Heart of Darkness* and persuaded the American historian Adam Hochschild to speak of a holocaust in which ten million died.

King Leopold used much of his private income to rebuild Brussels on a massive scale. The Congo revenue helped to fund major projects like the Avenue de Tervuren and the Cinquantenaire arch. The spoils of colonisation were proudly exhibited at the 1897 Brussels Exhibition and vast sums were spent constructing a spectacular museum on the scale of Versailles in Tervuren.

Until quite recently, the Africa Museum was an embarrassing bastion of colonial ideology, its glass cabinets crammed with exotic objects and trophies, its marble halls filled with sculptures showing Belgians bringing civilisation to Africa.

The museum began to change direction when Guido Gryseels was appointed director. He initiated a new debate on the colonial period, and brought in experts from the Congo to present the other side of the story for the first time. While the museum refuses to produce blunt judgements, it shows the Belgian colonial period as at best a mixed blessing. The Europeans brought schools, railways, gramophones and bicycles, but brutally exploited the people and the country's natural resources.

The colonial period came to a sudden end with independence in 1960. The museum now looks at independence as a joyous outburst of energy and music, rather than a black moment in Belgian history.

Brussels is full of reminders of the colonial period that barely get mentioned in tourist guides. The building that once housed Leopold's Congo administration is still standing at 13 Rue Brederode, in a quiet back street near the royal palace. In 1890, Joseph Conrad arrived here to apply for a job as a steamship captain.

Five minutes away, the Matonge district near the Porte de Namur is named after a quarter in the Congolese capital Kinshasa. This compact district has been settled since the 1960s by Congolese students. You pass greengrocer's selling blackened bananas, tailors dummies dressed in bright wax-printed cottons, and shops offering cheap phone calls to remote regions of Africa and Asia. The main streets of Rue de la Longue Vie and Rue de la Paix are particularly vibrant on hot summer nights.

Another side of the story is told in the Sablon district, where antique shops sell beautiful African masks, wood sculptures and spears. The African connection is far from over in this city.

Chinatown The area around Place Sainte Catherine is as close to a Chinatown as it gets in Brussels. Some 2,000 Chinese live in the city, and many shop in this area. If you're looking for ingredients to cook Pak Choi, head to the Rue de la Vierge Noire, off Boulevard Anspach, where Chinese and Korean supermarkets sell imported noodles, chopsticks and porcelain tea cups. The Kam Yuen Supermarket (Rue de la Vierge Noire 2) is a large friendly supermarket that sells a vast range of imported Oriental specialities. It also publishes a Chinese newspaper. Several long-standing Chinese restaurants are located in this neighbourhood, along with Thai and Vietnamese places which offer a more sophisticated cuisine in generally more appealing surroundings.

Moroccan Brussels The Moroccan community in Brussels totals about 42,000, making it one of the largest foreign populations in the city. Brussels as a result is dotted with Moroccan corner shops, Halal butchers and Moroccan bakeries. The Rue de Brabant, near the Gare du Nord, is the main street for Moroccan specialities. Here you find grocery stores next to shops selling battery-operated indoor fountains. The Moroccan community has had relatively little impact on the city's cultural life, but that may change with the opening of two new cultural centres in 2007. The first is a Flemish/Moroccan cultural centre, located in the abandoned Gaîte cinema, off Place de Brouckère. Funded by the Flemish and Moroccan governments, the centre aims to promote racial harmony in the city, with a wide-ranging programme of concerts, shows, plays, exhibitions and debates. The second project is a Moroccan cultural centre, Espace Magh, located in a building once occupied by the gay disco Who's Who's Land at Rue du Poinçon 17. Founded by a group of local actors with Moroccan roots, the centre aims to offer cultural events and language classes.

Belgium Facts

Size

Belgium is a small country, measuring 32,547 sq km or 1/329th of the total area of Europe.

Population

Belgium has a population of 10.4 million. About one resident in ten is foreign, including 177,000 Italians, 119,000 French, 109,000 Dutch and 81,000 Moroccans.

Density

The country has a population density of 333 people per sq km, making it the second most densely populated country in Europe, after the Netherlands (with 372 people per sq km). It is well ahead of Britain (239), France (105) and the United States (29).

Time Zone

Belgium is in the Central European time zone (CET), along with countries like France and Germany, but one hour ahead of Britain and Ireland (GMT). It is six hours ahead of Eastern Standard Time in the USA (EST) and nine hours ahead of Pacific Standard Time (PST). Clocks in Belgium go forward one hour on the last Sunday of March; clocks go back on the last Sunday of October.

Brussels and Europe

When asked to name the best thing about Brussels, a French diplomat once quipped that it was *'the Friday evening train to Paris'*. Belgians have learned to live with jokes like this. But they can take a certain pride in the fact that their small and modest capital has successfully turned itself into a hub of global political power. Brussels is the official capital of the world's biggest trading bloc, the second richest region in Europe, and one of the most desirable capital cities on the planet.

How Brussels became Europe's Capital

With 490 million inhabitants, 27 countries, 23 official languages and three alphabets, the European Union is a complicated international construction. Yet this unique political organisation has survived for more than half a century, and now includes countries that were under the iron grip of the Soviet Union when the idea of a united Europe was first discussed.

Brussels has always played an important role in the process of European integration. When the European Steel and Coal Community was created in 1950, marking the first hesitant step towards European unity, three countries out of six wanted to make Brussels the administrative headquarters, although France and Germany preferred Saarbrücken.

The Belgian government didn't push Brussels. Instead, it wanted Liège, a distressed industrial city, as the capital. The other countries rejected Liège, and the headquarters eventually went to Luxembourg, while the Parliament was located in Strasbourg. The Belgian government had learned an important lesson in European politics.

When the Treaty of Rome was signed in 1957, the Italian government suggested putting the EEC headquarters in the lakeside town of Stresa. But the majority of states favoured Brussels. They didn't go so far as to make it the official capital, but simply designated it as the provisional capital. That was enough for the Belgian government. It immediately started building offices for the new administration. The first officials moved into a building on the Rue Belliard, but they decamped within a few months to a new office building on the Avenue de la Joyeuse Entrée, next to the Parc du Cinquantenaire.

The administration gradually expanded, settling into several empty office buildings scattered across the 19th-century Leopold Quarter. In 1958, the government decided to construct a prestigious new building on Rond Point Schuman on the site of a Catholic school

The Charlemagne building

for girls known as the Convent of the Dames de Berlaymont. After moving the nuns to Waterloo and tearing down the buildings, the government commissioned three leading architects to design a modern office modelled on the UNESCO headquarters in Paris.

Completed in 1967, the Berlaymont was influenced by the Atomium Style of the 1958 Brussels Expo. Housing 3,000 staff, the star-shaped building was raised on concrete piles, giving the impression of a floating structure. It had a heliport on the roof, an underground garage and a petrol station reserved for Commission officials.

The government then demolished a block of 44 old Brussels townhouses to build a second administrative building known as the Charlemagne. A European Quarter gradually emerged in the streets and squares around Schuman. This happened pragmatically, *à la Belge*, without any form of rational plan. The new buildings were funded by private investors, usually banks or insurance companies, who used their own architects. Property speculators moved in on the neighbourhood, buying up old houses on promising sites and then leaving them to rot away, so that they could easily be torn down when more office space was needed.

The European Quarter is notorious for its failed urban planning and uninspired architecture. The result is an unappealing urban neighbourhood in which rotting buildings stand alongside gleaming office blocks, and brutal motorways cut through residential quarters. A short walk down Rue Belliard reveals the full destructive force of the EU on a formerly harmonious residential quarter.

Many Belgians can still remember growing up in houses that were later torn down to make way for the European institutions. They recall the old brewery that was replaced by the European Parliament, the artists studios that were sacrificed for office buildings and the lovely tree-lined Rue de la Loi before the traffic planners destroyed it.

The European institutions now occupy more than one million sq m of office space. The impact of Europe has been devastating. It has changed the appearance of entire urban quarters, driven out old residents, pushed up property prices, added to the traffic problem and led to English becoming the city's second most-spoken language. The people of Brussels have largely accepted the changes, although they have never really been given a choice.

Crossroads of Europe

Before it started calling itself capital of Europe, Brussels used to boast that it was the crossroads of Europe. The city stands at the point where six main European land routes converge. One route comes from the direction of Paris, entering the city by the Porte de Hal and following Rue Haute. Another route comes from the north-west, from Ghent and the coast, entering by the Porte de Flandre and Rue de Flandre. A third route comes from the south, from the Alps and Switzerland, entering at the Porte de Namur and descending to the Senne valley by the sloping rue de Namur. Other routes come from Antwerp, Cologne and Waterloo. But where precisely do they all meet? The answer isn't Grand'Place. It lies further south, at the bottom of the Mont des Arts, where the Boulevard de l'Empereur meets the ancient Rue de la Madeleine. A statue of Queen Elisabeth marks the spot.

What Has Europe Done for Brussels?

The European presence has brought successive waves of international residents who appreciate the old charm of Brussels, support its culture, eat in local restaurants and restore the crumbling houses.

A 2007 study by researchers at the Brussels University ULB proves that the EU presence has had a positive impact on the city, boosting its international image as well as the local economy. The EU generates some €7,000m in added value (13% of the total) and provides employment for 92,000 people, or one in eight jobs in Brussels.

The international community is responsible for raising the average per capital income of Brussels Region to €53,381 a year - the second highest in Europe. But the wealth is far from evenly spread. Brussels has high levels of unemployment and chronic poverty, with 27% of the population living below the poverty level, compared to 11% in Flanders and a European average of 14%.

The residents blame the Eurocrats for the destruction of Brussels, but the city was already changing before the Europeans arrived. Many of the new roads, tunnels and car parks were built for the 1958 Brussels Expo. Middle class Belgians were already leaving the old neighbourhoods and settling in modern American-style suburban villas. They were more than happy to sell their houses at extravagant prices to European civil servants.

Some of the most appealing areas of Brussels were saved by Europeans long after Belgians had left. Many houses on the Sablon were restored by Italians, while the St Géry neighbourhood was largely settled by young single Europeans. Many of the most impressive urban renovations of recent years have been carried out by foreign groups in the city. The Galician community renovated La Tentation, a former downtown department store, in the late 1990s, creating a cultural centre and restaurant, while the Asturian Region renovated an abandoned Socialist printing works to create the striking Casa de Asturias in Rue Saint Laurent.

It is hard to imagine Brussels without the Europeans. The city would probably be just as chaotic, but less exciting, more like a large town in France. It would have a different economy, different problems, fewer signs in English, cheaper housing, more parking spaces.

Summit Chaos

Four times a year the 27 EU leaders hold a summit in Brussels. The Brussels police cordon off the entire Schuman Quarter with razor-wire barriers, shut down Schuman metro station for two days and stop anyone from entering the area (apart from residents and EU pass holders). The summits used to be held in the country holding the EU presidency. Many countries took the opportunity to stage the event in a beautiful city or a glorious baroque palace. But in 2002, Belgium persuaded the EU to hold almost all summits in Brussels. The drab Justus Lipsius building became the venue every three months. Some would say that this shows a more serious EU. Others wonder if it serves any purpose. It certainly causes chaos for locals. The summit begins on Thursday. Early morning traffic soon becomes disrupted as police convoys escort the leaders to the Justus Lipsius building. The meetings last until about noon on Friday. Then the 27 leaders pose for a formal photograph. But what really happens behind the barbed wire? Does anything get debated? Or is it just a PR exercise, at the end of which each leader can announce to their national reporters that they have won a major concession in Brussels? Only a few insiders can say.

Is Brussels the Right City for Europe's Capital?

The main attraction of working in the European Quarter lies in the mix of languages and cultures, rather than the architecture. In a relatively compact district, you come across people from all 27 different countries of Europe, along with delegates from far-flung parts of the world. This is the unique selling point of Brussels as a working environment. *'The whole world is here'*, a European Parliament official explains.

Moving the European Parliament to Brussels?

The European Parliament is the world's largest democratic institution, serving the interests of 500 million Europeans. It has 785 members of parliament from 27 countries who speak 23 different languages. The MEPs represent 189 national political parties loosely organised into 11 broad political groupings. The parliament requires a vast staff of translators, interpreters, advisers and assistants if it is to function at all. But it also has to carry on its work in three different countries. It has two separate parliament buildings in Brussels and Strasbourg and a secretariat based in Luxembourg.

This is, almost everyone agrees, an unsustainable situation. Ten times a year, the 785 MEPs and their staff have to move from Brussels to Strasbourg, along with a fleet of lorries carrying essential paperwork. The MEPs then spend five working days in a shining glass complex near the Rhine before returning north to Brussels, a five hour journey away. The annual cost of the migration is estimated at €250m. It benefits no one apart from the hotels and restaurants of Strasbourg.

Most MEPs would prefer to be based in Brussels. They complain about the poor air and rail links to Strasbourg. The least happy are the MEPs from Eastern Europe, who often have to fly to Frankfurt and then take a coach to Strasbourg. A petition was recently signed by one million people calling on the EU to move the parliament permanently to Brussels. But the French refuse to budge on this issue.

The European Quarter

A Guide to Europe's Capitol Hill

The main European institutions are based in south-east Brussels close to the Schuman roundabout. Up until the middle of the 19th century, this was an area of rolling hills, ponds and watermills outside the city walls. The architect Tilman-François Suys then drew up a plan for a new district with grand classical mansions on broad tree-lined streets laid out in a grid pattern.

The Leopold Quarter, named after Leopold II, soon became one of the most fashionable quarters of Brussels. A second residential district was planned by the architect Gédéon Bordiau in 1875 on sloping land lying east of the Maelbeek valley. Bordiau's plan created a district of ponds, fountains and villas where some of the city's richest families settled.

The neighbourhood began to change in the 1960s when the Berlaymont was built on high ground above the Maelbeek valley. The first wave of demolition and construction was centred on the Schuman roundabout and the Rue de la Loi. A growing need for new buildings led to large office developments in the Leopold Quarter, where the grid layout designed by Suys was ideal for large office blocks.

The European Parliament project brought more heavy construction work to the European Quarter. The project, as usual, had to be done *en stoemelings*, on the sly, because the European Parliament was officially based in Strasbourg. The main sessions took place in the pretty Alsatian town, while committee meetings and parties met in a modest building on Rue Belliard in Brussels.

But MEPs wanted a more impressive place to meet in Brussels, close to the Commission. To meet the demand, a consortium of Belgian banks clubbed together to build the Espace Leopold. When work began in 1987, the building was officially described as an international congress centre, but everyone knew that they were building a new European Parliament. The result was that the European Parliament never discussed the design, or its effect on the neighbourhood.

The project involved the demolition of an old brewery and most of the neo-classical Gare du Luxembourg railway station, leaving just the central ticket hall as a token of the past. The train station is still there, but buried below ground. The first building to emerge on the skyline was regarded as a successful modern design. Housing the debating chamber, it comprised two parabolic wings surmounted by a large glass arcade which echoed the shape of the station clock. Locals noticed that

The European Parliament

Europe Statue on the Rue de la Loi

the parabolic wings looked like the box used for packing a French cheese called *Caprice des Dieux*. The name, 'Whim of the Gods,' seemed to suit a building that had somehow materialised without any public debate.

The cranes didn't go away. They continued putting up more buildings for the parliament, but now in a style that makes Ceausescu's Palace in Bucharest look positively benign. Even the names (D4 and D5) seemed to come from the mind of someone with a totalitarian agenda.

The biggest crisis to hit the European Quarter came in 1990 when dangerous levels of asbestos were discovered throughout the Berlaymont. The building was immediately closed down while the Belgian government tried to figure out what to do. The asbestos problem came at a particularly delicate time when the Belgian government was lobbying to become official capital of Europe. It was also trying to attract the European Parliament to Brussels.

The government rushed through the completion of a building called the Breydel to use as a temporary Commission headquarters. The move was engineered just before the crucial Edinburgh Summit in 1992, when the future role of Brussels was to be decided. Belgium won the vote in a late-night decision.

But the government still had to decide what to do with the building known to critics as the Berlaymonster. Many people were in favour of tearing it down and putting up something new, but some Belgians argued that it had become an iconic landmark of European architecture. The building was finally reprieved and a company named Berlaymont 2000 began renovation work. It turned out that the company had been overly optimistic when it put forward a completion date of 2000 and work continued for four more years before officials moved back.

After decades of allowing indifferent architecture, the Belgian authorities are now more concerned to create a good impression in the EU Quarter. There is now a serious urban development plan and a certain commitment to making the quarter more appealing.

The new policy has already led to some improvements, such as the curious Square Jean Ray next to the Leopold Park, and the romantic Parc de la Vallée du Maelbeek below the Charlemagne Building.

The government is now working on a railway tunnel to link the European Quarter with Brussels Airport and a new transport interchange at Schuman, which will integrate metro and rail links. Until that is finished (probably in 2012), the area is going to be a mess.

European Quarter

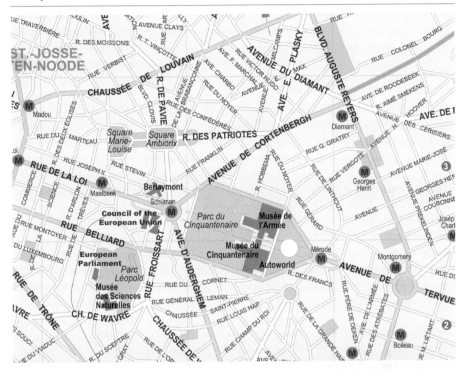

Waiting for the Museum of Europe

Brussels wants to be a worthy capital of Europe. Some people think that means investing in symbolic monuments. A group of pro-Europeans, many of them Belgian, one of them the daughter of the Belgian prime minister who signed the Treaty of Rome in 1957, see the creation of a Museum of Europe as a fitting monument. They proposed the idea back in 1999. The European Parliament was initially enthusiastic and offered to house it in the parliament complex. But now the project is stuck fast because of a row over funding. No one knows if it will ever open.

A tour of Euroland

A Walk in the Leopold Quarter

The European Quarter has been a permanent building site for the past 40 years and will remain that way for at least a few more years. Yet you can pick your way through the construction traffic and look at some of the inspired buildings that have gone up in recent years.

Timing is important if you want to see inside the European Parliament. Guided tours are organised every day, but you have to be outside the Parliament at 10am (Monday to Friday) or 3pm (Monday to Thursday). That means starting the walk after breakfast or lunch. In either case, you should begin on the Place du Luxembourg, an elegant 19th-century square surrounded by cafés and restaurants. You can order breakfast in Tout Bon, on the corner of Rue du Luxembourg, or eat lunch among MEPs and lobbyists in one of the restaurants on the square.

Station Preserved The 19th-century building on the far side of the square is all that remains of the Gare du Quartier Leopold, one of Europe's oldest railway stations, serving Namur and Luxembourg. The station closed down in the 1990s, replaced by a modern underground station. Most of the original building was torn down, leaving just the booking hall as a token of the past. It was originally intended as an exhibition centre, but this plan was quietly abandoned after the 11 September terrorist attacks because of security fears among MEPs. It was, however, used for an architecture exhibition in 2007.

Debating Europe Cross the open square behind the old station and go up the steps straight ahead. The European Parliament information office is on the left. It stocks some useful booklets on the EU in all 27 different languages. Continue through the passage and go down the steps. The building straight ahead with the 27 flags outside is the European Parliament, built on the site of an old Brussels brewery. The guided tours begin in an entrance hall to the left of the main entrance. You are given an audio guide with commentary in one of the 27 official languages and taken by lift to a viewing gallery above the main staircase. The tour lasts 45 minutes and provides a stimulating introduction to European democracy.

Vanished Zoo After you leave the building, turn left and you will see a fragment of the Berlin Wall almost buried by the greenery. Now go right into the Leopold Park, a romantic park created in 1847 in the grounds of an old country house. A private company turned the site into a pleasure garden with a zoo, and converted an abandoned convent on the hilltop into a festival hall, reading room and café.

The zoo was badly managed and poorly funded, and animals died in alarming numbers. It was finally forced to close in 1876, leaving no trace of its existence apart from the old name *Société Zoologique* carved on two lodges at the Rue Belliard entrance. The zoo was renamed the Leopold Park in 1880. But it didn't stay a park for long. The wealthy industrialist Ernest Solvay created a centre of scientific research in the park in the 1890s. This led to the construction of several impressive buildings, including the Solvay Library near the top of the hill, originally a research library but now occupied by one of the many European think tanks in the quarter.

Turn down the hill and you pass the Emile Jacqmain School on the right and the George Eastman Dental Institute on the left, built in 1933 and now occupied by the Brussels office of the European Court of Auditors.

Leave the park at the main gate, where the two gatehouses still have the inscription *Société Zoologique*. The square opposite is named Place Jean Rey after a Liège politician who served as president of the European Commission in the late 1960s. Cross the square (watching out for sudden jets of water) and turn left onto the Chaussée d'Etterbeek.

Notice the two older buildings on the left, on the Rue van Maerlant. These are exact copies of two buildings that once stood on the Rue des Sols, not far from Central Station. The red brick building is a copy of the Convent of the Dames of Perpetual Adoration, while the neat baroque chapel on the right is a perfect replica of the Chapelle Salazar. The two buildings were scheduled for demolition in 1907, during the construction of the Mont des Arts, and the city decided to build two exact copies next to the Parc Leopold. The planned demolition was never carried out, and the original chapels remained standing for almost 50 years.

The red brick convent is now occupied by the European Commission library, while the Chapelle Salazar is still a chapel. The chapel is open to the public, but the library is only open to those who can show an official EU badge or press pass.

Continue along the Chaussée d'Etterbeek, which follows the course of the vanished River Maelbeek. The huge Résidence Palace stands on the low hill on the right, built in the 1920s by the architect Michel Polak as a luxury apartment complex. Some apartments are still occupied, but much of the building is now used as an international press centre.

Art in the Metro Now walk under the railway viaduct, past the Schuman railway station entrance. A short distance further, and you pass under the bridge carrying the Rue de la Loi over the Maelbeek valley. Glance inside the metro station entrance on the left to see one of the quirky murals by the Belgian artist Benoît that decorate the station.

Once through the tunnel, cross the road and enter the little Parc de la Vallée du Maelbeek. Climb the steps to reach the paved terrace next to the Rue de la Loi. Here you can admire the gently curved façade of the Lex Building on the opposite side of the street, built for the 1,300 translators who work for the Council of the European Union.

Art by Benoît in the metro

The Charlemagne building overlooks the little park. This was a dull 1960s office building before the Murphy/Jahn partnership transformed it in 1998, wrapping the structure in spectacular glass curtain walls in an attempt to integrate it into the neighbourhood.

The dull grey building behind you, opposite the Europa Hotel, is home to the mighty DG AGRI, the department in charge of agriculture, which swallows about half of the annual EU budget in farm subsidies.

Walk to the far end of the park and turn right up Rue Joseph II. This cobbled street is typical of the European Quarter, with a row of traditional Belgian townhouses still standing on one side of the street and the huge Charlemagne building rising opposite. Look for the pub at the end of the street called the Old Hack. Journalists come here to drink Belgian beer and pick up the latest news and rumours from the Commission.

EU Headquarters The Berlaymont Building stands on the opposite side of the street. The lobby is open to the public, but the rest of the building is out of bounds unless you have a European Commission pass. A sombre stone block commemorating Robert Schuman stands in front of the building, next to a row of 27 flagpoles flying the blue EU flag.

You can pick up information at the EU Info Point on Rond Point Schuman, but there is little else of interest in the neighbourhood. Your best bet for a café is to head down Rue Froissart to reach Place Jourdan, a friendly neighbourhood square with a famous frites stand and several local cafés. The truly Belgian thing to do here is to buy *frites* at Maison Antoine, ask for them *emballée* (wrapped), and then take them to eat in the café Chez Bernard. The owner is perfectly happy for customers to bring their own frites as long as they buy a drink.

Now follow the short pedestrianised stretch of the Chaussée de Wavre which begins near Maison Antoine. This brings you back to the Chaussée d'Etterbeek. Cross to the other side and climb the Chaussée de Wavre, past little shops selling ethnic food and dusty antiques. After a few minutes, you will notice some steps on the right. They lead you to the Natural History Museum, famous for its collection of 29 dinosaur skeletons.

European flags outside the Berlaymont building

The museum was founded in 1772 as a cabinet of curiosities and moved in 1880 into an old convent on the hill. The collection became world famous in 1891 when the skeletons of 29 iguanodons were moved here. The iguanodons were found in a coal mine in southern Belgium and brought to Brussels to be reconstructed. They were originally displayed standing erect in special glass cases, but more recent research has shown that the iguanodons walked on all fours, forcing the museum to modify its displays (although not the wooden model outside the museum).

Romantic Artist On leaving the museum, turn right down the Rue Vautier. Look out for the gate on the left side painted with the words *Musée Wiertz*. It is worth taking a look inside this forgotten museum if it is open. You find yourself in the former home of the Romantic artist Antoine Wiertz, who in 1850 persuaded the Belgian state to build him a house and studio on the summit overlooking the Maelbeek valley. In return, Wiertz agreed to bequeath all his works to the state.

Wiertz had ambitious plans for Brussels which he set out in an 1840 pamphlet titled *Bruxelles capitale et Paris province*. His rousing manifesto still hangs in the corridor of the dusty little museum. *'Here is my plan, my new plan for Brussels as capital, capital of Europe,'* he wrote. *'Come along, Brussels! Stand up for yourself! Become capital of the world and then you can look down on Paris as a mere provincial town.'* The idea of Brussels becoming capital of Europe must have seemed like the rantings of a mad artist when Wiertz wrote his manifesto in 1840. But Monsieur Wiertz had the last laugh. The huge European Parliament at the bottom of the hill is proof enough.

Babble On

Brussels is the capital of Belgium, which has three official languages, but it is also the capital of the European Union, which now has 23 official languages. Some people see multilingualism as one of Europe's great strengths, but others ask whether Europe can survive under the increasing burden of so many languages.

It used to be much simpler. The original EEC had four official languages (French, German, Dutch and Italian). It was relatively easy for the founding fathers to make lofty claims about the linguistic rights of every European when meetings could be held with just four interpreters.

French was the main working language in the beginning and remained the dominant language even after Britain and Ireland joined in 1973, but the balance began to shift when the Scandinavian countries and Austria joined in 1995. The move towards English was accelerated when ten new countries joined in 2004, most of them more comfortable speaking English (or possibly German) rather than French.

The number of languages increased by three in 2007, when Romania and Bulgaria joined the EU and Irish became an official language. The sheer volume of work involved is clear from the EU's internet portal (www.europa.eu), which now provides a vast amount of EU information in 23 different languages and three different alphabets.

The EU spends some €1.1 billion a year on translation and interpretation. This money – about 1% of the EU's budget (or €3 per citizen per year) – pays for some 3,500 translators, interpreters and secretarial staff. Most are based in Brussels, but some are in Luxembourg or Strasbourg. Together, the translators deal with 1.3 million pages of text while the interpreters cover about 11,000 meetings. The costs have only increased slightly in recent years thanks to a fairly ruthless policy of staff cuts.

Many people were surprised at the decision to add Irish – one of Ireland's two official languages – in 2007. The language is only used by about 5% of the population, yet the Irish government argued that it was an essential part of Ireland's cultural identity. This has led to calls for Welsh and Scottish Gaelic to be added to the EU's official languages. It has also raised hopes for Catalan, Valencian, Basque and Galician speakers.

Yet not everything gets translated into 23 languages. Many EU reports are produced in just three languages – English, French and German. The other 20 EU languages are recognised, but only for important treaties. The reality is that English, not French, is now the main language in Europe. Europe's citizens can write to the EU in their own language, but they won't get the full picture if they don't speak English.

The EU Buildings

The European Union occupies about one million square metres of office space in Brussels. Many of the buildings are depressing concrete structures, but there are a few inspiring buildings dotted around the quarter.

European Parliament The controversial European Parliament building is the largest EU complex in the city. It is known locally as the *Caprice des Dieux* (Whim of the Gods), because the oval main building resembles a famous French cheese. The complex is occupied by 785 MEPs, and countless assistants and advisers, for three weeks every month. It lies almost empty during the other week, when the European Parliament meets in Strasbourg. The complex was begun by property speculators in the late 1980s as a 'conference centre'. It has slowly expanded with the bare minimum of planning controls and local consultation. A group of 16 architects from Rotterdam's Berlage Institute recently argued that the parliament should be demolished and replaced by a new building at Tour et Taxis. *'It would be an act of goodwill to the people of Europe,'* one architect said.

Berlaymont This landmark building symbolises the European Union. Named after a convent that stood on the site, the Berlaymont was constructed from 1963-69 as an office for 3,000 civil servants. It was closed and covered in white sheeting in 1991 to allow the removal of asbestos, and remained a construction site for the next 14 years. The renovated building incorporates sophisticated technology for conserving energy and water. The 27 Commissioners have their offices on the 13th floor.

Charlemagne The Charlemagne building was built soon after the Berlaymont in the subdued modern style of 1960s Belgium. It was radically transformed in 1998 by the Murphy/Jahn partnership, who wrapped the structure in glass curtain walls. The aim was to integrate the building into the neighbourhood. Several EU departments occupy the building, including enlargement, interpreting and trade. It is now considered one of the best EU office buildings in Brussels.

Lex Building on Rue de la Loi

Justus Lipsius A dull pink building opened in 1995 as the headquarters of the Council of Ministers. Some 2,400 civil servants work in this unassuming building. Yet this is where many decisions are made that affect the future of 500 million EU citizens. The big decisions are made every three months or so when the 27 heads of state hold EU summits here. Other important decisions are made in committee meetings when experts and diplomats from the EU states come to Brussels to discuss policy. The building is named after the Flemish philosopher Justus Lipsius, who was born in Overijse in 1547. The choice is accidental. It just happens that the building stands on the site of the Rue Juste Lipse. Yet Lipsius was something of an early European, travelling all over Europe and writing books on the Classical philosophers.

Borschette A dreary conference centre named after a Luxembourg Commissioner, Albert Borschette, who died in 1976.

LEX A new office building for the Council of the European Union completed in 2007 on the Rue de la Loi. The Council's translators work behind the gently curved glass façade.

Résidence Palace A huge residential complex built on Rue de la Loi in 1923-26 by the architect Michel Polak. Inspired by the great passenger liners, it was an apartment complex of unprecedented luxury, with 180 apartments, a rooftop restaurant, Art Deco swimming pool, theatre and shops. Yet the complex wasn't a great success. Some of the apartments are still occupied, but the main wing has been converted by the Belgian government into an international press centre. The theatre and swimming pool are currently closed to the public, and may never open again because of security fears.

Jacques Delors The old European Parliament building on Rue Belliard is now occupied by the Committee of the Regions and the Economic and Social Committee. This was a so-so concrete monolith until the Belgian architect Pierre Lallemand of Art & Build added a glass curtain wall supported by laminated wood arches. Huge bamboo plants now grow behind the glass wall, providing an unexpected tropical backdrop when Europe's mayors and regional ministers meet here to talk politics.

Madou Plaza A dull tower block in run-down St Josse commune was spectacularly renovated in 2005. The European Commission bought the building and moved in staff working for COMM (Communication), DIGIT (information technology) and the Intelligent Energy Executive Agency. The officials on the upper floors enjoy spectacular views of the city.

What Next?

A new headquarters for the Council of the European Union is to be squeezed onto a site between the pink Justus Lipsius building and the Résidence Palace. The winning design by architect Philippe Samyn involves an egg-shaped conference hall enclosed within a glass cube. The façade puts a new slant on recycling by incorporating hundreds of old wooden window frames from across Europe, torn out by home owners when they put in double glazing. Another plan, not yet approved, envisages two 250m skyscrapers on either side of Rue de la Loi. The Belgian architect Jean-Michel Jaspers believes the skyscrapers would provide the EU with a symbolic monument, but critics argue that high-rise projects have poor record in Brussels.

Guided Tour

The European Parliament offers a free 45-minute tour of the main building, including the debating chamber, on weekdays. Each visitor is given an audio guide which provides information on the Parliament, along with music, historical speeches and MEPs talking in all the languages of Europe. Commentary is available in 23 official languages. Rue Wiertz entrance, Monday to Thursday at 10am and 3pm, and Friday at 10am. ☎ 02.284.3457; www.europarl.eu.int

How Does the EU Work?

The EU bureaucracy employs about 25,000 staff in Brussels, one quarter of them Belgian. This may sound like a huge bureaucracy, but it is relatively small for the work it has to do. The city of Amsterdam, with a population 700 times smaller than the EU, has roughly the same number of civil servants. Some EU officials work very long hours and are highly dedicated, but the corrupt and lazy Eurocrat remains a popular tabloid myth.

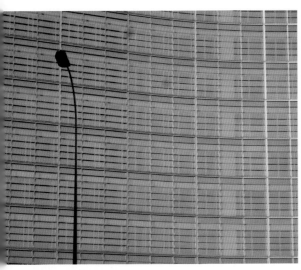

Berlaymont Building

The main work involves drafting new EU legislation that will apply to all 27 countries. Much of the legislation involves complex areas such as hazardous chemicals or transport safety. Those responsible for drafting new legislation rely heavily on input from outside experts, industrial lobbyists and pressure groups.

Anyone who deals with the EU bureaucracy soon discovers that it involves an exhausting amount of form filling. Even a modest contract worth a few hundred euro is accompanied by a massive weight of administration, most of it designed to prevent corruption. The EU is also deeply reluctant to deal with new organisations, so that many contracts will only be awarded to institutions that have an established EU track record. This has created a small inner circle of privileged research organisations that normally pick up every contract that is going.

Lobbying the EU: behind the scenes in the European Quarter

Lobbying used to be a discreet business in Brussels, but there are now an estimated 15,000 lobbyists based in the European Quarter. Some of them are hired by big multinationals, while others work for dedicated action groups who want to put their case to the Commission. The radical lobby group watchdog Corporate Europe Observatory keeps a close eye on lobbyists in Brussels and pinpoints the organisations involved in the persuasion business on an interactive map on its website *www.eulobbytours.org*

Understanding the EU

Europa: Official EU internet portal with information on every aspect of the European Union including official jobs. www.europa.eu

European Voice: Newspaper published in Brussels with extensive coverage of European politics. Produced by the same organisation as the Economist. www.europeanvoice.com

European Agenda: Find out what's happening in political Brussels. This useful site lists meetings, conferences and people. www.european-agenda.com

EU Observer: Useful online website with daily news on EU issues. www.euobserver.com

Infeuropa: European Commission information centre. Rond Point Schuman 14; ☎ 02.296.55.55

Europe Direct: Freephone line for information on the European Union in any EU language. ☎ 00800 67891011 (from any EU country). www.europa.eu/europedirect

European Bookshop: Bookshop near Mérode metro station with extensive range of books on the European Union. Rue de l'Orme 1; ☎ 02.231.0435; www.libeurop.be

Meet the 27 Countries of the EU

Brussels has been a city of immigration for many centuries. But the nature of immigration has changed over the years. Many British people retired to Brussels in the 19th century because of the cheap housing and low prices. French and German immigrants came in the mid-19th century as political exiles. The migrants who arrived in the 1950s were often escaping poverty in Spain, Italy and Greece. Others came to escape political persecution in Hungary or Portugal.

A different category of migrant comes to Brussels because of well-paid jobs in business or the European institutions. They often have little contact with poorer economic migrants from their home country, even if they speak the same language.

Austria The Austrians have links with Brussels dating back to the 18th century, when Brussels was capital of the Austrian Netherlands for more than 80 years (from 1713-94). The Austrians gave Brussels some of its most elegant palaces and squares, such as the Palace of Charles of Lorraine, the Place des Martyrs and Place Royale. More than a century after the Austrians period ended, the Austrian architect Joseph Hoffman made his mark in Brussels in 1905 by designing the sleek Palais Stoclet in pure Vienna Secessionist style. Just over two centuries after the end of Austrian rule, Austria joined the EU and Austrians began to settle again in Brussels. Yet their impact remains discreet. You can feast on *sauerkraut* or *goulasch* in the dated Alpine interior of the Tiroler Stüberl at Avenue de l'Hippodrome 124, or sign up for the annual *Wiener Ball* held in the faded ballroom of the Concert Noble, in the heart of the EU office district.

Britain The British have been in Brussels since before the Battle of Waterloo. There was a sizeable British colony living around Place Royale when Charlotte and Emily Brontë studied in Brussels in 1842-43. Other families settled in a British Quarter near Avenue Louise in the late 19th century, building an English Church in the Rue de Capitaine Crespel, now next door to a sex club and with a congregation largely drawn from the African community. There is also a neat Scottish church on the Chaussée de Vleurgat, built by Scottish architect in a traditional Baronial style. Famous British past residents include the Duke and Duchess of Richmond, who organised a ball on the eve of the Battle of Waterloo, and Edith Cavell, executed as a British spy by the German army in 1915.

The British community dispersed during the two world wars, but soon returned after 1945. A British School opened in Tervuren in 1969 and the British community swelled in 1973 when Britain was finally allowed to join the EEC. The city has countless British organisations, including the British Council, which organises English language courses, exhibitions and an annual Festival of British Film at the Palais des Beaux-Arts.

Bulgaria Bulgaria only joined the European Union in 2007, but the country wasted no time in acquiring a prestigious office building on the Square Marie Louise, formerly owned by the Belgian federation of chemical industries. There is also a Bulgarian church in Rue Victor Hugo.

Czech Republic The Czech Republic joined the EU in 2002. The country has a small cultural centre on Avenue A. Buyl in Ixelles.

Denmark Danes began to settle in Brussels after Denmark joined the EEC in 1973. The Danish Cultural Institute at Rue du Corner 22 organises concerts, exhibitions and language courses.

Finland The Finns have been settling in Brussels since Finland joined the EU in 1995. Their surprising and often eccentric culture is showcased at the Finnish Cultural Centre, Rue de Luxembourg 20 (www.finncult.be). The centre was founded in 1993 by the Finnish Seaman's Church of Antwerp and moved in 2002 to Brussels.

France The French have been in Brussels since the 15th century, when the Dukes of Burgundy spent long periods in the city. As a result, French became the language of the upper classes and Dutch gradually declined. The French influence increased in the late 18th century under Napoleonic rule and continued in the 19th century, when many French writers spent periods in Brussels. Victor Hugo lived on Grand'Place and admired the city, but Charles Baudelaire hated everything he saw in Brussels. The French population continued to grow after the Second World War, with some 3,000 French civil servants now employed by the European institutions. French language and culture is promoted by the Alliance Française, set up in Brussels in 1945, and the Lycée Français in Uccle. Yet the French are almost invisible in Brussels, barely distinguishable from French-speaking Belgians, except perhaps for their stubborn Gallic refusal to stop for pedestrians on crossings.

Germany German immigrants have been settling in Brussels since the 19th century. Karl Marx stayed in the city for three years (1845-48), and began writing the *Communist Manifesto* while living in a house in Ixelles. But Germany's relationship with Belgium hasn't always been positive. The country was occupied by German troops from 1914-1918 and again 1940-1944.

GRUPOS DE VISITANTES
NÁVŠTĚVNICKÉ SKUPINY
BESØGSGRUPPER
BESUCHERGRUPPEN
KÜLASTAJATE RÜHMAD
ΟΜΑΔΕΣ ΕΠΙΣΚΕΠΤΩΝ
VISITORS' GROUPS
GROUPES DE VISITEURS
GRUPPI DI VISITATORI
APMEKLĒTĀJU GRUPAS

The wounds healed after the war, and Germans began to settle in Brussels after the foundation of the EEC in 1957. Two years later, the Goethe Institute was founded to organise language courses and bring German art, films and music to Belgium. Each of Germany's Lander (states) now has an office in Brussels. Some of the offices are huge, like Bavaria's. The Dépendance gallery at 4 Rue du Marché aux Porcs (www.dependance.be) is a cool white art space run by two Germans. The Gutenberg Buchhandlung located behind the Belgian parliament (at Rue de Louvain 34) has a wide selection of German books. The one thing all Germans miss in Brussels is good bread. They are consoled by the dense black bread and bagels baked at The German Bakery (Rue H. van Dermalen 77). German restaurants come and go, but Maxburg at 108 Rue Stévin has been around for years, serving sausages and schnitzels to Germans working in the nearby European institutions.

Greece Greek immigrants have been settling in Brussels for more than a century. The most famous, Leonidas Kestekides, travelled to Brussels in 1910 to sell chocolate at the Brussels World Fair. He returned in 1913, married a Brussels woman, and started a chocolate business that eventually grew into Leonidas, a company with 1400 shops across the world. More Greek immigrants arrived in Brussels in the 1950s, often opening restaurants or shops near the Gare du Midi. The Greek population swelled again in 1981 when Greece joined the EEC. The city now has dozens of Greek restaurants and small shops. Most restaurants are basic, but some are highly sophisticated, such as Notos at Rue de Livourne 154 (www.notos.be) and Strofilia in the canal district. The main stores where Greeks go shopping for specialities are also in the canal zone.

Hungary Hungarians began to arrive in Brussels after the 1956 Revolution. The Hungarian Catholic Mission was founded in 1956 in a large 1870 townhouse known as the Hôtel Saintenoy with spectacular stained glass windows (at Rue de l'Arbre Bénit 123 in Ixelles). The building also accommodates a library with some 5,000 books used by Hungarian students. A new wave of Hungarians began to settle in Brussels after Hungary joined the EU in 2002. The new Hungarian Cultural Institute (www. hungarianinstitute.be) at Rue Treurenberg 10 organises art exhibitions, concerts and debates on Hungarian culture.

Italy Italian migrants have been settling in Brussels since the 19th century. The Italian community in Belgium grew rapidly after the Second World War, when migrants moved from poorer regions of Italy to work in the Walloon coal mines or run Italian restaurants. A second wave of Italians arrived after the creation of the EEC in 1957. The Italian Cultural Institute (www.iicbruxelles.be) opened in a 19th-century townhouse in the Rue de Livourne in the 1930s. Still located at the same address, the institute organises Italian language courses, exhibitions, film screenings and lectures. It also has an Italian library and newspaper reading room.

Ireland The Irish began to settle in Brussels after Ireland joined the EEC in 1973. The city has about 20 Irish bars, mainly concentrated in the streets around Schuman. The James Joyce was the first to open in Brussels, taking over a Pakistani restaurant in 1989. The Irish community also has an Irish Club and an Irish Theatre Group. The Irish butcher Jack O'Shea's (www.jackosheas.com) sells traditional Irish meat and cheese in a shop at Rue le Titien 30.

Latvia The Latvian community has slowly grown since the Baltic country joined the European Union in 2002. No one has opened up a Latvian restaurant so far, but there is a Latvian theatre group and a Latvian choir.

The Netherlands The Netherlands was a founding member of the EEC, and Dutch people have been settling in Brussels since 1957. But the community produces hardly a ripple in Brussels, perhaps because many Dutch families choose to live in the Flemish suburbs. The main venue for Dutch culture and debates is De Buuren, run jointly by the governments of Flanders and the Netherlands. But sadly there are no Dutch brown cafés anywhere in Brussels, nowhere to go for Dutch *appelgebak* or Grolsch beer.

Poland The Polish community in Brussels dates from the end of the Second World War, when many Polish soldiers settled in Belgium rather than return to Communist Poland. A further wave of Polish immigrants arrived soon after the fall of Communism, settling in old immigrant districts such as Flagey and Forest. This was followed by a third wave of Poles after Poland joined the EU in 2004. Most Polish regions have small offices in Brussels. Polsmaak (www.polsmaak.com) is a traditional Polish bakery selling bread, cakes, *paczki*, and Polish newspapers at five addresses in Brussels, including Chaussée d'Ixelles 311, Chaussée d'Alsemberg 399 and Place du Droit 5. Kuchnia Polskaat (Avenue d'Audergem 160) is a Polish grocery shop with a traditional interior. There is a Polish cultural centre at Rue du Croissant 68 in Forest.

Portugal The Portuguese migrant community dates from the 1960s, when immigrants began to settle around Place Flagey. The city now has a large expatriate community served by more than 100 Portuguese bars and restaurants and almost 30 Portuguese shops. When Portugal joined the EU in 1986, a new wave of Portuguese expatriates arrived in the city. A Portuguese bookshop called Orfeu opened in the European Quarter soon after Portugal joined (Rue du Taciturne 43; www.orfeu.net). Since then the Portuguese have settled all over Brussels, but Place Flagey remains the most vibrant Portuguese quarter, with numerous shops, cafés and football bars. The quarter is home to the delicatessen Los Sabores de Portugal (Rue de Vergnies 38), the football supporters' bar Clube de Futebol os Belenenses in the same street, the Portuguese bar Pessoa (Chaussée de Boondael 4) and even a Portuguese flower shop (Rue du Belvédère 8). A bust of the Lisbon poet Fernando Pessoa was recently placed in a leafy corner of Place Flagey, on a tiny triangle of grass named Square Pessoa. The Portuguese community has its own website with a full list of bars, restaurants and shops (www.portugalnet.be).

Slovenia Brussels has a small community of 500 or so Slovenians, most of them employed by the European institutions. Slovenia House opened in 2006 in a traditional Brussels townhouse on the edge of the EU Quarter at Chaussée de Wavre 402. The three-floor building contains a Slovenian restaurant and rooms for exhibitions and meetings.

Spain The Spanish ruled Brussels for much of the 16th century, but little remains from the period apart from the odd Spanish expression in the local Brussels dialect. The city experienced a wave of Spanish immigration in the 1960s, and many Spanish restaurants opened in the Gare du Midi and Marolles quarters. A further wave of Spaniards arrived in Brussels after Spain joined the EEC in 1986. The Spanish community is one of the most active and integrated in the city. The region of Asturias restored an abandoned socialist printing works to create a striking centre, the Casa de Asturias, at Rue St Laurent 36–38. The Galician community in Brussels did something different, and converted a downtown department store into a stylish restaurant and cultural centre. The Cervantes Institute at Avenue de Tervuren 64 organises Spanish lessons, and the bookshop Punto Y Coma at 115a Rue Stevin sells Spanish books and DVDs.

Sweden Sweden joined the EU in 1995, bringing fresh Nordic ideas to a city that previously had a strong Latin identity. The Swedes introduced new forms of fitness and nudged up property prices by buying old houses to convert into chic apartments and lofts. But Sweden's main impact on Brussels lies out in the suburbs, where three Ikea superstores provide city dwellers with neat furniture and smart lamps.

A Central Park for the European Quarter

Dating from the reign of King Leopold II, the Parc du Cinquantenaire on the edge of the European Quarter was the setting for the 1880 celebrations to mark fifty years of Belgian independence. The 'Jubilee Park' contains several cavernous museums located in the old exhibition halls, a neo-classical temple called the Pavilion of Human Passions (which contains a sculpture that once shocked Belgian sensibilities), a crumbling monument to the Congo colonisers and a circular panorama building in the style of a mosque (now used by the Muslim community). Despite its romantic charm, the park is bisected by a road tunnel and somewhat neglected. But the federal government (which owns the park) is working on a plan to bring new life to the neglected lawns and scruffy flower beds. The aim is to make the park an attractive green space close to the European institutions and, ultimately, link it to nearby parks such as the Leopold Park, to form a green urban promenade through the European Quarter.

National festivals

Burns Night, 25 January. The city's Scottish community celebrates the birth of the national poet Robert Burns with a meal involving haggis (bought from the Irish butcher), poetry and whisky.

St David's Day, 1 March. The Welsh community celebrates their patron saint with a meal involving imported Welsh lamb.

St Patrick's Day, 17 March. Irish pubs in Brussels are mobbed as the city's Irish community celebrates the country's patron saint.

Midsummer, 21 June. Expatriates from Scandinavian and Baltic countries celebrate the longest day of the year in Brussels with a party and bonfire.

American Independence Day, 4 July. The dwindling American community in Brussels holds Fourth of July parties to celebrate independence from British rule.

Belgian National Festival, 21 July. The national holiday celebrates the day when Leopold I ascended the throne as the first king of the Belgians, in 1831. The main festivities are concentrated in Brussels around the royal palace, where the King inspects a military parade as air force jets fly overhead trailing the Belgian colours.

Canadian Thanksgiving, second Monday in October. Canadians celebrate Thanksgiving with a family meal involving turkey.

American Thanksgiving, fourth Thursday in November. American expatriates celebrate the national festival.

St Nicholas Day, 6 December. Dutch and Belgian children normally get presents on St Nicholas Day, rather than Christmas Day. *Sinterklaas* visits schools during the day, accompanied by *Zwarte Piet*, a somewhat sinister black character from Dutch Christmas folklore.

Ramadan, dates vary. The Muslim community in Brussels celebrates the religious Fast of Ramadan in the ninth month of the Muslim calendar. This is traditionally a family-based religious festival in which Muslims fast during daylight hours and eat and drink in the evening.

Buying in Brussels

The Property Market

Many expatriates eventually decide to buy a property in Belgium, especially if they are staying for a long period. But the Belgian property market is complex and it is probably best not to rush into buying, especially as rented accommodation is plentiful. You should take time to get to know different areas and acquire a feel for the market. Property prices in Brussels can sometimes fall sharply, making it difficult to sell your house when you decide to move on. Some suburban areas such as Waterloo and Overijse are becoming less popular with commuters because of increased traffic congestion. Other areas are currently overheated because they are close to the main European institutions.

The situation for commuters might improve when the new suburban rail network RER is completed. This should make it easier to commute into Brussels by rail, though the new network may only affect those who live close to a station. House prices close to proposed RER stations have already increased by as much as 40% in recent years. But the project has been delayed, and is unlikely to begin operating fully until 2015-16.

House Prices in Brussels

The main demand in Brussels is for houses costing €250,000-€500,000. These properties are normally sold within a few days, whereas more expensive houses costing over €500,000 often remain unsold for many months.

The hottest properties at present are located in streets close to the European institutions, where a one-bedroom apartment will cost at least €300,000 and a two-bedroom apartment can easily fetch €400,000. Houses are even more expensive, and anyone looking to buy a house in this area will need to have at least €500,000 to spare plus a further €85,000 to cover the various taxes and fees.

Other areas of the city have also seen a spectacular rise in property prices, including the streets around Place Flagey and the Châtelain neighbourhood. It is possible that scruffy Forest commune could become the next hot area for cash-rich British and French investors following the opening of the Wiels art centre.

But older Belgians are cautious. They know that property prices can sometimes slump alarmingly. Many home owners have had to sell at a loss in Brussels because of falling prices. The city centre is now very expensive, but could suddenly lose its appeal. The European Quarter is currently popular, but people may return to the suburbs once the RER is running.

The much-praised quality of life in Brussels might gradually disappear if high earners continue to drive out local residents, creating expatriate ghettos where no one feels welcome or safe. In short, buying a property in Brussels is by no means a safe investment. Do it if you find the place of your dreams. But think twice if your sole aim is to make a profit after a few years.

Taxes and Fees

The main reason for not buying property in Belgium is the amount you have to pay on top of the selling price. The biggest shock to buyers is the registration tax. This amounts to 12.5% of the purchase price in Brussels and 10% in Flanders, though you can claim back 44% of the tax if you sell within two years. The registration tax has traditionally discouraged Belgians from buying a house until they were certain that they wanted to settle down. It partly explains why Belgians tend to spend most of their life in the same house.

Brussels Region is now trying to reduce the tax in an effort to persuade more people to settle in the city. The tax rate remains unchanged, but the first €60,000 of the purchase price is exempt, which means that the effective rate for an average house in Brussels is now about 10%.

The next bill comes from the notary, who charges a fee fixed by law for the various services offered. The rate varies according to the value of the property, but is generally about 1.6% of the selling price. Other costs include the mortgage lender's fee and a tax on the bank loan.

The end result is that Belgian home buyers pay about 17% extra on top of the purchase price. None of this can be recovered unless you move within two years, so you need to hold onto your house for several years to avoid selling at a loss.

When budgeting for a house purchase, you should bear in mind that many Belgian houses require a large amount of work, including electrical cabling and plumbing. Even relatively new houses can have unforeseen problems that cost huge sums to fix, like central heating boilers or hidden cracks. You should therefore have a financial reserve of at least €5,000 to cover renovation costs.

How to Find a House

The housing market in Brussels offers a wide choice of properties. You can find a cool architect-designed flat in the city centre, a spacious modern villa in the suburbs or even a turreted château in the green fields of Brabant. Several websites such as immoweb.be have extensive listings of houses for sale. You can, if you want, register with an estate agent, who can guide you to suitable properties and arrange appointments with sellers. The estate agent charges the seller a percentage (normally 3%) of the final price, but the buyer pays nothing. Some Brussels estate agents are dynamic and English-speaking, but others offer a poor service.

Once you are seriously interested in a house, it is probably worth asking a surveyor to visit the house and check that the building is in good condition. Count on paying about €200 for a survey in the case of a one-room apartment and more for a larger property. While there is no legal obligation to carry out a structural survey, it can give you some useful leverage in negotiating a price. For example, if the wiring needs to be replaced, you can suggest that the cost of the work is deducted from the selling price.

Sometimes there is no time for a survey. If you find the perfect house, you may have to make a quick decision, as some properties sell within a few hours of going on the market.

ABOUT BRUSSELS

The Notary's Work

You should contact a notary (*notaire/notaris*) as soon as you begin to think about buying and arrange an appointment to discuss the legal and tax procedures. The notary is usually willing to explain the process for free. It is important to find a reliable notary, as he or she is responsible for checking the title deeds and ensuring that the seller has the right to sell. All notaries charge the same fees, so you simply need to find one who will do the job properly. You can pick a name from the official notaries' website (www.notaire.be), or ask for a personal recommendation from a friend or work colleague.

Once you have decided to buy, you need to contact your notary immediately. The seller will ask his notary to draft an agreement to sell (*compromis de vente/ verkoopcompromis*). This is then sent to your notary for approval. You then meet with the seller and both notaries to read and sign the agreement. At this meeting, you have to hand over a deposit, normally 10% of the selling price. The agreement is now binding. You should insure the house from that date, as you are now liable for the property (even though you still don't legally own it). Your notary will then check the title deeds and draw up a final contract (*acte authentique/authentieke akte*). In the meantime, you have to arrange for a mortgage.

Four months after signing the *compromis*, you all meet again in your notary's office to sign the final contract and hand over the remaining money (usually a cheque from the mortgage lender) in return for the title deeds and keys.

Many Belgians like to avoid paying the full registration tax. They do this by declaring a lower selling price that the amount agreed. The buyer then pays the difference in cash. This is a risky strategy, as the tax authorities will sometimes spot an unusually low selling price and charge tax on a more realistic price. It's probably best to insist on honesty.

Mortgages

Belgian banks normally offer mortgages that run for 15 or 20 years, although you can sometimes negotiate a 30-year loan. Many people employ a mortgage broker to find them the best terms, but most stick with their bank. There are two types of mortgage available. In a fixed mortgage, the interest rate is set for the entire period of the loan. In a variable mortgage, the interest is adjusted after a certain number of years in line with the lending rate.

Banks in Belgium have been traditionally cautious about lending to borrowers, especially foreigners. Many banks will insist on carrying out a survey of the house before agreeing to lend. They will then decide the maximum amount they will lend on the basis of the estimated value of the house, which might be much lower than the price you have agreed to pay.

The strict lending limits are set by law to avoid people getting into debt. Salaried employees can usually borrow 40%-50% of their net monthly income, but self-employed workers might only be able to get a 30%-35% loan. Some banks might agree to lend you the purchase price plus the additional fees. They usually insist that you take out a life insurance, often with a specified company.

Local Taxes

The rateable value of your house (*revenue cadastral/kadastral inkomen*) determines the amount you pay each year in communal taxes. But the amount may go up if you carry out major improvements to the property.

Contacts

Home for You A house-hunting service that locates suitable houses for sale in Brussels and around and arranges for visits. www.hfy.be.

Royal Federation of Belgian Notaries Useful information on buying property in Belgium including a guide to fees and a list of notaries. www.notaire.be.

Renovation

Many houses in Brussels have not been repaired in decades. You may therefore have to get some major work done when you buy. Brussels Region encourages owners to restore their properties by offering various grants. Some apply to all houses in the city, whereas others are limited to a certain neighbourhoods. You can apply for subsidies for repainting the façade, installing a solar boiler or insulating the attic.

The state also offers an incentive to persuade Belgians to renovate older houses. The normal VAT rate for material and services is 21%, but this is cut to 6% when the work is done on properties older than 15 years. The contractor simply charges the lower rate of VAT in the final bill.

The best place for information on house renovation is the Centre Urbain/ Stadswinkel in the old market hall on Place St Géry. You can call in for leaflets on energy efficiency, sound insulation and renovation techniques. The staff can also explain the various subsidies and help you fill out the application forms. There is also a website (www.curbain.be) with information in English on renovation.

The government recently introduced a new measure that allows individuals to deduct the cost of home security improvements in their tax return. The measure, which applies to tenants as well as home owners, covers installation costs of fire extinguishers, alarms and security cameras, up to a maximum of €130.

Architects

Some people employ an architect to redesign an old house or build a new house on a vacant plot. But many simply rely on a general contractor to do the work using a team of professionals. The architect can provide a basic report on an old house for as little as €320, but it costs a lot more to employ an architect to design and supervise your project. But it is possibly worth the cost, since you will have someone who can deal with the various contractors involved and ensure that the work is done properly. You should expect to pay about 12-15% on top of the construction costs.

Finding Professionals

It sometimes seems as if Brussels is a permanent building site. There are several enormous projects going on in the city, along with countless small renovations and conversions. This puts pressure on firms and sometimes leads to long delays in getting work done. Plumbers and electricians are particularly overstretched and often difficult to contact. Many jobs take longer than expected, especially those involving old properties.

The simplest way to find a professional is to ask friends and work colleagues. Otherwise you can register free with the internet site Casius stating the work you need done. You will then be contacted by two or three local firms that are interested in doing the job. The next step is to ask for an estimate from each firm, and then pick the best offer. The agency has been running since 1999 and has built up an extensive database of reliable contractors. Its website is in three languages including English. ☎ 02.788.18.00; email info@casius.be; www.casius.be

The Discreet Charm of the Brussels Townhouse

The Brussels townhouse evolved in the 19th century as an elegant solution to urban constraints. It typically stands on a long narrow plot with its front door on the street and a long walled garden hidden from view at the back. The style of house often betrays the politics of the original owner. A Catholic voter would choose a Gothic façade, a liberal would prefer a neo-classical frontage, while an Art Nouveau façade often meant that the original owner was a socialist.

The basement is normally sunk below the street level, lit by small windows on the front side. The front room was originally the kitchen, while the back room served as a laundry room. Some houses also incorporated an extensive wine cellar in the basement.

Once inside the house, a flight of marble steps brings the visitor into a narrow tiled hallway, with a door on one side leading into the main rooms. Most houses were designed with three 'enfilade' rooms, with large glass doors separating the rooms.

Some houses have been altered over the years in response to changing fashions or economic factors. Sometimes ceilings have been lowered to conserve heat, fireplaces covered, and single-family dwellings converted into apartments.

The Centre Urbain on Place St Géry provides information on renovating period houses and protecting the architectural heritage of the city. It has a database with names of specialised craftsmen and information leaflets on different aspects of a Brussels house, such as railings, sgraffito, and balconies.

A quiet side street in Brussels

Appendices

Recommended reading

Culture

The Xenophobe's Guide to the Belgians: Antony Mason, 1999. An affectionate study of the Belgians. Not always accurate, but full of warm humour.

Historical Dictionary of Brussels: Paul F. State, 2004. Fascinating compendium of facts about every aspect of Brussels gathered by an American writer who spent several years living in the city.

Guidebooks

Brussels: A Cultural and Literary Companion: André de Vries, 2003. A fascinating guide to the writers and artists who have spent time in Brussels.

Brussels for Pleasure: Derek Blyth. An affectionate guide to the city in 13 meandering walks.

Time Out Brussels: Various authors, 2004. Lively guide to the city's bars, hotels and hotspots compiled by writers living in the city.

Food and Drink

Everyone Eats Well in Belgium Cookbook: Ruth van Waerebeek, 1996. How to eat like a Belgian by a Belgian woman chef who now lives in the USA.

Novels

Heart of Darkness: Joseph Conrad. A harrowing study of evil in Leopold's Congo with early scenes set in Brussels.

The Professor: Charlotte Brontë. Charlotte Brontë's first Brussels novel, unpublished in her lifetime, describes the experiences of a young man in Brussels.

Villette: Charlotte Brontë. Charlotte Brontë's final published novel describes a young English woman's experiences in Brussels.

Finding information

You can find a certain amount of information online, but some Belgian organisations are difficult to track down on the web. The contact details can be found in the white telephone directory or yellow pages, but you have to know where to look. Here are some essential terms in French and Dutch.

Administration

Insurance	assurance/verzekering
Tax office	administration des contributions directes/ bestuur van de directe belastingen

Work

Employment office	bureau de placement/arbeidsbureau
Job centre	intérimaire/uitzendbureau

Professions

Accountant	comptable/boekhouder
Beautician	institut de beauté/schoonheidsspecialist
Builder	entrepreneur/aannemer
Electrician	electricien/elektricien
Estate agent	agence immobilière/makelaar
Hairdresser	salon de coiffure/kapper
Lawyer	avocat/advocaat
Plumber	plombier/loodgieter
Removal company	déménagement/verhuizingen
Tax consultant	conseiller fiscal, belastingadviseur
Travel agent	agence de voyage/reisburo

Health

Chemist	droguerie/drogisterij
Childrens' hospital	hôpital pour enfants/kinderziekenhuis
Dentist	dentiste/tandarts
Doctor	médecin/huisarts
Ophthalmologist	optometriste/oogarts
Pharmacy (for prescriptions)	pharmacie/apotheek

Transport

Airline	compagnie aérienne/luchtvaartmaatschappij
Car dealer	auto concessionnaire/auto–dealer
Car hire	auto location/auto verhuur
Car repair	garage (in both languages)

Shopping

Bookshop	librairie/boekhandel
Childrens clothing	vêtements pour enfants/kinderkleding
Department store	grand magasin/warenhuis
Do It Yourself	bricolage/doe-het-zelf
Drugstore	droguerie/drogisterij
Dry cleaner	nettoyage à sec/stomerij
Electrical goods	electroménager/huishoudelijke apparaten
Furniture	meubles/meubelen
Garden centre	centre de jardinage/tuincentrum
Household goods	articles de ménage/huishoudelijke artikelen

On the web

Belgium is surprisingly backwards in website design, although some sites are outstanding. The following list points you in the direction of sites that will make life in Belgium easier.

Settling In

Brussels-Europe Liaison Office: Excellent website in English with an immense amount of useful information on living in Brussels. You can also subscribe to a free monthly email newsletter. www.blbe.be

Craigslist: This US listings site has been slow to take off in Belgium, but it might be useful for finding an apartment or possibly a job. www.brussels.craigslist.org.

Expatica: Expatica's Belgian site has useful articles on practicalities such as health and housing. www.expatica.be

Shopping

Amazon: For books, CDs and videos. Amazon doesn't have a Belgian site, but it's easy to order English books from the UK site, or French books from the French site. Items ordered from the US site may be charged import taxes. www.amazon.co.uk

Proxis: The Belgian answer to Amazon, in French, Dutch and English. Useful site for buying books, DVDs, CDs and videos. www.proxis.be

eBay: The massive online auction house has a Belgian site where you can buy almost anything, from Tintin comic books to used cars. You simply register, browse and bid. But watch out for online scams using your membership details. www.ebay.be

Caddyhome: Online shopping service operated by Delhaize supermarket chain. You order online at the same price as shops charge, but pay a €7.40 delivery charge. www.caddyhome.be

News

Xpats: Daily Belgian news in English. Site also has classified ads, a cultural agenda and an online Q&A forum where expats help one another solve problems. www.xpats.com

Flanders News: Excellent daily news site in English provided by the Flemish broadcaster VRT. www.flandersnews.be

Culture

Cinebel: Excellent cinema listing site in French and Dutch. Provides information on every cinema in the country, along with reviews, trailers and ratings. www.cinebel.be

Que Faire: Inspiring site that lists several thousand things to do, including exhibitions, festivals and activities for children. Focuses on Brussels and Wallonia, with excursions into France, but little on Flanders. www.quefaire.be

UGC: Online booking of cinema tickets for UGC cinemas. Not the easiest site to use. www.ugc.be

Nights

Brusselssucks: An enthusiastic guide in English to clubs, DJs and all that's wild in nocturnal Brussels. www.brusselssucks.be

Noctis: An essential source for news on raves, parties, clubs, night bars, museum nocturnes and anything else that happens after dark in Belgium. In English, French and Dutch.www.noctis.com

Travel

Ryanair: Low-cost Irish budget airline based at Charleroi airport. Flights are dirt cheap, but don't expect to find customer service when things go wrong. www.ryanair.com

Brussels Airlines: Virgin Express merged with SN Brussels Airlines in 2007 to create a new Belgian airline offering a choice of business and low-cost fares. Offers cheap flights from Brussels Airport to most major European cities. www.brusselsairlines.be

Brussels Airport: Clear site with information on facilities and flights. www.brusselsairport.be

Brussels Public Transport: Well-designed site with information on metros, trams and buses in Brussels Region. www.stib.be

Belgian Railways: Attractive site with information on national and international train services and online booking. www.b-rail.be

Eurostar: Online booking of Eurostar services from Brussels to London. www.eurostar.com

Thalys: Site dedicated to high-speed train services serving Brussels, Paris, Lille, Amsterdam and Cologne. www.thalys.com

Embassies and consulates

Most countries have an embassy or consulate in Brussels. Foreigners normally have little contact with their embassy, apart from an occasional visit to collect a new passport or register the birth of a child. The embassy can advise on obtaining a certificat de bonne moeurs, which is sometimes required in Belgium by the local administration. Some embassies and consulates charge very high fees for services such as issuing a passport or registering a birth.

Embassy Contacts

Australia: Rue Guimard 6-8; ☎ 02.286.05.00; www.austemb.be

Canada: Avenue de Tervuren 2; ☎ 02.741.06.11; www.international.gc.ca/brussels

Ireland: Rue Wiertz 50; ☎ 02.235.66.76

New Zealand: Square de Meeûs 1; ☎ 02.512.10.40; www.nzembassy.com

South Africa: Rue de la Loi 26; ☎ 02.285.44.00; www.southafrica.be

United Kingdom: Rue d'Arlon 85, ☎ 02.287.62.11; www.britishembassy.gov.uk/belgium

United States: Boulevard du Régent 27; ☎ 02.508.21.11; www.usembassy.be

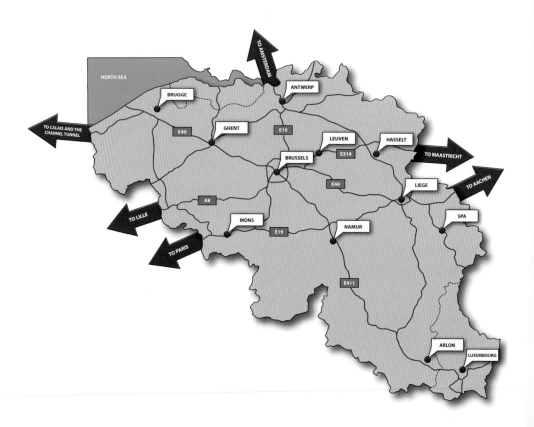

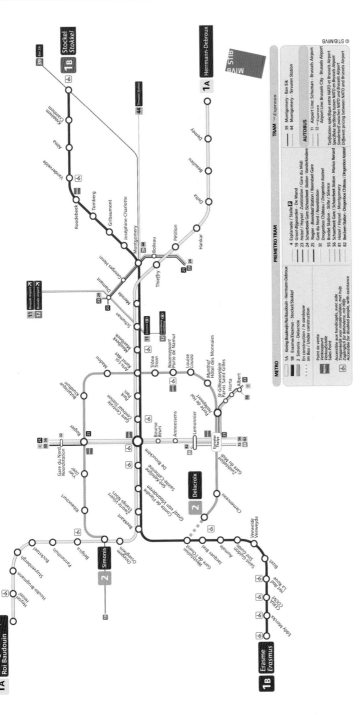

Source STIB/MIVB

Index

INDEX